Transnational Crime, Crime Control and Security

Titles include:

Vida Bajc
Security, Surveillance and the Olympic Games (*forthcoming*)

Paul Battersby
THE UNLAWFUL SOCIETY
Global Crime and Security in a Complex World

Jennifer Fleetwood
DRUG MULES
Gender and Crime in a Transnational Context

Sophie Body-Gendrot
GLOBALIZATION, FEAR AND INSECURITY
The Challenges for Cities North and South

Graham Ellison and Nathan Pino (*editors*)
GLOBALIZATION, POLICE REFORM AND DEVELOPMENT
Doing it the Western Way?

Alexander Kupatadze
Organized Crime, Political Transitions and State Formation in Post-Soviet Eurasia (*forthcoming*)

Jude McCulloch and Sharon Pickering (*editors*)
BORDERS AND TRANSNATIONAL CRIME
Pre-Crime, Mobility and Serious Harm in an Age of Globalization

Georgios Papanicolaou
Transnational Policing and Sex Trafficking in Southeast Europe
Policing the Imperialist Chain

(continued in page ii)

Leanne Weber and Sharon Pickering (*editors*)
Globalization and Borders
Death at the Global Frontier

Linda Zhao
FINANCING ILLEGAL MIGRATION
Chinese Underground Banks and Human Smuggling in New York City

---

Transnational Crime, Crime Control and Security
Series Standing Order ISBN 978-0-230-28945-1 hardback
Series Standing Order ISBN 978-0-230-28946-8 paperback
(*outside North America only*)

You can receive future titles in this series as they are published by placing a standing order. Please contact your bookseller or, in case of difficulty, write to us at the address below with your name and address, the title of the series and the ISBN quoted above.

Customer Services Department, Macmillan Distribution Ltd, Houndmills, Basingstoke, Hampshire RG21 6XS, England.

The Unlawful Society

Global Crime and Security in a Complex World

Paul Battersby
Associate Professor, RMIT University, Australia

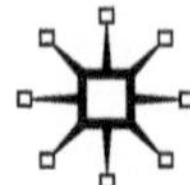

First published 2014 by
PALGRAVE MACMILLAN

Palgrave Macmillan in the UK is an imprint of Macmillan Publishers Limited, registered in England, company number 785998, of Houndmills, Basingstoke, Hampshire RG21 6XS.

Palgrave Macmillan in the US is a division of St Martin's Press LLC, 175 Fifth Avenue, New York, NY 10010.

Palgrave Macmillan is the global academic imprint of the above companies and has companies and representatives throughout the world.

ISBN: 978–1–137–28295–8

This book is printed on paper suitable for recycling and made from fully managed and sustained forest sources. Logging, pulping and manufacturing processes are expected to conform to the environmental regulations of the country of origin.

A catalogue record for this book is available from the British Library.

A catalog record for this book is available from the Library of Congress.

Contents

List of Figures and Table

Figures

Table

List of Abbreviations

ABC	Australian Broadcasting Corporation
ABDG	African Development Bank Group
ACC	Australian Crime Commission
ACFID	Australian Council For International Development
ADMA	Asian Digital Marketing Association
AFRICOM	United States Africa Command
AMLR	Anti-Money Laundering Regime
ANLM	Anzawad National Liberation Movement
AQIM	Al-Qaeda in the Islamic Maghreb
ASEAN	Association of Southeast Asian Nations
ATS	Amphetamine Type Stimulants
ATT	Arms Trade Treaty
AUC	Autodefensas Unidas de Colombia (United Self-Defense Forces of Colombia)
AusAID	Australian Agency for International Development
AWB	Australian Wheat Board
BAAG	British Agencies Afghanistan Group
BCBS	Basel Committee on Banking Supervision
BCL	Bougainville Copper Limited
BDS	Bureau of Diplomatic Security
BIS	Bank of International Settlements
BRIC	Brazil, Russia, India and China
BT	British Telecom
BTWC	Biological and Toxin Weapons Convention
BRA	Bougainville Resistance Army
CECP	Committee Encouraging Corporate Philanthropy
CEDAW	Convention for the Elimination of All Forms of Discrimination Against Women
CGC	Commission on Global Governance
CSIS	Center for Strategic and International Studies
CTOC	Convention against Transnational Organized Crime
DoJ	Department of Justice, United States
DoD	Department of Defense, United States
DoT	Department of Trade, United States
DoS	Department of State, United States
EC	European Commission

EIU	Economic Intelligence Unit
ELN	Ejército de Liberación Nacional (National Liberation Army, Colombia)
ENISA	European Union Agency for Network and Information Security
ENNA	European Network of NGOs in Afghanistan
EU	European Union
EU ISS	European Union Institute for Security Studies
EURIBOR	European Interbank Offered Rate
FAO	Food and Agriculture Organization of the United Nations
FARC	Fuerzas Armadas Revolucionarias de Colombia (Revolutionary Armed Forces of Colombia)
FATF	Financial Action Taskforce
FCPA	Foreign Corrupt Practices Act
GAM	Gerakan Aceh Merdeka (Free Aceh Movement)
GCHQ	Government Communications Headquarters
GSPC	Group Salafist pour la Prédication et le Combat
HBUS	HSBC United States
HRF	Human Rights First
HRW	Human Rights Watch
HSBC	Hong Kong and Shanghai Banking Corporation
IAEA	International Atomic Energy Agency
ICANN	Internet Corporation for Assigned Names and Numbers
ICEM	International Federation of Engineering, Chemical, Mine and General Workers Unions
ICFTU-ICEF	International Confederation of Trades Unions-International Federation of Chemical, Energy and General Workers Unions
ICRC	International Committee of the Red Cross
IEP	Institute for Economics and Peace
IISS	International Institute for Strategic Studies
ICG	International Crisis Group
ICJ	International Commission of Jurists
ICNL	International Center for Not-for-Profit Law
ICISS	International Commission on Intervention and State Sovereignty
ICTSD	International Centre for Trade and Sustainable Development
IDP	Internally Displaced Persons

ILO	International Labour Organization
IMF	International Monetary Fund
IMO	International Maritime Organization
INLEA	International Narcotics and Law Enforcement Affairs Bureau
INSCR	*International Narcotics Control Strategy Report*
IOM	International Organization for Migration
ISAF	International Security Assistance Force
IWM	Information Warfare Monitor
LIBOR	London Interbank Offered Rate
LRA	Lord's Resistance Army
MDG	Millennium Development Goals
MEND	Movement for the Emancipation of the Niger Delta
MSF	Medicins Sans Frontières
MUJAO	Movement for Unity and Jihad in West Africa
NATO	North Atlantic Treaty Organization
NIC	National Intelligence Council
NIF	National Islamic Front, Sudan
NSA	National Security Agency, United States
OECD	Organization for Economic Cooperation and Development
ODA	Overseas Development Assistance
OFAC	Office of Foreign Asset Control, Department of Treasury, United States
OIC	Organization of the Islamic Conference
OPA	Office of Public Affairs, Department of Justice, United States
OPCW	Office for the Prohibition of Chemical Weapons
OPM	Organisasi Papua Merdeka (Free Aceh Movement)
PMSC	Private Military Security Contractor
PRI	Penal Reform International
SIPRI	Stockholm International Peace Research Institute
SWIFT	Society for Worldwide Interbank Financial Telecommunications
TPLF	Tigrayan People's Liberation Front
TNI	Tentara Nasional Indonesia (Indonesian Armed Forces)
UCC	Union Carbide Company
UK ISC	United Kingdom Intelligence and Security Committee
UK JCHR	United Kingdom Joint Committee on Human Rights
UNCHS	United Nations Commission on Human Security
UNCTAD	United Nations Conference on Trade and Development

UNCLOS	United Nations Convention on the Law of the Sea
UNDP	United Nations Development Programme
UNECOSOC	United Nations Economic and Social Committee
UNEP	United Nations Environment Programme
UNFPA	United Nations Population Fund
UNGA	United Nations General Assembly
UNHCR	United Nations High Commission for Refugees
UNMOVIC	United Nations Monitoring, Inspection and Verification Commission
UNODC	United Nations Office on Drugs and Crime
UNSC	United Nations Security Council
USAID	United States Agency for International Development
USTR	Office of the United States Trade Representative
WDC	Whale and Dolphin Conservation
WVA	World Vision Australia

Acknowledgements

The Unlawful Society is the culmination of more than 15 years of teaching and research at the Royal Melbourne Institute of Technology (RMIT) University. It is my privilege to have been involved in the forging of a new kind of humanities discipline, Global Studies, to which the multiple interconnections of globalization, culture and language are defining concerns. From the outset I was afforded the opportunity and encouragement to design courses and pursue research projects that addressed the socio-cultural and political dimensions of risk and governance, all of which laid the intellectual foundations upon which this book is built. I have, along the way, been privileged to teach a great many critically engaged and globally minded undergraduate and postgraduate students. The classroom, perhaps more so than the academic conference or workshop, is the toughest testing ground for new concepts and new approaches. There is a perennial tension in globalization analysis between the intricacies of different local contexts in which global issues are played out, and the belief that events or patterns evident in these localities need to be viewed with a "global" lens. The analysis presented in the chapters that follow exemplifies a "global" mode of inquiry, where local patterns and events are mapped out on a planetary landscape. My approach here is expansive, and necessarily ambitious, but because of this it is also innovative, if not entirely unique, and I make no apologies for any part of it. In my investigations into human unlawfulness I have striven to be as objective as is possible. No one is spared from criticism, but then neither is anyone singled out for condemnation. If at the end of the day my analysis provokes outrage from all quarters then this book will have served its purpose. It is after all is said and done an argument against the partisanship, the polarization and the hardening of ideologies that plague the modern global age.

Inevitably, fragments of my past and concurrent writings filter into the text at various stages. Many of the ideas presented here evolve out of my earlier work on globalization and human security with Joseph Siracusa (2009) and on global crime, law and political violence with Joseph Siracusa and Sasho Ripiloski (2011). There is, too, some cross-fertilization between this project and selected individual contributions to the *Handbook of Globalization* (2014), co-edited with Manfred Steger and Joseph Siracusa. Still, such material as is reinvented here has been subject to significant reconceptualization, updating and extensive reworking so as to complement and extend this book's central arguments. I offer the reader a fresh synthesis and the fullest expression of my take on globalization to date, within a single book that is both a distinctive and coherent whole.

Debts of gratitude are owed to those people without whom this book would never have come to pass. Firstly, I am indebted to the editors of this Palgrave series for their interest in my ideas and their confidence in ability to deliver. I am grateful for the generosity of the School of Global, Urban and Social Studies. Without the allocation of precious time to think and write I could not have made it to the finishing post. I owe thanks to Joseph Siracusa and to Manfred Steger for their mentorship at RMIT over the years and for the opportunities given to collaborate with scholars of their global stature. Timely and expert editorial assistance was provided by Candice Maddison without whose attention to detail the final stage of manuscript preparation would have been much more arduous. I am very fortunate to work alongside a highly productive and creative team in the discipline of Global Studies and to be associated with RMIT's Globalism Research Centre, which continues to provide excellent opportunities for intellectual debate and collaboration with prominent national and international scholars. I have travelled a very great distance from the northeast of England to the northwest of Western Australia, to James Cook University in Queensland, to Thailand's northeast, and to my current home in Melbourne. This is a journey that I could never have undertaken entirely on my own. To my wife, Carmel, all I can say is thank you once again for sticking with me, and for tolerating my protracted inattention and frequent absent-mindedness.

Introduction

What should we make of those legal "grey areas" where, to paraphrase Hedley Bull, there is often no clear differentiation between what is lawful and what is not (Bull, 2002, p. 132)? How can we be so certain that law and democratic process cannot be subverted by the weight of numbers to sanction the extermination of an entire social group (Arendt, 1958, p. 299)? In the networked "information age" (Castells, 2009), is there any greater surety that the truth about the nature of international or global order will be known, let alone told? When American whistle-blower Edward Snowden revealed to the world details of the US National Security Agency's systematic "bulk" surveillance of global telecommunications, US allies and rivals alike reacted with feigned outrage. Some argue that the age of political impunity is over (Farrell and Finemore, 2013). But *cause célèbre* leaks of official records, detailing routine governmental violations of agreed principles and protocols governing interstate relations, are a sharp reminder that trust in the global system remains limited and deception is still the norm.

The exposure of extensive state surveillance of global telecommunications arguably explodes many of the utopian or "digitopian" myths accompanying the globalization of telecommunications – and the "*informationalization*" of society (Castells, 2009; 2012; Lovink, 2011; Morozov, 2011; Mathiesen, 2013). Technology liberates but also ensnares us in an evolving complex web of informational relations, within which information gathering has become a compulsion, or pathology, a "reflexive" response to uncertainty on the part of state agents but also private actors (Giddens, 1994; 1990; Beck, 1999; Elmer, 2012). The global sensation generated by Snowden's disclosures also draws attention to a central paradox in international and global relations, that is, the use of "unlawful" means by lawfully constituted actors to achieve organizational or political objectives, and, equally significant, the "unlawfulness" of those who transgress or test law in the name of a higher moral code. There is a common thread connecting many disparate instances of arguably justifiable or tolerable transgressions of law, just as there is a common thread linking many disparate instances of the deliberate subversion of globally accepted norms through the pursuit of power and private gain. *The Unlawful Society* explores these anomalies and the disorderly, but not ungoverned or rule-less, spaces in which they arise.

This is not a book about technology *per se*. Rather, it is principally an exploration of crime – understood here as the violation of codified law – and criminality, and also the struggles to define how law is encoded into social relations. In so doing, it necessarily veers into analysis of the political compromises and systemic tolerances that shape the contemporary global system. What is presented, then, is a photographic "negative" of global relations, not to reveal some "dark logic" but to contest assumptions about the relation of crime to security. Globalization multiplies opportunities to connect, to cooperate and to challenge illegitimate power, but it also increases the opportunities to do harm, to perpetrate crimes against property and people – and against vital complex systems upon which people and peoples depend. The securitization of crime is a reflexive response to this new layer of global complexity, but this securitization in no way guarantees greater security – for anyone at any level.

National and global security is today synonymous with the anxieties and realities of terror and transnational crime. So much so that security policies require little or no public elaboration beyond the deployment of the key words "terrorists" and "criminals" to legitimate the latest surveillance operation or interception. Organized and decentralized transnational criminal entities are allegedly corroding the foundations of global order by extending the scope of transnational crime economies and compromising or capturing weak links in otherwise "virtuous" chains of global governance (Galeotti, 2004a; Naim, 2005; Hanlon, 2009; Mandel, 2011; Farah, 2013). Since 9/11, a "literalized" Global War on Terror has tied security institutionally and intellectually to crime prevention and law enforcement, with terror and crime used interchangeably to privilege "reasons of state" and to diminish international humanitarian principle in the public mind (Roth, 2004, p. 178; Open Society Justice Initiative, 2013). Indeed, national security narratives elevate "transnational organized crime and terror" to the status of a singular convergent risk through the conscious detachment of crime and criminality from the systemic contexts in which crimes are perpetrated, defined, sanctioned or condoned.

Notions of a subterranean global "underworld" or a "dark underside" of globalization, however, focus our attention only to one dimension of the crime–security equation – the world of illicit gangs, terrorist groups, money launderers, traffickers and crime "godfathers." There is no single or monolithic cabal of global criminals and terrorists lurking within the dark caverns of global society. Reality is much more fragmented and criminality is not the preserve of "hardened" criminals. In their daily operations, legally constituted actors (namely, sovereign states), registered private and public companies and even humanitarian non-state organizations, routinely straddle an indistinct "line of control" between legality and criminality. This dimension extends far beyond conventional "white-collar crime" into a world of ambiguity where laws are deliberately set aside, for reasons of state, commercial advantage or higher moral principle, and where "bright lines" are either absent or inadequate to distinguish clearly between lawful and criminal acts. Such ambiguities are magnified and their scope enlarged by the exponential growth of global connectivity. "Cyber space" is a social space that accommodates the extension of familiar human behaviour into a new "virtual" domain, facilitated by the tangible hardwires and wares of fibre-optic cables, satellites, servers, mobile telecommunications devices and computers. Here, cyber criminals, terrorists and "hacktivists," synonymous in the eyes of many, operate in virtual anonymity beyond the reach of law – but so too do corporate and freelance data harvesters – and "faceless" agents of the state, who hover precariously at the edge of law.

Escalating communications intercept activity by governments of democratic states in particular, which can be read as an index of rising insecurity in a global context where security threats are increasingly invisible and diffuse. Warrants are a cumbersome means by which to trawl through the trillions of gigabytes of data communicated between the rapidly growing numbers of Internet users globally. Enhanced computational power and increasing network densities give some security agencies at least the power and the motive to appropriate and process vast quantities of telecommunications data. That this power is used and abused should, of course, come as no surprise.

The trajectory of surveillance is, depending upon your point of view, either a grave risk to individual liberties, including the right to privacy and anonymity, or a necessary evil. From a purely utilitarian view, surveillance is also, arguably, of systemic benefit because it can compensate for the absence of global governmental authority and oversight, and the determination of many governments to avoid invasive scrutiny by international agencies (Baker, 2003). The "mission creep" evident in governmental security practice is but one more issue area that exemplifies Stephen D. Kranser's assertion of the "organized hypocrisy" of an interstate system to which sovereignty is a fundamental legal principle but where all states routinely violate the sovereign rights of others (Krasner, 1999). Radical and liberal globalists alike view the state as a hindrance to the emergence of a liberated (read denationalized and deterritorialized) global community (Ohmae, 1996; Castells, 2011; 2012). That human systems can self-organize is not in dispute; the question posed here is whether such collective self-organization will necessarily follow a normative, cosmopolitan trajectory.

The codification of crime

With the ascendancy of Internet-mediated communication it has become fashionable to conceive law as a series of codes and protocols that govern human relations in both the virtual and the "real" world (Lessig, 2006; Deibert and Rohozinski, 2010; Coleman, 2013). All human social interactions involve coded communication in the form of language, and are necessarily constrained by tacit behavioural norms and protocols. From a systems perspective, law, national and international, can usefully be imagined as "grid codes" that define the limits of acceptable social behaviour across a highly complex global mosaic. International laws, writes Antonio Cassese, represent "values considered important by the whole international community" (2008, p. 11). The contested nature of international legal principles and their application arise from a "gap" between formalized legal codes and divergent "source codes" of constituent polities, but also the basic operating principles of the "anarchical" society of states (Bull, 2002). That said, the evolving corpus of international law suggests a transnationalist if not internationalist evolutionary trajectory that reflects the degree to which state and non-state actors accept the need for structures of governance beyond the state to address matters of global concern.

The most widely known area of international law – international criminal law – concerns "war crimes," "crimes against humanity" and "genocide," objectively defined as crimes in the Rome Statute and drawing authority from the Geneva Conventions and Nuremberg

Principles (Cassese, 2008, p. 11). International criminal law assigns criminal responsibility to individual transgressors, whether acting on behalf of a government or privately, but not to states. Within international criminology especially, however, there is an evolving critique of state crime where states, rather than individual agents of the state, are viewed as criminally responsible and hence, by implication, criminally liable. But international criminal laws fall well short of providing the legal means to bring an entire state to trial (Bassiouni, 2011).

Distinguishing between international criminal law and public international law, Cassese remarks on how the latter, consisting principally of conventions, treaties and agreements to govern interstate relations, serves to "facilitate a minimum of peaceful intercourse between states" rather than establish the grounds on which to bring a state to trial (Cassese, 2008, p. 9). That said, there are international legal avenues to bring cases against states before the International Court of Justice, for example, on questions of border demarcation, resource rights and violations of international laws, including international human rights laws. The imposition of United Nations (UN) Security Council sanctions against states, deemed under Chapter VII of the UN Charter to be acting contrary to "international peace and security," represents another form of "punishment"; however, these are coercive actions designed to enforce compliance with Security Council resolutions rather than criminal penalties imposed by a court of law.

Still another category involves transnational corporate actor violations of national and international public laws and international criminal law. Investment in countries gripped by intrastate violence and under the control of authoritarian regimes entails a degree of tolerance for state brutality, gross human rights abuses, corruption and more. In weakly governed contexts, corners can more easily be cut and safety considerations set aside for reasons of cost and profitability because the costs of possible prosecution are judged a lesser risk. There are many legal sleights of hand that potentially allow those responsible for human tragedy to escape prosecution by exploiting international jurisdictional gaps or gaps in national legislation, to evade or otherwise limit legal liability, and to escape being judged criminal in a court of law – even though individual and collective moral culpability might be indisputable (Wilks, 2013, pp. 182–183).

Transnational crimes are a separate category, again involving primarily "serious" market crimes, committed by private individuals or organized groups for commercial gain in violation of international conventions outlawing fraud, corruption and trafficking in narcotics, persons and armaments, and specified collectively, though not exhaustively, in the UN Convention against Transnational Organized Crime (CTOC) (2004). Here again, individuals or "legal persons," including those belonging to criminal gangs, are liable for apprehension and prosecution under national laws enacted in compliance with the Convention. Yet, here too, states can be judged complicit in crime, in the transfer of weapons to insurgents, or in the tolerance of narcotics trafficking by critical strategic allies. Corruption, defined broadly as bribery and favouritism, criminalizes human actions once considered the norm in many societies and, perversely, criminalizes many actions of good intent. If not so, how then do we judge the humanitarian worker operating at the end of some hellish conflict where the overriding priority is to save the lives of innocent and not-so-innocent victims – whatever the asking price? Virtue, writes David Kennedy, has an unpalatable "dark side" (Kennedy, 2004).

There is thus a vast body of international law which prohibits acts deemed harmful to people and property – and the natural environment – and allocates substantial responsibilities to state authorities. And yet, states break many of these laws, in some cases as a matter of routine. Spying, for example, is a violation of the laws of war and all states have criminalized spying *against* the state, while establishing protocols to permit spying *by* the state – "cloaked" as surveillance – where national security is presumed at risk. The crime of espionage as variously construed in law essentially entails the clandestine acquisition of information, including the use of deception, to gain or provide an advantage. This implies a peremptory disdain for secrecy or covertness, which is counted as synonymous with unfairness at best and treachery at worst. There are, however, many other "covert" state actions that are likewise a part of international routine. State sponsorship of armed groups perpetrating acts of violence and terror in foreign countries remains a salient feature of international relations; indeed, many security planners would argue that to uphold the law of nations, these "covert" operations are a "proportionate" and "protective" security strategy. Such are the moral dilemmas created by the adoption of the doctrine of the Responsibility to Protect (R2P), evidenced in the international intervention in Libya during 2011 and thrown into relief by the international community's "failure to protect" in the Syrian Civil War of 2011–2013. The Syrian state is accused of perpetrating war crimes and crimes against humanity, as are the rebels, but the "international community" (which, by the way, includes Russia, China and Iran) is complicit in the perpetuation of this conflict, for the supply of arms to government forces and to rebel groups and, thus, arguably, for the deaths of civilians – women and children – on all sides.

How, then, should we conceive these global tolerances? David Held and Tom Weiss write of "governance gaps" between international rules and practice, democratic principle and "executive" authority, as well as the many jurisdictional gaps that restrict the enforcement of compliance at the global level (Weiss, 2000; Held, 2003; 2010). Helpful though this logic is, the notion of a "gap" implies a clear distinction between institutionalized legitimacy, on the one hand, and "deviance," on the other, when what we confront is a much more deceptive and ambiguous or complex terrain, littered with confounding antinomies that test our faculty for "practical judgement" (Kant, 1788; Rawls, 1971; Linklater, 2011).

The term *unlawful* captures the faults and incongruities encountered along an extensive, unstable and unruly frontier where legal, but often morally questionable, actions are perpetrated or tolerated in the name of security or justice, necessity or right. In this contested space there are no absolutes, no unambiguous rights or wrongs, but neither is this space a haven for the morally bankrupt.

Actions can be either illegal, but arguably justified, as in unilateral interventions to prevent massive loss of civilian life, or legal, but unconscionable, as paradoxically is the case with most if not all forms of organized state violence (Holzgrefe, 2003). Accommodated within this conceptual space are acts that directly contravene international criminal law but also the "lesser offences" of non-compliance with non-binding international norms or non-observance of customary law. It accommodates instances where lawful people find themselves trapped in circumstances dominated by ill-intentioned and criminal actors or shaped by the "perplexities" of unintended consequences, where the pursuit of ethical ends entails the transgression of sovereignty, criminal law and even the abandonment of some humanitarian standards. Incorporated, too, are acts which, though not strictly illegal or criminal, can be construed as "unconscionable" to the extent that they test the "intent" of a law. Reasoning thus in Kantian and Rawlsian vein, *unlawfulness* serves as an intermediate category between legality and criminality where the rightness of an action is conceived according to the extent to which it advances (affirms) or retards (denies) universally agreed principles (Figure 0.1).

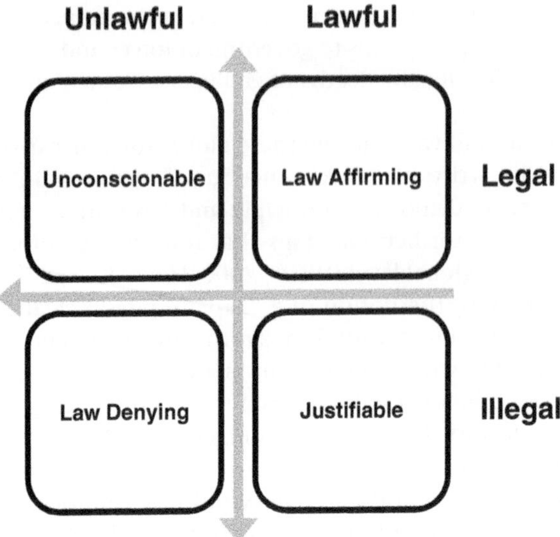

Figure 0.1 The scope of unlawfulness

Complicity

There is a "diabolical" paradox where moral people pursuing moral ends, nonetheless, find themselves induced or compelled by circumstance to commit immoral or "morally dubious acts" (Weber, 2008, pp. 200–204). Unfortunate circumstance or unintended consequence is no defence against the charge of complicity in crime. If anything, the chain of criminal causality and hence responsibility is lengthening in judicial and political theory. For the International Commission of Jurists, complicity is defined as action contributing "in greater or lesser ways to harm suffered by another" (ICJ, 2008, p. 5.). This raises many questions about the attribution of responsibility across the broad expanse of human suffering. Drawing on Arendt's seminal study of normalized evil in *The Origins of Totalitarianism* (1958), Patrick Hayden's *Political Evil in a Global Age* (2009) argues that the persistence of poverty, war crimes, crimes against humanity and human displacement is evidence of widespread and knowing complicity in routine if not systematic harm by governments and government officials, and intergovernmental agencies. Indeed, the reach of Hayden's cast net of complicity draws in virtually anyone and everyone who gains in some way from the denial of justice to others.

Perversely, global regimes have inbuilt tolerances for harm, albeit within prescribed limits. "Collateral damage" to civilian infrastructure and the unintended killing of civilians by states in wartime or during "humanitarian interventions" is "acceptable" according to the laws of war, as are civilian casualties incurred through justifiable military operations (Battersby et al., 2011; Battersby, 2012a; Kennedy, 2004). The destruction of livelihoods and the abuse of other human rights through the construction of economic infrastructure, roads, pipelines, industrial estates and hydroelectric dams is a frequent occurrence in developing countries where economic development is prioritized over the welfare of disempowered rural communities (White, 2008; Battersby and Siracusa, 2009). The consequences of regulated "environmental harm," in terms of polluted food chains and diminished biodiversity, draw attention to the ethically questionable nature of much legal international business practice, while also highlighting the costs of inaction to prevent unlawful environmental practices by both legal and illicit organizations (Elliot, 2007; White, 2008). Absolute compliance is, at best, a dangerous mirage because the integrity of those in charge can never be entirely guaranteed or the risk of repeat catastrophe ever excluded (Arendt, 2000a; Weber, 2008, p. 204).

Modern neo-liberal management is predicated upon new technologies of social control that seek to manufacture uniformity as a means to maximize efficiency and minimize the risk of deviations from the mean. However, standardization without a reflexive appreciation of the nature of human and global complexity incurs many "unintended" costs and forces many invidious trade-offs in the pursuit of social and political ends, whether economic gain or global security. The imposition of austerity measures to address the assumed root causes of the Eurozone crisis of 2011–2013 and the devastating and counter-productive consequences of these measures is but one example of official failure to grasp the unruly nature of global complexity (Blyth, 2013). The professionalization of management and the adoption of sterile economic and managerial discourse sanitize the "unconscionable" nature of much human behaviour validated by the allegedly mechanical laws of the marketplace.

Arguing from a different standpoint, Joseph Stiglitz's *Globalization and Its Discontents* (2000) and *Freefall* (2010) and Ha-Joon Chang's *Bad Samaritans* (2007) explore and explain how and why liberal development policies in the twentieth century failed to universalize liberal freedoms but instead perpetuated underdevelopment and poverty, indebtedness and political volatility. But who is to bear criminal or legal responsibility for the harm occasioned by grand but flawed systems of governance, be they state- or market-oriented, the instigators or the system's functionaries and apparatchiks – or the system itself? Karl Polanyi's assertion of the "unnaturalness" of market competition implies a systemic origin for the many flaws in human economic judgement that continue to undermine stability in the global economy. The tension between individuating market values and the social values of community, can, arguably, be thought of as potentially criminogenic (Polanyi, 2001, p. 258). Market pressures can and do force companies and their normally law-affirming employees to take risks and to stray or step into unlawful territory, just as potential windfall gains create an incentive to manipulate market conditions, as unambiguously demonstrated by events surrounding the 2008 Global Financial Crisis when the unlawfulness of a few inflicted serious economic and social harm on a global scale.

Whether we adopt Weber's "diabolical" paradox, Krasner's "organized hypocrisy" or Bull's "anarchic society" as the starting point for our analysis, the pursuit of absolute justice is indeed a precarious enterprise in a global environment in which laws are contested, rule breaking commonplace, security broadly defined and contingent on moral trade-offs that legalize the use of violence, for example, as an exceptional (but not unexceptionable) political expedient (Krasner, 1999; Bull, 2002; Weber, 2008, p. 204). Put another way, war might well be a horrific way for peoples to settle disputes or resolve differences, but the international community struggles to criminalize war in its entirety, only those aspects most repugnant to international sensibilities (Simpson, 2007, pp. 147–148). Notions of collective security aside, tolerances for violence remain encoded and codified in international norms.

Within realist thought, the historical record of frequent conflict, power struggles and atrocities serve as evidence of a fundamental truth about human nature and the nature of human societies (Mearsheimer, 2001). Seminal realist philosophers such as Reinhold Niebuhr caution against ignoring the human drive for power, for self-glorification and for wealth, because these human flaws allegedly defeat the pursuit of a universally moral international order (Niebuhr, 1934, pp. 20–25). Self-preservation and system maintenance are, in Bull's reasoning, prior to universal ideals of justice, law and rights and, thus, define the "base" operating codes of the international society of states. State criminality can, therefore, be defended as the consequence of breaks in the code between human aspirations for a moral world and the encoded operations of the global system. Yet Bull acknowledges the possibility of systemic transformation through the incremental "extension of cosmopolitan culture" (Bull, 2002, p. 305). Even realists can accommodate the idea that international order is socially constructed and that human society is malleable (Guilherme, 2011). Realists and cosmopolitans diverge as to the degree to which base operating code can be overwritten and the "system" as a whole reprogrammed.

The idea that "human nature" is constant is, argues Samuel Barkin, a "transhistorical" claim that can be dismissed as ahistorical if we accept the premise that human societies are "historically contingent" and subject to change (Barkin, 2010, pp. 44–45; Wendt, 1999). Advances in neuroscience and cognitive psychology are filtering into economics and political science, challenging notions of a fixed and calculable human rationality (Denzau et al., 2007; Ferguson, 2013). Steve Pinker in *The Better Angels of Our Nature: Why Violence Has Declined* (2011) writes, "humans are wired for violence," but this is not the same as arguing that the human propensity to use violence is a historical constant (Pinker, 2011, p. 483). Moral behaviour is learned, but while evidence of evolutionary learning can be read into statistically declining frequencies of conflict, and to advances in the provision of public welfare, ethical practice is often discouraged or defeated by the "anarchic" nature of international society (Al-Rodhan, 2008; Pinker, 2011). The message from Pinker is that we must be on guard lest the "dark side" of the human psyche wins out. Perhaps the greatest global danger then is not so much the transnational criminal or terrorist – "globalization's bastards" (Pollard, 2002) – but the complacency that comes with the mistaken belief in the human capacity to mitigate uncertainty through the management of risk (Giddens, 1990).

There are parallels to be drawn here with Arendt's warnings against seeking sanctuary in dreams of an arrested or "transcendent" utopian condition, which in reality can be nothing more than a complacency-inducing equilibrium. Complacency, Arendt argues, threatens the bases of democracy because, in this comatose state, the very conflicts – of ideas and interests – that sustain political vibrancy are stifled (Arendt, 2000a, pp. 36–40; 2000b, pp. 508–509). The drive to control the future through the quantification of risk feeds into myths of human perfectibility. The aggregation and manipulation of "big data," which, following Castells, manifests *informationalization* taken to the extreme, suffocates the very social dynamics upon which open and democratic societies depend because the mistaken faith in the distillatory omniscience of bulk information denies the infinite variability and unpredictability of human thought and behaviour (Arendt, 1972; Rihani, 2002; Silver, 2012). Deviations from the global mean cannot be standardized, and the pursuit of a standardized taxonomy of crime and criminality is fundamentally an illiberal enterprise.

Complex securities

The globe is connected in many complex ways and our thinking about global complexity has "evolved" considerably since the early pioneering International Relations work of Keohane and Nye (2012). There is increasingly much cross-fertilisation between political science and the natural sciences concerning the multidimensional and chaotic nature of human interactions and behaviour. John Urry and Samir Rihani have done much to "translate" scientific models of complexity into a language that social scientists can understand. Jim Whitman's *The Limits to Governance* (2005) maps out a path for genuinely global analysis of the perplexities of the contemporary global system. This book draws upon the ideas of biologist Niklas Luhmann who writes of the dynamism and chaos of complex biological systems in which "the continuing dissolution of the system becomes a necessary cause of its *autopoietic* reproduction" and within which "arbitrariness" and "unpredictability" are "unavoidable" (Luhmann, 1986, pp. 179–180). Models of biological systems complexity, applied to questions of human development, provide a sufficiently flexible conceptual framework within which to accommodate the observable irregularity or "chaos" (Rihani, 2002; Bird, 2003; Lorenz, 2004; Moeller, 2006; Smith, 2005; Mitchell, 2009). Complexity theory also opens wider the window on the possibility for error, in the measurement and analysis of human behaviours and in drawing conclusions about the nature, extent and strength of human social networks. A little disorder, or a lot, might be necessary for social adaptation. Yet the tendency, even in societies governed to serve liberal markets, is towards the pursuit of greater control achieved through the internalization of market values and individual self-regulation (Rihani, 2002; Elmer, 2012; Taleb, 2012). The same logic applies also to the security governance "scripts" dispensed by the global "executive" which threaten to replace global anarchy with something conceivably much worse (Kavalski, 2008; Held, 2010).

Even if political scientists agree that security is a "contested concept," in the world of security planners the word retains the status of a moral axiom and a moral imperative (Buzan, 1983; Buzan et al., 1998). Framed negatively as the absence of threat, physical or otherwise, security can be conceived as safety and protection from harmful or aggressive acts through the preservation of national strength or the disablement of presumed or actual enemies – or both. Framed positively, security can mean the creation or maintenance of conditions that enable the pursuit of individual and collective aspirations, with the proviso that the same rights and privileges are not denied to others. For realists, peace, the corollary of security, ensues from an orderly system or society of sovereign nation-states where security is synonymous with stability and is to be preserved by overlapping and often interlocking global and regional power balances of limited durability (Waltz, 1979, p. 112). Realism is the global "default code," but this realist "mental model" of order, as with all "imaginaries," offers or generates prescriptions fraught with error, not least because a risk is merely a future possibility, an apparition or spectre, yet to materialize, and which is therefore demonstrably unreal (Denzau et al., 2007; Steger, 2009).

Prefiguring critiques of modernist risk management, Arendt warns of the hubris that leads decision-makers into a mist of false assumptions and self-deceptions. This perplexity was evident in the Pentagon's reductionist "problem-solving" approach to the Vietnam War, which, she argues, perpetuated self-deceits and conceit as strategists and US political leaders alike convinced themselves and the American people that, on paper, the war was winnable (Arendt, 1972, pp. 38–39). Gregory A. Daddis's study of US military strategy in the Vietnam War indicates that poorly conceived and gratuitous "performance" metrics can have a blinkering effect on the perceptions and concerns of decision-makers, including those close to the seat of action and those far removed, leading to erroneous conclusions, futile strategies and fruitless policy (Daddis, 2012). The course of international interventions in Iraq and Afghanistan at the start of the twenty-first century gives strong indication that today's security planners are often similarly deceived and too willing to accept generic explanations and simplistic military solutions to complex questions of political dissonance. Even in the most brutal of conflicts, after all the bodies are counted, negotiation and compromise are still necessary for lasting peace. Peace is not a metric but a state of mind.

The "failed state" is pivotal to contemporary analysis of the crime–security nexus, attached to which is the assumption that the liberal state is the axiom towards which all developing countries must gravitate if the future of the globe is to be secured (Lambach, 2006; Duffield, 2007). Ashraf Ghani and Clare Lockhardt cite expanding criminal networks and crime economies, and corruption, as corrosive influences on state structures that, if unchecked, contribute to political "dysfunctionality" and "state failure" (Ghani and Lockhart, 2009, p. 82) According to this post-Cold War "domino theory," a collapsed state in which governmental authority is minimal to non-existent becomes, metaphorically speaking, a "black hole" into which violent and criminal opportunists are drawn by the attraction of zero governance. These lawless spaces – or "delinquent" states – become potential havens for criminals and terrorists unless corrective action is taken early and decisively.

The identification of indices and predictors of state failure renders security challenges visible and governable and makes "state failure" one of the catch-cries of twenty-first-century global governance (Duffield, 2007; 2010). This securitizing discourse invites the conclusion that managed interventions can "correct" deficiencies in national-level governance and engender greater societal stability at the global level. As Kenneth Waltz writes, however, "saying that stable states make for a stable world amounts to no more than saying that order prevails if most states are orderly. But even if every state were stable, the world of states might not be" (Waltz, 1979, p. 64). Liberal peace theory skirts around the unwelcome reality that democratic states can be callous and brutal when prosecuting war against authoritarian rivals and when promoting liberalism abroad (Reiter and Stam, 2002, p. 198; Rummel, 2008, p. 2). Missing from much insecurity analysis is the uncomfortable truth that the prosecution of secular liberal capitalism is necessarily disruptive. Historical experience suggests that inequality and political dissonance are inescapable consequences of rapid economic development and that both are potentially generative of violence and revolution (Velasco, 2005, p. 143; Huntington, 2006). The notion, therefore, that democratization (and, by implication, greater security) is attainable merely through the extension of liberal principles to illiberal states makes light of deep, enduring and intractable political divides within many countries – developed and developing – that give oxygen to crime and political violence.

Structure and scope of the book

The structure of this book maps out different but not separate categories of unlawfulness, beginning with the most deceptively straightforward category of transnational organized crime. Chapter 1 investigates the claim that global or transnational organized crime represents the most "clear and present danger" to global security. Measures of conventional crime are juxtaposed against obvious, and not so obvious, legal but arguably unconscionable corollaries to draw attention to the incongruities in prevailing conceptions of the categories "transnational criminal" and "organized crime." Much has been written about the crime–terror nexus and an alleged global crime–terror convergence since September 11, 2001. Chapter 2 questions the empirical and ideological bases of these interpretations by surveying the conditions of criminality in globally significant crime–security complexes in sub-Sahara Africa – from West to East – and in Southeast Asia and Latin America. Each complex is linked in different ways, and without denying local agency, to the interventions and disengagements of powerful states in the Global North and Global South. Convergence thinking is, arguably, a manifestation of the modernist drive to create order in the midst of complexity that constructs "individuated" crime and terror subjects but ignores the overarching forces that disrupt and destabilize the global system. Security risk management, or securitized public policy, is, viewed from this perspective, merely another case of the late modern state's drive to reassert control through "biopolitical" means (Giddens, 1990; Duffield, 2007).

In calculating the systemic sources of criminality, the crimes of networked states and state agents surface as, potentially, of greater disturbance to the global security environment. Chapter 3 inquires into crime–security dimensions of the non-observance of domestic and international law by state officials and their justifications for stepping over the "edge." In many instances, it seems, the claim of "necessity" occasioned by the apparent absence of trust in interstate relations is an all too convenient form of self-deception that helps to bridge a "moralization gap" (Pinker, 2011, pp. 491–492). International laws are not being violated so much as reinterpreted to serve state security aims in a globalizing world where subterranean challenges to state power are proliferating. In the absence of codified laws to govern global technological connectivity, cyber space is being refashioned by an invasion of war protocols, "deterrence," "defence" and "offence" that confound the idealized self-organizing logic of digital society. Here cyber crime and cyber security merge to create a new and disturbing amalgam where traditional conceptions of law and justice appear alien, even naive.

Concern over the extent to which networked states are subject to the influence of transnational capital encroaches unavoidably into this analysis of state power and practice. Chapter 4 evaluates the transgressions of the corporate world, and challenges the orthodox assumption that globalization necessarily weakens the bargaining power of states vis-à-vis transnational corporations. It argues that the vulnerabilities of the global economy are to be found not simply in the increasing sophistication and scale of illicit finance, but in the disruptive "economic warfare" of market competition and the reluctance of the world's most powerful companies to submit to regulatory restraint. Globalizing market forces corrode legal or regulatory protections – that is, they "destroy" in order to renew, which, market protagonists claim, impartially and thus justly serves a greater common good. Laws once enshrined in national legislations are consequently rendered into vaporous non-law, leaving the most vulnerable to grapple with the disappearance of certainty and the moral sureties that certainty provides.

The right to oppose illegitimate authority is fundamental to liberalism and, yet, in undermining the sovereign authority of states in order to achieve commercial objectives, corporate actors subvert liberalism. The subversion of sovereign authority is not, however, the preserve of "evil" corporations. Chapter 5 explores the conditions under which well-intentioned private individuals and non-state entities transgress law to oppose governmental regulations in the name of universal morality. This dimension of unlawfulness encompasses contradictions inherent in the pursuit of humanitarian objectives in "wicked" environments defined by political oppression and internecine conflict. Here we confront the perennial danger that steadfast adherence to universal principle merely perpetuates the very harms that humanitarian action is meant to prevent. The same can be said of civil disobedience taken to the "ignition point" of blind intransigence. This chapter, therefore, presents a disquieting critique of a very different category of expert claims, the counter-hegemonic claims of the development professional, the advocate and the political activist.

The analysis of crime and security needs must travel through a disquieting meta-logical universe to reach the cosmic heights of conceit from which to glimpse negative impressions of contemporary global society. In a complex global system, the pursuit of absolutes invites disappointment. The "judicialization" of international relations is, from this perspective at least, a partial answer at best to the global tolerance of harm. The globe is a system in which the Internet and cyberspace are but coded subsystems but which might yet reformulate global operating codes – for neither better nor worse, but for the sake of system maintenance. Chapter 6 conceptualizes the unlawful society thus as a society constructed upon amoral foundations, where the analysis of global crime and the pursuit of global security allows us to travel through the airlock between amoral and cosmopolitan space. It re-evaluates the proposition that governance frameworks and policy responses to the globalization of crime and the increasing complexity of security concerns at all levels can be conceived through a reflexive appreciation of paradox and perplexity – in other words, through a Rawlsian notion of "rough" or flexible justice. There is no dialectical synthesis, no grand "solution" provided for the crimes and insecurities explored in the chapters that follow, merely the unsatisfactory grappling with untidy notions of "integrity," "resilience," "restraint" and "reflexivity."

The quantifiable spread of transnational crime directs our attention towards itinerant deviants and maliciously inclined global vagabonds, and shades out larger considerations to do with the nature of global systemic change. Global society is entering a period of major disruptive transformation – a global inflection point. Taking the long-cycle view, the world is pushing forward towards a new peak of human achievement, carried on a wave of technological invention, but this brings with it many challenges of which the globalization of crime is but one. In analysing both the terrestrial and meta-logical connections between crime and security, it arrives at the conclusion that crime–security risks and threats are not external to global society but embedded in the social relations that constitute this global system. Complexes of insecurity are inextricably linked to systemic patterns of global change and the variable human interpretations of, and responses to, these patterns and their impacts. This, more so than transnational organized crime and/or terror, is the pervasive "dark logic" of globalization.

1 Criminal Measures: Counting the Costs of Transnational Crime

How substantial are criminal or illicit transactions relative to licit economic exchange? The globalization of crime or "deviant globalization" is, from one perspective, merely globalization unrestrained by law or principle, save for the necessary "black protocols" that facilitate criminal organization and exchange (Deibert, 2013). Indeed, the extension of criminal enterprises across time and space is but one more manifestation of the fluidity or "liquidity" and "compression" that are engendered by, and accelerate, globalization (Harvey, 1991; Baumann, 2000). Parallel to the diversification of corporations in the licit economy, criminal entities are "networked," "diversified," strategically managed and "vertically" integrated to achieve "upstream" and "downstream" business "synergies" (Naim, 2005; UNODC, 2007). Yet, the value of transnational criminal activity, such as can be gleaned from publicly available sources, is only a fraction of total global economic activity or gross global product.

Strong objections are often raised against the "securitization" of crime and the claim that transnational criminal networks are "winning" a global crime war (Andreas, 2011). Peter Andreas and Ethan Nadelmann highlight the growth of security as a domain of expert knowledge, encompassing both military and policing affairs, and the consequential growth in the number of experts and "expert systems" with a vested political or commercial interest in threat inflation (Giddens, 1990; Andreas and Nadelmann, 2006). Viewed systemically then, "securitization" perpetuates a global "state of emergency" that serves to entrench established power structures and negates inquiry into the sociological and political dimensions of crime (Duffield, 2007, p. 33). Clearly, the nature and extent of criminal activity is changing, but the dominant transnational organized crime narrative focuses attention on conventional "identikit" profiles of the protagonists of crime, with little or no consideration given to their social context. To achieve a genuinely global perspective in crime, therefore, conventional and unconventional profiles of crime need to be assembled, juxtaposed and analysed, and criminal relativities measured, not to exonerate the guilty but to recalibrate the scales of criminality.

Securitizing transnational crime

Security doctrines are first and foremost doctrines designed for the control of people as either the referents or the enemies of security. Pre-emptive or "prudential" intervention to correct or control deviance in the international systems is both sanctioned and "normalized" through two non-traditional security doctrines framed in response to the emergent complexities of the post-Cold War era. The first doctrine, "human security," prioritizes the well-being of peoples and communities above the security of states and frames human security as a development-oriented security domain addressing the interrelationships between poverty, human rights, public health, education, political participation and peace (UNDP, 1994). Marking substantial refinement of the concept, the United Nations (UN) Commission on Human Security declared in its 2003 report, *Human Security Now*, "the international community urgently needs a new paradigm of security," not least because the state, for so long the "fundamental purveyor of security," cannot be relied upon to guarantee the welfare of its people (UNCHS, 2003, p. 2). Defining security as "enablement," the Commission revisits the UN Charter and the Universal Declaration of Human Rights to objectively state a connection between respect for the rule of law, justice and peace. Reprising the "ethical realism" espoused by US presidents Franklin D. Roosevelt, Harry S. Truman and Dwight D. Eisenhower, the report re-represents respect for rights to self-determination and to freedom from persecution, famine and disease as the essential building blocks for an ordered new post-Cold War world (UNCHS, 2003; Lieven and Hulsman, 2006).

As a comprehensive framework for analysis and as an organizing principle for the mobilization of institutional resources, human security is a ground-breaking idea that captures the complexities of peace and security in the contemporary world. But like all ideas it can be subverted, not least because any human weakness and any systemic vulnerability could be interpreted as a threat to the organic security of global society and thus rendered "actionable." Human security is a concept not only conceived in opposition to materialist or realist notions of state-centric security but also to broaden the scope for state action to address a longer menu of security "problems" (Nuruzzaman, 2006, p. 300). The idea can be recruited to serve traditionalist ends, whether framed as militarized security or securitized crime, with the result that the repertoire of governance is culled of creative options to law enforcement and the use of force.

The second doctrine, emphasizing the dangers of "terror and transnational organized crime," gained ascendancy in Washington post-9/11. Security thinking in the US and among close US allies veered towards pre-emptive "threat disablement," distorting the problem-solving logic of human security to seek to control political outcomes in parts of the world deemed critical to US national security through strategic interventions (Boot and Kirkpatrick, 2004; Kagan, 2008; Rieff et al., 2008). In the logic of this terror and transnational organized crime imperative, anti-state terrorism and transnational crime are conceived as threats to US interests and to global order. Despite the discrediting failures of interventions in Afghanistan (2001–2014) and Iraq (2003–2011), residues of this interventionism – labelled, for better or worse, as "neo-conservatism – continue to inform conceptions of national and global security (Fukuyama, 2007).

Crime and terrorism thus constitute a new *raison d'être* for state interventions. Extensive inventories of political risk detail the structural causes of state failure and global insecurity. Replete with models outlining the conditions under which societies become destabilized, these inventories offer logic and legitimacy to "corrective" prescriptions including pre-emptive actions by interested parties (Farah, 2013). Much effort was invested in the study of state failure in the 1990s, for example, by the State Failure Task Force (also Political Instability Task Force), funded initially by the Central Intelligence Agency's (CIA) Directorate of Intelligence during the Clinton Administration. In quantifying political risk, the Task Force *matricized* a long schedule of "risk factors" that included, *inter alia*, widespread poverty, extreme inequality, lack of economic opportunity and the political and economic marginalization by the state of political groups claiming distinctive identities and rights. A "global model" is used to profile states and security risks according to regime type, with "democracies" identified as security enhancers. Authoritarian states with brittle regimes, weak economies and unresolved internal political tensions were placed high on the "at risk" list, with most located in the "badlands" of the developing and underdeveloped world, especially the underdeveloped Muslim world (Esty et al., 1998). The Institute for Economics and Peace adds to the wealth of security metrics with its Global Peace Index, offering a further refinement of the risk management approach to security. Adding to the weight of evidence in favour of liberal governance, the Index identifies 23 state-level factors or indicators of risk to global peace (IEF, n/d). Of these only four refer directly to crime: imprisonment rates, murder rates, criminal violence, perceptions of criminality and corruption. Indeed, crime ranks lower, relative to political legitimacy, economic opportunity or freedom, while the entire transnational dimension to crime is left to the reader to infer.

The compilation of compelling "big data" offers no guarantee that the data is either collected or interpreted without bias, especially where fiscal and political pressures are at play (Kavalski, 2008; Silver, 2012; Richards and King, 2013). Neither can we be assured that insecurities are likely to be addressed holistically where conceptions of the security challenges faced are narrow and bureaucratically partisan, or where the requisite security responses are limited to police surveillance, law enforcement and the militarization of diplomacy.

Parallel worlds

Official crime narratives detail an alarming global crime surge over the first decade of the twenty-first century. Transnational financial crime is, according to the US State Department, a serious threat to US security and global order. In its annual *International Narcotics Control Strategy Report* (INCSR), the Bureau of International Narcotics and Law Enforcement Affairs (INLEA) estimated a ten-fold increase in transnational financial crimes – ranging from money laundering to identity fraud – and warned of the new possibilities and vulnerabilities generated by the exponential growth of Internet traffic. The main security challenge identified, predictably, is "terror finance," which brackets terrorist organizations with organized crime and attaches greatest significance to the illicit activities of traffickers and terrorists (INLEA, 2008; US DoT, 2011; INLEA 2011, pp. 3–4). The growth and sophistication of financial crimes is a matter of concern for the risks posed to individuals and to the global financial system as a whole. There is, however, a conceptual gap between financial crimes detailed in the INCSR and the more complex issue of "shadow economies" that fall outside the remit of the International Monetary Fund's (IMF) Financial Action Taskforce and the global terror finance regime (Schneider et al., 2010, p. 4). The aggregate annual value of global "shadow" economic activity, encompassing both illegal and legal but also unconscionable economic behaviours, could be as high as US$15 trillion, of which as much as US$11 trillion is attributable to tax evasion and other forms of financial obligation avoidance – and much of this to the unlawfulness of otherwise lawful economic actors. The failure to abide by or to ensure payment of nationally legislated minimum wage rates could thus be conceived as a form of transnational financial crime and one that would draw in many footloose transnational corporations, in the textile, clothing and footwear industries especially (Schneider et al., 2010, p. 5; Tax Justice Network, 2011). Conventional money laundering, or illicit finance, conservatively estimated to be the equivalent of four to five per cent of global Gross Domestic Product (GDP) – approximately US$4 trillion – accounts for much of the remainder. But then what, under the expanded definition of financial crime offered here, is the absolute value of "stolen" money washing through the global financial system? This is to say nothing of the annual underpayment of overseas development assistance obligations by developed country governments spanning more than four decades (see Chapter 5).

Allowing for the impossibility of gathering reliable and comprehensive data on all forms of criminal finance, the aggregate value of transnational crime involving conventionally defined criminal entities is comparatively small, surprisingly, when considered in the context of a global economy worth US$83 trillion Purchasing Power Parity (PPP) in 2012, and a global financial system in which tens of trillions of dollars are traded lawfully each day. Valuations of financial crime are all too easily exaggerated. In one example, counterfeit bonds found in a Zurich bank vault in 2012 were claimed by police investigators to have a face value of US$6 trillion. Allegedly controlled by an Italian syndicate but attributed to an "international network" of criminals, the fakes were held up as an example of the increasing scale of criminal efforts to subvert the global financial system. As a single instance of attempted fraud, this appears a globally significant sum in a global bond market worth US$96 trillion (c. 2010–2011), and there were suggestions of a link to international terrorism, but it was, surprisingly, downplayed by US security officials as a wishful, amateurish and easily detectable "routine scam" – akin to running-off reams of bond certificates from a home office bubble-jet printer (Accenture, 2012, p. 3; Donadio, 2012). There is a very wide gap between monetary aspiration and market value. Exaggerations and misrepresentations contribute to an image of a world economy awash with illicit capital and in danger of falling into the clutches of organized crime syndicates. Yet, expansion in the illicit global economy might well be interpreted as an inevitable but *relatively* minor corollary of the rapid expansion of the licit global economy that has more than doubled in GDP terms since 1990.

It is possible both to overstate and to underestimate the relative significance of all forms of transnational criminal activity. The global trade in narcotics doubled in value in the first decade of this century, inflicting misery upon millions of addicts and their immediate families but, as noted, the global economy has also grown rapidly. United Nations Office on Drugs and Crime (UNODC) statistics indicate a "stable" prevalence of illicit drug use and "problem" drug use at, respectively, 5 per cent and 0.3 per cent of the global population aged 15 to 64. The actual number of persons addicted to or experimenting with illicit psychoactive substances rose from 180 million to 210 million, an increase of 30 million, but roughly proportionate to the growth of the world's population from six to seven billion over the same period (UNODC, 2011, p. 22; 2013a, p. 1). UNODC reports that the bulk of global illicit trade earnings (excluding investment returns) is derived from trafficking in cocaine (US$72 billion, 2008) and heroin (US$55 billion). Criminalized Amphetamine-Type Stimulants (ATS) are, however, today's designer drugs of choice (noting that there are many legal methamphetamine and amphetamine drugs used to treat respiratory and neurological conditions including depression; Benzedrine and Dexedrine for example). Illicit ATS manufacture and use is in a major growth phase and – because of their disaggregated production and distribution and the seemingly limitless chemical combinations available to synthesise new varieties of illegal stimulant – represents a more insidious global challenge (UNODC, 2013b, pp. 49–52). Mirroring patterns of transnational exchange in the licit global economy, nearly two-thirds of the "street value" or "surplus value" of exported narcotics is realized at point of sale in the US and European markets (UNODC, 2010, pp. 16–17). The gross yield from narcotics trafficking is of course much higher, incorporating returns from the investment of "drug money" in illicit and licit enterprise. Gross harm is likewise higher than monetized returns on narcotics transactions, and the balance of harm is likewise unevenly distributed across the globe.

Governments give character to the claimed transnational "threat" posed by narcotics trafficking and money laundering by associating crimes with established stereotypes: mafia dons, terrorists (read Islamists), "drug barons." In some instances, parallels are drawn for rhetorical effect between crime economies and states, to imply the solidification of criminal entities into a singular geostrategic menace. In its 2003 foreign policy white paper, the Australian federal government cast transnational organized crime as a major national security threat (DFAT, 2003, p. 46). The document stressed how aggregate transnational crime values exceeded the GDP of large developing countries, like Australia's nearest Asian neighbour, Indonesia, but such comparisons are misleading. Narcotics trafficking and money laundering are deterritorialized market activities, despite the intentional association of such endeavours with imaginary "narco-states." The terms "organization" and "organized" invoke an impression of structured and powerful institutions, on the scale of government agencies and private corporations. Yet, such actors are the very opposite of relatively small, localized, dispersed and opportunistic criminal enterprises that fit within the definitions of organized criminal groups provided in transnational criminal law, and without which much larger and well-known criminal operators could not profit. The narrative further entrenches transnational crime and transnational criminals as distinct categories of security risk thus setting to one side the systemic environment in which crime is generated.

Allowing for exaggeration, miscalculation and the plain wishful thinking of counterfeiters, the multiplier effects associated with transnational crime are nonetheless substantial. The Federal Bureau of Investigation (FBI) estimates the value of narcotics-generated finance spilling across the US–Mexico border to be in the range of US$18–38 billion (INLEA, 2013). This encompasses trade values but also the licit and illicit banking and investment returns to drug trafficking syndicates. The corrosive impacts of drug trafficking and drug-related crimes of course extend to the destabilization of communities and entire countries. Government officers can be corrupted and governmental institutions captured or at least severely compromised. The public health impacts include not only drug-related deaths – there were 211,000 such fatalities in 2011 – but also the cost to healthcare systems of treating those with drug dependencies, HIV and also those affected by drug-related violence (UNODC, 2013a, p. ix, pp. 4–8). These interconnections underpinned US government budget allocations for counter-narcotics operations of approximately US$24–25 billion per year between 2009 and 2013 (Mueller, 2011; ONDCP, 2013; Wyler, 2013, p. 24). For Australia, with a population of 23 million, the multiplied cost of crime "as a whole," including social and economic costs and crime control, is, according to the Australian Crime Commission, A$10–15 billion (US$10.5–15.5 billion) annually (Australian Crime Commission, 2011). There is no point in dismissing the harm done by illicit drug production and use, and it is not the purpose of this book to argue the case for decriminalization or otherwise. There is, however, a case to argue as to the patterns of public choice by which certain psychotropic substances are declared illicit and others not.

Heroin and cocaine are rendered illicit because of their addictive qualities and harmful neurological impacts, but the primary and historical origins of their criminalization are found in the convergence of Christian evangelist morality and the political economy of the global drug industry. The genesis of the global anti-narcotics regime is traced to the moral objections to opium and alcohol among evangelical Christian groups in the US during the nineteenth century, a sentiment that proved strategically advantageous to both the US government and American pharmaceutical companies. Global criminalization of opium weakened the market power of European, principally German, drug companies and removed an important economic mainstay of European, principally British, imperialism in Asia. Beginning with the International Opium Convention, 1912, the international community has sought through successive legislation to control the production and sale of harmful "psychotropic" drugs. The success or otherwise of these efforts is debatable given that criminalization of opiates and cocaine created the lucrative market for the illicit narcotics that we have today. The global ascendancy of the US post-1945 facilitated the growth in narcotics trafficking and paradoxically gave Washington greater strategic leverage over major narcotics-producing countries through the strident assertion of a global anti-narcotics norm (Tyrrell, 1991; Trocki, 1999; Andreas and Nadelmann, 2006; Okrent, 2011). Perversely, a major contributing factor to this global heroin trade was intervention by the US in Vietnam and Laos in the 1960s. Although the level of heroin addiction is disputed, and criminal involvement denied by the CIA, the war in Vietnam generated an appetite for many varieties of stimulants, including lawfully supplied amphetamines, among US service personnel seeking to cope with or temporarily escape the trauma of conflict (McCoy, 2003; Kuzmarov, 2009; Hersh, 1972). Criminalization set the market price for illicit opiates; disruptive, amoral globalization fanned market demand.

How much more harmful might opium and cocaine trafficking or trading be, in public health terms, if trade or traffic in these illicit substances flourished under the same legal and political protection as nicotine? Moral objections to tobacco and other legal but deadly substances cross ideological divides but are unlikely to gather critical mass without an enabling confluence of hegemonic commercial and geostrategic self-interest. Nicotine is an addictive stimulant that, in addition to the harm done to tobacco users, causes severe physiological and psychological distress to those who seek to break their dependency. Tobacco is a global industry, valued at US$450 billion, and also a global health curse. The World Health Organization (WHO) has calculated that tobacco smoking kills six million people per year and imposes substantial cost burdens on health systems forced to cope with tobacco's many harmful side effects, including but not limited to lung cancer, emphysema, cardiovascular disease, eye disease and the increased risk to maternal and infant health (British American Tobacco, 2011, p. 8; WHO, 2011, p. 12).

Yet, tobacco continues to be produced, processed, packaged and sold, indifferent to the harm done to those who consume the end product. There can be no claimable negligence, and no possibility of plausible denial, and yet the formal criminalization of tobacco is impossible because of the strategic influence exercised by the global tobacco industry. Combative tobacco companies deploy substantial strategic cash reserves to pressure, even capture, governments and direct them to block stricter tobacco controls, and to bankroll international trade "lawfare" against noncompliant states through the World Trade Organization (WTO) (Seccombe, 2013; Voon and Mitchell, 2013). There is no tangible public benefit from tobacco production – beyond state tax revenues, employment and profit generation – and if these are sufficient justification for legal status then there could be little objection to the decriminalization of opium, cocaine, cannabis or hemp. The susceptibility of the principal norm globalizer, the US, to corporate influence means, however, that the global benchmarks for both intolerable drug-inflicted harm and acceptable drug-related killing are set too high.

Crime and criminality become much more complex non-traditional security issues once measured or considered against licit or tolerated correlates. Another contentious "traffic" – the illicit trade in human beings – survives in a global system where slavery was outlawed almost two centuries ago. In addition to the 214 million people moving around the world as temporary and permanent international migrants, the International Labour Organization (ILO) estimates that there are around 2.4 million internationally trafficked persons in an illicit global business valued by UNODC as in excess of US$32 billion (ILO, 2008, p. 3; UNODC, 2010, p. 16; IOM, 2011, p. 49). The scale of this issue, however, reaches far beyond illegal cross-border transfers of human beings. When all forms of forced labour, within as well as between states, were included in the count, the number of trafficked persons was not less than 27 million and as many as 30 million or more for 2012 (US DoS, 2013; Walk Free Foundation, 2013). Criminal laws and law enforcement agencies target "traffickers," "people smugglers" and their confederates in legal as well as criminal businesses as the protagonists of exploitation (FBI, n/d). Yet, as Maggy Lee argues, "trafficking" is not simply a problem of "irregular" international transfers of people for money but is part of larger patterns of gender discrimination and labour exploitation, and also the governance systems created to criminalize and penalize those caught in the complex webs of the global people trade (Lee, 2011, p. 149).

Refugee flows are indices of the uneven geographic distribution of human insecurity (Table 1.1). The 1951 Refugee Convention and the United Nations High Commissioner for Refugees (UNHCR), created to protect people displaced by war, confront escalating responsibilities in an increasingly volatile global system. According to Barnett and Finnemore (2004), the global policy balance has, over the course of the last 60 years, tilted against resettlement towards "voluntary" repatriation of refugees (p. 93). This shift in emphasis, they continue, is due to the increased reluctance of developed countries to accommodate refugees following the mass exodus from Indochina after 1975 (ibid., pp. 94–103). Indeed, repatriation is celebrated by the UNHCR as a "durable solution" to refugee crises and the measure most responsible for a decline in refugee numbers in recent years (UNHCR, 2006a, 2006b). While responsibility for such human suffering is popularly attributed to military dictators and their corrupt regimes, modern mass refugee movements highlight significant structural weaknesses in the evolving global system which governments in the developed world and global institutions are best placed but reluctant to tackle. Statistics on refugee movements represent an unacceptable social and, for the most part, hidden cost of power politics at the local and global level reflecting the broad "bandwidth" of tolerance for human misery in contemporary global society.

Table 1.1 Tolerable distance: Human displacement and resettlement, 2012

	Official population	**Refugees (and asylum seekers) by country of origin (2012)**	**IDPs (2013)**
Iraq	31.8 million	747,440 (23,920)	2.1 million
Syria	22.4 million	728,542 (25,671)	6.5 million
Somalia	10.2 million	1.1 million (32,978)	1.1–1.3 million
Sudan	34.8 million	569,212 (21,525)	2.5 million
Colombia	45.7 million	394,122 (18,850)	4.9–5.5 million
Afghanistan	31.1 million	2.58 million (51,834)	493,000
Myanmar	55.1 million		430,400
Global Total		15.4 million (937,000)	26.4 million
Global Refugee Resettlement 2012 – 88,578 (all countries)			

Sources: UNHCR, IDMC, Refugee Council of Australia, CIA *World Factbook*, 2012

The empirical connections between tectonic power shifts and irregular migration are undeniable, as are the dangers that confront those displaced by conflict. Trafficking in persons is defined in the UN Trafficking Protocol as "the recruitment, transportation, transfer, harbouring or receipt of persons, by means of the threat or use of force or other forms of coercion, of abduction, of fraud, of deception, of the abuse of power . . ." (UN Trafficking in Persons Protocol, 2000, p. 2). A useful distinction is made between trafficking and smuggling in the two UN protocols appended to the CTOC and which govern unlawful people movements on the basis of the relationship between the perpetrators and their victims or clients. While trafficking almost always involves coercion, smuggling implies a degree of consent between the smuggler and the persons smuggled (UNODC, 2004, pp. 42, 54–55). Women and children living in poverty or escaping conflict are particularly susceptible to trafficking and to exploitation at the hands of smugglers, and in practice, the level of "consent" involved in a smuggling transaction can quickly diminish in favour of the smuggler/s. Feminist economists Smriti Rao and Christina Presenti contend that poverty is not necessarily the primary driver of the international illegal labour trade as much as relative economic opportunity. Indeed, they argue that relatively affluent women, meaning those who are not poor within their country of origin, often willingly submit to smuggling rings (Rao and Presenti, 2012, pp. 254–257).

There is still reason, however, to stress the economic vulnerability of women and young children to forced labour because of extremes of income inequality, and a case to be made for economic justice as one avenue for the reduction of women's exploitation. One major and underresearched issue of social injustice is the lawful but unjust non-payment of women for work done, primarily in the household. One early study of gender and income inequality, by the United Nations Development Programme (UNDP), estimated that in global aggregate terms "all non-monetized work" was worth $16 trillion in 1995 (equivalent to 70 per cent of "visible" global GDP), of which women accounted for US$11 trillion (UNDP, 1995, p. 97). More recent analyses indicate that between one-third to one-half of all work done by women is unpaid (UNDESA, 2010, p. 102). In countries with welfare states that pay income supplements and social benefits for parenting and caring, there is still a significant issue with women's underpayment or unequal payment relative to men for comparable work. Universal welfare coverage, meaning access to adequate income support, subsidized services and the like, is a myth even in many advanced industrial countries. However, the attractiveness of work in developed countries, even if illegal, remains strong, despite rising unemployment in the wake of the Global Financial Crisis (GFC).

Representations of mobility crime focus, in the public domain at least, on "people traffickers" and the victims of trafficking as criminal subjects. Selective attention draws analysis away from systemic considerations, and the circle of unlawfulness is therefore restricted. Trafficking is one part of a global illegal labour trade, the scale of which is unknown. Undocumented workers, illegal immigrants employed as cheap and compliant labour, are vulnerable to exploitation through underpayment or non-payment of wages – which as discussed above is a form of financial crime – and politically voiceless on account of their illegal status. As much as half of US agriculture's one million strong immigrant workforce is thought to be illegal. Across all industries, there are estimated to be 11 million such undocumented workers, overwhelmingly from Latin America (primarily Mexico) and the Caribbean, roughly equivalent to the total number of illegal immigrants residing in the US (Baragona, 2010; Dwoskin, 2013; Passel et al., 2013; Romanelli, 2013). The demand for illegal labour is evidently substantial, as is the available supply, and one principal reason for this is substantial inequality in economic opportunity between nations. Undocumented migrants are not necessarily trafficked or smuggled, but neither are all trafficked persons the victims of kidnapping or labour recruitment scams.

This use of antinomies destabilizes conventional framings of transnational crime and aids reconceptualization and recontextualization of the issue of criminality. The approach draws out structural and semantic considerations that shed light on the nature of criminal activity and also focus attention on official conceptions of criminality. Switching location and focus, piracy over the past decade has become closely associated, spuriously, with terrorism and Islamism in East Africa. Article 101 of the United Nations Convention on the Law of the Sea (UNCLOS) (1982) defines piracy as "any illegal acts of violence or detention, or any act of depredation, committed for private ends by the crew or the passengers of a private ship, or a private aircraft" (UNCLOS, 1982, p. 57). The survival and growth of piracy as a market enterprise is attributable to the growth of maritime commerce globally and to the evolution of interconnected subregional crime complexes linked to intrastate armed conflicts. Piracy has emerged as a global security priority in terms of policy and public media profile because of the audacious exploits of pirate gangs operating off the east coast of Africa and the identification of North and East Africa, with globalized concern regarding the emergence of an extreme Islamist element in Somalia. Costs to shipping companies from piracy in the Gulf of Aden, measured in ransoms paid to Somali pirates, is estimated to be between US$339 million and US$413 million for the period 2005–2012. A critical multiplier effect becomes apparent when we consider the aggregate annual costs to companies, in terms of increased insurance premiums, rerouting of shipping and the like, which is US$18 billion annually (UNSC, 2013a; World Bank, 2013b, p. 40). As will be discussed in Chapter 2, this transnational crime is neither specific nor endemic to East African waters.

Piracy is but one form of maritime crime; it brings into focus illegal and unregulated fishing, toxic-waste dumping, and smuggling and trafficking across maritime boundaries. The maritime shadow economy is broad and broadening, encompassing actors as diverse and divergent as conventional criminal entities, Somali clansmen, Indonesian and Russian fishermen, shipping companies and oil traders. Contraband and forged goods, narcotics, light weapons and endangered and protected species of animals and plants are moved across the surface of the globe in containers carried aboard legally registered vessels on routine shipping runs. Such is the scale of maritime commerce and the limited surveillance capabilities of customs and port authorities that a substantial proportion of shipping containers are not closely checked (Griffiths and Jenks, 2012). This is no minor point because the global rule of law, such as it is, depends upon the legitimacy of international laws and the institutions that administer them. And yet, as will be discussed in Chapters 3 and 4, many legal entities, including both state and private commercial actors, frequently bring the global rule of law into disrepute.

Environmental crimes

The grid of maritime crime encompasses the violation of national and international environmental laws, including environmental protections and prohibitions. In the strictest sense, environmental crimes are human actions that are both harmful to the natural environment and proscribed by law. As with all forms of market or transnational crime, environmental crimes are conceived as crimes against state law, perpetrated by criminal individuals or gangs but not by states (Rice, 2008; Bricknell, 2010). Landmark international- and national-level environmental protection laws pre-date or parallel the development of what we know as international environmental law today – with one or two exceptions. The International Convention for the Regulation of Whaling (1948) and the Antarctic Treaty (1959) are key foundational agreements that, in the case of the former, opened the way for a total ban on whaling in the 1980s and, in the latter, the prohibition of mining in the Antarctic under the Protocol on Environmental Protection to the Antarctic Treaty (1998). The earliest and best-known instance of modern national environmental legislation is the 1872 Act of US Congress that created the world's first national park, Yellowstone National Park, and the first of many established in the US. This incorporation of environmental values into US law grew from middle-class civic campaigns of mobile and mobilized urban professionals, writers, adventurers and artists, influenced to an extent by the Romantic Movement's celebration of the "sublime" power and "picturesque" beauty of "wilderness." But the purpose of national parks legislation was protection or "conservation" rather than the criminalization of environmental harm *per se* (Antolini, 2009).

Pollution was first criminalized under US federal law in 1899, but the creation of a robust environmental governance regime within the US occurred in tandem with the rise of modern environmentalism as a global political phenomenon in the 1970s (Uhlmann, 2009; Cohen, 1992, p. 1056; Meadows et al., 1972). Globally, the institutionalization of environmental governance accelerated appreciably in the last decades of the twentieth century, driven in part by grave concerns that the global environment could not withstand the stresses imposed by rapid industrialization and increased consumption of non-renewable resources (WCED, 1987). Diminishing public tolerance for environmental harm created the political opportunity to expand the scope of environmental criminal law, and to attempt to impose stricter criminal sanctions on offenders (Marald, 2001). Environmental conservation and environmental protection are today established international norms given prescriptive force in a wide range of international conventions. A substantial body of international law is emerging around environmental issues ranging from the Montreal Protocol on greenhouse gas emissions (1987), which led to a measurable reduction in the use of ozone-depleting chlorofluorocarbons (CFCs) over the next decade, followed by other landmark agreements including the Basel Convention on the Movement of Hazardous Waste (1989), the Convention on Biological Diversity (CBD) (1992) and the Convention on International Trade in Endangered Species (CITES) (1973). Even so, the dividing lines between lawful and criminal harvesting of natural resources are fiercely contested and complicated by jurisdictional disputes and the oftentimes qualified acceptance of environmental responsibility by governmental authorities.

UNCLOS defines extensive protections (and obligations) for the governance of marine environments claimed by signatory states as part of their Exclusive Economic Zones (EEZ), one reason why the US, until recently, was reluctant to ratify the treaty (Patrick, 2012). The extension of these exclusive zones to up to 200 miles offshore has two effects. Firstly, it enlarges the maritime space within which national fishing regulations can be enforced and, secondly, it widens the net of maritime surveillance. Logically, this extension of national jurisdiction should reduce the incidence of Illegal, Unreported and Unregulated fishing (IUU). If anything, however, the issue has become more acute because either political commitment or enforcement capabilities are weak in many states, and because fish remain vital to the food security of millions. The growth of unlawful fishing is a consequence of the expansion of fishing capacity worldwide, from an estimated 585,000 fishing vessels in 1970 to 4.36 million in 2010 (FAO, 2010, p. 47). In tandem with these systemic pressures comes the *informationalization* of fishing, a necessary regulatory step, but also a challenge to the unregulated "traditional" fishing practices of coastal communities. The Food and Agriculture Organization (FAO) estimates a global population of 54.8 million people reliant to some degree on fishing for their livelihoods. Of these, 97.8 per cent live in the Global South and depend upon small-scale coastal or inland fisheries for their subsistence, and who now find themselves "captured" in the vast "trawl nets" of global environmental governance (FAO, 2012, p. 10).

The cost of unlawful fishing, measured as lost potential earnings, is estimated at between US$10 billion and US$23 billion (MRAG, 2009; Agnew et al., 2009). In net financial terms, therefore, illegal fishing could conceivably be a more serious global problem than maritime piracy. The key difference, however, is that with illegal fishing, poorer countries suffer, whereas with piracy, it is the richer countries and larger corporations that are most affected. More important, unlawful fishing is not simply a case of the Global North exploiting the Global South with impunity. Vessels flagged as Chinese, Russian, Panamanian and Indonesian join ships from Europe and Japan in the global unlawful fish harvest. Another factor, the collapse of state-controlled fishing industries in the former Soviet Union, created the opportunity and incentive for private operators to disregard Russian and international fisheries laws. To this list should be added the smaller flotillas of illegal fishermen operating inshore and offshore in claimed traditional fishing grounds but acting in contravention of national fisheries legislation.

If the scale of illegal fishing is significant, more so, again, is the legal overexploitation of fisheries pushed to or beyond the limit of sustainability to feed the world's growing demand for protein sourced from fish meat. Critical fisheries such as the Atlantic bluefin tuna are placed under increasing pressure through legal overexploitation, which continues despite international agreements to curtail their exploitation (FAO, 2012, p. 12). Global environmental laws are often "gamed" by countries seeking concessions that contravene the spirit of international conventions. An international ban imposed in 1986 by the International Whaling Commission (IWC) suspends indefinitely the practice of commercial whaling everywhere. The intent of the law is the recovery of whale species endangered by over a century of intensive harvesting. Although Norwegian whalers hunt commercially for minke whale, Japan has attracted the greatest international condemnation for breaching the terms of its special permit for "scientific whaling" by hunting minke whales in Antarctic waters (specifically Australia's declared Southern Ocean Whale Sanctuary) – now confirmed as a treaty violation by judgement of the International Court of Justice (ICJ, 2014). The Norwegian minke whale quota was set at 1,286 for 2011, although less than half that number was harvested – or slaughtered. Japan's "scientific" whale catch of 266 animals in 2012 is also well below the quota and substantially less than the previous year's inshore "small cetaceans" catch of over 3,000 mammals (killer whales, dolphins and porpoises) (Kishiro, 2012; WDC, 2013). The point is that a return to full-scale commercial exploitation on the high seas, on the evidence of past and present whaling practice, is likely to put certain whale stocks under extreme stress. Contrary to neo-liberal ideals of self-regulation, the operating costs, and risks, involved in large- and small-scale commercial fishing, to say nothing of high variability of returns, render species collapse a distant and second-order concern for many – too many – operators.

Risk subjectivities aside, the scientific evidence suggests that many under and un-regulated human impacts on marine environments threaten global food security. Depleting or collapsed fish stocks and a growing global population mean that pressure on the world's remaining marine environments will intensify – from legal as well as illegal activities. Where, on land, responsibility for policing crime is determined by sovereign jurisdiction, in the world's oceans, maritime jurisdiction is often contested, not least in international waters beyond the internationally recognized maritime zones. In the EU, measures to suppress IUU include the blacklisting of fishing vessels known to have engaged in illegal fishing and extend to market-based measures to reduce consumption of illegally procured marine produce through strict labelling standards (EC, 2009). The EU is acutely conscious of the costs of illegal fishing globally and is taking steps to prosecute ships and shipowners for maritime crimes; however, the collapse of fish stocks and the attendant loss of livelihoods cannot be rectified through punitive measures alone. This is because, for the millions who depend upon coastal fisheries for essential protein, the curtailment of fishing entails a radical change of livelihood and cultural practice.

What was once lawful or traditional practice quickly becomes unlawful and illegal when localized cultural economies are incorporated into global systems of governance. The illegal harvesting of rainforest timber is another site of intersection where global control is compromised by gaps between national and international monitoring and enforcement regimes, and by inequalities in wealth within and between countries. The scale of illegal logging is extensive, and, from a climate change perspective, potentially more harmful in global terms than any other form of environmental crime, and, yet, land clearing is essential for swidden agriculture and practised widely by those people clinging precariously to their traditional way of life. Virgin or primary rainforests are still disappearing in equatorial Southeast Asia and the Amazon and, while logging companies are to a large extent responsible for the most intensive deforestation, it is important to recognize the complex array of factors involved in land clearing, including population growth, urban sprawl, industrial development, poverty and farm profit incentives (Ramage et al., 2013).

Illegal logging involves the felling of timber, usually free-standing, in contravention of the national, state or provincial forestry laws of the country where the practice occurs. This includes felling without a permit, falsification of tags or markings, and certificates and the movement and trade in illegally harvested timber. It becomes a transnational crime when this timber is exported. In the case of Indonesian timber, illegal felling historically outstripped legal supply, a reality compounded by the price competitiveness of illegally sourced wood (Schloenhardt, 2008, pp. 48–53). Indonesia holds roughly 10 per cent of the world's remaining rainforest, and there are grave fears that this is fast diminishing due to a combination of legal and illegal logging. Tentative estimates furnished in a 2010 Chatham House study suggest a "dramatic" decline in the volume of illicit timber from three quarters of all known Indonesian production to perhaps as low as 40 per cent of the annual timber harvest, in line with a global downward trend in the international trade in illegally procured wood and wood products since 2000 (Schloenhardt, 2008, p. 49; Lawson and MacFaul, 2010, p. 94). That said, calculations do not capture the effects of the GFC, nor the possibility that this environmental crime occurs masked by unlawfully procured government concessions, as acknowledged by the authors of the Chatham House report (Lawson and MacFaul, 2010, p. 95). Also within this governance complex there sits an uncomfortable ambiguity. Governments are under enormous informal and indirect commercial pressure to legislate to open new areas to logging; that is to enlarge the scope of lawful but damaging timber harvests (Dauvergne and Lister, 2011).

The global logging industry thrives when global demand for downstream products like plywood and paper is strongest and also because timber is a more readily exploitable source of income and domestic capital accumulation in developing countries (Katchadourian, 2011, p. 188). Because Indonesia in one of the world's last regions of extensive rainforest coverage, unlawful logging threatens global environmental harm. But forest governance is complicated by the patronage structure that supports the timber industry. In a fast developing country such as Indonesia with a wide disparity in wealth, and a patronage system that continues to link big business with powerful political leaders, the dynamics of illegal logging are entrenched. According to Peter Dauvergne, Japanese general trading companies, the *sogo shosha*, which invested heavily in the development of Indonesia's forestry industry during the early decades of former President Suharto's rule, courted and to an extent "captured" powerful political patrons (Dauvergne, 1997). The legacy is a politically powerful domestic timber "lobby" and rapid and extensive deforestation; a pattern repeated across developing Asia and the Pacific, driven by demand in Japan and China but in which Western consumers are to a degree complicit (Dauvergne, 2011; 1997; Elliot, 2007; Katchadourian, 2011).

Concern for climate change is less a motivating factor – if a factor at all – in international efforts to suppress the illegal timber trade. In order of priority, the main drivers of global forest regulation are: the suppression of transnational crime, the promotion of sustainable economic development and then wildlife protection. More directly, the US pursues its legislative options through amendments to the 1900 Lacey Act introduced in 2008. The amendment states unequivocally that it is "unlawful to import, export, transport, sell, receive, acquire, or purchase in interstate or foreign commerce any plant, with some limited exceptions, taken or traded in violation of the laws of a US state and most foreign laws" (US Code Title 16, Ch. 53, Sect. 3372). Australia's Illegal Logging Prohibition Regulation of 2012 extends the scope of the 1901 Customs Act to address the importation of illegally felled timber and illegal timber products. These developments are not without tensions because, among those countries party to CITES, there is a wide divergence in regulatory capacity – including the capacity to sift out illegally sourced wood and deter environmental criminals (Brack, 2013; Lawson and MacFaul, 2010, p. 30; Dauvergne, 2001, pp. 60–64). Australia's recalibration of its customs regime met with objections, from Indonesia, for example, for allegedly imposing a restraint on international trade, implying a breach of WTO regulations, but reflecting official Indonesian concern for the enormity of the regulatory burden imposed (Alford, 2012; Brack, 2013; ICTSD, 2012). As with many if not most areas of global environmental regulation, legal jigsaws do not fit smoothly at the point where national and international pieces meet. Prevention of environmental harm necessarily therefore must go beyond criminalization to include investment in reforestation programmes, alternative income generation, effective domestic law enforcement, as well as programmes to raise consumer awareness. However, these alternative measures are all too easily confounded by vested interests – or ill-conceived development policies.

It is the most vulnerable who are at the "receiving end" of official policies and actions deemed necessary to progress national development. Dams, because of their extensive human and environmental impacts, have generated strong public opposition – in countries where opposition is tolerated – because of their disrupting impacts upon those who live within catchment areas. Signatories to the CBD acknowledge the "close and traditional dependence of many indigenous and local communities embodying traditional lifestyles on biological resources" (CBD, 1992, pp. 1–2). Dam construction is for governments in the developing world symbolic of modernity and also a relatively expedient means to provide water and generate cheap hydroelectric energy for their populations. It is not that relocation of indigenous communities is unconscionable but rather indigenous rights are frequently swept aside. Under the CBD, signatories are urged to "respect, preserve and maintain knowledge, innovations and practices of indigenous and local communities embodying traditional lifestyles relevant for the conservation and sustainable use of biological diversity" (ibid., p. 6). The indigenous people of Malaysia, or the Orang Asli, confront the ongoing destruction of their forest habitat to make way for dam projects to provide water and energy for Malaysia's industrial centre in Selangor's Klang Valley. Environmental impacts extend to the dismantling of rainforest ecosystems which, environmental and community rights campaigners argue, threaten the region's biodiversity.

The UN Declaration on the Rights of Indigenous Peoples (2007), to which Malaysia is also a signatory, states that the government must "consult and cooperate in good faith [. . .] prior to the approval of any project affecting their lands or territories and other resources, particularly in connection with the development, utilization or exploitation of mineral, water or other resources" (Article 32, 2, UN DRIP). Consent can, however, be "engineered" by breaking down community consensus through the offer of direct compensation payments – as occurred with the Klang Valley project. Once communities are relocated, and traditional lands appropriated, the urgency for state authorities to fulfil obligations rapidly diminishes – or so it is apparent (Swainson and McGregor, 2008, p. 160). This is not a failing specific to dam construction in Malaysia.

The world's largest hydroelectric dam construction project, the Three Gorges Dam and its reservoir on China's Yangtze River spans 1,045 square kilometres, and, it is estimated, displaced 1.3 million people up to 2012. Allegations have regularly leaked about the failures of resettlement strategies, which were deemed as woefully inadequate and leaving vast numbers of displaced villagers in greatly reduced circumstances. Environmental and human rights take second place to national economic development priorities in the policies of authoritarian and liberal democratic states alike. The CBD requires signatory states to assume "responsibility to ensure that activities within their jurisdiction or control do not cause damage to the environment of other States or of areas beyond the limits of national jurisdiction" (CBD, Article 3, p. 4). The local effects of the Three Gorges Dam have, according to environmentalists, been devastating – including destruction of downstream ecosystems, loss of biodiversity and geological destabilization (International Rivers, 2012a). More controversial are the transboundary effects of dam construction along the upper reaches of the Mekong River in southern China; neighbouring countries that rely upon the Mekong for irrigation allege that the construction is impacting river flows to the detriment of food security in the Greater Mekong (Tolson, 2013).

The intergenerational consequences of poorly planned dam projects are exemplified by the plight of the Aral Sea. Today the Aral Sea straddles the border between the Central Asian republics of Kazakhstan and Uzbekistan. Fifty years ago, both countries were states within the former Soviet Union, and it was Soviet central planning that caused the swift ruination of what was then the world's fourth largest freshwater lake. Water from tributary rivers in the Aral Sea Basin was diverted to irrigate state-controlled cotton farms in the steppes of Uzbekistan, Tajikistan and Kazakhstan, and for hydroelectric projects, causing water levels in the Aral Sea to decline by 90 per cent and water salinity to quadruple. This environmental legacy is today primarily the responsibility of Uzbekistan and Kazakhstan, countries heavily reliant upon natural resources industries for their economic development, and whose diplomatic relations are tested by the sensitivity of this issue (Peimani, 2009, p. 203). Where such transboundary issues occur between relatively stable states, the potential for common environmental concerns to be managed peacefully is high. The opposite obtains in zones of intense resource contestation and a rapidly evolving complex of crime, politics and insecurity (see Chapter 2).

Dysfunctional states and "liquid" crimes

As highlighted in the preceding discussion, the governance capacities of states vary markedly across the globe. Samuel Huntington's seminal inquiry into political change in the developing world stresses that inequality and political dissonance are inevitable consequences of rapid economic development and that both are potentially generative of violence and revolution, and by implication the same processes affect law enforcement capacity. At the very least, his historical analysis indicates that political development does not follow a predictable, linear path (Huntington, 2006, pp. 56–71). As Jose Velasco writes, "the establishment of democracy through peaceful and democratic ways seems to be a historical rarity" (Velasco, 2005, p. 143). The notion that democratization is attainable merely through the extension of liberal principles to illiberal states makes light of deep, enduring and intractable political divides within many countries – developed and developing – that give oxygen to crime.

The most compelling argument used to elevate transnational crime to a security threat is the alleged corrosive impact of crime gangs and powerful crime figures on bodies politic. Yet neither the Cosa Nostra nor the Yakuza prevented the US or Japan, respectively, from becoming global economic heavyweights. The heroin trade did not break Afghanistan, to give one example of an alleged "narco-state," nor turn the country into a zone of protracted internecine war. Afghanistan's swift emergence as the epicentre of global heroin trafficking reflects as much the fraught conditions of everyday life as it does the political aspirations of Islamists. Critically, the polar vectors of Cold War geostrategic rivalries intersected with the realities of Afghanistan's location on the western fringe of a South Asian security "complex," defined by

India–Pakistan rivalries and complicated by localized resource conflicts borne of tensions between landowners and the landless in northern Pakistan (Homer Dixon, 1999, p. 148). Separating the Afghan heroin trade out from these multi-scalar historical trajectories and its wider geographical context denudes security analysis of essential detail and deep perspective.

There are many global narcotics hubs and transnational narcotics networks emanating from Latin America were converging on West African countries like Nigeria and Ghana decades before the rise of Islamic extremism in Central Asia (Ellis, 2011). Guinea-Bissau, for example, regarded by many observers as a fully fledged "narco-state," today serves as a narcotics *entrepôt* supporting a transoceanic supply chain of networked crime gangs. But while cases like Guinea-Bissau highlight the possibility of criminal capture, there are very few if any "wholly owned" criminal states in the world today. There are, however, many "virtual" or "shadow" states, occupying physical self-governed spaces outside the reach of centralized authority. Shadow states manifest in physical form as insurgent armies in control of territory or as networked crime groups, which, though composed of dispersed gangs, exhibit a degree of social cohesion sufficient to thrive even in the most well-ordered societies.

As David Kaplan and Alec Dubro's seminal study makes plain, the Japanese Yakuza, despite a distributed authority structure, constitute a state within the Japanese nation-state. Counter-intuitively, it can be argued that "organized" criminal groups have some social utility by ordering the lives of sociopaths and psychopaths through gang discipline, itself a form of private authority and law. The now legendary Yakuza culture maintains a sense of identity, while a strict code of conduct, system of internal taxation, and a centralized decision-making hierarchy ensures a measure of group cohesion among a multiplicity of Yakuza gangs (Kaplan and Dubro, 2003). The Yakuza were once a social, if not a national, institution that emerged from the ranks of the urban poor in early Meiji Japan. With an estimated 80,900 gang members in 2011 – less than half the number active half a century before – they constitute a very small minority in a country of 237 million people (Corkill, 2011; Leonardsen, 2010, p. 80). Grouped within decentred hierarchical networks rather than as a singular criminal monolith, these entities, once structurally "embedded" in Japanese society, have become competitive economic actors whose social purpose and cultural traditions are increasingly subordinated to the pursuit of financial gain (Rankin, n/d).

The value of Japan's Yakuza-controlled "shadow" economy, estimated at between US$70 billion and US$80 billion annually in the 1990s, translates into what Kaplan and Dubro claim is extensive "structural corruption," linking the Yakuza with compromised government officials, business people, politicians and police officers, that weakens the foundations of government and administration (Kaplan and Dubro, 2003, pp. 151–152). Yakuza gangs have contributed significantly to Japan's asset bubble economy that crashed spectacularly in the early 1990s and that initiated a decade of economic malaise (Hill, 2003). Yet, Japan was then the world's second largest economy and still ranks third in the world behind the US and the People's Republic of China with a nominal GDP at US$5 trillion (2011). So brazen did Yakuza influence become, however, that police efforts to constrain Yakuza power and curtail escalating inter-gang violence enjoyed wide civic support. Law enforcement strategy was not only conventional in targeting consumer demand for illicit goods but also innovative in addressing Japan's shame culture that gives oxygen to extortion – one of the principal techniques used by the Yakuza to manipulate politicians and bureaucrats and ordinary Japanese citizens conditioned by society to "save face" at any price (Corkill, 2011; Kaplan and Dubro, 2003, p. 154). Yet, despite these claims of major gains against the Yakuza, US crime authorities cite Japan for official complacency towards organized crime (INLEA, 2011, pp. 123–124).

There are evidently two divergent views of organized crime in Japan, one where Yakuza influence is cast as pervasive and deeply ingrained, and the other in which the significance of organized crime is placed in a broader social context. Crime data reported by Dag Leonardsen suggests that over the latter part of the twentieth century, when Yakuza power was allegedly in the ascendancy, no more than one-quarter of Japan's exceptionally low murder rate can be attributed to criminal gangs (Leonardsen, 2010, p. 80). Japan has one of the world's lowest rates of firearm ownership and a record of low, if fluctuating, rates of violent crime, suggesting some aspects of crime control are very effective (Fisher, 2012; Bangalore and Messerli, 2013). Poorly conceived counter-crime strategies in contrast can multiply the quantum of crime, especially where violent crime gangs infiltrate the police, the military and the halls of government or where policing methods are themselves violent. In Mexico, following the election of the Calderon government in 2006, cities became battlegrounds in an escalating war between the state and drug trafficking syndicates and between rival syndicates vying for a share of the cocaine trade out of the Andean Ridge. The intrasocietal armed conflict that erupted is a "product" of state action to quash a regional drug production and trafficking "industry" that had been tolerated for decades. Mexico's recent "drug wars" are held up as a measure of the Mexican state's dysfunctionality, which, in turn, is arguably a consequence of the "shallowness" of Mexican democracy that liberal economic policies adopted since the 1990s have not altered (Velasco, 2005, pp. 132–138; Beittel, 2009, pp. 8–12). A pivotal member of the North American Free Trade Agreement, a recipient of substantial investment from North America and a country with nearly two centuries of independent government, Mexico does not fit the profile of a "failed state," let alone a derelict "narco-state." And yet, an estimated 60,000 people have died since the attempted purge of drug cartels began (Beith, 2013).

The protracted nature of Mexican "drug-related violence" is attributable to the transnationalized nature of narco-trafficking which, despite official and popular perceptions, is not dominated by powerful drug barons but by flexible and efficient networks – usually described as cartels – that transcend national boundaries. This is a consequence of both Mexico's proximity to the main coca-producing countries of the Andean Ridge and protracted civil conflict in Colombia but there is also a global systemic dimension. Under the conditions of globalization specified by sociologists like Manuel Castells and Zygmunt Baumann, flexible networking is the new modus operandi for all organizations in a fluid or "liquid" and infinitely reconfigurable global economy (Baumann, 2000; Castells, 2009). Narco-trafficking, as with other forms of trafficking, involves extensive, flexible and adaptable supply chains that connect multiple actors and that are resilient or organic enough to withstand the elimination of one link and to repair and regrow (Kenney, 2009). These networks are chains of amoral micro-systems driven by the "pure" pursuit of profit, with executable codes for torture and murder built-in and activated for maximal resilience.

The virtual crime–security complex

Criminal network theory draws extensively on the work of biologists and sociologists concerned with patterns of network formation and function. Niklas Luhmann, in particular, was a pioneer of cybernetics in the 1980s, long before the prefix "cyber" became entrenched in public discourse. The scale of information networks has grown rapidly and exponentially since then, and digital communications technologies have become today's symbols and agents of technological modernity. We live in "networked societies" where the power of "knowledge" is daily realized by the exponential growth of global information flows (Luhmann, 2013 Castells, 2009). From a mere hundred million Internet users in 1998, there were more than one billion people connected to the Internet by 2006, with rapid penetration being registered in Mainland China. In the first decade of the twenty-first century, the aggregate length of undersea fibre-optic cables, the principal routes through which the world's Internet traffic passes, crossed one million kilometres, which is a reminder of how "hardwired" cyberspace is (Carter et al., 2009, p. 29). By 2013, the number of Internet users globally had more than doubled to 2.4 billion, half of whom subscribed to the social media site Facebook (Internet World Stats, 2013). The digital share of global telecommunications capacity is set to nearly triple to reach 1.4 zettabytes by 2020, out of a total projected telecommunication capacity of four zettabytes (ITU, 2012; Cisco, 2013). Assuming as inevitable the incremental transition from analogue to digital in developing countries, global digital communications capacity is set for a substantial growth surge. As prefigured by Luhmann's model of *autopoietic* networks, Internet connectivity has sprawled as much as rolled out across the globe, driven by an overpowering internal "cellular" logic (Luhmann, 1986). But, as already alluded to, there are serious "downside risks" to the real and potential freedoms offered by this organic informational revolution.

Internet communications encourage creative, cooperative, exploitative and destructive behaviours across space and time. Cyberspace is a virtual human networld inhabited by digitized human imaginings – games, avatars and the like – and, therefore, susceptible to criminal imaginings. Cybercrime is defined by Douglas Thomas and Brian Loader as "computer-mediated activities which are either illegal or considered illicit by certain parties and which can be conducted through global electronic networks" (Thomas and Loader, 2000, p. 24). An extensive and lengthening taxonomy of Internet crimes includes bulk email fraud (phishing) to online trading in illicit goods to more sophisticated hacking of government and company databases, resulting in theft of classified official documents and social security or bank account numbers. This latter virtual corollary of "breaking and entering" crimes is achieved through the skilled manipulation of the codes and protocols that govern Internet communication and computer systems configuration. The costs of cybercrime are impossible to gauge because, beyond stolen bank balances, losses include many unknown variables such as the market value of stolen intellectual property, the loss of customer confidence and the costs associated with shutting down and repairing systems in the wake of adverse infiltrations or "cyber security incidents."

Targeted cyber security incidents range between 42,000 and 46,000 per year, while random "attacks," estimated at 247,350 per day in 2012, exceed one trillion. (Symantec, 2013; Verizon, 2013) Of the 621 "serious data breaches" (actual access to or infiltration of an information technology system) reported by Verizon, 75 per cent were attributed to financial motives and another 21 per cent to state-sponsored espionage. In Symantec's analysis, "data breaches" – systems infiltration and exfiltration of information – on average result in the exposure of 604,826 identities each (Symantec, 2013). Internet security providers like Symantec are accused of overstating the impacts of Internet crime. But Symantec's estimate of US$388 billion in lost income globally for 2010 trails McAfee's estimate of US$1 trillion in losses attributed to cyber crime for 2009, equalling the US government's upper estimate of US$1 trillion in combined losses and costs to US industry from Internet Protocol and data theft in 2008 (Pachio, 2011). McAfee has since reduced its estimates of cyber crime impacts to US$300 billion annually. This is still, relatively speaking, only a fraction of the aggregate value of global productivity and less than five per cent of the value of global e-commerce (Du Rausas et al., 2011, p. 1).

The picture for global cyber crime is complicated by the evolutionary nature of communication technologies: by their rapid take-up by cyber criminals, by the adoption of cybercrime techniques by states and by the emergence of Internet activist or "hacktivist" entities. The realities of Distributed Denial of Service (DDoS) attacks, hacking and Internet fraud make Internet security professionals focus on the potential vulnerabilities of computer-mediated communications. The projected three-fold increase in digital communications could reasonably be presumed to generate a similar rate of increase in targeted and random web attacks, which would test the capabilities of existing cyber security systems. All modern communications networks – telecommunications, logistics, banking, finance and defence systems – are increasingly reliant upon uninterrupted information flows and are perpetually updated and upgraded because consequences of system-wide disruption are potentially catastrophic. The risk sensitivities generated by fears of systemic collapse in part explains the overstatement of the costs of cybercrime – just as fear of the unknown explains the appeal of dread scenarios of global cyberwar.

Banking institutions, in fact all institutions, that are connected to the Internet, have reason to be concerned about their cyber security vulnerability. Security agencies have reason to fear infiltration of defence information systems and the information systems of private contractors by equally capable "hackers." Thus, the reflexive response of governments and banks to rising security concerns about Internet crime, and the hidden threats of terrorism, is to gather more information and to create new categories of crime, to constrain the promised freedoms of Internet communication by devising new techniques of forensic investigation to trace cyber crimes to their source. This again reveals the double-edged nature of informationalism and *informationalization*.

Inevitably, the "holy grail" of cyber detection is attribution of crimes, and the apprehension of cyber criminals, but freedom of speech includes the right to anonymity (Reich et al., 2012). The potential for anonymity offered by the Internet is, from a crime-security perspective, however interpreted as both a source of vulnerability and a threat. "The Onion Router" or "Tor" networks are computer networks through which communication paths are randomized to avoid surveillance and interception. Unlike encryption, the standard method Internet exchanges are legally masked from unverified observers; randomized communication adds another layer of complexity that confounds algorithmic means of detection and decryption. Tor networks are used by online narcotics traders, the most notable being Ross William Ulbricht, the "Dread Pirate Roberts" and operator of the Silk Road website, who was apprehended in the US in 2013 with an estimated fortune of US$80 million in encrypted Internet currency, "bitcoins" (Matthews, 2013; *SMH* October 3, 2013). Cases such as this are "grist to the mill" of states and their law enforcement agencies

Non-state groups exploit the anonymity of Tor networks to mobilize, organize and execute counter-hegemonic activities. The global "Occupy" movement maintains an extensive global communications culture mediated through Tor networks (see Chapter 5). Unlike market criminals, cyber activists claim cosmopolitan legitimacy through the pursuit of higher moral codes. Cyber activist organizations, Wikileaks and hacktivist entities like Anonymous pursue informational campaigns against a presumed global capitalist conspiracy orchestrated by the US and the world's leading transnational corporations. Hacking into the web database of Strategic Forecasting, Inc. (StratFor), the US open source intelligence aggregator, in 2011, members of the Anonymous network obtained bulk email records and credit card numbers of "StratFor" subscribers and declared the intention to transfer funds "Robin Hood" style to social welfare causes. While there are doubts as to whether these threats were acted upon, the event cost StratFor US$1.75 million in damages (Constantin, 2011; RT USA, 2012). But, with a mere two per cent of reported adverse system infiltrations attributed to hacktivism, the scale of the cyber activist "threat" is marginal (Verizon, 2013).

What is perhaps much more threatening, although denied by those involved, is the extensive surveillance operations of the US and UK governments – paralleled without doubt by similar state surveillance in many or most other states. The alleged development by the CIA of a five-zettabyte data processing facility is, if true, an absolute measure of the scale of securitization of cyberspace (Gorman and Valentino-Devries, 2013). The exponential growth of information databases and the all too apparent vulnerability of computer-mediated information systems create a security imperative that presents undeniable challenges to basic human rights. This much was presaged by Simon Garfinkel more than a decade ago in *Database Nation: the Death of Privacy in the 21st Century* (2000) in which he criticizes the new science of absolute identification on the grounds that absolute security is an impossible dream. His point is not that information has no social or law enforcement purpose, but that those responsible for controlling the surveillance "datasphere" are human, and thus susceptible to human failings – curiosity, complacency and much worse (Garfinkel, 2000 pp. 44–65). Herein lies the weakness of claims, made by security agencies and digitopians alike, that "if you have nothing to hide then you have nothing to fear." There is "nowhere to hide" in cyberspace anymore and guarantees of freedom of speech are fragile, at best, even in democratic states; while the advocates of digital integration prove very agile in their quest for global transparency. It is also the case that law is an ever-shifting slide rule along which normative considerations are calculated against commercial and political utility.

In the global knowledge economy, all knowledge is potentially strategic and profitable and, thus, private companies have a strong economic interest in harnessing the power of bulk data. The legal collection and processing of customer information by companies is reaching such a level of sophistication and scale, and computing power *so vast*, that, with the right algorithms, it is possible to profile individual customers, even where they have left no indication of their identity. The notion of privacy, regardless of what protections might be imposed upon the National Security Agency (NSA) or the UK Government Communications Headquarters (GCHQ), is rapidly evaporating. Strong privacy regulations can be circumvented easily by moving data to a third country with much weaker or no privacy laws. From there, private data can be relayed around the global public domain.

The Internet remains a relatively open and, in a formal sense, lawless frontier even if states and their security agencies are developing techniques to police it. It is not, however, an "ungoverned space." As Lawrence Lessig writes, "code is law" and the codes or protocols that enable computers and information systems to communicate constitute a set of agreed rules that "govern" Internet exchange (Lessig, 2006, p. 19).

What renders the Internet a lawless frontier is the absence of formal international legal agreements that set binding limits on the harmful use of Internet technologies and clear principles that apply where digital communication codes intersect with laws protecting individual privacy, human rights, commercial transactions, intellectual property and state security.

Governments have legislated against Internet crimes and law enforcement agencies have developed sophisticated tracking and interdiction techniques to trap cyber criminals. There are, however, no international conventions that address the governance of cyberspace in the way that UNCLOS provides a framework for oceans' governance. There is the EU's Budapest Convention on Cybercrime that defines Internet crimes and calls for common cooperative solutions from signatories (Council of Europe, 2011). National regulatory agencies can exercise a degree of extraterritorial control over the global actions of locally based service providers. The Internet Corporation for Assigned Names and Numbers (ICANN) is held up as an example of "multi-stakeholder" governance by non-governmental actors, but critics argue that while ICANN is indeed an NGO, its remit is defined by its licence to issue network names conferred by the US Department of Commerce, and to which ICANN is thus subordinate. At the international interstate level, coordinated Internet regulation is still "virtually" non-existent, despite the attempted extension of International Telecommunications Union (ITU) interest into digital telecommunications regulation. The number and scope of global Internet-mediated activities, together with the potential for harm arising from nefarious Internet use, points to a need for globally coordinated oversight. But, while intergovernmental regulation is possible, governments are far from unanimous in supporting a norm of global Internet control (*Economist*, December 14, 2012).

The "Great Firewall of China" is evidence, as much as can be gleaned, that Internet communications can be filtered and blocked, not merely surveilled. The Chinese state allegedly employs a large army of officials across multiple agencies to monitor and filter China's vast and surging data flows. The reach of state surveillance not only limits freedom of information but, equally importantly, enables the state to accumulate surveillance expertise and refine its code-breaking and inspection technologies so as to decipher even the most advanced encryption algorithms. China has, by far, the greatest number of Internet users of any country and the largest number of social networkers and gamers online in the Asia Pacific. Chinese "netizens" gravitate towards the local equivalents of Facebook and Google. The country records the highest regional e-commerce revenues for online shopping and hosts the largest concentration of Asia's most visited Internet sites (ADMA, 2012). There is thus a rich pool of data processing expertise in China, which decants into a deep reserve of surveillance and hacking capability, which, simply for reasons of scale, quite possibly outstrips that of any rival. For these reasons, then, international attention focuses on China for its untapped e-commerce potential but also for the Chinese state's curtailment of Internet freedom and the alarming increase in international cyber crimes attributed to Chinese hackers – allegedly linked to the Chinese state (IWM 2010; Mandiant, 2013).

The Internet in China is effectively nationalized. Commercially, the majority- state-owned enterprises, China Telecom, China Unicom and China Mobile control the country's informational hardware, while state surveillance agencies monitor the "software" of China's informational society (Reporters Without Borders, 2013a, pp. 19–20). This hierarchical control network is confirmation that, given the means and the motive, any government can in theory suppress freedom of speech. The demonstration effects are apparent in other one-party states, in Vietnam, for example, where 35 bloggers were imprisoned in 2013, but also in authoritarian democracies, like Thailand, where *lese majesté* laws are used to silence web debate and prosecute alleged critics of the Thai royal family (Reporters Without Borders, 2013b). Telecommunications companies are subject to state prerogatives to yield communications data where security breaches or crimes are suspected and, as with Yahoo in China, this can lead to conflicts between commercial priorities and international legal obligation, with the latter sacrificed to commercial expediency. The Yahoo precedent is perhaps the clearest proof of the enduring power of states over private capital, namely the power to deny access to wealth.

Conclusion

The terrain of global criminality is vastly more complex than is allowed in official narratives of crime prevention and control. Transnational criminals depend upon state structures to create spaces within and through which they can procure illicit goods, trade and invest the proceeds of crime. But criminal entities do not constitute states in the conventional sense. There is no single or coherent state structure, virtual or otherwise, that can be targeted in a militarized "war on crime," no standing global criminal army, no integrated command, no uniform convergence of political interest, even if evidence points to greater transnational or global cooperation between rival syndicates. Instead, crime and terror constitute disaggregated security challenges that reflect the disaggregation and fluidity of contemporary patterns of globalization. The construction of a global transnational crime and terror threat using standard national security concepts actually distorts the nature of the security risks involved.

Criminal networks are "pure" capitalist entities formed in the pursuit of profit maximization, with few if any moral restraints beyond what is necessary to sustain network cohesion. The scale of transnational crime economies relative to legal or lawful commerce is, however, relatively small – although far from negligible. The diffuse societal impacts of criminal harm are substantial but, and here is the crucial point, not as substantial as the harm done by legal actors operating just within or across the very edge of law. This is where analysis of crime in terms of antinomies of legal–illegal practice aids analysis by broadening our perspective. As argued, unlawful acts can be both legal, but unconscionable, and illegal, but justifiable, in terms of agreed international principles. Legal but unconscionable actions that undermine or deny agreed moral principles present a significant challenge to the realization of a just or broadly legitimate global order. This argument, imperfect as it is, drags transnational crime "out of the shadows" and places crime in the same frame of reference as the unconscionable behaviours of actors that belong to the global "overworld" of states and powerful commercial entities. It allows us to explore the complexities of global criminality and to interrogate claims that we are witnessing a global crime–terror convergence.

2
Converging in the Shadows: Complex Crime, Complex Security

While the causes of conflict and human suffering are well known, global governance measures to mitigate human security risks have had at best limited effect. US President Woodrow Wilson's Fourteen Points – presented to the US Congress in January 1918 and played out at the Treaty of Versailles in 1919 – prefigure what are today widely accepted as major sources of insecurity, including the absence of state political legitimacy, economic protectionism, territorial rivalry, state secrecy and arms proliferation. A nascent international community, in 1945, conceived the tragedy of World War II in systemic terms, as a consequence of unrestrained power (Wilson, 1919; Roosevelt, 1945). There is evidence of significant systemic adaptation since 1945 to accommodate the stresses created by the growth of industrial market economies. Still, political violence remains a feature of inter- and intrastate relations. The convergent search for "solutions," prescriptions and metrics with which to end war and promote economic development reflects a common tendency to associate peace and prosperity with democratic order – the theory of "liberal peace." But order, and its corollary, equilibrium, is not a natural or permanent condition in human affairs or in the natural environment (Luhmann, 1986). Globalization is a multi-scalar process comprising multiple and commonly irregular complex systems evidencing divergent or convergent patterns – frequently both at once.

The shifting terrain of global relations ensures that security challenges of any kind can appear unexpectedly and rapidly change in shape and scope. Security issues can, therefore, usefully be thought of as "polymorphous," in that they are multi-faceted, part of an evolutionary trajectory but also the "product" of a confluence of "trajectories" that are themselves the "downside" to social change. Security "trends" are in reality non-linear – and sometimes cyclical – patterns or "pathways," connecting across different domains: military, political, societal or environmental. Ideological or psychosocial factors also inform the creation, identification and prioritization of strategies of control or resistance. Borrowing from the field of sociological risk theory, governmental strategies to address identified security challenges, in the current global context, can paradoxically be generative of new threats and new vulnerabilities (Beck, 1999; Beck, 2005, pp. 12–14). To attribute a crime, terror, rebellion or societal collapse to a single source or "enemy" is, therefore, to downplay the strings or threads of interconnected happenings, decisions, ideas and beliefs that shape the dynamics of security "risk."

Some divergent thoughts on convergence thinking

Writing before constructivism became *de rigueur*, Robert Jervis recognized the human predisposition to rely upon images or models of reality to compensate for the incompleteness of information, and to reflexively imbue the actions of adversaries with hostile intent (Jervis, 1976). As is now widely recognized, impressions of reality or "mental models" are constructed from imperfect evidence, sometimes leading to error in the attribution of motives and coherence to the disparate actions of others (Denzau et al., 2007). It is possible, using the quantitative tools of network analysis, to quantify connections and nodes, scale and expansion, and communication frequency of illicit networks of traffickers and terrorists. Care, however, is needed where horizontal data is used as a proxy for organizational "depth" and intention. A realist view of human nature, combined with entrenched suspicion of peoples with differing value systems, can lead to the presumption that evidence of a network connection between declared or suspected adversaries necessarily translates into convergent action. Also, the psychological "dread" of terror violence perpetrated by subterranean terror cells and random individuals far exceeds what is justified by the scale of physical harm inflicted by terrorism, measured in human lives lost to terror attacks relative to other forms of violent death (Pinker, 2011, pp. 344–347).

Terrorism is a crime under international law and those who engage in acts of terror, as defined and criminalized by a growing body of international legal instruments, are criminals. Yet, links between terrorism and market crime, significant though they are, do not translate axiomatically into a crime-terror nexus as conceived in Western counter-terrorism strategies. The linkage of transnational crime and Islamist extremism in US global strategy since 9/11 reflects a tendency, common in the developed world, to view the developing world – especially the developing Muslim world – as a threatening deterritorialized "locale" of global security risk. There is, what conservative Christian Whiton argues in *Smart Power: Between Diplomacy and War* (2013), an inherent inability in US strategic culture to shed outdated modes of thinking about Muslim-majority states and accept the reality of substantial political achievements and democratic aspirations across the Muslim world, as displayed for example in Cairo's Tahrir Square during and since 2011 (Whiton, 2013, p. 16). Transnational criminals and international terror entities are indeed cooperating for tactical gain and, in some instances, out of ideological affinity, but there are significant differences between those groups or entities "lumped" together as constituents of a convergent terror threat (Hanlon, 2009). To this we can attach the further reservation, based on the observable inherent fractiousness of criminal groups that makes any crime-terror compact unpredictable at best.

Armed and coordinated al-Qaeda-linked terror groups operate in northern Africa and Asia, and there is ample evidence of global jihadi networks of varying levels of sophistication and violent intent across the globe (Chivvis and Liepman, 2013). David Kilcullen refers to al-Qaeda-inspired terrorism as a "globalized insurgency" that takes advantage of both the globalization of communications, finance and transport, and the globalization of Islam (Kilcullen, 2009, p. 12; Kilcullen, 2010, p. 184). But this reality in and of itself does not indicate global crime and/or terror network convergence or cohesion. Complexity, in theory, works against order and permanency, and too much can too easily be read into the chaotic tumbling and churning of global society. The global connections of this insurgent movement are, writes Mark Juergensmeyer, "tenuous," and the movement itself is divided and relatively weak (Juergensmeyer, 2008, p. 211). Terrorist groups are also allegedly and, for the most part, relatively short-lived and volatile political phenomena (Cronin, 2009). Despite their global connections, extreme Islamist groups in the Middle East, including the Taliban in Pakistan and Afghanistan, concentrate their efforts and resources on securing influence or power within existing state structures closer to home. Parallel to communist-inspired insurgencies in Asia of more than half a century ago, local political objectives dominate the counter-hegemonic agendas of today's armed alter-globalist non-state actors.

In *New and Old Wars* (2001), Mary Kaldor writes presciently of a new kind of conflict that will dominate the early twenty-first century, in which disparate armed non-state groups become more salient in the local security landscape. Against a backdrop of the secessionist wars that accompanied the disintegration of the former USSR and Yugoslavia,

Kaldor avers that a new generation of warfare is emerging in which wars are increasingly fought not between but within nation-states, between the state and groups defined by a shared sense of cultural identity and a politically manufactured sense of common grievance that "their" interests are not served by centralized authority. In this crucible, crime becomes the means by which political players achieve strategic advantage over competitors and through which connections between those with crime as their *raison d'être* and those more committed to political power find common if unstable ground. This, she argues, is a consequence of globalization stripping away the protective layer of international stability provided by the Cold War bipolar balance, and also the diminution of state control by the inexorable processes of economic globalization. In this new state of flux, criminal actors merge with politically motivated rebel groups, rendering it increasingly difficult to distinguish between criminal and political entities. Crucially, however, and to reiterate the point made above, the politics of these new wars will, she asserts, be local, whatever the ideological fault lines exposed or chosen by belligerents and their criminal associates (Kaldor, 2001). And this pattern is perhaps most in evidence in the aftermath of the collapse of Soviet power in Central Asia and the upsurge in drug-fuelled political violence where contests over state power are fed by the Afghanistan–Pakistan narco-terror complex (Cornell and Jonsson, 2014).

Security risk analysis, if it is to be of value, should accommodate both empirical and subjective considerations (Buzan, 1983, p. 1). Barry Buzan's objective in proposing the idea of the "security complex" as a geographically defined patchwork of overlapping security interests and substantive concerns was to draw attention to multi-layered linkages between contiguous states and their real and subjective securities. All too easily complex circumstances become reduced into convenient binary oppositions that belie the intricacies of international and regional interactions between different categories of security actors. Buzan, and others at the Copenhagen School, critiqued the utility of national security in a world where national securities were becoming increasingly internationalized and where states could only logically achieve security through participation in their neighbourhood "security community" (Buzan et al., 1998). Proposing a convergence of a different kind, Buzan asserted that state-led regionalization is a significant global peace dynamic and a logical corollary to globalization (Buzan and Waever, 2007). Much therefore depends upon which dynamics and which evidence crime and security analysis rests.

None of this is meant to imply that insurgencies or terror groups are trifling nuisances. Concerns that insurgency, Islamism and crime are closely connected are borne out in conflicts and political turmoil from Chechnya through to the borders of Pakistan and India (Cornell and Jonsson, 2014; Engvall, 2014; al-Sishani, 2014). There is a danger inherent in dismissing the germ of genuine grievance, against either the governments or the international system, and its manifold flaws (Kilcullen, 2010). As it unhinges established political orders and unleashes the criminally inclined, globalization also provokes reactions from those most disadvantaged or "disenfranchised" by the pace and direction of change (Giddens, 1990; Castells, 2012). In many parts of the world, globalization is not so much leading to the demise of the state as exacerbating conflicts over the very legitimacy of states that have smouldered for decades. Many of the world's states are nations in name only, with political elites exercising little or no direct control over every part of their sovereign territory. Contemporary conflicts in North Africa, the Middle East and South and Southeast Asia need to be analysed against a backdrop of decolonization and persistent disputes over the legitimacy of states in which the institutional furnishings of independence – bureaucracy, parliament, the judiciary and territory – were not accompanied by popular acceptance of the "idea of the state" or its founding ideology (Buzan, 1983). A framework of analysis is required that can assimilate these different systemic dimensions of crime, political violence and security.

The history of marketization and democratization in Eastern Europe, Central Asia and East Africa bear out Huntington's point that political and economic developments often follow divergent non-linear paths (Huntington, 2006, pp. 37–39). To escape linearity, the four-dimensional model (given in Figure 2.1) permits emphasis to be placed upon any quadrant or any combination of quadrants. Political violence and crime are as much structural phenomena as they are matters of individual market choice or "deviancy," or both. Revolutionary and terrorist "movements" propound utopian imaginings driven by aspirations for the recovery of a golden age of authentic community, and sustained by a deep-felt sense of "injustice–dishonour" suffered by the group at the hands of adversaries (Battersby et al., 2011; Midlarsky, 2011, pp. 56–67). "Mortality salience," contends Midlarsky, strengthens extremist sentiment, which translates into a heightened danger or risk of armed extremism in societies with high rates of violent death (Midlarsky, 2011, p. 57). Feelings of anomie arising from the collapse or dissolution of an established social order render some people more attracted or vulnerable to the criminal opportunities created by the fluidities of "transition." This is evident in Russia and the former Soviet Bloc countries where, in the 1990s, state socialism was swiftly replaced with market systems, the principles and practices of which cut against the grain of a century of state socialization (Findlay, 2000). Not that the Soviet system was ever crime-free. Soviet Gulags were incubators of organized criminal groups, but the Russian *mafiya* welled up through a split in society caused by the traumatic collapse of the protective institutions and ideology of the Soviet state, and by the rich opportunities arising out of the West's determination to build Eastern European market economies from the ruins of the Berlin Wall whatever the price. Still, the Russian *mafiya* is not a monolithic entity but rather a constellation of several thousand disparate groups, some of which have become very influential at home and successful, resilient globalizers abroad (McCarthy, 2011, pp. 55–62).

There can be little doubt that the many civil conflicts that broke out following the collapse of Soviet-style communism in Eastern Europe fed and camouflaged the spread of *mafiya* networks. Criminal entities, revolutionaries and separatist groups, where they are converging, do so because the globalizing dynamics present in the security complexes

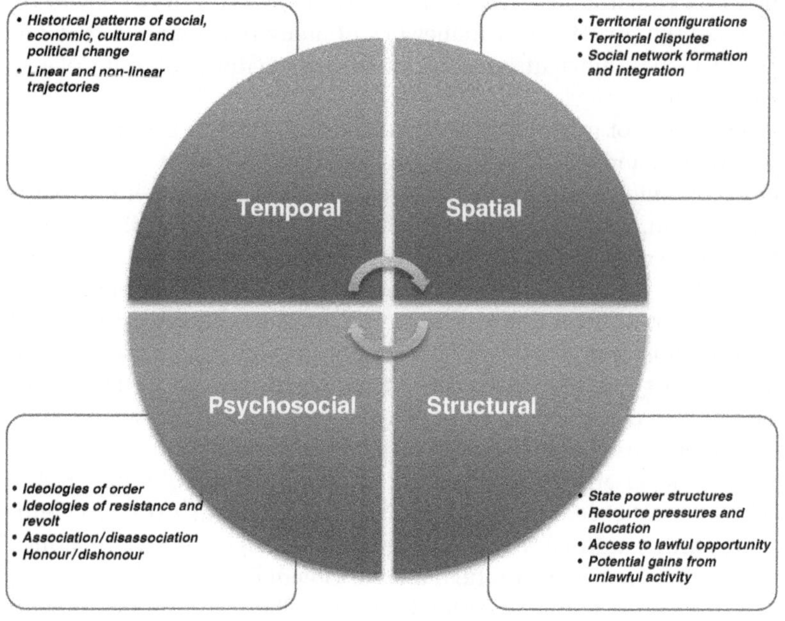

Figure 2.1 Four-dimensional crime-security analysis

they inhabit encourage and facilitate more extensive interconnections. But, as with globalization, deepening and more frequent interactions do not necessarily lend concreteness or durability to alignments and alliances between disparate licit or illicit entities. Narcotics and light-arms trafficking were and remain synonymous with insurgency and organized crime in mainland Southeast Asia and the Andean Ridge countries of South America where legacies of underdevelopment, social exclusion and internecine conflict shape the terrain of relations between states and peoples. But the major protagonists fight against each other for a share of the cocaine trade and, in Mexico and Colombia, the state is fighting back with, in the Colombian case at least, significant success. So, there are many subtle and less-subtle links between crime and political violence, and many gradations in criminal involvement in politics, but, to reiterate, care must be taken not to detach these links from their sociopolitical and socioeconomic contexts and conflate distanciated connections into the substance of empire.

The following case studies examine divergent patterns of "convergence" in Africa, Southeast Asia and Latin America in which transnational crime and political violence remain persistent features of everyday life for millions. Transnational crime is further explored through the illegal and irregular movement of people and also through state responses to perceived non-traditional security challenges in national policy and through the practices and doctrines of intervention. These issues, in different ways, exemplify the intersection of four distinct but interrelated dimensions. This "four-dimensional" approach is both systematic and systemic in orientation, but it serves only as a guide to exploration and not as a roadmap for the mitigation of risk.

Complex convergence

In a special feature edition on Africa in 2011, the *Economist* celebrated the startling and unprecedented demographic and economic growth rates of African economies in the west and south of the continent (December 3, 2011). Africa, long dismissed as a singular place of endemic internecine conflict, underdevelopment and HIV/AIDS, is changing rapidly, but rapid societal change brings new challenges and new risks on the "upside" and the "downside." State capacity in many countries is constrained by the limited remit of central authority, a consequence of colonial inheritance and of decades of economic hardship and attendant long-running "centre–periphery" tensions (Herbst, 2000, Loc. 352). The 2012 Tuareg Rebellion in northern Mali was widely construed as incontrovertible proof of the spreading influence of al-Qaeda in the Islamic Maghreb (AQIM). The ethnic Tuareg rebel group, the Azawad National Liberation Movement (ANLM), entered into a tactical alliance with Islamist militants to prosecute its historical claims for an independent Tuareg state. What was in reality a three-cornered contest – between ANLM and AQIM cadres that sought to "merge" with and "acquire" the Tuareg Rebellion, and the Mali government backed by French troops – became yet another "site" in a spreading global struggle between Islamist terrorists and "good states," aligned to the West (CSIS, 2010; Halperin and Blair, 2012; Hirsch, 2012; *Deutsche Weller*, September 9, 2013).

AQIM is at its core a gang of mainly Algerian Islamist fighters, numbering little more than 500 active cadres, many of them the defeated and dishonoured remnants of the Salafist Group for Preaching and Combat or Group Salafist pour la Predication et le Combat (GSPC) which fought in the Algerian Civil War of the 1990s and now includes Algerian volunteers who trained and fought in Afghanistan during the 1980s. Narcotics and people trafficking, and kidnapping and theft, provide the financial resources necessary to sustain core group operations and, equally important, influence over affiliates and favour with the real al-Qaeda, to which it pays "tax" (Mohamedou, 2011; Masters, 2013). While there are fears of a widening of the AQIM network in northern Africa, there is also evidence of rifts between its leadership and the central command of al-Qaeda. Volatility and disorder is evident both within this offshoot and its alliances of disparate, even mutually hostile, armed non-state groups. Government forces regained control over northern Mali in early 2013, and the Mali government then sought to engage the ANLM in a dialogue to find a durable peace settlement. Even before this setback, AQIM was splintering into the Ansar al-Din and the Movement for Unity and Jihad in West Africa (MUJWA). Reports of ideological differences and internal friction point to weak institutionalization and also frustration on the part of AQIM's central leadership with the opportunistic freelance terror operations of former core members turned affiliates, like the notorious Mokhtar Belmokhtar (Chivvis and Liepman, 2013; Masters, 2013; McElroy, 2013). AQIM has the capacity to recruit and to mobilize, but not to bind people in sufficient numbers to be anything other than a destabilizing militant entity.

The sudden collapse of order in Mali, once held up as an exemplar of African development, demonstrates the limited effects of strategic assistance to countries experiencing high levels of political dissonance. Substantial financial and military aid from the US during the presidency of George W. Bush did not insulate Mali from the southward and westward extension of vectors of insecurity generated by ideological disputes over the "idea" of post-colonial states as coherent territorial polities. Insurgencies and secessionism in Sudan and Somalia especially have endured for decades and are not amenable to foreign diplomatic or military interventions (Samatar, 2011; De Waal, 2004). So, too, are lesser-known and "localized" territorial disputes spanning the borders of northern Kenya, Somalia and Ethiopia. Long-running "low-intensity" conflicts, save for reports of piracy, kidnappings and occasional acts of terror, remain in the shadows while larger conflagrations have drifted out of global public consciousness in the wake of the so-called "Arab Spring" and the humanitarian catastrophe of the Syrian Civil War.

Despite the 2005 Nairobi Comprehensive Peace Agreement, which brought an end to the Second Sudanese Civil War (1983–2004), Sudan and the now independent state of South Sudan still engage in sporadic fighting along their disputed and resource-rich common border. Estimates of the death toll – from what is widely termed a "genocide" – in Darfur range between 200,000 and 400,000, with most killed as a result of fighting between the government-backed nomadic Arab militia and the *Janjaweed* (a Fur word meaning "hordes"), on the one hand, and the multi-ethnic Sudanese Liberation Army (SLA) and the Justice and Equality Movement (JEM) on the other. The parallel 2006 Darfur Peace Agreement between the SLA–JEM rebels and Khartoum was doomed from the outset. Fighting resumed within a year of the settlement despite the presence of African Union peacekeepers (ICG 2007a; Battersby and Siracusa, 2009; Klomegah, 2013; Tubiana, 2013). From the 1980s to 2007 at least 9.5 million people were displaced by conflict in Sudan. Sudanese refugees are scattered across the globe, but most remain crowded into camps in their own country, 2.7 million of these clinging precariously to life in Darfur where their fate is further complicated by the fragmentation of conflict parties fighting over land, oil and now gold (Laessing, 2013; UNHCR, 2013). The lethal "dynamic" of combat, famine and disease which claimed 1.9 million lives during the civil war threatens to return, not just because of rival territorial claims between Sudan and its new neighbour but also because of enduring conflicts over land and resources within both states. It is these systemic "disorders" that represent the greatest challenge to international or global security, and which reflect gross failures of governance by Western and African powers.

Any notion that "development" is an orderly process is dispelled by even the most attenuated discussion of Sudan's recent past, trace elements of which can be discerned in the present. As with many colonial inventions,

Sudan was a state in name only, with Khartoum barely in control of its assigned sovereign territory. A patchwork of different tribal groups divided by ethnicity and by the currents of Islamic and Christian conversion were incorporated into a single political entity by Britain and Egypt at the end of the nineteenth century. The trajectory of state formation reflected the consequences of unresolved tensions surrounding tribal, religious and state identity. Because of its proximity to Egypt and the Middle East, northern Sudan was drawn into the Islamic and Arab orbit by Egypt in the early nineteenth century with Islamization and Arabization proceeding in tandem. British–Egyptian collaboration in creating a new state on the Upper Nile to protect British interests in the Middle East further strengthened the position of the Islamized north vis-à-vis the underdeveloped South. Applying the traditional colonialist "divide and rule" principle to governing the Sudan as a British protectorate, Britain treated the south as a separate entity to the economically more advanced north, thus creating and perpetuating regional rivalry. State formation inevitably fostered animosity towards the northern-dominated government among geographically and culturally distant and marginalized rural peoples. Resentment between "Arab" and "African" Sudanese was, however, well entrenched before independence in 1956. The northern Sudanese were Muslim; also, they were better educated and enjoyed better economic opportunities (Johnson, 2004; Meredith, 2005).

The western area of Darfur was integrated into the larger entity of Sudan through a combination of Mamluk Egyptian and British imperial expansion. The sultanate was, according to M. W. Daly, a premodern African Muslim polity in which African Muslim rulers presided over a multi-ethnic and multi-religious population (Daly, 2007, pp. 28–34). Under British tutelage, Darfur suffered from the same neglect accorded to southern Sudan, adding a second layer of resentment towards Khartoum that compounded the long-standing objection to northern political influence and the increasing inward migrations of nomads from northern Sudan and Chad seeking new pastureland. Independence brought no tangible change of fortune (Battersby and Siracusa, 2009).

Economic grievances, rather than a shared sense of regional or cultural identity, maintained unity among the disparate multi-religious and multi-ethnic South Sudan Liberation Movement (SSLM) (Daly, 2007, p. 205). The movement grew sufficiently strong to field armed forces grouped under the banner of the Sudan People's Liberation Army (SPLA), but the southern rebels were viewed in Washington as ideologically more inclined towards the Soviet Union – this despite a Christian preponderance in the South. US economic and military assistance inevitably flowed towards the anti-Soviet Khartoum government while Washington turned a blind eye on the brutality of the Sudanese state towards southern rebels and their supporters. From independence until the late 1970s, the state in Sudan was secular. President Colonel Muhhama Nimayri (1969–1985) enshrined secularism in the 1973 constitution that confirmed a major condition of the peace between north and south. However, a reinvigorated and radicalized form of Islam, manifest in the Muslim Brotherhood, changed the complexion of national politics and government.

The growing electoral appeal of Sudan's religious right gradually translated into political influence at the centre and, following well-established patterns in other postcolonial African countries, further strengthened anti-Khartoum sentiment to the south and west of the capital (Herbst, 2000; Meredith, 2005). To better navigate factional politics in Khartoum, Nimayri admitted Muslim Brothers into senior government posts – a move that opened the way for Islamists to press for the alignment of Sudanese and Shari'a or Islamic law. Before his removal in 1985, Nimayri abandoned secularism, declared his intention to convert all of Sudan and tore up the 1972 peace agreement, plunging the country back into civil war. Islamization was vigorously pursued by President Al-Saddiq al-Mahdi, leader of Sudan's largest Islamic political organization, the Umma Party. Al-Mahdi was the first to arm local Arab militias and use them against rebel forces, in this instance the *muraheleen*, presaging the tactics later used by his successors in Darfur (Kindiki, 2007, p. 3).

Precipitated by the military's disapproval at the prospect of a new peace agreement between the government and southern insurgents, yet another coup in 1989 installed General Omar Hassan al-Bashir as president and he, in return for electoral support, granted substantial governmental authority to Hassan al-Turabi, a Muslim Brother, and his National Islamic Front (NIF). That the NIF did not command majority support among Sudan's Muslim population did not dissuade al-Turabi from pursuing his vision for an orthodox Islamic society. He manoeuvred the government to the far right of political Islam, presided over an increasingly murderous, some would say genocidal, counter-insurgency, and drew the country into a dangerous if loose liaison with jihadist groups (Taylor and Elbushra, 2006; De Waal and Abdel Salam, 2004, pp. 102–106).

Religion and identity do not map out precisely the lines of division in Darfur. Distinct tribal identities, religious beliefs, languages and competing economic interests between sedentary and nomadic peoples cut across issues of land ownership and support for or opposition to the central government. The Arabic or Arabized nomadic camel-herding tribes, *Abbala*, are constantly in search of adequate grazing lands in a region where decades of desertification have taken their toll. African tribes, including the Fur, Masalit and Zaghawa, are predominantly farmers and form the majority of Darfur's population. Skirmishing between tribal groups became commonplace during the 1980s creating the perfect incubator for both inter- and intracommunal malice to evolve. When conflict in Darfur escalated into "low-intensity" warfare, the *Janjaweed* were already well established (Kindiki, 2007, p. 3). Into this mix poured armaments and an increasing array of armed militia from neighbouring Chad. Darfur became a safe haven for Chadian militia and the Libyan-backed Islamic Legion fighting against the non-Muslim African government in N'Djaema. In political science terms, these "factors" created an environment conducive to the escalation of violence, including extensive and, a common problem in conflict situations, underreported predations by non-Arab rebel groups against Arabs in Darfur (Flint, 2009).

Conflict trajectories in Darfur reflect the gestation of long-held rivalries exacerbated by a constellation of contemporary systemic factors. Successive major climate change-related droughts have hastened desertification in Darfur, placing additional pressure on land and food resources (UNEP, 2007, pp. 7–10). Cross-cutting religious and tribal rivalries over land and political influence are, according to Daly, crucial to understanding the vectors of conflict in Darfur and Sudan. Western analysis, he argues, has too easily succumbed to the simplifications of Huntington's clash of civilizations thesis, leading to erroneous conclusions of religious war between Muslim and non-Muslim, Arab and African. Daly further explains that the violence in Darfur has the characteristics of both an intercommunal conflict and a civil war, inflamed by Khartoum's support for pro-government Arab Muslim militia (Daly, 2007, p. 273).

The ideologies, preconceptions and commercial interests of external powers have a bearing upon the course of intrastate conflicts. Egypt's influence endures along its southern geostrategic flank, tilting the balance of forces in Cairo's favour whenever possible. US interest in Sudan derived from Cold War strategic concerns, which bore upon interpretations of the Second Sudanese Civil War and the SPLA. In the late 1970s and early 1980s, socialism appeared to be gaining ground in the Horn of Africa and across North Africa and the Middle East. After the discovery of oil south of Sudan's Nuba Mountains on the Upper Nile, the American oil major Chevron secured concessions from Khartoum, which hoped oil would eventually be piped to a government refinery on the Red Sea. Reflecting the official thinking that influenced Washington's relations with the entire Islamic world, US strategists believed Islam presented an impenetrable shield against communist ideology. US political leaders and geopolitical strategists did not consider the anti-Western orientation of reform Islam as a serious threat until the 1990s and the rise of al-Qaeda – by which time the seeds of jihadism had long since taken root in East Africa (De Waal, 2004, pp. 220–222).

Political Islam in the NIF-dominated government was shaped by the teachings of the Muslim Brotherhood, of which al-Turabi was the leader in Sudan. An anti-imperialist protest movement originating in Egypt in the 1920s, the Brotherhood advocated a return to "pure Islam" drawn from a literal translation of the Qur'an. Jessica Stern writes that the Islamist message of its founder, Hassan-al-Banna, was inspired by extreme ideologies at both ends of the political spectrum (Stern, 2003, pp. 45–46; Tibi, 2007. The Brotherhood's appeal was broadened in the 1950s by the viscerally anti-Western Sayyid Qutb, whose militant rhetoric garnered support among the millions of Muslims left behind by the post-war global economic boom. Driven out of Egypt, for a time, the movement spawned offshoots across the Middle East (Hamas being the most notable), also reaching into North Africa and South Asia (Nassar, 2005; Stern 2003).

With the Muslim Brothers ensconced in Khartoum, Sudan became a haven for Islamic militants from the Middle East. Osama bin Laden used Sudan as a haven in which to incubate al-Qaeda and turn it into a transnational terror network committed to jihad against the US (Kahler, 2009, p. 106). It was from his base in Sudan that bin Laden allegedly forward-planned the 1998 attacks on US embassies in Tanzania and Kenya. Bin Laden later relocated to Afghanistan after al-Turabi, acting under intense US pressure, expelled him in 1996; he established new training camps under the protection of a triumphant Pakistan-backed Taliban government, but his terror cells and plans in Africa remained intact (9/11 Report, 2004, pp. 59–62; Coll, 2005, 162–164; Meredith, 2005, pp. 590–593). It is this ecology of conflict that enabled, and continues to enable, groups like al-Qaeda and AQIM to spread their ideology and gain traction with at least some of the millions affected by economic hardship and disaffected with the prevailing order, however disordered it might be (Battersby and Siracusa, 2009).

Counter-terrorism and counter-Islamism have come to dominate the US agenda in East Africa to the degree that less attention is paid to the humanitarian crisis in Darfur. Also, Washington's influence has been eroded by the rapid expansion of Chinese investment into African resource industries. As civil war raged across its oil concessions, US oil major Chevron pulled out of Sudan in the early 1990s, after which al-Bashir developed the country's oil infrastructure, including the Red Sea pipeline, with investment from Chinese and Malaysian oil interests (Suliman and Badawi, 2010). China's instinctive opposition to international interventionism at the UN and substantial investment from the China National Offshore Oil Company (CNOOC) places Khartoum in a stronger position to resist international calls for large-scale intervention in Darfur. Al- Bashir's 2009 indictment for war crimes by the International Criminal Court (ICC) did not prevent him from being feted in China by former Chinese President Hu Jin Tao in 2011. China has not ratified the Rome Statute and is, therefore, not bound to abide by ICC warrants, but major African states that have ratified the Statute, Nigeria for example, are likewise reluctant to act on their international obligations and take Bashir into custody (Wines, 2011; Gladstone and Kushkush, 2013). Relations between Washington and Khartoum are strained by the latter's association with Islamist terrorism and by the former's memory of 9/11. Washington's diplomatic switch to support an independent South Sudan also, and perhaps more disturbingly, reflects the rising influence of both Christian conservatives and progressives over U.S. geo-strategy (De Waal, 2004, pp. 228–229). Sudan remains designated by the US as a "state sponsor of terrorism" but the Sudanese regime stands resilient despite concerted international pressure.

Concerned that any visible increase in its military presence in North Africa could likely backfire by engendering further radicalization and enhancing the appeal of the Islamists, the US covertly expanded its counter-Islamist operations in East Africa, working with amenable governments, principally Ethiopia, Eritrea and Uganda, to suppress Islamist activities through its Africa Regional Command (AFRICOM). AFRICOM's presence is both suspected and welcomed by African governments fearful of the appeal of radical Islamism. Stronger criticism is aired through the non-Western media accompanied by inevitable accusations of neo-colonialism (Deen, 2013). Within US government circles, however, tensions exist between those committed to waging covert war against Islamists and those who voice dissent over the potential for US diplomacy and development assistance in Africa to become militarized and punitive, and hence counter-productive (Ploch, 2011, p. 29). The proliferation of terror incidents across northern and eastern Africa from 2011 to 2013 raises questions about the strategy and the tactics employed to arrest the spread of extremism, which is not, it must be repeatedly emphasized, purely Islamic extremism. A case in point, the Lord's Resistance Army (LRA) is a volatile amalgam of syncretic, fundamentalist Christian, "anti-modern, anti-developmental and anti-state" beliefs that originated in northern Uganda, with the aid of Khartoum. This "alliance" represented, writes De Waal, a pragmatic compact designed to destabilize Uganda and weaken the SPLA, which drew support from Kampala (Jackson, 2010, p. 4; De Waal, 2004, p. 198). Despite AFRICOM's attention – and temporarily that of the whole international community when LRA leader, Joseph Kony, became an overnight social media celebrity – the LRA has established footholds outside Uganda, in South Sudan and the Central African Republic. Al-Shabaab is *the* terror group of Western concern in East Africa, and yet the chaos upon which it thrives is informed by many conflicts, including those with little connection to radical Islam.

Regional fissures

With the benefit of hindsight, US Cold War opposition to the South Sudan rebels ignored popular political aspirations and intensified the traumas of decolonization and self-determination in East Africa. Ideology, personal preferences, fears and the arguments of vested interests serve to cloud as much as clarify the development of state security strategy – everywhere. With Moscow-dominated communism in retreat across the world in the 1990s, the US turned to support secular states in Muslim-majority countries against Islamic extremists in the hope that stability and rising global prosperity would gradually diminish the appeal of Islamist ideology. The "Arab Spring," however, exposed the fragility of authoritarian order and the incapacity of governing elites in Tunisia, Libya and Egypt to accommodate the social transformations and stresses generated by economic modernization. Conflict in West, Central and East Africa tests the resolve and resources of the African Union and Arab League, and yet it is concerted action on the part of both groups that is most likely to produce a coordinated regional response sufficient to yield politically viable resolutions. One step in that direction is the systematic "unveiling" of crime–security complexes so as to foreground structural, more than ideological, sources of criminality (Battersby et al., 2011). To put it another way, our interpretations of crime and conflict need to be both systematized and "deradicalized."

Topographies of conflict signal breakdowns in political relations attributable to a long list of interrelated factors. Africa's east–west conflict arc spans northern Kenya, Somalia, Ethiopia, Sudan, South Sudan, Chad, the Central African Republic, the Democratic Republic of Congo, Mali, Nigeria, Guinea-Bissau and Senegal. The illegal arms trade contributes to a complex feedback loop that aids the transference of organized violence from one regional hotspot to another. Trafficked arms – legally manufactured but illegally acquired – are available everywhere thanks to Western military support for anti-Gaddafi rebels in 2011, arms shipments from China and the attentiveness of Russian arms dealers like Victor Bout. Simply put, the roots of effective, legitimate government run very shallow across this east–west belt, allowing political and criminal violence to escalate. The freshly minted state of South Sudan descended into headline-grabbing internal chaos in December 2013 following a reported mutiny within government forces that escalated into interethnic violence and brought the country to the verge of civil war. The scope for democratic governance is constrained by serious internal political conflicts at the micro or local level and the violent means by which state security forces have sought to deal with militant groups and their supporters (ICG, 2009a; Herbst, 2000; UNODC, 2005, pp. 6–8; Oshita, 2009, pp. 33–36; Amnesty International, 2013). Yet, while crime is integral to the supply chains of violence, the coexistence of criminal networks alongside rebel groups does not necessarily signal convergence or "threat solidification."

International attention focuses on Africa's east coast maritime piracy, but there is a substantial and underacknowledged frequency of piracy on Africa's west coast. The International Maritime Organization (IMO) reported 64 incidents of maritime piracy and armed robbery for the West African region in 2012 – compared to 86 for East Africa (IMO, 2013). Along the West African coast pirate havens exist in zones of periodic political upheaval characterized by fragile or repressive states where state power is weak. In West Africa's recent history, Sierra Leone and Liberia have experienced protracted civil wars, both of which fuelled lucrative crime economies based on diamond smuggling. Future projections of global systemic transformation designate Nigeria as the African country most likely to rise to a position of regional leadership (EUISS, 2012; NIC, 2012). Many structural factors contribute to Nigeria's current internal security challenges, not least rapid population growth and severe income inequality. The country's oil-dependent economy has, despite rising levels of economic growth and aggregate prosperity, not led to any appreciable reduction in the chronic prevalence of poverty (AfDB, 2013a, p. 5; AfDB, 2013b, p.15). Armed sectarian violence persists in the predominantly Islamic north of the country. Jama'atu Ahlis Sunna Lidda'wati Wal-Jihad, the vaguely constituted Islamist group better known by its Hausa sobriquet Boko Haram (variously translated as "books are sinful" or "Western education is sacrilege"), has graduated from robbing banks and kidnapping (its core business since its formation in 2002) to waging a guerrilla war against the Nigerian state since 2009. Whatever links there might be with elements of al-Qaeda or AQIM, Boko Haram is principally a collection of robber bands, at liberty and at large, and but one manifestation of the deep-rooted sectarian rivalries dividing the north and the predominantly Christianized south (Bavier, 2012; Campbell, 2013; Jacinto, 2013; de Montclos, 2008).

The idea that Nigeria should be an Islamic state is not a recent invention of Islamists, and violence in Nigeria is not confined to Boko Haram attacks against civilians and the state. Human rights violations by the Nigerian military against communities in the oil-rich Niger Delta are linked to armed struggles with militia groups, operating under the umbrella Movement for the Emancipation of the Niger Delta (MEND), for control over oil resources. MEND sustained its war economy through oil theft and maritime piracy. Nigeria's "oil insurgency" is reportedly subsiding in the Delta following the amnesty offered by the Nigerian government of Goodluck Jonathan in 2009, but a splinter group persists, committing environmental crimes by setting fire to oil pipelines, and seeking to recast MEND's agenda in sectarian terms as anti-Boko Haram (Boas, 2009, p. 9; Junger, 2011; Bavier, 2012; Chinwo, 2013; Hirsch, 2013). It might be the case that the triggers for organized violence by and against the state in southern Nigeria have been to some extent removed, but the structural conditions that sparked anti-state mobilizations have not. Noticeably, the incidence of piracy off the West African coast, linked to conflict and crime, in particular the trade in "blood oil," has not subsided but rather doubled since 2006 (Batterbsy et al., 2011, p. 127; IMO, 2013).

There are parallels to be drawn between West Coast and East Coast piracy, but "piracy" is as disparate a crime category as narcotics. Pirate gangs operating off the Horn of Africa take refuge along the northeast African coast beyond the reach of international law and where internal political chaos creates a force field against nominally sovereign central authority (Gunaratna, 2009; Ploch et al., 2010. The collapse of state power in Mogadishu in the 1990s created a vacuum that was filled by semiautonomous "substate" polities (Kinsey et al., 2009, p. 151). These notional states sought to provide a semblance of political order and attempted to suppress illegal fishing by foreign ships operating in Somali waters. Piracy was countered effectively, for a time, through the recruitment of private contractor, British-based Hart Security, to train local coastguards and direct them in surveillance and interdiction in 2000 (Kinsey et al., 2009, pp. 152–154). Interpretation matters when determining how to engage with such regimes. The International Crisis

Group, for example, regards Puntland as a pivotal pirate refuge and a virtual criminal state (ICG, 2009b, pp. 7–9). Yet, governance is clan-based in these notional polities and piracy is, in fact, a clan-specific activity that renders suppression problematic from both a cultural and a political standpoint (Sorensen, 2008; Kinsey et al., 2009, p. 153). Piracy on this subregional level seems more aligned with the ambiguities of governing across indistinct lawful/unlawful divides than with Islamist terror *per se*. The phenomenon is arguably a form of terrestrial overspill, where land-based criminal groups extend their activities seaward aided by the "smog" of war and the limited reach of the state (Battersby et al., 2011).

Piracy became closely associated in the Western mind with Islamic radicalism post 9/11. Brazen acts of piracy by maritime raiders, operating mainly out of Eyl, a port city on the Puntland coast of Somalia, attracted international concern both for the ease with which the hijacking of container ships are effected and for the fear that financial benefit might flow to Islamist extremists in the Horn of Africa, namely, the Somali group known as al-Shabaab. Ironically, this conflation of Islamic radicalism and crime contributed to self-defeating US policies in the region, in particular, the decision to back Ethiopia's intervention in Somalia to remove the Union of Islamic Courts (UIC) regime in 2006. Until replaced by combined Ethiopia–AFRICOM action, the UIC briefly brought order to Somalia and had effectively curtailed piracy off the Somali coast (Thompson, 2007; Samatar, 2011). The IMO reports that in 2006 there were 31 attacks on shipping along Africa's east coast. Two years later, the number climbed to 134 (IMO, 2006; IMO, 2009). The alignment between Islamism and piracy is unclear, and there is evidently much antagonism between pirate clans and the Islamists. Pirates, or their leaders, are more concerned to accumulate riches in this world, and despite evidence of forced cooperation or pragmatic compromise with extremists, mutual antagonism is the norm. Ironically, when piracy incidents again declined in 2010–2011 it was because al-Shabaab denied land bases to Somali pirate groups that refused to pay "tax," and also the presence of the Kenyan military, retaliating against al-Shabaab cross-border attacks. (IMO, 2011; IMO, 2013; Singh, 2013; Yousef and Gismatullin, 2013; McCarthy, 2011, pp. 214–216).

Criminogenic trajectories

Violent actions by armed non-state actors stem from disparate causes, historical unresolved grievances and resource rivalries especially. It is not the convergence of criminals and terrorists *per se* but the convergence of crime complexes comprising multitudes of individuals and criminal entities – flexible, reconfigurable, fragmented and thus resilient – which undermine or corrode governance (Battersby, 1998–1999; Kenney, 2007a; Kenney, 2007b; Kenney, 2009). As the preceding foray into African politics indicates, the trajectories along which crime–security complexes form are multi-layered, reflecting an accumulation of parallel and linked vectors of risk along which the severity and intensity of violence is inflamed by Midlarsky's "mortality salience." The linear representation of this conceptual approach implies forward movement, continuity – even predictability, but the layering of trajectories at least serves to illustrate the "compound structure" of crime–security risk (Figure 2.2).

As obvious as it might seem, criminals thrive on illegality. The modern system of sovereign nation-states, to which codified law is central, defines the boundaries of what is legal and illegal and, perversely, influences the market price of contraband. Demand drives one side of the market for these goods and services, but the risks of detection and imprisonment set the premiums. Without national legislation to outlaw certain drugs – heroin, cannabis, cocaine and a suite of amphetamines and methamphetamines – there could be no illegal global drug trade. Without strong motives or incentives to disregard the rule of law, there would be no supply of illicit drugs to foster and to feed addiction. What is still more perplexing is the resilience demonstrated not by criminal groups per se, but by the phenomenon of transnational illicit traffic, which survives frequent "changings of the guard" in different world regions. This tendency is evident in illicit drug economies in Southeast Asia and Latin America where decades of drug suppression, while successful in limiting the trade in illegal narcotics, have not extinguished sources or vectors of supply or demand.

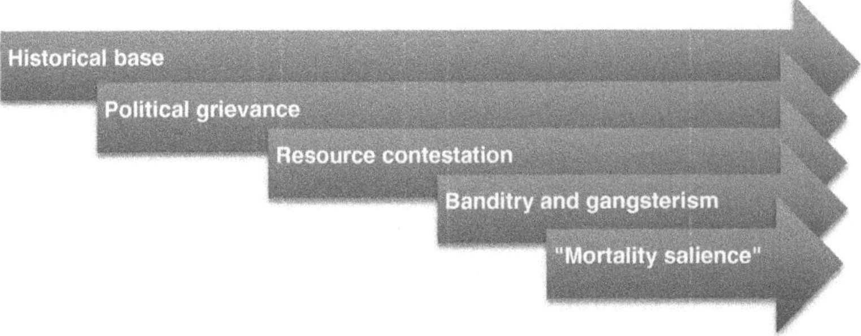

Figure 2.2 A compound trajectory of criminal and intrastate political violence

Political and economic imperatives created the global heroin trade, first as a legitimate business pursuit and then as a criminal endeavour. In British Burma, colonial officials collected opium in lieu of taxes from northern hill tribes where opium cultivation flourished. Opium production in other British colonies likewise grew rapidly to service the China market forced open by the Opium Wars (1839–1842). In this way Britain maintained a favourable trade balance with China and ensured the viability of its Asian empire (Trocki, 1999. Poppies coloured the countryside of Bengal and what is now northern Burma, Thailand and Laos (the Golden Triangle). Criminalization in the twentieth century altered the dynamics of opium cultivation and heroin trafficking. Political chaos arising from civil and international conflict across Asia after 1945 created the conditions in which this illicit cottage industry could thrive (Gibson, 2011; Kuzmarov, 2009; Chin, 2009; McCoy, 2003).

The legitimacy of the Union of Burma (Myanmar) was challenged from its inception in 1947. Under the Panglong Agreement, Burma's largest ethnic minorities (the Shan, Karenni, Karen, Mon and Chin) were granted individual states within the union, but only two, the Shan and Karenni, won the right to secede. Independence demands from the remainder went unheeded by Burmese and British constitutional negotiators. Karen, Mon and Arakhanese preparations for armed struggle were already well-advanced before formal independence was received. Once British troops withdrew, fighting erupted between the state and ethnic separatists, initiating five decades of secessionist war that acquired an ideological dimension with the Burmese Communist Party's (BCP) entry into the fray. Constitutionally agreed upon rights to secede were never recognized by the central government, which, despite being civilian and democratic, was dominated by the military upon which it relied to govern the country. Unlike India, where mass political parties emerged under British rule, Burmese politics was shaped by ethnic rivalries and the military. After 15 years of parliamentary rule, military control was entrenched when General Ne Win seized power in 1962, putting an end to Shan and Karenni hopes of independence.

With the legitimacy of the state thus fractured, secessionist wars flared along Burma's borders with China and Thailand. From the 1960s until its disbandment in 1989, the BCP funded its guerrilla activities primarily by drawing rent from poppy cultivation and opium trafficking in Myanmar's richest poppy-growing areas in the Shan state. External interventions served the strategic priorities of neighbouring states. To counter the ideological and military threat posed by the BCP, Thailand gave assistance to Karen rebels and also to Shan drug lord, Khun Sa, whose personal influence as a member of the Shan aristocracy and control over Shan militia groups made him a pivotal Thai ally. Khun Sa's Shan United Army was permitted to use bases in northern Thailand to mount military campaigns against the Ne Win government and maintain an extensive opium trading empire. Despite these protections as well as independent income from narcotics trafficking, logging concessions, and donations from sympathizers, communist movements in both Myanmar and Thailand were vulnerable to loss of support from external benefactors. China's thawing relations with the West and its "Open Door" policy of the 1980s spelt the end for communist movements in Burma and neighbouring Thailand – but not the drug trade. Kachin, Shan and Wa separatists assumed control over trafficking routes out of Myanmar, and dwindling external military assistance merely gave added impetus to the production and trade in opium (Chin, 2009; Wyler, 2013).

The systemic transformations that occurred globally and in Asia during the 1980s and the 1990s were not beyond the human capacity to anticipate. The capacity of governments and intergovernmental institutions to control the course of events is quite another matter. Despite intense efforts since the late 1990s to eradicate poppy cultivation in former separatist-controlled areas, the State Peace and Development Council (SPDC) has compromised narcotics suppression in the interests of defeating remaining insurgent armies. Poppy eradication remains hindered by the twin dynamics of narcotics demand and intrasocietal conflict – and residual external intervention in the form of continued Chinese military assistance to the Wa (Shearf, 2013). For the Burmese government, eradication complements the strategic imperative to deny economic resources to insurgents. For remote rural communities, economic uncertainty coupled with economic hardship strengthens the appeal of insurgents offering protection in return for support. There is also credible evidence of Burmese army officers' tolerance of opium cultivation and methamphetamine manufacture by militia groups allied to the SPDC, extending to the collection of an informal opium tax to supplement meagre army salaries (Wyler, 2013 pp. 4–5). Myanmar's integration into the Association of Southeast Asian Nations (ASEAN) and its international rehabilitation following the adoption of parliamentary democracy has not lessened its primacy in the illicit drug trade (Battersby et al., 2011; Battersby and Siracusa, 2009).

It is no coincidence that opium cultivation is most prevalent in countries affected by prolonged civil war. Without sufficient land under opium cultivation, heroin could not be produced in large-enough quantities to serve the interests of traffickers and insurgents. Afghanistan's slight reduction of the global share of opium cultivation (down to 74 per cent in 2012 from 82 per cent in 2007) is explainable, in part, by a steady resurgence in cultivation in Myanmar and Lao PDR (UNODC, 2007; UNODC, 2012; UNODC, 2013b, p. 10). Decades of regional counter-narcotics actions driven by the US have failed to rein in the production and trade in heroin. If one looks deep into the institutional structures of modern states, legacies of Cold War conflict can be found in residual sympathies for Shan and Wa insurgents within senior ranks of the Thai military – an institution long implicated in the Southeast Asian heroin trade (McCoy, 2003; Goswami, 2013; Gibson, 2011, p. 163). Transnational networks formed during decades of insurgency provided many of the "switch-tracks" of subregional criminal enterprise, from opium trafficking to illegal logging and arms smuggling, that flourished in the immediate post-Cold War era (Battersby, 1998–1999; Wille, 2006, pp. 28–29). Still, given the rapid technologization and diversification of drug production, physical and human geographies are today much less of a constraint.

The Southeast Asian crime–security complex is extensive and no longer routed principally through nodal points marked by protracted civil war. Globalization is deterritorializing narcotics production to the extent that synthetic drugs do not require large swathes of territory to be produced in commercially viable quantities. A few chemicals and a makeshift laboratory are all that is required to produce crystal methamphetamine and other "party drugs." Internet sites, like the now defunct "Silk Road," connect producers with customers through the post, thereby fragmenting the shipment of illicit drugs. African, Iranian and Chinese traffickers now supply the Asian market, as do significant numbers of Australian and New Zealand illicit Amphetamine-Type Stimulants (ATS) labs in a globalized illicit cottage industry (UNODC, 2013b, p. 9).

The neutralization of armed conflict is only the first step in dismantling crime–security complexes and, for this step to be effective, negotiated peace settlements are infinitely preferable. Although United Nations Office on Drugs and Crime statistics indicate an overall decline in the area of land under coca cultivation along the Andean Ridge, cocaine trafficking out of Columbia, Peru and Bolivia through Mexico to the US and Europe is rising due to more efficient production techniques (UNODC, 2013a, p. 38). The cocaine industry in Colombia is driven by complex demand–supply dynamics. Michael Reid writes of a pattern of governance failures that can be detected across Latin America, most glaringly, the failure to adequately address poverty and inequality – one that fuels the thriving Andean coca trade. At the centre of these failures Reid finds vested class interest, corruption and widespread police brutality as key drivers of political and criminal violence (Reid, 2007, pp. 147–158). While Chile, Argentina and Brazil have developed stable democracies, government in democratic Mexico is seriously compromised by narco-gangs and escalating gang violence, which, as mentioned in Chapter 1, is a legacy of military and police tolerance of and involvement in the lucrative Andean Ridge cocaine trade. It is, thus, the criminality of individuals within legitimate state institutions, as much as the criminal actions of people outside the state, that degrades political legitimacy and generate political estrangement.

Colombia's location at the epicentre of a Western hemispheric cocaine trafficking economy is attributable to that country's violent past (Eakin, 2007). Failure to establish common ground sufficient to accommodate Conservative and Liberal elements in Colombian society saw their common front splinter during the twentieth century with many dissidents joining with Marxist revolutionaries to form the Fuerzas Armadas Revolucionarias de Colombia or the Revolutionary Armed Forces of Colombia (FARC), and the Ejército de Liberación Nacional or National Liberation Army (ELN). Left-wing insurgents in their early days funded their campaigns through the sale of coffee beans, but coca production and trafficking became the economic staple of conflict by the 1980s. It was during this period that the "people's war" degenerated into a struggle for control over territory and cocaine crops as paramilitaries and insurgents fought for a share of the lucrative global cocaine trade. Resource demands increased parallel to this expansion, adding organizational pressures to the corrosion of rank-and-file ideological commitment. Unlike the Wa in Myanmar, the FARC did not develop an elaborate international syndicate of its own but instead relied upon working relationships with established transnational and global narcotics-trafficking networks (Guaquetta, 2003, pp. 93–94; Chernick, 2005, pp. 190–192; Reid, 2007, p. 259; Saab and Taylor, 2009; Purdue, 2012, pp. 147–208).

A lesson from the dismantling of long-running insurgencies in the Niger Delta, and the longer still insurgencies in Thailand and Malaysia, is that some form of accommodation with rebel forces is necessary in the form of a peace settlement to bring internecine wars to an end. In 2013 FARC and the Colombian government resumed negotiations for a peace agreement and the reintegration of FARC cadres into Colombian society – and indeed for FARC to be recognized as a legitimate political force in Colombian politics (Amnesty International, 2013; Bargent, 2013; BBC, 2013; Brodzinsky, 2013).

Colombia's strategic repositioning as a centre of regional economic dynamism, however, masks considerable and unresolved societal fractures.

Not least, Colombia's protracted drug wars have left between 4.2 million and 4.7 million persons internally displaced (Anyadike, 2013; UNHCR, 2013). The Colombian government's efforts to neutralize the FARC through counter-insurgency was only partially successful in that, despite weakening its military strength, which declined from 20,000 armed cadres in 2002 to around 7,000 by 2008 (according to official Colombian government claims), the movement, through its revolutionary message, retains a broad regional appeal under the banner of the Continental Bolivarian Movement (Purdue, 2012, pp. 196–206; FARC-EP, 2014). Three remaining societal conflict dimensions allow the cocaine trade to survive: between the Colombian state and left-wing revolutionaries, between the Colombian state and drug-trafficking networks that replaced the larger cartels such as the Medellin in the latter 1990s, and between the Colombian state and residual elements of right-wing paramilitaries formed to protect the interests of landowners against left-wing insurgents. Tenuous and expedient links between Latin American radical groups, traffickers and armed non-state entities from the Middle East, and with Iran, are bruited as evidence of the global crime–terror convergence reaching the territorial gates of the US, regardless of the ideological inconsistencies within and between extremist elements, or between Iran and al-Qaeda (Purdue, 2012). That states, like Iran, should be engaged in such pursuits is not that unusual for, as will be discussed in Chapter 3, this is after all the essence of "organized hypocrisy."

Paralleling tactics used in Thailand to combat the spread of communist influence and to counteract Islamist militancy in the south, the Colombian military created a system of local defence groups, *convivirs*, comprising armed but ill-disciplined volunteers. Colombian right-wing paramilitaries were formed initially to protect the property and interests of wealthy landowners, who were among the insurgents' prime targets. As with the FARC/ELN, however, these paramilitaries moved into drug trafficking and used extortion to fund their expansion, bringing them into conflict with communist guerrilla forces for commercial, rather than ideological, reasons. One critical factor in reducing paramilitarism was Executive Order 13224 (EO13224), issued by President George W. Bush in 2001, which outlawed payments to known terrorist organizations, including the Autodefensas Unidas de Colombia or United Self-Defense Force of Colombia (AUC). This listing made cooperation between the Colombian military and paramilitaries more and more difficult while exposing the Colombian state to potential sanctions. Former Colombian President Alvaro Uribe Velez succeeded in negotiating the demobilization of the AUC in 2003, but question marks remain over the scale of disarmament. Official estimates claimed as many as 31,000 disbanded AUC fighters, but there is a high degree of recidivism and enduring paramilitary political influence. Human Rights Watch reported a revival of paramilitaries in Colombia (Hanson, 2008; HRW, 2010). One last observation, prefacing critiques of civil society and social activism in Chapter 5, concerns the scope for "people power" to curtail the actions of criminals and paramilitaries. In areas once dominated by drug warlords, such as the city of Medellin, people no longer cower in fear of drug gangs but the return to normalcy and the recovery of civic pride and identity are the result of a resurgent Colombian state (aided by US counter-narcotics programmes) – not the spontaneous flowering of popular "grassroots" democracy (Villarreal, 2013).

"Soft" power and "smart" governance

Our understanding of the nature of conflict and human suffering has grown rapidly through the investment of time and financial resources into the study of peace and security. Critiques of the indexation of security governance aside, the search for a systematic approach to guide policy at the national and global levels is justifiable if only because the scope of security risk and the potential scale of impact have grown exponentially through globalization. The evolution of state security doctrines in the post-Cold War era is evidence of acceptance that the roots of conflict, crime and terror are to be found in broader social and economic contexts and not merely in the ill-intentioned actions of "deviant" individuals and criminal groups. Yet the crime–terror narrative is today proving the most virile expression of a non-traditional security rationale. The reality of global security relations is that the military option, through direct intervention or the militarization and paramilitarization of state security strategies, is the preferred option through which to dissolve crime–security complexes. The attendant equation of all forms of radicalism with terrorism and terrorism with all forms of market crime is as compelling a justification as it is convenient – but it is also erroneous.

The distinction between security – defined as human security – and security defined in reference to a crime-terror nexus is accentuated by the so-called Global War on Terror. The end to the Cold War was supposed to herald the dawn of a new age of peace and prosperity. The changing polarities of global politics in the 1990s created a moment in time where a different kind of world order became possible. Aspirations for world peace were fed by the Western triumphalism that greeted the Soviet Union's demise, but within a decade of the dissolution of the Soviet Bloc the world was plunged into a different kind of cold/hot war. No single global actor bears responsibility for this global transformation, just as no single global actor can single-handedly reorder the globe by dint of its policies and diplomacy.

With the Cold War officially over, global leadership was split, and thus diluted, between a reluctant US and a re-energized UN. The financial burdens of war, argues Robert Keohane, and the costs of underwriting the liberal international economic order that it had created at Bretton Woods, severely eroded the capacity of the US to direct global economic and strategic affairs after 1971 (Keohane, 2005, p. 207). The demise of Moscow-dominated communism, when it came, swiftly altered the global landscape of security policy and allowed the partial relaxation of the US global strategic posture but not US Cold War doctrines. Global, regional and national policy settings were recalibrated and policy prescriptions outlined to bring stability to global affairs. US presidents hinted at a new world order, but it was the multilateral institutions, the UN and the World Bank, that gave shape and substance to the debate. Acknowledging the multiple links between poverty, illiteracy, malnutrition, disease and political chaos, the World Bank adopted poverty alleviation as its prime focus. This was recognition that decades of development assistance had largely failed to bring "development" to much of the developing world. The Bank's approach and policy prescriptions, however, remained economistic and largely generic (or ideological) with insufficient consideration given to the many idiosyncrasies of national and subnational developmental challenges (CGC, 1996, pp. 133–134, 222–224, 301, 333–334; Whitman, 2005).

In framing development challenges as Millennium Development Goals (MDGs), and incorporating human security into its conceptual repertoire, the UN created a broad platform from which to advocate for systemic change. Conflict prevention, disease eradication, poverty alleviation, sustainable economic development, food security and the promotion of human rights were acknowledged as interlinked security concerns that required a globally coordinated but locally effective response (UNCHS, 2003). Human security acquired traction with "middle power" countries like Japan and Canada. "Soft power," diplomacy, development aid, police cooperation and defence assistance underpins Europe's new approach to the post-colonial world. Clearly, the international community has many policy instruments at its disposal. Yet, at the many critical global intersections of crime and political violence, where extremes of poverty and inequality combine with the denial of political rights, these instruments have had, at best, limited effect. From the perspective of those who advocate a different approach, these are merely instruments of a different kind of violence against cultural identities and the social relations that sustain human diversity (Escobar, 1995; Hayden, 2009).

Intended or not, the conflation of human security with the doctrine of humanitarian intervention or the Responsibility to Protect (R2P) limits the effectiveness of both. The "new security" proposed by former Secretary-General Boutros Boutros-Ghali (1992–1996), in his *Agenda for Peace*, rested on the argument that the international community had an obligation and a right to override the sovereign rights of states "when all peaceful means have failed," to put an end to intrastate conflicts where the risk of mass civilian casualties is immediate (Boutros-Ghali, 1992). The scope for unilateral action by states to prevent mass civilian casualties was not discounted, nor the grounds for intervention limited to the impending threat of genocide (ICISS, 2001; Holzgrefe, 2003). The Commission on Intervention and State Sovereignty, formed to address the international response to humanitarian tragedies in Rwanda and the former Yugoslavia, concluded that sovereignty bears with it the responsibility for "states to protect persons and property and to discharge the functions of government adequately within their territories" (ICISS, 2001). The adoption of R2P by the international community in 2005 marked a significant moment in international post-Cold War diplomacy but the efficacy of intervention and indeed the legitimacy of UN-mandated interventions remain in question.

The two most significant and protracted military interventions of the early twenty-first century were led by the US in Afghanistan and Iraq. Neither intervention referenced humanitarian aims, but both were effected in the name of international peace and security with legitimacy claimed under the UN Charter; both also served US geostrategic interests. Following 9/11, the US aggressively prosecuted a new form of *realpolitik*, pursuing Osama bin Laden and his al-Qaeda organization into Afghanistan. US forces were decisive in bringing about the removal of the Taliban Islamist regime in 2002. Occupations of Afghanistan and Iraq, although supported by America's European NATO allies, and Pacific allies Australia and Japan, were first and foremost US-directed military operations and represented a significant shift away from the tentativeness with which security issues were addressed in the 1990s under the Clinton Administration.

Military security, which slipped down the scale of global priorities after the Soviet bloc's demise, returned to the top of the global agenda where it fused with terrorism, weapons of mass destruction and transnational crime. In Washington, the UN was viewed as an institution that had lost its way, that was hostage to factionalism, stymied by diplomatic trade-offs, bloated, bureaucratic and quite possibly riddled by corruption. The limits of unilateralism, however, became more and more exposed as the Iraq and Afghanistan occupations turned into counterinsurgency operations. Smarting from sustained international condemnation for the unfolding debacle in Iraq, President George W. Bush reminded the UN members of their responsibilities. Referring to the Universal Declaration of Human Rights in a speech to the General Assembly in September 2006, President Bush appealed to the legacy of American idealism embodied in the UN Charter and Universal Declaration of Human Rights:

> Achieving the promise of the Declaration requires confronting long-term threats; it also requires answering the immediate needs of today. The nations in this chamber have our differences, yet there are some areas where we can all agree. When innocent people are trapped in a life of murder and fear, the Declaration is not being upheld. When millions of children starve to death or perish from a mosquito bite, we're not doing our duty in the world. When whole societies are cut off from the prosperity of the global economy, we're all worse off . . .
>
> This great institution must work for great purposes – to free people from tyranny and violence, hunger and disease, illiteracy and ignorance, and poverty and despair. Every member of the United Nations must join in this mission of liberation (Bush, 2006).

In a not-so-veiled accusation that UN member states were not shouldering their share of the burden of global security, Bush cast the US as liberator in a global war recast as a war to end humanitarian suffering – neither claim is borne out by the evidence. In Iraq, despite the reinstitution of a democratic system of government in 2005, and the withdrawal of occupation forces in 2011, thousands of civilians die each year from politically motivated violence with a marked increase in 2013 (Iraq Body Count, 2013). Civilian casualties in Afghanistan are surprisingly much lower, even with the continuation of International Security Assistance Force (ISAF) military operations to 2014, and Taliban offensives (Rogers and Chalabi, 2013). In hindsight, neither Operation Iraqi Freedom (2003–2011) nor Operation Enduring Freedom (Afghanistan) (2002–2014) has yielded any durable political gains – in terms of the creation of stable democratic regimes in either Iraq or Afghanistan or the enhancement of US power or the legitimacy of global institutions, primarily the UN.

Estimates of the cost to the US alone of the Afghanistan and Iraq interventions range from US$2 trillion in direct costs to US$6 trillion, once the long-term liabilities of military pensions, for the families of nearly 7,000 American war dead, and lifelong social and healthcare benefits for injured service personnel are factored into the equation (Blimes, 2013; National Priorities Project, n/d).

Critics of US policy speak with a common voice in the charge of misdirected and mis-informed American power. Not that interventionist, counter-insurgency or counter-terrorism strategies uniformly meet with failure. Lessons are being drawn from significant counter-insurgency gains outside the Middle East in the first decade of this century. The title of Ahmed S. Hashim's book on the Sri Lankan civil war, *When Counterinsurgency Wins* (2013) speaks to the aspirations of counter-terrorist and military strategists worldwide for swift and decisive solutions to protracted intrastate conflicts. There are grave dangers however in extrapolating too much from the military defeat of the Tamil Tigers by the Sri Lankan state in 2009, or the FARC's apparent denouement. Though fed by a global Tamil diaspora, the Liberation Tigers of Tamil Ealam was not part of an international counter-hegemonic movement nor was it contiguous to ideologically aligned or criminally inclined insurgencies. The defeat of the FARC was one objective of "Plan Colombia," through which the US aimed to extinguish the Colombian cocaine trade. A case is made here however that the catalyst for Colombian state gains against the FARC was the criminalization of right-wing paramilitaries by the US, a by-product of the War on Terror, which was in turn a reaction to the attacks of 9/11, and a strategy perhaps unimaginable a decade before.

Conservatives, such as Whiton, advocate for the "smart" redirection of diplomacy to broker solutions to crises that threaten US interests while those of a more liberal view call for greater support for multilateralism, or for popular democracy (Keohane, 2005; Castells, 2012; Whitton, 2013). A shift in US policy towards the world is prefaced in President Barack Obama's acknowledgement of the limits of US power in an address to the UN General Assembly in September 2013:

> We live in a world of imperfect choices. Different nations will not agree on the need for action in every instance, and the principle of sovereignty is at the center of our international order. But sovereignty cannot be a shield for tyrants to commit wanton murder, or an excuse for the international community to turn a blind eye to slaughter. While we need to be modest in our belief that we can remedy every

> evil, and we need to be mindful that the world is full of unintended consequences, should we really accept the notion that the world is powerless in the face of a Rwanda or Srebrenica? If that's the world that people want to live in, then they should say so, and reckon with the cold logic of mass graves.
>
> I believe we can embrace a different future. If we don't want to choose between inaction and war, we must get better – all of us – at the policies that prevent the breakdown of basic order. Through respect for the responsibilities of nations and the rights of individuals. Through meaningful sanctions for those who break the rules. Through dogged diplomacy that resolves the root causes of conflict, and not merely its aftermath. Through development assistance that brings hope to the marginalized. And yes, sometimes, all this will not be enough – and in such moments, the international community will need to acknowledge that the multilateral use of military force may be required to prevent the very worst from occurring (Obama, 2013).

Replete with references to Weberian perplexities, and even a hint of Kantian antinomy, Obama's remarks imply a "smart" turn in US foreign policy. The speech evidences acceptance that rigid grand strategies are inappropriate in a complex world, where diplomatic gains are only ever marginal, incremental and conditional. But if AFRICOM's operations are any guide, the "whole-of-government approach" advocated by influential voices in the US security community, and encapsulated in Obama's UN speech, is in reality constrained by the persistence of a strategic culture of defence through offence, be this "light footprint" interventionism or the global policing of transnational criminals and terrorists and all the compromises that this entails (Farah 2013, p. 10).

In the post-9/11 global context, in which both China and Russia have grown more assertive and inclined to block US diplomacy at the UN, humanitarian interventions to end the violence in Syria or human rights violations in Tibet, Chechnya, Burma or Sudan are unlikely to gain Security Council approval. China and Russia, both permanent members of the Security Council, oppose humanitarian intervention, because both countries are sensitive about their respective positions in Tibet and Chechnya, and both seek to inhibit the evolution of an interventionist norm at the UN. This new global reality greatly increases the stakes of military interventions of any kind.

The adoption of "soft power" strategies has greater appeal for those states with less military firepower at their disposal. After failing at its formation in 1993 to deal effectively with the break up of the former Yugoslavia, the EU has matured as a regional security actor evolving towards a "security community." The EU is a global actor with substantial diplomatic resources at its disposal to pursue the advancement of both social and economic priorities within and without (Hix and Hoyland, 2011, 206–209). Europeaid, the EU's international development arm, spent US$16 billion in 2011 on programmes designed to promote human rights, democratization, "South–South" cooperation and MDG implementation. This spending complements the US$69 billion in overseas development assistance given separately by EU member states for that year directed primarily towards Africa, the Middle East and Eastern Europe in keeping with the Union's primary geostrategic interests (Battersby and Siracusa, 2009; EC, 2011, p. 170).

The Union's Common Security Strategy, adopted in 2003, encapsulates the broad sweep of security defined in non-traditional terms, outlining an approach not dissimilar to the UN's human security agenda released in the same year, nor one repugnant to Obama's take on smart power (UNCHS, 2003). EU strategy connects terrorism, state failure, regional conflict and organized crime as key contributors to insecurity to be countered, militarily where necessary, but primarily through "soft power" diplomacy (EU, 2003). This, of course, has not limited the ability of member states to pursue independent security policies, for the UK to join in the invasion of Iraq or for France to intervene in Mali. Since the EU's formation in 1993, membership has expanded from 12 to 25, with more countries applying to join. Enlargement, though derided by detractors, demonstrated the attraction of economic security in numbers – especially for the smaller European states. Marking the transference of significant sovereign functions to a supranational organization by states seeking to control a complex global environment through collective action, this European initiative is, perhaps, the prime exemplar of Buzan and Waever's ideal of regional security convergence (Buzan and Waever, 2007). The veracity of this observation is undiminished by the impacts of the Global Financial Crisis (GFC) of 2008 and the Eurozone Crisis of 2010–2012.

When the UN was founded there were no significant regional institutions that could serve as a bridge between the global and the local. In terms of mediating global programmes for regional security, regional institutions are beginning to play a pivotal role in global governance. A "demonstration effect" from European integration is evident in Asia, where the ASEAN is evolving towards a wider Asian economic union with the expansion of institutional connections with China and India

(Ba, 2009). European economic cooperation is today acknowledged as the reason for the absence of a major European war since 1945, and while this is explicable in terms of mutual economic self-interest, the institutional constraints imposed on unilateral action through regional policy integration are significant. In this late modern age, states are becoming networked, and the "network state" requires cooperative international frameworks to sustain critical risk management functions (Giddens, 1990; Castells, 2000).

The "informational logic" of regional and global "interdependence" was prefigured in Australia's 1989 regional security strategy. The Australian government adopted a prototypical "network security" model to outline policy responses that spoke to apparent interconnections between traditional and non-traditional security risks confronting Australia and the Asian region. Development and defence were recognized as interdependent issue areas requiring a "whole of government" response, incorporating military, diplomatic, economic, social and cultural measures. This matrix of regional security "management" reflected deepening regional interconnectedness in Southeast Asia, driven in part by a dynamic of actual and planned infrastructure integration. Australia's security strategy mapped an informational grid onto these regionalizing patterns through which economic, development and military cooperation was calibrated and cross-referenced (Evans, 1989).

Policy was reset to "manage" the risks of economic integration, as opposed to the threats of ideological confrontation (Richardson, 2005, p. 364). Judicious interventions to remove the vestiges of Cold War conflicts were part of the approach. Australia played a significant role in the Cambodian peace settlement, and took a lead role in the UN Transitional Authority for Cambodia with Australian soldiers overseeing the demobilization of the Khmer Rouge. Although Foreign Minister Gareth Evans was one to the first to advocate for the principle of R2P in the diplomatic aftermath of the Rwandan genocide, Australian regional interventions were technical and developmental rather than military, save for limited peacekeeping roles under the UN banner. Collaborative multilateral approaches were favoured to meet potential challenges to Australian sovereignty at source, with foreign governments taking the lead in return for Australian financial assistance – and advice. In what was considered a "benign" regional environment, security was envisioned and fashioned through the frame of a systematic hazard reduction programme.

Australia's regional strategy became overtly interventionist and increasingly militarized in the late 1990s. One catalyst for this shift was the identification of non-traditional security risks arising from the1997 Asian Financial Crisis. The spectre of chaos across the Indonesian archipelago refocused the minds of Australia's security community and Australians became more actively involved in regional security affairs. Australia played an influential role in persuading Indonesia to accept a referendum on East Timor's independence and then applied R2P in practice by sending in Australian troops under a UN mandate to end the intracommunal violence that followed the referendum vote. Following on the deployment of Australian forces to Iraq and Afghanistan, the stationing of Australian troops and federal police in the Solomon Islands from 2003 under the Regional Assistance Mission for the Solomon Islands (RAMSI) underscored the doctrinal switch. Logical connections between terrorism, transnational crime, political chaos, "poor governance" and state failure were clearly evident in foreign policy and defence thinking. "Transnational crime, including people smuggling and trafficking, drug trafficking and money laundering, threatens the sovereignty of Australia and other nations," it was claimed (DFAT, 2003, p. 46). Policy signalled out South Pacific states as facing potential violent social unrest and "vulnerable to the activities of terrorists," hence the urgency accorded to RAMSI (DFAT, 2003, p. 37).

Failing Pacific states, it was thought, presented opportunities to transnational criminal syndicates and terrorist groups evidently seeking a base from which to flood Australia with narcotics and mount terrorist attacks on the Australian mainland (DFAT, 2003; Wainwright, 2003). It was a much larger archipelagic state, Indonesia, that attracted most investment in security network building following the 2002 Bali terrorist bombings, which killed 202 people, including 88 Australians (Battersby, 2007). Australian–Indonesian police cooperation to suppress terrorism in Indonesia has been effective, but policing and law enforcement in isolation do little to address the deeper societal tensions that encourage terrorism, criminal violence or drug production and trafficking. Connections between drug-related criminality and "underdevelopment" should not, however, be overdrawn. Gun trafficking and drug manufacture thrive in established democracies, and Australia is no exception. There is a substantial illegal trade in light weapons within Australia. Though reports suggest an increase in illegally imported handguns, arms trafficking experts claim that, by far, the majority of illegal guns are "acquired" unlawfully from lawful sources in the country (Alpers and Twyford, 2003; Rubinsztein-Dunlop, 2012). Amphetamines pop from pill presses in every Australian city, and significant quantities find their way into Asian markets. And while Australian crime authorities focus on "Asian" threats, one of the most dangerous recent transnational entrants into the world of Australian organized crime is the Mongols, a "motorcycle gang" – not from some remote Pacific island but from Australia's closest ally, the US (Mann, 2013).

Conclusion

The anticipatory logic of security risk is fraught with potential for refractive error. *Informationalization* makes distant sociopolitical phenomena "knowable," in the sense that data can be collected and impressions formed, but are not necessarily "understandable" or "governable." Historical perspective matters but the conventional security "risk matrix," fashionable in the early 2000s, is, at best, a two-dimensional tool, devised to guide time-bound security "projects" with defined but artificial end points that might or might not be the "end" of the matter. There are deeper processes working to change the interaction dynamics of the global system, of which terrorism and the transnationalization and globalization of crime are symptomatic. This is not the same as arguing that terrorism and transnational crime do not present challenges to governance and to social order either locally or globally. Globalization engenders and is engendered by ephemeral, tactical and spontaneous convergences between nefarious and malevolent entities. But, if it is the global norm for global business executives to meet in five-star hotels, or confer through the Internet, or for intellectuals to converge to share knowledge at international conferences, is it any surprise that sophisticated criminals and terrorists are following suit?

3
The Globalization of State Crime

States have need of laws, including international laws, and yet states, or their agents, claim the prerogative to reinterpret, rewrite or even transgress the law – where necessity dictates. For this reason, state crimes are entirely absent from the corpus of international criminal law – as they are from domestic criminal codes (Bassiouni, 2011, loc. 248). Even the Rome Statute of the International Criminal Court (ICC) implies individual and not state criminal liability. Unlike civil law, where responsibility can be apportioned and penalties imposed upon state and corporate entities, responsibility for criminal acts committed in the name of the state is individuated so that individual culprits can be identified, isolated and punished, but not the institutions they represent. Yet, the concept of state crime enjoys wide currency among international jurists, political scientists, criminologists and humanitarians. The terms "pariah state," "narco-state" and "state sponsor of terrorism" surface in official security discourse to justify punitive actions against "rogue" foreign governments. The "failed state" is a special category of political deviance, where, under the Responsibility to Protect (R2P) norm, the rights and privileges of sovereignty are abrogated because "national authorities manifestly fail to protect their populations from *genocide, war crimes, ethnic cleansing and crimes against humanity*" (emphasis added) (UNGA, 2005, p. 31). There are evidently strong moral as well as political grounds for regarding certain state actions as criminal and assigning collective responsibility for them.

There is a countermovement, however, to the progressive extension and expansion of international criminal law and international humanitarian law. Many state actions once considered unlawful are being rendered lawful in a formal legal sense – in the name of state and international security. What was once considered covert and objectionable is now overt and negotiable. For example, "running guns" to insurgent groups is normalized under R2P. *Informationalization* is "dehumanizing" war and enlarging the scope of state power but also weakening the legal foundations of basic human rights. Total war is taken to a new level through the securitization and militarization of cyber space. The global politics of networked states is rapidly destabilizing long-established legal categories of war and crime and the laws defined to protect people from the arbitrary exercise of power. This is a new dimension to the globalization of crime in which states are the pivotal actors.

Globalization, anarchy and criminality

States have not withered in the full force of economic globalization and are not set to depart the global scene anytime soon (Lachmann, 2010). Rather, state power is transformed by the opportunities and imperatives generated by the ongoing integration of economic, technological and financial systems. As emphasized at the beginning of this book, the US can, subject to judicial authorization, compel telecommunications multinationals to yield information on demand and to employ specialized staff to filter and collect telecommunications data, then surrender this information on demand (Gellman and Blake, 2013; Timberg and Nakashina, 2013). The Communications Assistance for Law Enforcement Act, 1994, empowers US government agencies to direct the configuration of telecoms technologies to facilitate data collection. This is one of the less well-known laws that, in combination with the US Patriot Act, delivers substantially enhanced surveillance powers to the US government that intelligence gatherers are unlikely to yield, even in the face of rising public privacy concerns. Similar directives impose requirements upon telecommunications companies operating within the EU and its member states (Pillsbury et al., 2010, pp. 51, 87). From one perspective, then, the exponential growth of telecommunications systems has extended the power of the executive, and more so in one-party states.

The "networked state" still seeks to exercise power, through institutionalized cooperation or "smart" diplomacy and by manipulating or regulating international flows of money, people and ideas. It is perhaps no coincidence that at a time of heightened tensions between the US and China over trade and alleged cyber espionage, historical interest returns to economic warfare, meaning the historical pursuit of geostrategic advantage by economic means, as a precursor to armed conflict (Lambert, 2012; Taillard, 2012) New technological capabilities unsettle established system hierarchies and the geopolitical interests that they serve. Looking to the integrated conduits of global trade and finance at the end of the nineteenth century, power was exercised through strategic control over terrestrial networks, and this power to control was fought over intensely, first, by economic and, then, by military means. Britain – or, more precisely, influential figures in the British Naval Intelligence and the Admiralty – writes Nicholas Lambert, was concerned about the potential disruption of international trade and communications, credit and finance arising from this new networked world, and yet some were prepared to contemplate manipulating this global system to restrain German economic and geostrategic competition (Lambert, 2012, pp. 109–126). Communications technology advances today are unlikely to level out disparities in economic and military power globally, but the vulnerability of the evolving global system to disruptions arising from the uses and abuses of new transformative and globalizing technologies does focus the mind.

Deliberate destabilization of global markets today would be a form of state unlawfulness, a violation of international agreements but not a crime in the strict legal–technical sense. Indeed, it is not so straightforward a task to distinguish between intentional "warlike" ruination and economic self-preservation through, for example, competitive currency devaluation. The world is not thought to be on the verge of a major interstate war even if the BRIC (Brazil, Russia, India and China) economies and emergent regional influencers, like Indonesia and Nigeria, are thought likely to reshape the prevailing global order in the next 20 years (EU ISS, 2012; NIC, 2012). Historically, however, major technological changes, aligned with major shifts in economic capacity, are associated with heightened interstate rivalries and an increased risk of armed conflict. Long cycle theories of global change stress correlations between major systemic disruption caused by technological innovation and rapid economic transformation and interstate conflict (Modelski and Thompson, 1999; Wallerstein, 2004). It would be complacent, therefore, to assume that mutual economic interest and mutual economic gains will be sufficient over the short to medium term to sustain a global cooperation dynamic when the international system created at the end of World War II is under enormous strain. Accordingly, it is unwise to place too much faith on rationalist models of international relations and human behaviour to determine the precise conditions of war and peace.

The sheer scale of potential harm arising from the collapse, engineered or otherwise, of globally networked systems is substantial. The ongoing global extension and enmeshment of information infrastructure can be interpreted as the continuation of the "time–space compression" and "world systems" formation that define the integrative dynamics and tendencies of the modern global system (Harvey, 1991; Wallerstein, 2004; 2011; Curran, 2008). A counter-movement is, however, discernible in the firewalling national telecommunications systems, a form of digital ring fencing or fence building. There are two distinct patterns evolving in this regard, one driven by the international response to the exposure of US and UK meta-surveillance strategies and the other by the control sensitivities of authoritarian and one-party states. Given the Internet's dependence upon physical infrastructure, "balkanization" is a possibility insofar as *de facto* "nationalization" is a reality in China (Brown, 2013). With global informational relations thus poised, the advancement of particularistic state interests through the manipulation of systemic interconnections clearly risks system disintegration. Globalization, in all its forms, evidences both centrifugal and centripetal tendencies, and cyberspace is perhaps the best exemplar of this material reality (Choucri, 2012).

Are current cooperation dynamics sufficiently robust to withstand the disintegrative dynamics of state unlawfulness? The density of global interconnectivity, while adding to the global quantum of cooperation, cannot be read as an absolute indicator of diminishing mistrust (Keohane and Nye, 2012, p. 264). There is no automatic positive correspondence between connection and cooperation. Systemic integration alters the ways in which industrially and technologically advanced states pursue their interests globally. But this is no protection against nefarious intent, or unintended disruption. Trade tensions are often identified, in light of the European experience of Franco-German rivalry, as a potential cause of interstate war. World War I demonstrated how states acting rationally according to the unwritten rules of the European balance of power system, could launch themselves into a grinding war of attrition that proved a costly and, for the most part, futile exercise. The creative potential of an entire generation of Europeans was squandered in the madness. Military historian John Keegan writes in *A History of Warfare*, "the First World War was . . . an extraordinary, a monstrous cultural aberration, an unwitting decision by Europeans . . . to turn Europe into a warrior society" (Keegan, 1993, p. 58). Descent into even greater irrationality was arguably prevented by the post-World War II bipolar order. Trade tensions between the US and Japan, and the US and Europe, in the 1980s were ultimately manageable within a Cold War alliance framework. Today's US–China economic rivalry, involving trade, technology and investment competition, however, occurs in an entirely different global context, without parallel alliance constraints, and perhaps without historical parallel.

"Techno-strategic" competition between the US and China has a clear economic dimension, in which economic competition is tied to the pursuit of geostrategic advantage, and technological primacy is analogous to the topographical high ground. But, today, decision and reaction times are substantially reduced in an evolving complex of humans and technologies, dubbed the "automaton" by Manuel Castells (Castells, 2000, p. 53). Consequently, the likelihood for misperception to trigger a serious security incident involving both countries is high. Informational competition in cyber space does not, however, constitute "cyber war," in the sense that war and cyber war are not analogous, and yet the Internet, as with all network forms, can be used to inflict harm (Libicki, 2009; Clarke and Knake, 2010; Carafano, 2012; Rid, 2013). The risk of global disorder is thus structural, in the sense that power competition occurs within an anarchic state system, in real space and cyberspace, but there are also ideological and ideational dimensions. While in theory, and in the strategic imagination, critical government information systems can be infiltrated and disrupted to cause widespread societal chaos, there is only a remote possibility, if plausible, that such catastrophic systems failure can be manufactured so as to bring a state to its knees (Deibert, 2013, loc. 2505; Rid, 2013). Of equal if not greater concern is the consolidation of risk imaginaries that authorize the development of offensive/defensive "cyber weapons." The Cold War logic of "deterrence," is being transposed, uncritically it would appear, into the cyber security domain. This development runs parallel to the construction of a global terror threat to compensate, unintentionally or otherwise, and largely within the Atlantic strategic policy community, for the disintegration of the former Soviet Union and communism. Strategic "risk-talk" of cyber war, crime and espionage feed into a deepening risk aversion that poses a more insidious and invisible threat to global order. Complexity thinking helps illuminate this global "gridwork" of risk vectors, throughout which security sensitivities and risk imaginaries are laterally interconnected with extensive temporal patterns of crime and violence.

Covert authority

To what extent is "political evil" – to borrow from the title of Patrick Hayden's book – a crime (Hayden, 2009). The killing of Osama bin Laden by members of a US Navy SEAL team in Abbottabad, Pakistan, in May 2011 was, on the public record at least, an acknowledged violation of Pakistan's sovereignty and, therefore, an illegal act within the state of Pakistan. It was also either a "combat incident" or an extrajudicial killing involving foreign forces in a foreign country not in a state of war and, thus, arguably a transgression of international law or, at the very least, a violation of the UN Charter. And yet, the mission was hailed as "victory" within the US, and bin Laden's death greeted with relief by UN Secretary-General, Ban Ki-moon (Ban, 2011; Bowden, 2012). The SEAL team's actions were legally protected within the US by presidential authorization for the mission; this legal legitimacy was drawn from a special 2001 Congressional *Joint Resolution* extending the 1973 presidential war powers to permit authorization of unilateral attacks against "organizations and persons" judged to pose a terrorist threat to the US, without the requirement for a formal declaration of war (Congress, 2001, PL 107–40; 50 USC 1541, Ch. 33, Title 50). Bin Laden's killing, again, as far as can be judged from the public record, occurred in the confusion of a military operation conducted at close quarters against largely unarmed occupants in the bin Laden compound, during which bin Laden was shot by "return fire." There was no official order to kill bin Laden but, in Mark Bowden's detailed account, neither was there any commitment by those involved to capture him alive (Bowden, 2012, pp. 252–253).

Even within the "overworld" of "black ops" and international espionage, legalities matter only insofar as law is used to protect the covert actions of government agents. There is general public acceptance of the reality of spying and the need for spies to operate in a legal "twilight zone," but only insofar as espionage is directed against potential foreign enemies and where "collateral damage" to innocent civilians is minimized (Barry, 2008, p. 287). The assassination of Hamas commander Mahmoud al-Mabouh by Israeli intelligence (Mossad) agents in a hotel room in Dubai in 2010 drew public attention to the extent of state-sanctioned criminality. The agents involved travelled with stolen identities, on forged passports, to kill an ostensibly unarmed civilian – surely multiple criminal offences of a transnational if not international nature, committed with the collective sanction of the Israeli state (Lewis et al., 2013). Deception is standard practice for spies who use false identities to penetrate defensive barriers, infiltrate organizations and gather information of strategic benefit to their country or their employer. Spies operate by winning the trust of people with access to intelligence and influence, and by securing access to both through means of deception or blackmail. Only with official authorization, and tacit acceptance, could such elaborate systems of transnational identity theft and fraud, and a multitude of other crimes, be tolerated – as a form of customary and collective "hypocrisy."

The illegality of spying is a question of jurisdiction and geographic proximity. Spying in a foreign country, on a foreign country, is a crime under the laws of that country. Spying on one's own government for a foreign power is likewise a crime and, under the US *Espionage Act of 1917* for example, a capital offence in instances where the passing of information to a foreign power leads to the death of US citizens (USC 794, Ch. 37, Title 18). Extreme penalties for spying in, and on, one-party states are more likely to be summarily enforced. But while spying for, or to, the benefit of a foreign power is outlawed domestically, spying is not criminalized under international law, save during wartime. The 1907 Hague Convention (hereafter Hague II) defines a spy as someone "acting clandestinely or on false pretences" behind enemy lines with the intention of acquiring intelligence about an enemy force during time of war. Though limited by wording to the operational area of an enemy's armed forces, the clear implication is that any act to secure intelligence by deception about an enemy and within enemy territory is spying (Hague Convention, IV, Ch. 2.29, 1907). The denial of prisoner of war status, and associated protections to spies under both the Hague and Geneva conventions, implies that the practice, though wide, is, nonetheless, outlawed (Geneva IV, Additional Protocol I, Art. 46.3). The reality is that in peacetime, in addition to the crimes detailed above, states routinely engage in clandestine power struggles and proxy wars, perpetrate sabotage and foment political unrest. In the era of asymmetrical and "post-national" war, distinctions between war and peace are breaking down, and international criminal law is slow to adjust.

Interpretations of law can be moulded to redefine "vague" or "ill-defined" terms and categories used in the objective or substantive definition of crime. Indeed, the problem of legal grey areas is not that there are grey areas *per se*, but that indistinctness is an invitation to perverse "clarification" to suit the agendas of the governments of the day. Former Secretary of State under George W. Bush, Condoleezza Rice, betrayed a "moralization gap" (Pinker, 2011) in the US approach to global security, admitting to a World Economic Forum meeting in Davos in 2006 that "our ideals and interests may be in tension in the short term, and they are surely tested by the complexities of the real world" (Rice, 2008). The history of the so-called War on Terror, a term and concept to which the US state and its key decision-makers and legal advisers subscribed, indicates that when these ideals are tested, an acute sense of insecurity or vulnerability usually sways the official interpretation of state legal obligations. To put it bluntly, presumed operational imperatives subvert moral principle, and with such regularity that one can only conclude that such deviation is indeed systemic.

At the very beginning of its global anti-terror campaign, the Bush Administration made clear its belief that the US and the West faced an implacable enemy in al-Qaeda and a presumed global Islamist movement that presented a vast monolithic threat to (Western) civilization. *Raison d'état* was thus invoked to reinterpret domestic and international legal obligation (De Nevers, 2006, pp. 369–371). Hence there was the suspension of habeas corpus for inmates at the US military detention centre at Guantanamo Bay in Cuba, who were consigned, captured combatants from Afghanistan and Iraq. The ghosting away of captured, suspected terrorists for interrogation in secret locations is in contravention of international human rights law – the euphemistically termed practice of "rendering." For senior US government officials, including those responsible for the administration of justice, the argument was not whether the use of torture against suspected terrorists would be a violation of US treaty obligations, which it clearly was, but whether a conceptual gap within the US Criminal Code between torture and interrogation could be exploited to permit certain moral "declensions." Legal advice provided to the CIA recommended nuancing interpretations of intentionality and severity to permit the physical abuse of detained terror suspects in US military facilities under the guise of "enhanced interrogation" (Bybee, 2002; Bradbury, 2005).

Threat ideation, ideology and fear influence the psycho-social dimensions of strategy and policy by engendering extremes of "self-deception" that encourage gross deviance (Pinker, 2011, pp. 491–492). US covert assistance to Nicaraguan "contras" fighting against the left-wing Sandanista government in the 1980s, for example, rendered the Reagan Administration complicit in the atrocities committed by what were counter-revolutionary "death squads" recruited and trained with US material support; indeed, the CIA broke US law by continuing to provide assistance to the contras in contravention of a Congressional order to desist. Denied a budget for its insurgency operation in Nicaragua, the Reagan Administration brokered international financial backing for the contras, which included substantial profits realized on sales of US-made weapons by Israel to Iran in return for the release of American hostages (US Senate, 1987, pp. 4–7, 450; DeFronzo, 2011, p. 271). The fact that American public opinion was decidedly against supporting US intervention in Nicaragua, and the fact that Congress, through the 1984 Boland Amendment, sought to restrain the Executive, do not absolve either from collective responsibility for clear violations of US law and international law. Despite clear evidence of official complicity in weapons trafficking to the contras between 1984 and 1987, after which Congress approved the resumption of military aid, no Reagan Administration official faced criminal charges. Weighing the meaning and official US definition of terrorism in the wake of 9/11, Noam Chomsky draws debate back to the US sponsorship of "state terror" in Central America during the Cold War, not to justify the actions of terrorists, but to emphasize inconsistencies in official policy rhetoric and state security practice (Chomsky, 2003). Nicaragua's Sandanista movement could not be proved to represent a clear and immediate strategic threat to the US. It was mainly an ideological challenge to US regional interests, born of grievances and political tensions common across Latin America, and this was evidently sufficient reason for US and international law to be set aside.

The shifting terrain of international law complicates the extension of cosmopolitan values, not least because new security doctrines render many formerly criminal and covert state actions legal. William Lind coined the term "fourth generation war" to capture a doctrinal shift in war fighting and foreground the civilian dimension to hostilities in what are today known as "asymmetrical conflicts" (Lind et al., 1989). It is standard state security practice to lend covert support to non-state groups in foreign countries for geostrategic advantage. In effect, it was, and is, "understood" that states will conduct espionage operations, and possibly engage in sabotage, in rival states or against the interests of rival states in third countries. But in the new "spaceless" theatres of emerging warfare, covert military operations are conducted within civilian spaces, "against" civilians as much as armed combatants, because modern "special ops" involves political operations to win popular support for campaigns against dispersed adversaries (Nagl, 2002; Hammes, 2006; 2008). This is where Krasner's notion of "organized hypocrisy," Bull's "anarchical society" and the work on networked states and societies by Giddens and Castells intersect.

Here emerge the contradictions within global crime–terror narratives that decry all radicals as terrorist threats, yet sanction the pursuit of geostrategic advantage by criminal means, in the "great game" of states. US sponsorship of the Afghan *mujahidin* fighting against first the Soviet-backed Afghan state from 1979 to 1989, and then the Northern Alliance against the Taliban regime is legendary, as is the support given to Hmong fighting the socialist government in Laos during the 1960s and 1970s. Arms and material transfers were commonly directed through intricate deals, Iran–contra style, involving third parties to give governments scope for "plausible denial." Covert US assistance for the disparate elements resisting the armed Soviet intervention in Afghanistan was predicated on the same thinking applied in Sudan: that Islam could be mobilized to counter Marxist ideology and arrest communist expansion. Washington was determined to turn Afghanistan into a quagmire, a Soviet Vietnam that would further degrade Moscow's capability to challenge US interests elsewhere. Determined to break Soviet resolve, the CIA failed to recognize the risks inherent in sponsoring radical Islamic forces that were as much anti-West as they were anti-communist. American-supplied arms and combat expertise materially assisted Pakistan's intelligence organization to build up its Islamic front in Afghanistan. Pursuing a short-term Cold War objective, the authors of US policy in Central and South Asia, from CIA station chiefs up to the State Department and the White House, did not, or could not, foresee the consequences of their strategy for strategic security in South Asia or the global heroin trade – which blossomed with deepening civil conflict in Afghanistan (Coll, 2005).

In the wake of the Soviet withdrawal in 1989, and the consequent suspension of US assistance, Afghan factions turned to the illegal opium trade to fund their internecine struggle for control of the state, feeding a cycle of violence and corruption that engulfed neighbouring Pakistan (Rangsayagam, 2005, pp. 184–188). Backed by Pakistan, the Taliban succeeded in imposing a harsh Islamic regime over much of the country, including the capital, Kabul, which fell in 1996. But the harshness of the regime and the ongoing armed struggle between the Taliban and forces loyal to *mujahidin* commander Ahmad Shah Massoud, and grouped under the banner of the Northern Alliance, fuelled the production and trade in opium. The history of Afghanistan post 9/11 need not be rehearsed here, but despite ending Taliban rule in 2001, the US-led coalition and an elected Afghan government grapple with persisting ideological, factional and economic divisions that suggest the reconstruction of Afghanistan is a substantial and long-term challenge. The future for Afghanistan without long-term international assistance is bleak. The post-intervention government of President Hamid Karzai failed to establish popular legitimacy among the country's multi-ethnic population. Unable to control all parts of the country, the Afghan state was powerless to prevent the movement of civilians and Taliban combatants across the frontier between Afghanistan and Pakistan.

Cross-cutting strategic objectives of the US and Pakistan governments exacerbated the refugee crisis along Pakistan's Northwest Frontier, which is the seedbed of Islamic radicalism in Central Asia. The Pakistan military has long coveted a submissive, or at least pro-Pakistan, government in Kabul, while Pakistani politicians see Afghanistan as a gateway to Central

Asia, in particular a passageway for Central Asian oil to reach the Indian Ocean through Pakistan. It is a double irony that Pakistan's entry into the geopolitics of oil should rebound on it to the extent that the Islamist militants defying central authority along the Northwest Frontier are so well endowed with Saudi finances. The jihad against the Soviets and, then, the US-led international forces in Afghanistan, has created a terror industry in which the children from poor tribes are drawn into radical *madrassas* and inculcated with the Islamist mission to drive the US from the Arabian Peninsula, rescuing Islam from the corrupting influences of secular Western culture. The mission and the message resonate throughout the Middle East to South and Southeast Asia. It appeals to the poor and undereducated, who resent Western affluence, and for whom jihad is as much an economic as a religious calling. It also appeals to the educated middle classes who, like those who flew the planes into the Twin Towers and the Pentagon, resent the secularizing tendencies of hegemonic globalization (Battersby and Siracusa, 2009).

In practice, then, interventions whether strategic or undertaken in the name of humanity and international justice, necessarily stray into unlawful territory, and beget law-denying criminality. The doctrine of humanitarian intervention includes a responsibility to rebuild countries in the wake of military action, but rebuilding and reconstruction programmes are notoriously vulnerable to corruption. Financial monitoring of interventions and attendant aid flows is limited. An International Crisis Group (ICG) report on aid in Afghanistan highlighted the extensive and ostensibly gratuitous payment of poorly accounted cash to purchase approval for the International Security Assistance Force (ISAF) mission and convert wavering Taliban supporters. From the 2001 intervention onwards, the overriding imperative to defeat the Taliban both militarily and politically resulted in less than rigorous accounting for expenditure, and the impacts of poorly regulated aid investments in the Karzai government (Savage et al., 2007, p. 13; ICG, 2011, pp. 20–21). Ironically, ISAF was, despite efforts to eradicate opium cultivation, dependent in critical areas upon provincial drug lords for social order and assistance in countering the Taliban. These tactical compromises are again justified by the exceptional circumstances of war, but sent the wrong political message to the Afghan people and did little to engender the kind of trust necessary to construct a viable and lawful state as a beacon of democracy in Central Asia (Norland, 2010; Caulkins et al., 2011).

The course and consequences of international intervention in Afghanistan and Iraq demonstrate the unpredictability of political transformations and the limits of military power. The uncertainties confronting a remade Afghan state bear distinct resemblance to conditions in the country following the Soviet withdrawal. Guiding assumptions about the potential to force political redevelopment in both countries to fit the liberal globalist template have proven mistaken. Military assessments of the achievements of both interventions are mixed. Humanitarian and academic assessments foreground violations of transnational criminal law and international criminal law by foreign civilian and military elements, stripping legitimacy away from the vaunted international "rule of law." Neither intervention affirmed any international principle, or affirmed any laws, beyond the operating principles of Bull's anarchic society of states.

Declensions of responsibility

The course of events dubbed collectively as the "Arab Spring" began with demonstrations in Tunisia in December 2010 and spread quickly through Libya, Egypt, the Gulf States and to Syria. The rebirth of democracies proved problematic and chaotic, reflecting the strains of long-suppressed but quickly re-energized political pluralism. The 2011 UN-sanctioned intervention in Libya materially helped rebel forces topple the regime of Colonel Mu'ammar al-Gaddafi (hereafter Gaddafi). Predicated on R2P, the actions of the international community reflected a popular conviction that the removal of a reviled dictator would lead towards a democratic future for Libya, but the episode also exposed the malleability of the "responsibility" principle in international affairs. The trigger for the NATO-led intervention was the claimed imminent danger of mass civilian casualties as Libyan government forces bore down on the rebel stronghold of Benghazi. Under UN Security Council Resolution, 1973, NATO forces were authorized to use "all necessary measures [. . .] to protect civilians and civilian populated areas under threat of attack" (UNSC, 2011a, S/RES1973). In practice, this meant, first, the creation of no-fly zones over rebel-controlled areas, but quickly extended to direct attacks on advancing Libyan troops, aircraft and military infrastructure. In effect the intervention lent material and moral support to the enemies of a sovereign state, the government of which was judged to be in "default" of its political obligations under international law.

The case of *NATO v. Gaddafi*, pressed in the theatre and not the high court of war, is an exemplar of how swiftly, and effectively, states can move both individually and collectively to override the principle of state sovereignty, stretching the interpretation of international law. Tracking ahead of the arc of legal authorization, France supplied arms directly to rebel forces before the UN arms embargo imposed under the preceding UNSC 1970 was lifted, and thus technically in violation of UNSC, 1973. Diplomatic recognition from the National Transition Council in September normalized hitherto covert support given to Libyan rebels, opening the way for more substantial military assistance and the eventual defeat of Gaddafi forces. In so many ways, this episode advanced the normalization of hitherto unlawful state practices. While the UN Charter permits military action to uphold international peace and security under Chapter 7, it is stretching the scope of Article 42 to cover actions involving cooperation with an assembly of untrained rebel militia and defecting Libyan military personnel, some of whom, according to credible accounts, perpetrated war crimes against supporters of the regime and bear responsibility for Gaddafi's extrajudicial killing in the town of Sirte in October 2011 (Amnesty International, 2012a, pp. 217–221).

Intervention in Libya occurred with the support of Arab nations and the acquiescence of rebel leaders – without which the intervention could not have proceeded. From a strategic security standpoint, and allowing for disagreements between NATO members over their respective roles in the air war against Gaddafi, tactics deployed by NATO demonstrated the effectiveness of what Pentagon strategists term "light footprint" military operations, where air power is used in conjunction with local military forces to prosecute a ground war against an unpopular incumbent regime (Daadler and Stavridis, 2012). Yet there was, and continues to be, generous embellishment of the details by those who portray the NATO action as a success. Alan Kuperman's analysis raises fundamental questions about the relationship between inadequate "real time" reporting of humanitarian crises and official interpretations of international law used to justify intervention. He argues that, contrary to mainstream media coverage, the Libyan "Spring" was, from the outset, an armed rebel uprising. Furthermore, Gaddafi's forces did not target civilians in their counter-offensives against rebel strongholds, and, pivotally, Western journalists habitually, perhaps instinctively, overstated civilian casualties (Kuperman, 2013, p. 109). Without seeking to rehabilitate Gaddafi, Kuperman's critique suggests that law and evidence were judiciously massaged to serve a NATO geopolitical objective, namely, regime change in Libya (Kuperman, 2013, p. 113).

As argued with regard to United States Africa Command's (AFRICOM's) efforts to alter the course of political change in East Africa, societies are complex systems, and, as noted, the course of political evolution is unpredictable and non-linear. Events in Libya throughout 2013 gave little indication of stability or democratization. Following the collapse of the Gaddafi regime, Libya was, regardless of the existence of an elected national government, *de facto* divided among rebel groups reluctant to disarm or submit to central authority. The intervention generated new, or replenished old, supply chains of violence, through the filtering of small arms into conflict zones across the Sahel – and westwards into Syria (Sullivan, 2013).

"Compelling human need," one of the triggers of R2P-compliant intervention, must be balanced against "reasonable prospects" for success (ICISS, 2001, pp. xi, 37). The civil conflict in Syria is the most traumatic consequence of the pressure for political change across North Africa and the Middle East from 2011. The international response, and non-response, to the conflict and conflict-related deaths of over 100,000 people in Syria during 2011–2013 demonstrates the limited reach of international law – and the enduring systemic tolerance for human suffering. The accumulated and concentrated imperatives of regional and global power politics negate all avenues for legal or UNSC-mandated solutions. Neither Russia nor China is prepared to authorize military intervention in Syria, and Russia, along with Iran, provides material military support to the regime of Syrian President Bashar Hafez al-Assad. Instructively, Gareth Evans, co-chair of the International Commission on the Responsibility to Protect, and a champion of the Libyan intervention, argues against the too-frequent enforcement of the R2P norm and is concerned about the ramifications of intervention in Syria, which is riven by internal sectarian rivalry and stands at a sensitive intersection in the escalating power competition between regional and global geopolitical interests (Evans, 2011).

Crime and security converge along multiple vectors in Syria through the subterranean underworld of arms traffickers, al-Qaeda sympathizers and the violation of Syrian sovereignty and international law by states seeking to precipitate or prevent regime change (Mazzetti et al., 2013). The conflict degenerated into a virtual proxy war between Sunni-majority Saudi Arabia supporting Syrian co-religionists and the Alawi-Shi'ite "alliance" that was formed by Syria's governing elite and the Iranian state. Russia's continued sponsorship of the Ba'ath Party regime of al-Assad implicates it in war crimes perpetrated by the Syrian government, including the use of sarin gas against civilians in August 2012, confirmed by the UN Mission to Investigate Allegations of the Use of Chemical Weapons by the Syrian Arab Republic (2013, A/67/997-S/2013/553). Weapons transfers into Syria from all interested external parties to different elements within the country, both state and opposition, without

UN authorization, contributed to a murderous stalemate that precipitated the fragmentation of the National Coalition of Syrian Revolution and Opposition Forces. The implication of elements from the Free Syrian Army in both transnational and war crimes coincided with the ideological and material disintegration of the opposition front to a point where no coherent alternative to the Assad regime existed by the end of 2013 (Sherlock, 2013; UN News Centre, 2013).

War machines

The Libyan and Syrian cases serve as reminders of the state of systemic unlawfulness in contemporary global affairs. States security practices spanning the line of control between lawful and unlawful betray the concealed "tolerances" built into the prevailing system of "executive" global governance (Held, 2003). "Small arms" are responsible for more battle-related deaths than nuclear or chemical weapons combined, and there is a thriving global business in "transitioning" legally traded and stolen armaments onto the illegal arms market. Military campaigns, of any kind, merely assist in the transfer of weapons across the licit–illicit arms trade frontier and across physical state frontiers into new spheres of conflict; both the Libyan intervention and the Syrian non-intervention are no different in this regard (*Defence News*, 2011; Feinstein, 2011a, 2011b; Spencer, 2011). The governance challenges presented by the trade in Small Arms and Light Weapons (SALW) thus stem from the scale of legal armaments production and trade, which the world intends to regulate through the Arms Trade Treaty (ATT), by imposing legal obligations upon arms exporting countries not to provide armaments that could be used in violation of international humanitarian law (ATT, 2013, p. 7). This is the latest in a growing list of conventions that seek to civilize non-international armed conflict by creating disincentives for states to supply arms directly, and indirectly, to non-state forces implicated in international criminality.

Weapons proliferation is a clear measure of a crippling absence of trust and political legitimacy in the international system. Annual legal small arms and ammunition sales are estimated to be between US$7 billion and US$8.5 billion globally (UNSC, 2011b, S/2011/255, p. 2; UNSC, 2013c). Governments engage lawfully in the distribution of armaments and war fighting capabilities, with the US amongst the most active in military diplomacy, spending US$17.8 billion on foreign military aid in 2011, a substantial increase on the US$14.5 billion "allocated" in 2010 (covered largely by a US$4 billion increase in expenditure on Afghanistan)

(USAID, 2013). The global conventional arms trade was estimated at US$43 billion in 2011, declining marginally in 2012, presumably because of ongoing contraction in the global economy. Obviously, the value of trafficked illegal global arms is unknowable, but with major intrastate conflicts affecting countries in the Middle East, Central Asia, the Sahel, Latin America, and with significantly high rates of "lethal violence" recorded in 58 countries globally during the first decade of the twenty-first century, the demand for illegal weapons is doubtless as substantial as is their illegal use (Feinstein, 2011a; Geneva Declaration, 2011, p. 44; SIPRI, 2013a; SIPRI, 2013b).

Legal arms manufacturers and retailers both produce and distribute SALW that eventually find their way into the hands of criminals and insurgents. Feinstein (2011a, b) writes of a global "shadow world" of arms trading that verges on trafficking by virtue of the clandestine, and often illicit, nature of many state-sanctioned transactions. There is a vast web of underground arms dealers that connects indirectly with the legal arms trades of the US, the EU countries, Russia and China, all of which provided arms to Libya under the Gaddafi regime (Feinstein, 2011a, pp. 492–493). The ATT can be counted as an evolutionary step in arms regulation, and an accountability tool to promote increased transparency in arms transfers. It is unlikely to prevent the transfer of weapons by states to insurgent groups, or to pariah states where this serves state security interests. Even the suspension of US arms transfers to Syria in 2013 was prompted by fears that weapons would fall into the hands of Islamist factions and not because there were concerns about the alleged complicity of Syrian opposition forces in war crimes. The ATT therefore, argues Feinstein, while right in its intent, faces the twin obstacles of multi-level power competition and criminal incentive that "drive" the unlawful trade in weapons, weapons components and materiel (Feinstein, 2011a, pp. 529–530).

No one state really trusts another to self-regulate nuclear, chemical or biological weapons, which is why there is, in order of substance, a Nuclear Non-proliferation Treaty (NPT), a Chemical Weapons Convention that entered into force in 1997, the earlier Biological and Toxin Weapons Convention (BTWC) in 1972 and a global bureaucracy committed to arms control and disarmament. While the development of nuclear technologies is lawful, within limits set by the International Atomic Energy Agency (IAEA) and the NPT, as with any system, individuals with specialist inside knowledge are, for reasons of ideology or personal economic gain, able to circumvent even the strictest controls to trade their expertise on illicit markets. The same logic applies to chemical and biological weapons technologies and capabilities. "Control" is an unattainable policy goal without an international consensus between the P5+1 (the US, Russia, China, the UK and France, plus Germany) at the very least, on all aspects of arms limitation. The global arms regime evidences a familiar pattern of vulnerability or weakness arising from variations in national-level legislation to monitor weapons movements and the trade in components, precursor chemicals and lethal biological toxins. In countries where monitoring regimes have been tightened in response to the threat of terrorist attack, ports and border crossings (and entire populations) are subject to intensive surveillance, but globally border controls and state surveillance capabilities are variable and limited in reach and effectiveness (Battersby et al., 2011).

That there are only a handful of nuclear-armed states in the world is either testimony to the effectiveness of the non-proliferation control regime or simply a factor of there being only a handful of states capable of developing nuclear arms. Technological diffusion and the emergence of new regional and global economic powers are quickly altering the global nuclear landscape. There is little to stop states that decide to develop Weapons of Mass Destruction (WMD) provided they have the political will to resist international pressure and hinder the work of UN weapons inspectors. The lessons of WMD inspections in Iraq during the 1990s illustrate the weaknesses of global arms surveillance in the absence of unified commitment from UNSC permanent members. Inspection, monitoring and verification techniques have become more sophisticated, largely as a result of the UN's experiences in Iraq (UNMOVIC, 2007b). Still, weapons inspection regimes depend upon extensive cooperation, including cooperation from states under inspection and suspicion. That cooperation is difficult to achieve globally, as is underscored by the reluctance of the US to submit to biological weapons monitoring under the BTWC, on the grounds that control of dual-use biological technologies is impossible (Lynn, 2009).

Developments in the fields of computing and biochemical technology radically challenge definitions of offensive and defensive capability and, hence, complicate the task of wording international conventions to control the development of new weapons. The Iraqi Ba'athist regime of Saddam Hussein demonstrated what a developing state could achieve with rudimentary facilities, but richer states are engaged in a legal, high-tech bioarms race, with many more far-reaching implications for international law, crime and war. New generation technologies made possible by ground-breaking research into the molecular structures of life mean that our notions of biological and chemical weapons and biological warfare need to be reconsidered – if not for the immediate term most certainly for the not too distant future (Williams, et al., 2008, pp. 75–76; Dando, 2009). Biotechnologies give us the tools to reformulate human life, and disrupt physiological and psychological processes, in more fundamental and invasive ways than was possible before the discovery of the human genome. The potential to disrupt human neurological systems with invisible new pathogens, trigger impulses through the deployment of nanomagnetic particles, or shut down functions critical to stasis, creates a new subcategory of WMDs – weapons of mass distraction (Kelle et al., 2006; Dando, 2009). The invasiveness of this Taylorist imperative for deep control takes Giddens' "in-here" dimension of globalization to an even more "intimate" level.

The military applications of new gene and nano technologies raise disturbing questions about the relationship between individual and collective responsibility for war crimes in combat. Science tells us that human behavioural reactions to stimulants vary greatly between individuals. If it were possible in the future to develop drugs that could enhance kill rates and at the same time reduce the psychological trauma of battle, the unintended consequence might be an out-of-control combat soldier, chemically programmed to attack without mercy, killing civilians as coldly and efficiently as they would kill an armed adversary on the battlefield. In such cases, would culpability for war crimes, applying the Nuremberg and Tokyo complicity test, rest with the soldier or with those administering the performance-enhancing stimulant? The challenge of WMD regulation, and elimination, re-emphasizes the reality that the risks of major systemic harm are intrinsic to globalization, in this case from the pursuit of scientific innovations that have a dual civilian and military use, and where control depends upon the acceptance that all members of the global scientific community constitute a critical part of the social assemblage of this crime–security complex (Miller and Selgelid, 2007; Dando, 2009; Nasu, 2013).

Systemic recalibrations

Weapons technologies are evolving far ahead of, and far quicker than, the legal regimes invented to limit their destructive potential, and there is every reason to believe that the pace is quickening. Landmark conventions to extend weapons control to land mines and cluster munitions, for example, suggest the enlargement of cosmopolitan responsibility, but the dynamics of the so-called global knowledge economy, to which science and scientific research is critical, generate new patterns of deviance from the norm of arms limitation. Viewed in this light, where anything is potentially weaponisable, "disarmament" seems outmoded and an ever less workable principle in practice. The limits of law as a tool of governance are apparent in the ongoing contravention of established principles concerning the development and use of lethal technologies, and of the laws of war in general. Part of this complex, these laws contain "permissions" and omissions that give rise to creative interpretation. There is also the obvious point that the ATT does not criminalize the trade in lethal technologies and, like many accommodations between power and principle, thus "merely" succeeds in placing constraints upon the conduct of and preparations for organized state violence (Kennedy, D., 2004 and 2006).

The evolution of international criminal law is closely associated with the experience, and the laws of war. Hence, the Fourth Geneva Convention (hereafter Geneva IV) (1949) should be interpreted in conjunction with its three antecedent conventions and subsequent additional protocols: The Hague Convention (1899) (hereafter Hague I) and Hague II (1907); and the Genocide (1948), Refugee (1951) and Torture (1975) conventions. The Geneva conventions are an example of international humanitarian law emerging out of a sense of common humanity and moral revulsion at the increasingly visible inhumanity of war. Central to each of the four conventions is the concept of protected persons being those who, by virtue of their civilian or non-combatant status, present no immediate battlefield threat and are, therefore, entitled to safe passage or medical treatment or both. The Geneva conventions primarily address the civilian consequences of war, but also extend limits to the prosecution of war defined by Hague I and II (Battersby, 2012a).

As with military strategy, war law tends to reflect the experiences of wars just passed and, as with all law, is subject to interpretation and to derogation. Hague II outlawed the use of poisonous substances as weapons of war, and yet in World War I, moral revulsion at the effects of gas warfare quickly succumbed to tactical and strategic imperative. The Third Geneva Convention (hereafter Geneva III) (1929) granted formal protections to Prisoners of War (POWs), but this condition was likewise victim to circumstance and strategic consideration. The moral universalism embodied in the Geneva conventions was tested in the crucible of war. In the Pacific theatre of World War II , bitter fighting between Japanese soldiers and US marines allegedly degenerated into a race war in which combatants regarded each other as less than human; accordingly, no quarter was given and few prisoners taken (Dower, 1986; Aldrich, 2006, pp. 30–40). On the Russian front too, fighting between Russian and German forces was relentless and merciless in which soldiers from ostensibly civilized societies routinely demonstrated the human capacity for cruelty and inhumanity (Bellamy, 2007).

At the level of global multilateral regulation, one can reasonably argue that all WMDs violate the Geneva Conventions, because they are designed to maximize damage to large and densely populated cities and the natural environment upon which people depend for sustenance (Battersby, 2012a). Of particular note is the incorporation of arms control provisions in the Protocol Additional to the Geneva Convention of August 12, 1949, Relating to the Protection of Victims of International Armed Conflicts (hereafter Additional Protocol I), especially Article 35, which could be interpreted as a prohibition against the use of a range of war-fighting technologies, including chemical defoliants that inflict "superfluous" harm. The Article expressly prohibits the use of weapons designed to "cause widespread, long-term and severe damage to the natural environment" (Additional Protocol I, Art. 35.3). This protocol evidently had chemical substances like Agent Orange in its sights, for which reason the US withheld ratification.

While the intent of the conventions is clearly to minimize human suffering, the additional protocols go much further in criminalizing the deliberate targeting of civilian populations, and in requiring that conflict parties take all possible steps to prevent civilian loss of life during combat operations. Indeed, the protocols criminalize many actions that for decades have been standard military tactics, and particularly advantageous to the prosecution of proxy wars. The evolution of the norm against attacking civilians in wartime remains hindered by the caveat of clear military objective. Hague II forbids the bombardment of civilian settlements with certain exemptions, namely, that the settlements are undefended or that, when an attack takes place, civilian deaths are unavoidable but not deliberate. Geneva IV reaffirms the illegality of attacking civilians in time of war but leaves open the option to target combatants and military infrastructure located in civilian population centres. Subsequent additional protocols to the Conventions addressing the treatment of civilians as distinct from combatants in interstate and civil wars retained the caveat of "necessity" (Battersby, 2012a).

The status of civilians and combatants in intrastate conflicts is rendered difficult, however, because insurgent armies often do not wear combat uniform. Acts of terror are explicitly prohibited under the conventions, including the tactics used by terrorists to gain advantage and maximize civilian casualties. For example, "perfidy," objectively defined in Article 37 of Additional Protocol I, as the use of deception to win the confidence of an enemy in order to kill them, including the use of false emblems and markers, is prohibited. The "feigning of civilian, non-combatant status" could arguably extend to the use of civilian disguise by suicide bombers and gunmen. To secure the status and protections of combatants, including the right to prisoner of war status, fighters must be clearly distinguishable as such, or otherwise clearly in possession of a weapon, unless surrendering their arms upon capture. Guerrilla fighters disguise their weapons or hide them only to rearm when tactically advantageous before melting away into the civilian population – and, bearing no formal legal relation with any armed group, surely as unarmed civilians. Carrying arms openly in combat zones preserves the rights of combatants set out under the first additional protocol. Combatant status in non-international warfare is harder to determine as the wording of the Protocol Additional to the Geneva Convention of August 12, 1949, Relating to the Protection of Victims of Non-International Armed Conflicts (hereafter Additional Protocol II), merely restricts civilian protections to those who take no "direct part in hostilities" (Additional Protocol II, Art. 13.3). And, yet, civilians are cast as protagonists in the "4-G" spectrum of post-modern asymmetric war (Battersby, 2012a, b).

The US has not ratified either the first or the second additional protocol undoubtedly because of sensitivity over the possible legal ramifications for US service personnel and the federal government for the pursuit of US geostrategy in Latin America and the Middle East. In non-international or intrastate conflicts, including insurgencies and counter-insurgency operations, tactical logic calls for the elimination of command structures through the targeted killing of decision-makers – armed or not. Assassination is practised with impunity by insurgent forces, sanctioned not by international law but by revolutionary ideology. For lawfully constituted armed forces, however, the legality of "targeted killing" is open to question and interpretation. Deferring to tactical expediency, experts on military law argue that the laws of war permit the use of this kind of force in counter-insurgency operations and here law is being reinterpreted to comply with what appears to be common counter-insurgency practice (Gross, 2010; loc. 122; Cullen, 2008).

The impulse to justify the use of force remains as strong as ever, as is the imperative to appear just in the application of military power – but only by those who submit to the laws of war. Legal advisers were not fully integrated into US military operations until the Second Gulf War (1990–1991) when the US and its coalition partners recognized the inevitability, and hence the need, to limit legal liability of civilian casualties in the air war against Iraq and the reoccupation of Kuwait (Borch, 2001).

Even though the US is not a party to Additional Protocol I and II, under customary international law, signatory states that have not actually progressed to ratification are still obliged not to act in a manner that undermines the treaties or conventions concerned. Military lawyers have since become a fixture in tactical planning for international peacekeeping and peace enforcement operations but so, too, have "unmanned" weapons systems and distanciated attack (Borch, 2001). Despite efforts to conduct battlefield operations within a framework of war law, the "accidental" killing of civilians – once termed collateral damage – remains a grey area (Battersby et al., 2011).

Like national laws and legal institutions, international regimes are a battleground of competing interests, and yet international law experts recognize objective principles that guide the interpretation and application of international criminal law. The Rome Statute, for example, specifies categories of actions that constitute war crimes, crimes against humanity and genocide. Crimes of war include *inter alia* the intentional killing of persons protected under Geneva IV and its associated protocols, torture and inhumane treatment, and intentional attack against civilians and civilian settlements without a clear military objective or on a scale considered excessive. Derogations on grounds of national interest are, according to the International Committee of the Red Cross (ICRC), increasingly unjustifiable in the face of what are now, allegedly, accepted by states parties as universal customary law (Meron, 2009, p. 624). From a legal transnationalist or internationalist perspective, then, tolerance for derogations from international norms is narrowing. In terms of actual state practice, however, outside the spheres of international diplomacy and international legal process the interpretation of these objective clauses suggests otherwise. Determining which wartime actions are justifiable and which are not is a fraught exercise but one that brings us closer to appreciating the often rough nature of justice in international affairs and the challenges of the shifting and continually evolving terrain of combat.

A mercenary according to Additional Protocol I (Art. 47) and the International Convention against the Recruitment, Use, Financing and Training of Mercenaries (1989) (hereafter Mercenary Convention) is "any person recruited locally or abroad [who is] motivated to take part in hostilities essentially by the desire for private gain" (Art. 2). The mercenary accepts, indeed, seeks, a combat role where they have no stake in a conflict other than the receipt of their contract price in return for their combat skills. Both conventions were framed in an international atmosphere of revulsion at the activities of mercenary units in Africa during the 1960s, and thus the definition reflects a desire to criminalize paid private soldiers regarded as little more than contracted killers. As of 2013, there are only 33 state parties to the 1989 convention, and another 10 signatories, none of which include the world's major military powers or their principal allies (ICRC). This reluctance to endorse or further expand the definition and prohibition of mercenary activities warrants some attention. While the Geneva protocols deny legal protections to mercenaries, the Mercenary Convention is much more restrictive and prescriptive. The latter criminalizes anyone who "recruits, uses, finances or trains mercenaries," (Art. 1 a–b) which could conceivably incorporate the widespread use of insurgent forces by governments to supplement combat missions in foreign territory. The definitions of mercenary provided in both conventions are neither watertight nor conclusive in stating objectively the criminality of many categories of military freelancer.

One major issue is the growing preference for Private Military and Security Contractors (PMSCs) in modern armies and the potential for such contractors to become combatants *de facto* where caught in the midst of a fire fight. As Tony Coady argues, the ambiguities surrounding the affiliation and motivations ascribed to mercenaries in international war law have the potential to criminalize a broad spectrum of military actors (Coady, 2009, p. 206). This was but one complication that led former Secretary-General Boutros Boutros-Ghali to abandon the idea of an independent standing UN armed force for rapid deployment in peacekeeping operations. The EU's rapid multinational deployment force avoids this moral and legal obstacle by virtue of a common EU foreign policy, which connects the actions and purposes of this professional fighting unit to the collective interests of EU member states (Battersby et al., 2011).

The term "contractor" lends legal respectability to the paramilitarised private security profession, but to appreciate the phenomenon of private security contracting from a global perspective, we have to acknowledge the widespread use of paramilitary and insurgent forces for political and commercial reasons in countries riven by violence. In academic and public policy debates, the word mercenary has come to bracket the now ubiquitous PMSCs, synonymous with Blackwater (now Xe) and Dyncorp to name but two. The role and legal status of PMSCs are sensitive political issues for the US, which has increased its reliance on private companies since the end of the Cold War to provide support to its peacekeeping and combat operations in the Middle East and Africa. While mercenaries are outlaws under international law, along with terrorists and gangsters, international law is less clear about the status of militias, paramilitaries and insurgent armies, unless proscribed and subject to extraterritorial sanction under EO13224.

PMSC field operatives are not combatants in the sense of regular military personnel, but they are also not civilians. The term militia does not cover the category, because armed PMSCs are only supposed to discharge their weapons in self-defence. And, as they are usually deployed overseas, they do not fit the civilian defence profile. Under Hague II and Geneva III, PMSC operatives fall under the category of "non-combatant" rather than "civilian" by virtue of their entitlement to POW status if captured (Geneva III, Art. 4.4; Hague II, 1907, Ch. 1, Art. 3). Contractors are subject to international law and the law of states to which they are contracted, but the confusion created by multiple contractual masters makes regulation extremely difficult. US PMSCs, while subject to US commercial law, are not subject to US military law unless contracted specifically to the US military. Blackwater, however, held many contracts with the US State Department to provide personnel security services to embassy staff in Iraq, for example, which saw armed private guards venturing out into Baghdad's urban combat zones but without the restraining influence of military law, military codes of conduct and, by virtue of negotiated legal immunity, Iraqi law also (IISS, 2007, pp. 1–2; Hedahl, 2009). As David Kennedy explains, military law, if it is to be effective, must be woven into the routines and thoughts of service personnel (Kennedy, 2004, pp. 289–291). There are questions as to whether such high levels of discipline are or can ever be maintained within the ranks of PMSCs.

In Iraq, especially, Blackwater field operatives demonstrated their willingness to "escalate the use of force" on a weekly basis during 2005–2006, indicating the degree of danger in which they were placed by their employer but also their cavalier attitude to their contractual obligations (Human Rights First, 2008, p. 1). The most widely condemned Blackwater action was the September 16, 2007, "Nisoor Square Incident" in which Blackwater guards allegedly shot dead 16 Iraqi civilians and a police officer, injuring one other (Bureau of Diplomatic Security, 2007). Militias and paramilitaries might be entitled to the full protection under the Geneva protocols but, if so, militia fighters are also liable for prosecution as war criminals for war crimes committed in an international or non-international conflict – and so, too, should be the states that sponsor them. Within states where such paramilitary actors are tolerated and, indeed, created by the state, private soldiers can enjoy extra-legal status and virtual immunity from prosecution for actions undertaken in the name of the state or national economic interest (Battersby et al., 2011).

Killing distance

The idea of controlled violence is central to modern warfare and war law, yet even the organized violence of interstate war is a wildly chaotic affair, at both the strategic and tactical battlefield levels (Clauzewitz, 1982; Malesevic, 2010). This notion of the controllability of violence permits the normalization of legal limits – or permissions – governing the use of military force. Conventions and protocols explicitly acknowledge the legitimacy of "military considerations" and "military necessity" in determining the extent to which civilian protections can reasonably be respected and enjoyed *in bello*. The Just War concept of proportionality is invoked by clauses which prohibit "unnecessary" and "indiscriminate" killing. Violence or force is a legitimate part of statecraft in the sense that law sanctions war making, albeit within certain limits. Legal scholars and practitioners debate the tolerances within which war or violence can be justified, but this is usually done without consideration of the nature of violence itself. Force is treated as amoral in the language of strategic security and law; it is the purposes to which force is put, therefore, that render the use of force legitimate or illegitimate.

Dave Grossman's analysis of soldiers in warfare makes the large claim that humans are by nature reluctant killers, citing evidence of non-firers in wars from the American Civil War to World War II (Grossman, 1995). With the exception of sociopaths, he argues, humans must be conditioned against their natures to kill and to cease killing on orders (Grossman, 1995, pp. 250–256). His conclusions rest upon the controversial findings by Samuel L. A. Marshall, a US brigadier general, in his seminal book, *Men against Fire: The Problem of Battlefield Command* (1947). Marshall claimed US army combat "kill ratios" during World War II were astonishingly low, because soldiers resisted killing the enemy even in the midst of battle. His counter-intuitive and hotly contested findings shaped the preparation of US officers and soldiers for combat in Korea and Vietnam; the latter, according to Grossman, were the most mentally conditioned killers ever put into the field by the US Army (Grossman, 1995, pp. 250–256; Malesevic, 2010, pp. 219–220). Marshall's conclusions were both challenged and championed by his contemporaries suggesting that the conduct of men in battle was, and remains, highly variable and dependent upon the character of the soldiers and the commanders (Marshall, 1947; Glenn, 2000).

Training can negate the possibility that combat soldiers might empathize with those whom they are trying to kill. So too can the repeated psychological trauma of close-quarters fighting, but what of the evidence of "exhilaration" in killing? Joanna Bourke in her confronting work, *An Intimate History of Killing* (1999), asserts that soldiers, men and women, can be trained to enjoy the act of killing in combat – indeed, the purpose of training is to engender the "offensive spirit" (pp. 18, 60–64). Battlefield killing does not stop when one conflict party retreats and is quite evidently beaten, and loses nothing of its intensity as the pursuing army hunts down the defeated enemy and dispatches them with extreme prejudice. The fates of untold numbers of surrendering or captured soldiers in twentieth-century wars is sufficient evidence perhaps to dispute the claim that the reluctance to kill in or outside of battle is universal (Bourke, 1999, p. 170). In combat, it would seem, if we accept Grossman and Bourke's analyses and evidence, violence becomes normalized and combatants gradually become desensitized to death, a condition akin to Midlarsky's "mortality salience" (Grossman, 1995, pp. 264–269; Bourke, 1999, pp. 18–21; Docker, 2008, pp. 15–28). If soldiers are reluctant to fire directly at the enemy, does this reluctance reflect some innate code that must be broken to prosecute war? If so, how is this to be squared against the evidence of "orgiastic" violence, for example, in genocides (Docker, 2008, p. 27)? What should be of even greater concern is the degree to which cognitive and behavioural psychology, battlefield management, kill ratios and other advanced technologies of social control reflect more general tendencies towards mass control in post-industrial societies.

Killing in combat is made easier with distance from the enemy, whether the distance is physical or cultural (Grossman, 1995; Bourke, 1999, p. xviii). War crimes were perpetrated on all sides during World War II, but the treatment of POWs once removed from the battlefield was a point of difference. Japanese atrocities in China from 1931 to 1945 and throughout Southeast Asia during the Pacific War were extensive. Contravening both Hague conventions, to which Japan was a signatory, the rights of POWs to humane treatment were ignored. Allied POWs were subjected to torture and summary execution, and were used as slave labour on the notorious Thai–Burma railway where thousands died from malnutrition, beatings and disease. A martial tradition based upon a corrupted derivation of Bushido – the Japanese "way of the warrior" – is said to have encouraged an ethic of fighting to the death (Tanaka, 1996, pp. 206–211; Nitobe, 2007, pp. 100–105). The "culture" of the Japanese Imperial war machine cultivated the emotional detachment necessary for close-quarters killing without mercy, and a sense of contempt for those who chose the dishonour of imprisonment over the sacred glory of death in combat, but, as discussed, emotional detachment in battle is something that all armies seek to instil.

Martial cultures repugnant to international law were not eliminated with the defeat of Imperial Japan and Nazi Germany in 1945. As argued, post-1945 the US military sought to increase the killing efficiency of US forces, albeit within the laws of war. However, the killer impulse requires strict discipline if a soldier's propensity to violence in combat is to be kept in check. The challenge to military discipline is increased by proximity to an enemy indistinguishable from civilians and where enemy combatants have no regard for the laws of war. This is the case with modern post-national asymmetric conflicts where modern armies are pitched against, or placed alongside, ill-disciplined combat forces. For insurgent groups, there were/are no grey areas concerning the legality of violence in the name of ideology or religion. Terror tactics discount any notion of moral or legal obligation to international law by appealing to a higher authority – in the case of Islamists, an extreme interpretation of the Qur'an. In interventions from Vietnam to Iraq, there were no front lines, increasing the psychological strain on even the most well-trained soldiers. Bourke's claim that most combat war crimes go unreported suggests that available statistics on criminal killings in war understate the brutality of all sides in any conflict. The massacre of some 500 Vietnamese villagers by US soldiers in the hamlet of My Lai in 1967 is a reminder that, even in a modern military machine, the propensity for discipline to collapse in the ambiguous space of an open and wide-ranging war front is high (Bourke, 1999, pp. 159–163). Furthermore, there is no guarantee that the military cultures consciously cultivated in modern armies post-1945 will follow a purely linear trajectory guided by law towards an "arrested state" of professional and virtuous efficiency (Battersby et al., 2011). Acknowledgement of the potential, if not the propensity, to cruelty among service personnel is surely then pre-requisite to addressing concerns raised in the preceding discussion. But with so much political capital and national morale invested in a nation's martial traditions and military forces, critiques of military practice and the search for evidence of criminality in combat encounter substantial hostility and secrecy – justified by operational "necessity."

War law struggles to accommodate the realities of the fast-changing terrain of combat, the collapse of distance and the detachment of human emotion from the act of killing. The nuclear bombings of Hiroshima and Nagasaki in 1945 arguably ended what would have been a long and costly war of attrition as the Allies prepared to invade Japan. For the hand-picked crew of the *Enola Gay*, which dropped the bomb on

Hiroshima, the mission was, as far as can be judged from pilot Colonel Paul Tibbets' recollections, a routine bombing flight (Harden, 2005). The legality or morality of the bombings remains a matter of heated debate. After nearly four years of horrendous war in the Pacific and nearly six years of devastating conflict in Europe, the possibility that aerial bombing campaigns could hasten victory cancelled out the potential and actual costs in terms of civilian casualties. Take, for example, the Allied bombing raids on Dresden on February 13 and 14, 1945. The bare details of the raids are horrific. Britain's Bomber Command attacked the older, more densely populated quarter of the city with a high percentage of incendiary bombs generating a merciless firestorm that left 25,000 civilians dead and 30,000 civilians wounded according to Allied and German post-war estimates. The military value of the target remains a matter of controversy. Dresden was a major transport and communications hub for the German military and a centre of arms production and storage. However, US, British and Soviet strategists also believed that air strikes on Dresden and other civilian population centres would weaken German morale ahead of a final Allied and Soviet push to invade Germany (US Strategic Bombing Survey, 1945).

It is the purposes to which force is put that render the use of force legitimate or illegitimate in the minds of security planners and tactical decision-makers. Geneva IV established civilian protection in war as a global peremptory norm. Perversely, this has increased the incentive for signatory states to devise more precise means of targeting. Force is increasingly disaggregated in the post-industrial state as technologies increase the physical and emotional decision distance between targeter and "target." These are the tactical realities and moral challenges presented by twenty-first-century warfare. States perennially push the legal envelope to achieve presumed security gains. The US military's targeted killing campaigns in Afghanistan and Iraq, and their use of unmanned aerial vehicles (UAVs or "drones") to launch surprise attacks against putative enemies in Afghanistan and Pakistan, test the laws of war which prohibit attacks on the unarmed and civilians. UAVs flying across the Northwest Frontier between Afghanistan and Pakistan are "flown" or controlled by "pilots" located in mainland US, thousands of kilometres away from danger, and yet intimately close to their prey. In strictly quantitative terms, drones are an efficient means by which to hunt and dispatch the enemy and reduce the civilian "kill ratio." Still, the number of civilian deaths from drone strikes in Afghanistan and Pakistan is high enough to have substantially undermined ISAF's political and strategic objectives (Bryman, 2013, pp. 33–37; Cronin, 2013). But the alarmingly consistent drive to *distanciate* and *disembed* combat killing, to reduce the "human equation," indicates a direction in military technology and strategy towards minimizing impediments to performance, with empathy occasioned by proximity to target being one major contributor to sub-optimal outcomes on the battlefield (Giddens, 1990; Der Derain, 2001, p. 133). These "advances" occur in an international context where there are few laws specifically limiting "state of the art" weapons technologies and new battle spaces where even the basic concepts of conventional warfare are destabilized. The laws of war were devised after all for wars with humans and humanity in mind.

Economic warfare and war economics

The relationship of war and war law to economics does not require that much of an imaginative stretch, unlike the connections between economic war and state crime. The concept of economic warfare became unfashionable as economic history slipped from favour because of its many historically grounded but discomfiting critiques of econometrics and economic liberalism (Sewell, 2012). For Marx and the Marxists of course, war is a necessary feature of capitalist interstate relations; indeed, capitalism is, in a Marxian sense, a warlike system in which the owners of capital compete for supremacy amongst themselves, by whatever means necessary. States are cast as the "agents of capital" and wage war to secure economic advantage for their capitalist sponsors. All forms of warfare are criminal, save for revolutionary wars of proletarian liberation. Critical neo-Marxist readings of international affairs go one step further to equate capitalistic competition as a form of war in which capitalists deploy superior market power to seize the resources of the poor and destroy livelihoods, communities and entire nations. European empires are the historical referent for this critique because of the close association between colonization and violence. Yet, this more critical reading merges "real war" with war in the rhetorical and figurative sense, in which all forms of social harm inflicted by capital and the capitalist state are manifestations of "violence" (Gilbert, 1978; Lenin, 1994, p. 97; Malesevic, 2010, p. 22). One does not need to be a Marxist to explain the complex connections between interstate war, economics and crime.

Mass or total war, exemplified by twentieth-century world wars, is a creature of industrializing nation-states in which finance capital and the labour of entire national populations are mobilized to operate national war machines. Economic capacity or industrial power was crucial to the conduct of war and to victory. For this reason air attacks on industrial and civilian centres, made possible by the development of long-range bomber aircraft, designed to weaken an enemy's industrial base and public morale, were integral to the war-fighting strategies of the principal belligerents. But these, as with many other wars before and since, were pursued through many avenues of "attack" many of which were non-military, and, yet, still counted as warfare of a kind. The Union blockade of the Mississippi during the American Civil War wrecked the South's cotton bond scheme, thus choking off vital financial support and military supplies to the Confederate army (Forland, 1993). Britain created its own British Ministry of Economic Warfare (BMEW) to coordinate efforts to limit or weaken the industrial and financial capabilities of Germany and Japan during World War II and the US, its own American Board of Economic Warfare. Economic tactics used by the Allies encompassed the denial of access to strategic resources like oil, rubber and tin, physical blockade and trade embargo, asset seizures and financial exclusion, all of which required the compliance of private commercial banks and transnational resources and manufacturing companies (Cox, 2001; Taillard, 2012).

Before the outbreak of hostilities in the Pacific in December 1941, the US Department of State and the BMEW pursued a vigorous strategy of strategic denial towards Japan by limiting the availability of strategic commodities, oil, rubber and tin. Unlike oil, produced within the Allied sphere, rubber and substantial volumes of tin ore were produced in Thailand, an independent and neutral state leaning heavily towards Japan in anticipation of a new order in Asia. British, Australian and Chinese miners sold the vast bulk of alluvial tin recovered from the waterways and alluvial plains of southern Thailand to British-owned Malayan tin smelters. Tin was an essential component in alloys used to make gunmetal and machine bearings and thus vital to arms production. British, US and Australian governments believed that tin concentrates, produced in Thailand and which the Thai government was hoping to buy under compulsory purchase order, would be processed at a proposed Japanese-built smelter and transferred to Germany through Japan. Elaborate steps were taken to bring pressure to bear on British and Australian tin companies operating in Thailand during 1940 not to yield any tin ore to the Thai government. Under instructions from the British government and BMEW, all companies renewed long-term production contracts with Malayan tin smelters, thereby denying the Thai government any legal means, short of nationalization, to obtain a portion of the tin extracted from within Thailand's sovereign territory (Battersby, 2007).

This was a strategy pursued in a context of rising tensions in Asia, but where no state of war existed between the colonial powers, Britain, the US and the Netherlands, and independent Asian powers, Japan and Thailand. Tactical manoeuvres entailed the disruption of market processes, and the careful management or manipulation of private and public international law (Thailand was bound by separate commercial treaties not to take adverse action against British or US business interests). Yet this was more than just "strategic trade" or strategic investment for that matter. Economic strategies employed were intended to have direct impact on the military and industrial capabilities of competitor states. In emphasizing military as opposed to political objectives, economic warfare defined here, therefore, is differentiated from trade or tariff wars, policy contests designed to wrest largely commercial concessions from one or both the protagonists. It is the political purpose of an economic act that defines it as hostile and warlike, but divining the purpose of a state's action in the absence of a formal declaration of intent, or of accurate intelligence, can a matter of educated guesswork where tactics are not as explicit as blockage or embargo, or asset freeze, and even then absolute certainty is elusive.

Wars of a kind can be fought by economic means but to what extent does economic competition lead to conflict? Arash Abizadeh argues that human conflict is fundamentally a matter of "disagreement" over principle, ideology or identity. Contrary to realist theories of resource scarcity as a cause of war, and citing Hobbes, he argues that, paradoxically, "humans are most prone to war when material goods are *abundant*" (Abizadeh, 2011, p. 301). As already mentioned in the preceding chapter, European integration is driven in part by the belief that both World War I and II were a consequence of Franco-German economic rivalry. Governments compete for access to what they perceive to be vital economic resources indispensable to their national economic welfare. The evidence for resource scarcity as a cause of war is, however, weak, writes Shlomi Dinar, with a relatively small number of interstate wars fought over resource issues compared to instances of resource sharing through cooperation and mutual agreement (Dinar, 2011, p. 22). Then again, Iraq's invasion of Kuwait in 1990, which triggered the First Gulf War, entailed seizure of Kuwait's rich oilfields and the financial resources of the Kuwaiti state by an Iraq state economically weakened by almost a decade of war with Iran.

The potential for resource competition to escalate interstate tensions and contribute to intrastate conflicts cannot be entirely discounted. Historically, war in the Pacific was arguably precipitated by the Allied denial of Southeast Asian strategic resources to Japan. There was a resource element to Hitler's decision to dispense with the Molotov–Ribbentrop Pact and invade the Soviet Union. Oil was a factor in Iraq's invasion of Kuwait in 1990 and its subsequent ejection by the international community the following year. But resources are rarely the principal source of conflict between states. Simmering antagonism between China and Japan over rival territorial claims to the allegedly oil and gas rich Senkaku/Diaou Islands in the East China Sea, in the midst of a global unconventional oil and shale gas bonanza, perhaps exemplifies Abizadeh's point about abundance and war. In the China–Japan dyad there are multiple "escalators" to conflict, including nationalistic sentiment in both countries, and, for China, the memories of past Japanese war atrocities. Economic considerations, be they resource-orientated or financial, are contributing factors to patterns of complex causality.

There is another area of economic geostrategy that sits outside the ambit of economic war but falls within the scope of international peace and security. Sanctions are used by the international community to bring pressure to bear upon governments deemed to be acting contrary to international law or in violation of a major international principle. Such measures range from the cancellation or denial of diplomatic visas to the suspension of all diplomatic and economic relations. These do not constitute economic warfare in that they are measures directed towards affirming and upholding international principle, for example, international sanctions imposed upon South Africa's apartheid regime during the 1980s, and against the Burmese junta during the 1990s. The UN sanctions regime imposed upon Iraq after the First Gulf War is a different case.

The brief First Gulf War ended in March 1991 with Iraq's expulsion from Kuwait. Conscious of regional sensitivities, the US opted to remove Saddam Hussein through economic sanctions rather than military force. Sanctions were imposed and administered through the UNSC, with the clear political purpose of choking the Iraqi state and forcing the removal of Hussein and his Ba'ath Party from power. When it became obvious that economic measures were inflicting unconscionable harm on civilians as supplies of food and medication dwindled, the sanctions regime was eased to permit limited sales of Iraqi oil, the proceeds of which would be used to purchase essential foodstuffs and medicines. The point here is that blanket sanctions disproportionately affect civilians. Because the UN embargo was imposed *post bellum*, and because Iraq was not then an occupied state, these did not technically violate the letter of the Geneva Conventions, but, arguably, ran contrary to the intent of international humanitarian law. The subversion of this UN Iraq Oil-For-Food Programme is addressed in the next chapter, but the fact that so many prominent international companies chose to circumvent UN sanctions also highlights the precariousness of economic controls imposed as tools of international strategy.

The logic of globalization suggests a steady decline in the capacity of states to regulate economic activity. The "retreat of the state" thesis popular among liberal globalists holds true in the sense that the globalization of trade and investment relations has, in the developed world, diminished the relative scale of government enterprise and institutionalized the principle of trade liberalization, despite the failure of states to agree to draw down agricultural protection during the Doha Round of trade negotiations. With the rise of China, India and Brazil, command and control within the global economy is becoming more diffuse. The complexities of contemporary economic warfare derive, in part, from the increasingly fragmented and networked nature of transnational business and by the integration of production and finance through complex share transactions, mergers and acquisitions and the emergence of hedge funds and other forms of equity management – *financialization* – to which the fates of companies and governments are increasingly subject.

There are, however, areas of international and global economic activity where the power of states to regulate has, if anything, increased or, more to the point, the nature of power in a networked world has altered. After the September 11, 2001 twin attacks on the World Trade Center in New York, global anti-money laundering efforts were intensified once the circulation of "terror finance" through the global financial system became a recognized national security priority. Globally, the Financial Action Task Force (FATF) became the coordinating body for measures directed towards achieving greater transparency in all forms of transnational capital transfer, including the substantial informal banking sector.

The global Anti-Money Laundering Regime (AMLR) comprises, at the international level, the International Monetary Fund (IMF), the World Bank-sponsored FATF and the UN Counter-Terrorism Committee (CTC), which track suspect transactions through myriad informal and informational exchange networks. International agreements designed to tackle transnational crime were linked in an evolving global web of criminal law through the 2004 UN CTOC. This sophisticated global regime can be, and is, vulnerable to capture or at least manipulation to serve state strategic policy.

US foreign policy and the AMLR converge along a number of vectors of which the US–Iran "relationship" is the most salient. The Clinton Administration initiated a sanctions campaign against Iran in 1995, declaring Iran an "extraordinary threat" and prohibiting US citizens and business entities (juristic persons) from trading, directly or indirectly, in Iranian oil (EO12957, 1995). While the precise nature of the threat which Iran was supposed to represent was not stated, there were, as then still unsubstantiated, concerns of an unauthorized Iranian nuclear programme. In the context of a vigorous sanctions regime imposed on Iraq for its presumed development of nuclear weapons, similarly unsubstantiated but strongly suspected, the economic restrictions were at the very least in keeping with US security thinking about the Middle East at the time. Sanctions have strengthened incrementally and globally with the passage of UNSC Resolutions S/Res 1737 (2006), S/Res 1747 (2007), S/Res 1803 (2008) and S/Res 1929 (2010) in response to Tehran's resistance to IAEA inspections (Taylor, 2009). From the Iran Sanctions Act (1996) to the Comprehensive Iran Sanctions Accountability and Divestment Act (CISADA) (DoT, 2010), the US government gives financial regulators, principally the Department of Treasury and the Department of Justice, the legal means to block financial dealings by anyone residing in the US with the Iranian government, Iranian banks and the Iranian Republican Guard, and to impose heavy penalties for violations, with the Hong Kong and Shanghai Banking Corporation (HSBC) being the most recent high-profile case (see Chapter 4).

The extent of US "lawfare" and economic warfare against Iran extends to choking off global credit facilities and curtailing Iranian oil exports to countries heavily dependent upon access to the US market, especially China. Through the EU, the Society for Worldwide Interbank Financial Telecommunication (SWIFT), a private company registered in Belgium, was "instructed" to expurgate a substantial part of Iran's banking sector from its system, and by default, ostracize Iran from much of the global economy (SWIFT, 2012; Younglai and Rampton, 2012). China's rising demand for oil and related energy resources complicates the enforcement of US and UN sanctions designed to dissuade Iran from developing its nuclear technologies. As Iran's principal customer for oil, China, with oil dependence approaching 60 per cent and with no potential domestic source of supply, is reluctant to suspend imports of Iranian oil. To secure China's support for international sanctions and to navigate around alliance sensitivities, Washington granted oil import waivers to China, Japan and other significant trading partners with no viable alternative source of supply (Downs and Maloney, 2011; Gardner and Hampton, 2012). Such denial-of-access measures constitute an "oblique parallel reflection" of the archetypal Distributed- Denial-of-Service (DDoS) "attack."

The "dark cloud" of cyber war

Power within the global system is becoming ever more diffuse, but this does not prevent states from seeking and exploiting new networked power resources for geostrategic gain. Herein lies one of the principal vulnerabilities of the global system. The proliferation of systems integrating technologies and practices through the global economy, in telecommunications, transport, defence information systems and financial services, generates a spectrum of vulnerability. From demonstrable susceptibility to hostile disruption, this spectrum extends into the psychosocial domain to anxieties over the possibility of systemic collapse occasioned by technical malfunction, unintended damage to critical hardware or software, random interference or nefarious acts of criminal or political intent (Klibi and Martel, 2013; Ghadge et al., 2013). Global systems of all kinds are subject to hostile "pulses" emanating from within the strategic policy communities of states that possess significant network power. To appreciate the complexities of techno-strategic competition in cyberspace, therefore, the widely misconstrued phenomenon of cyber warfare has to be placed in this broader context of deepening systems and systemic interconnectedness, and the human interpretations of this global merger.

"Cyber war is real," declare Richard Clarke and Robert Knake, and "cyber security" is necessarily a militarized domain (Clarke and Knake, 2010, pp. 51, 62). "Cyberspace," they argue, is a distinct sphere or layer of international relations, bristling with critical security vulnerabilities that, at the national policy level, can only be addressed with specific "cyber security" or "information security" strategies and the means to target hostile and "malicious" threats and "take down enemy systems" (Clarke and Knake, 2010, p. 62). They provide an insight into the cyber "risk imaginary" that has evolved and "matured" in US national security circles in the first decade of this century. The term risk imaginary used here draws upon Charles Taylor's idea of the "social imaginary" as "the ways people imagine their social existence, how they fit together with others [. . .] the expectations that are normally met, and the deeper normative notions and images that underlie these expectations" (Taylor, 2007, p. 23). This, in combination with the shared mental models approach, frames "communities of security practice" built around shared interpretations of threats that manifest in cyberspace and the steps "necessary" to secure the state from "cyber attack." For the creative and the conspiratorial mind, the Internet is a space of infinite social possibility and risk.

Professional risk managers, argues Cass R. Sunstein, determine risks systematically and according to available scientific information, not emotion or normative concern (Sunstein, 2002, p. 54). But scientific inquiry, from a critical viewpoint, is less ordered and manageable and more chaotic and unpredictable than many interested in the science of prediction are prepared to admit (Feyerabend, 1991, pp. 14–24; Silver, 2012). The world of risk management, therefore, and despite the appearance of mathematical clarity, is a world of the imagination shaped by feelings and calculations of vulnerability, expressing the desire to control, mitigate or prevent future harm. It is also a world where power is exercised or claimed through explanation and prediction, and where the future is "ordered" according to the designs of the most powerful (Dean, 2000, p. 131). Imaginaries of risk are paradoxically disruptive and potentially disintegrative, and nowhere are these realities more evident than in the sphere of cyber security.

The rise of the networked state is accompanied by the rise of the "risk society," in which, state Beck and Giddens, uncertainty is "manufactured" out of ill-conceived reactions to the perceived future possibility of harm (Giddens, 1990; Beck, 1999). "Manufactured uncertainty" occurs because, Giddens writes, "knowledge reflexively applied to the conditions of systemic reproduction intrinsically alters the circumstances to which it originally referred" (Giddens, 1990, p. 59). Paradoxically, the pursuit of cyber security and the use of cyber systems to advance state security interests by the US and other world powers threatens to undermine President Obama's ideal of "an open, interoperable, secure, and reliable cyberspace," one shared by the EU (Obama, 2011, p. 11; Ashton, 2013). Governments, or more precisely, their security advisers, are reacting to real and perceived vulnerabilities in their information security systems by developing both defensive and offensive strategies to counteract perceived threats from state and non-state entities without adequate reflection on either the nature of these alleged threats or the processes by which they are constructed (Rid, 2012). Evidence is mounting that states are prepared to counter perceived sources of cyber threat through retaliatory measures justified with claims that "cyber offence" capabilities are essential to "cyber deterrence" (Libicki, 2009; Gellman and Nakashima, 2013). These defensive strategies, however, risk the openness of the Internet, which arguably is the fundamental principle upon which to construct a global system that is both resilient and of greatest global public benefit (Rid, 2012, pp. 169–170). In other words, the preparation for cyber war ensures that it is, to quote Ronald Deibert, "unlikely that nothing bad will happen" (Deibert, 2013, loc. 2505).

Of the two principal vulnerabilities in computer-mediated information systems DDoS, in which a website is shut down by a snowstorm of email messages, is the least invasive. "Hacking" or systems infiltration poses the greater threat, or the greater opportunity to acquire sensitive information or cause serious damage to equipment and informational capability. As detailed in Chapter 1, systems breaches are common occurrences and only a fraction of recorded "incidents" fit the models of cyber war proponents. Encryption codes are numerical passwords used to protect all sensitive information, from a person's identity or their bank details to intellectual property and details of military operations. All encryption codes can potentially be hacked, although the computing power necessary to break long encryption keys used for the most sensitive and secret information, measured in Million Inputs Per Second (MIPS), is currently available only to significantly resourced entities, like government security agencies or large private corporations.

Alternatively, and most commonly, malicious codes can be written into electronic documents attached to innocuous and inviting emails where it passes undetected through protective firewalls until accepted by the system the invader seeks to subvert, either automatically or by an unsuspecting user inside the target organization. The code remains dormant until activated by an external computer, or a "botnet," a network of computers over which control is established, often with the knowledge of the computer's owner. Once "malware" impregnates a computer system, everything on the host computer, and every computer connected to it, is potentially compromised and potentially killable. Electronic documents can be, have been and are "exfiltrated" while the compromised insiders, human and machine, are asleep. In this amorphous world of codes and electronic pathways, digital footprints evaporate as soon as they are set down – as if they were mere shadows drifting across cyberspace – or "shadows in the clouds" (Information Warfare Monitor, 2010, pp. 38–41).

Cyber espionage raises perplexing challenges for the governance of cyberspace, not least because, unlike conventional spying, cyber spies operate from their home country using the dispersed networks of the Internet to disguise their identities and traverse the "web". In this new wired and wirelessly interconnected world, the international "agent" is not a human being but an electronic code. International law provides few protections against cyber threats if for no other reason than that it is almost impossible to attribute attacks or espionage directly to any state or non-state actor unless responsibility is admitted publicly.

It is possible to imagine scenarios where coordinated and sustained use of computer malware, delivered through a maliciously coded email, cripples a country's information networks to the extent that its war-fighting capabilities are degraded. However, there are some problems with defining this as "war" in the conventional sense and treating "cyber war" as the virtual corollary of "total war." The pursuit of strategic advantage through the use of "malicious" Internet technologies is only effective when conducted covertly – meaning, in the simplest sense, that states are likely to be reluctant to identify themselves as combatants by declaring cyber war on a strategic rival. So-called "kill switches," built into computer operating systems to shut down industrial machinery in an emergency or to lock computers using pirated software, are common enough. Suspicion that such switches have been illegally and covertly implanted in imported security and command systems software and hardware negates any strategic advantage that might be gained from their deployment. For this reason alone, there is a strong disincentive for any state to declare cyber war on a rival.

The current fluidity of global relations calls into question the serviceability of Cold War security concepts, specifically deterrence. Nuclear deterrence "worked" in a global context where two nuclear-armed states maintained a rough equivalence of power sufficient to ensure the destruction of the other in the event of nuclear war. Neither the technologies of cyber offence nor the multiplicity of "cyber capable" entities today can replicate the nuclear threat of Mutually Assured Destruction (MAD). Cyber "incursions," however extensive and targeted, can be disruptive but are unlikely to deliver a decisive strategic blow. States prove resilient in the face of catastrophic systems collapse. For example, bombing campaigns by the Allies and Germany during World War II, and indeed the US bombings of North Vietnam, substantially degraded infrastructure, and materials, and killed tens of thousands of civilians, but systems were quickly rebuilt, or surviving ones adapted, to compensate. Even if one state were able to severely disable the informational control systems of a rival, decisive victory would still require the deployment of conventional forces.

Nonetheless, virtual strategic competition between states is a reality. Cyber "breaches" of US defence systems are reportedly increasing. Notably, the tide of accusations tends to flow in an East–West direction evidencing more than a ripple of old Cold War hostility. Russia was thought to have mounted DDoS attacks on Georgian servers prior to the invasion of South Ossetia in 2008, while China is allegedly employing a form of Trojan spyware to hack into government databases in South and Southeast Asia and compromise the Dalai Lama's communications (Information Warfare Monitor, 2010). In all cases, cyber security professionals suspect collusion between state security agencies and the cyber crime syndicates – roundly denied by the accused. Anonymity enhances deniability, but if we look back to the history of Cold War covert operations the possibility that states and criminal entities might still be cooperating for mutual benefit, only this time in the cyber domain, is hardly far-fetched, and neither can we presume that only "the enemy" engage in such clandestine and unconscionable alliances.

Violence in law involves the threat of or the infliction of physical harm on civilians. Just because retaliatory cyber offensives would be directed against information infrastructure and not human beings does not mean that an "attack" or act of violence has not occurred, merely that the attack does not violate the letter of international war and humanitarian law (Additional Protocol I, Art. 49.1; Art. 75.2). Computer viruses are new weapons of war and not only are these technologies used by states against perceived and actual enemies, they are evolving rapidly both in complexity and in operational impact. The development of offensive capacity thus becomes the corollary of defence, and crime becomes both a tolerated counterforce strategy and another by-product of enhanced defence capability. Stuxnet, a malicious self-replicating "worm" code, deployed by Israel and the US, disabled critical equipment and disrupted Iran's nuclear programme in 2010 (Sanger, 2012; Deibert, 2013). But this is "war" in the figurative sense only and, as argued previously, is not analogous to conventional conflict. This is the realist version of the neo-Marxist construction and conflation of real war with economic harm. To understand the relationship between technology and war requires a shift in our conception of war, and the abandonment of distinctions between conventional and unconventional combat. Moreover, we must also appreciate that this conceptual shift challenges both the laws of war and traditionalist modes of strategic thought.

Applying the "logic" of mainstream security studies, we can surmise that rival states will strive to equalize power imbalances by replicating each other's strategies and tactics, whatever the legal or political objections, and develop offence capabilities (Broad et al., 2011; DoD, 2011). US, UK and Australian suspicion centres on the growing global reach of the Chinese telecommunications company Huawei, which, US analysts allege, colludes with the Chinese military to spy on foreign governments (Mandiant, 2013; Rogers and Ruppersberger, 2012, pp. 7–8; UKISC,

2013). Cyber resilience and "cyber defence" is to be achieved in Europe through the convergence of European civilian and military technological capabilities, a virtual military–industrial complex, developed with the most compelling of discursive practices (Ashton, 2013, p. 11). The European Agency for Network and Information Security (ENISA) claims that by April 2013, 34 countries had developed explicit cyber security strategies, in some of which the distinctions between cyber defence and offence are blurred or eliminated in the construction of a "full spectrum" cyber security posture (ENISA, n/d; Hammond, 2013). These new crime–security dynamics are emerging in globalized "self-governing" spaces where there are no international agreements to control or limit the malicious use of Information and Communication Technologies (ICT) by states and where the distinctions between enemy and ally, criminal and combatant (and criminal and state official) are rendered increasingly indistinct.

Surveillance and espionage are two sides of the same coin, each designed to gather information on the unknown to inform the mitigation of uncertainty. Surveillance, as demonstrated in the US,UK, and also Australia, can be invasive and yet sit within the law, where laws are interpreted flexibly and in favour of the state. Bulk meta-data about people's Internet behaviour is freely traded as commercial marketing data, and yet such data, when subjected to algorithmic analysis in high-powered information processors, yields highly sensitive information about a person's habits that can be acquired by state security agents and used to target them if judged a security threat. Surveillance, in this sense, is a form of monitoring but security agencies have, in the age of quantum computing, the capacity to decipher encryption keys and infiltrate personal computers at will. The trajectory of state privacy protections, where matters of national security are concerned, is trending downwards, as are tolerance levels for the exercise of freedom of speech where judged contrary to the national interest.

Conclusion

Questions of governance and the rule of law within this space raise some important concerns about the current status of civil if not political rights globally. Liberal democracies, it seems, prefer "uncensored" cyberspace where control is exercised through clandestine means, and where rights are circumscribed covertly, on a case-by-case basis, in the name of national security. Authoritarian states seek to regulate away most or all civil liberties in the interests of tighter national control (Deibert, 2013, loc. 2477). At both ends of the cyber governance spectrum, the power of the networked state is paradoxically enhanced.

The capillaries of cyberspace are mostly in private hands; hence any retaliatory – or pre-emptive – cyber offence, if it is to be effective, must be prosecuted through civilian infrastructure and civilian social networks. Cyber offence or cyber attack is likewise necessarily a military strategy pursed through economic means – a form of economic warfare in other words. Such forms of warfare exemplify the perplexing governance challenges created by the *informationalization* of security. The Geneva Conventions expressly prohibit attacks on civilians and imply a prohibition on attacks harmful to civilian infrastructure in war, albeit medical infrastructure (Additional Protocol I, Art. 51). In a cyber attack, however, it would be nigh impossible to distinguish between civilian and "enemy" computers, if for no other reason that PCs (and their owners) are surreptitiously and unwittingly recruited to serve in malicious botnets. An added complication involves the psychological bonds that people form through social media, and the psychological harm potentially caused to a person by any disruption in their social connectivity compounded by the realization that they are the target of state-sanctioned violence. The vulnerabilities of computer-mediated systems are very real and exploitable, for which reason, the global governance of cyberspace requires, in addition to consensus, principles and agreements, a more balanced "risk imaginary," one that accommodates the systemic and social nature of cyber threats and which is not "martialled" by self-perpetuating doctrines of cyber war.

Convergent security risk imaginaries "externalize" threats. But global insecurity is a manifestation of deeper insecurities and vulnerabilities arising from the nature of competition between states, and also between non-state entities, in the global political economy. Without this appreciation of the intimate connection between system and human imagination, the evolution of global norms to govern competition in cyberspace will be, at the least, a very slow, ill-directed process. And, beset by the mistrust and "misperceptions" that shape traditional international security practices and relations, politics in cyberspace could easily degenerate into a pattern of exclusion and competition between antagonistic "virtual" blocs. The course of global trade liberalization is dogged by the perennial risk that states will return to protectionist practices and form closed regional economic groupings. That this has not occurred is testimony to the ideological power of "market globalism" and the material returns from global trade (Steger, 2009).

4
Good Corp, Bad Corp: Market Crimes and Systemic Risk

Collective responsibility for criminal acts is easier to apportion when the collectivity concerned is a private corporation subject to state and international law. For example, BP and Transocean, the lessee and the owner respectively, of the oil rig *Deepwater Horizon* accepted criminal liability for the pollution in the Gulf of Mexico following the spillage of some 4.9 million barrels of oil from BP's deep-ocean Macondo well in 2010. Criminal charges, to which BP pleaded guilty, covered not only environmental damage but also fraudulent behaviour by BP executives in misleading US Congress as to the severity of the disaster (Ramseur and Hagerty, 2013, pp. 5–6). The National Commission appointed to investigate cited a collective "failure" attributable to a corporate culture of risk taking and safety cost aversion, with primary responsibility falling to BP as a corporate entity and not merely to individual employees, even if some liabilities were subsequently defrayed to subcontractors (Chief Counsel's Report, 2011, pp. 248–249; Oil Spill Commission, 2011, pp. 2, 90–93, 95). Whereas responsibility for international or state crimes is apportioned to individuals, whether they are acting under orders or not, national-level corporate criminal laws increasingly acknowledge collective guilt. Under US law, as in all jurisdictions that accept corporate criminal liability, corporations are liable for the criminal actions of individual employees where such acts are committed within the framework of their contractual obligations to their employer (Pieth and Ivory, 2011, p. 7). That a large multinational corporation such as BP can be compelled to accept extensive liabilities in excess of US$20 billion, including costs of restoration, compensation and government fines, is one more reminder of the power that states can exert over private corporations – when they so choose. Globalization has eroded but not curtailed the capacity of states to control the activities of transnational businesses operating within their borders. That said, state capacity to regulate capitalism as a system is weakening under sustained, incremental and insidious challenge from within the global private sector.

Capitalism, observes Joseph Schumpeter, is an "evolutionary" and "organic" system to which "creative destruction" is central for regeneration and renewal (Schumpeter, 2012, loc. 1838). Viewed critically, then, capitalism thrives by "smashing up" and remaking the equally "organic" social entities that support or resist it (Polanyi, 2001, pp. 171–172). As such, acceptance of capitalism's fundamental norm entails individual tolerance, and, arguably, therefore, collective authorship of all the harms that capitalism inflicts upon those least equipped to survive (Escobar, 1995; Swanger, 2007; Hayden, 2009, p. 103; Henry, 2011; Linklater, 2011). But merely asserting that "capitalism is violent" or "capitalism is evil" does not lead to any sharper appreciation of precisely where deficiencies or failings are to be found in a mode of economic organization that thrives still, despite frequent catastrophes and abundant systemic contradictions. Global capitalism, in aggregate terms, has lifted hundreds of millions out of poverty and raised human well-being, measured in terms of life expectancy, health, literacy and the like, to unprecedented levels. Yet, while capitalist enterprises and those who govern capitalism trade on assurances of control, capitalism is a chaotic system beset by complexities and uncertainties where risk taking, loss and atrophy are intrinsic to systemic growth and regeneration.

The cutting edge

The *Deepwater Horizon* disaster offers multiple insights into the horizontal and vertical symbioses that connect individual human actions to system-wide dynamics in the contemporary global economy. US federal investigators found that the quest for new oil is pushing exploration and extraction towards more costly and "technically difficult to access" reserves, into the unknown in fact, where exploration and extraction become experimental. The commission of inquiry cited as contributing factors to the disaster the very systemic interactions that drive the global economy to new heights. The commercial pressures, or incentives, to control costs encourage operational compromises, or "flexibilities," the pursuit of military precision through the *informationalization* and *individuation* of responsibility, which transparently places employees under enormous stress to prioritize cost efficiency at every turn. Thus the decisions along the chains of corporate command are governed by axial cost–earnings ratios, which at once measure individual "performance" and signal risks to global market returns. Despite sophisticated technologies, advanced human and process micromanagement techniques, and an extensive history of environmental and social catastrophes from which to learn, such human and ecological disasters continue (Chief Counsel's Report, 2011, pp. 248–249; Oil Spill Commission, 2011, p. 62). If we switch industry focus from resources to finance, parallel consistencies are also evident in the recurrence of financial crises and corruption scandals involving some of the world's most advanced economies and most "trusted" companies – all of which are in one way or another "systemically significant." This is the mercantile overworld, analogous to Stephen Krasner's political world of "organized hypocrisy," where the edge of law is tested and principles subverted as commercial necessity dictates, to be constrained only when "misbehaviour" threatens systemic continuity, by which time catastrophe can already have struck hard and deep.

There is of course the invidious paradox created by the legal imperative for directors and executives to maximize company earnings and profits. This is both an expression of the *raison d'être* of "the corporation" and a reflection of the historical evolution of industrial capitalism. The "compression of time and space," writes David Harvey, is a defining dynamic of modernity, a reflection of the commercial drive to bring the entire globe under control (Harvey, 1991). At the beating heart of capitalist enterprise is the reflexive impulse to conquer, control and reduce or eliminate costs. This was evident in the technological innovations of the industrial age, and in today's "informational age" in which time and space are no longer impediments to production and exchange on a global scale. When engineers chose to reduce the number of stabilizers used in the Macondo Well's production casing in the days leading up to the oil spill catastrophe, they were merely submitting to the incessant imperatives of industrial time. The pursuit of greater speed and efficiency comes at a price, however. Beset by cost overruns, the *Deepwater Horizon* programme was running behind schedule, and time was at a premium. The regime under which the engineers worked compelled them to be cost-averse in their behaviour, and despite internal disagreements about how to proceed in the technically complex and highly uncertain circumstances of offshore drilling, time and cost considerations overrode all else (Oil Spill Commission, 2011, pp. 92–99). This was not simply a case of human error under pressure but also a measure of the deep undertow of commercial forces that fashioned the reasoning of those involved.

As in the political sphere, global economic order is contingent upon the reliability of individual decision-makers along long global value chains of production, finance and trade, and these chains are both vast and intricate. Recurrent financial crises underline the vulnerability of these value chains to human error and criminality. Transnational Corporations (TNCs) occupy critical junctures in this global system. As the primary agents of economic globalization, even if the rise of global finance is gradually strengthening the grip of capital markets (and capital market players), their scale and the intensity of interactions between them shape the redistribution of wealth along vast and increasingly flexible global production lines. Globally, there are an estimated 82,000 TNC parent corporations with the vast majority headquartered in the developed world. An indication of the scale and density of global production and exchange networks is that as much as two-thirds of global trade occurs between TNC parents and their 780,000-plus affiliates (UNCTAD, 2007, pp. 217–218; UNCTAD, 2010, p. 17; Dicken, 2011). The geographic division of the world economy, between the industrialized "North" and underdeveloped "South" is, to a large extent, breaking down. A sharp rise in TNC formation within developing countries since 1992 is accompanied by a rise in South–South investment (UNCTAD, 2010, pp. 17–18). Not only, therefore, is the volume of critical economic decisions made increasing almost daily, but so too is the variety and variability of the corporate cultures within which these global decisions are taken.

Taking the classic liberal view, corporate decision-making reflects the contractual basis of "the firm" in which employees, from executive board level to factory floor, are under contractual obligation to company shareholders to maximize financial returns (Barry, 2003; Klausner, 2006). In an attempt to counteract this shareholder imperative, and impose legal obligation to include "stakeholders," the UK government has introduced into its *Companies Act* of 2006 the requirement for directors to pay regard to the "impact of company's operations on the community and environment" (172.1d) – what Andrew Keay terms the principle of "enlightened shareholder value" (Keay, 2007). Yet, there are limits to the capacity of legal systems to constrain dynamic entities operating in dynamic global markets. An alternative view, and one by no means peculiar to Marxist and neo-Marxist objectors, is that corporate actors seek to influence their operating environment by ruthlessly exploiting market power, manipulating legal and regulatory systems to their advantage, and by cultivating political influence. Indeed, the globalization of production was, in part, propelled by US firms seeking to manoeuvre around anti-trust (anti-monopoly) legislation, of the kind that led to the break-up of John D. Rockefeller's Standard Oil Company in 1911, and to transcend protectionist barriers (Picciotto, 2011, pp. 114, 134–136). Clearly, the joint-stock model of capital mobilization has proven highly effective in generating profitable returns to investors. However, there is growing international concern that some corporations are too powerful and too easily evade scrutiny and sanction (Wilks, 2013).

Often the term "wicked" is used to describe hypercompetitive markets, but wickedness implies morality, whereas from the systems perspective advanced in the book the global system is fundamentally amoral (Nesvetailova and Belli, 2013, pp. 46–49). It is possible to place constraints on corporate practice and to enforce corporate laws, provided the political will exists. Indeed, as noted, corporate practice is extensively regulated and corporations submit as a matter of routine to national and international laws – while also seeking to evade them, however. At the very minimum, then, companies have to comply with national rules of incorporation, registration, financial auditing and reporting, intellectual property or patent laws, and taxation laws (Picciotto, 2011; Nesvetailova and Belli, 2013). Even if they are able to negotiate favourable terms with governments that either lack equivalent negotiating expertise or are willing to heavily discount regulatory requirements to attract foreign investment, companies rely upon governments to provide a safe and supportive operating environment. The imbalance of negotiating power in the global system, however, frequently favours the largest actors, and the largest actors in many "public–private" bargaining relationships are TNCs.

In contrast to the stereotypical corporate monolith characterized by the Ford Motor Company of the early twentieth century, today's "post-Fordist" TNCs are, because of the scope of their operations, disaggregated into network formations where affiliates have a greater or lesser degree of autonomy from the parent company and head office. Companies cooperate in networks or "clusters" of corporations, to achieve efficiency gains from "internal" comparative advantages. Investments are prioritized according to market demand, resource and market location but also the prevailing "investment climate" or, more colloquially, the "cost of doing business," primarily business taxation, minimum wages, exchange rates, transport and communication infrastructure and conditions of employment. Post-World War II, transnational manufacturing companies mastered the arts of vertical integration, corporate alliance building and globalized investment agendas to maximize returns and minimize political risk. Even resources companies, struck by the wave of economic nationalism, out of necessity developed vertically integrated transnational structures to extract value from globalized commodity markets – to put it another way, they dealt with whomsoever and did whatsoever was necessary to secure pay dirt.

"Influence" within business networks is highly and deceptively concentrated and the exercise of power is well disguised (Vitali et al., 2011). Networked firms connect the globe in highly variable circuits of capital, but this does not mean that corporate power is diluted or that networked capitalism necessarily complements democracy or egalitarian social practice any more than did industrial capitalism under Fordism. From a statist and realist standpoint, markets are battlegrounds for competing interests where power is fundamental to market outcomes. Global commerce is of course conducted primarily by private companies, and the largest corporations in today's global economy are household names: Ford, General Motors, Mitsubishi, Sony, Nestle, the Hong Kong and Shanghai Banking Corporation (HSBC) and Barclays. These TNCs have achieved a position of global economic power where they can, if not dictate terms, place enormous pressure upon governments to accommodate their interests. By virtue of their advanced technological capacities, capital and their grip on intellectual property, corporations extract "regulatory arbitrage" and exploit the weakened bargaining position of individual states and national-level contractors competing to attract lucrative investment dollars or supply contracts (Strange, 2004; Dicken, 2011, pp. 221–238).

Industry policies in the Global South aided the formation of local business conglomerates and, through successive waves of liberalization, allowed Western corporations to establish regional footholds. Strict foreign investment controls popular with the governing elites of newly independent post-colonial nations were gradually modified through the incorporation of market globalist elements that included generous incentives for foreign manufacturing corporations to invest in export processing zones, for example. In the 1980s, Asian and Western Foreign Direct Investment (FDI) helped fund the economic booms experienced by Southeast Asia's tiger economies, although the rapid withdrawal of Japanese capital from Thailand in the early 1990s precipitated the Asian Financial Crisis of 1997. Rising FDI did not curtail domestic capital accumulation in Asia, as evidenced by the rapid growth in the number and size of developing country TNCs. The potential local impacts of sudden economic collapse in China, Europe or the US are much greater today. Volatile investment capital flows are one consequence of Finance Driven Globalization (FDG) and it is argued that *financialization* leaves many developing countries at a severe disadvantage (UNCTAD, 2012b). North–South capital flows have grown consistently but the bulk of northern investment is concentrated in a handful of states, principally China. This leaves billions perched precariously on the "edge" of global capitalism.

There are many varieties of capitalism globally, and, despite receiving a "bad press," aspects of the so-called "Asian way" have proved highly durable. Indeed, studies of Asian corporate entities offer insights into the nature of power and influence within networked corporate entities globally, and to the salience of cultural practice in global capitalism, if only because so many Asian corporations have become "globalizers" over the twentieth century (Sklair, 2003, pp. 51–53; Sklair, 2002). In Japanese *keiretsu*, personal relations and finance combine to foster organizational coherence in diffuse business agglomerations or what Michael Gerlach presciently terms "complex networks of cooperation" (Gerlach, 1992, xiii). In contrast to the individualist and competitive culture of Western corporations, "stakeholder" culture of Japanese corporations ensures that business clusters are not held together purely by market logic but also by a sense of mutual dependence founded upon deeply rooted social norms (Wilks, 2013, pp. 243–249; Dicken, 2011). For example, the Mitsubishi Group today is a vast and expansive network of companies, likened to a "family" in company public relations. Within the Group no single agency exercises apparent control but Mitsubishi's Japan-based CEOs sustain a "mutual understanding" through the routinized informalities of the *kinyokai* or "Friday Club," a social group with access to substantial financial power. *Keiretsu* were traditionally built around a single financial anchor that could be relied upon to provide finance to meet the needs of the group and its members. In the case of Mitsubishi, the Bank of Tokyo-Mitsubishi UFJ (BTMU) is today a globally significant banking institution that enjoys "leverage" in key global financial centres (Tudor and Lucchetti, 2010). Cultural dynamics shape capitalist business interactions but such dynamics lie beyond the reach of corporate regulators, even where systems of business regulation are relatively robust.

Asian "business empires" were built and remain held together through a combination of kinship relations and cultural obligations, as well as mutual financial interest. In Japan's post-war industrialization growth spurt, corporate power was held in check by the Ministry of International Trade and Industry (MITI), which set industry policy aided by a protective "developmentalist" state. Government–business power balances in Southeast Asian industrializers were altogether different and, as discussed in Chapter 1, Japan's *sogo shosha* exploited this to their advantage. Patron–client ties bound together the interests of overseas Chinese "entrepreneurs" and local political elites in Indonesia and Thailand's industrialization. Such "marriages of convenience" allowed business people and groups to navigate a path through the ambiguities of highly personalized systems of law and government. Liem Sioe Liong (Sudono Salim) migrated from the Fujian province to the then Netherlands' East Indies in 1938. As a key supplier to Indonesian Republican fighters in central Java during the 1945–1949 war of independence, he built a firm "understanding" with one guerrilla officer of the Diponegoro Division, Suharto, later General Suharto, president of Indonesia (1967–1998). Liem, who adopted his Indonesian name to align with the nationalist mood of the Sukarno era, and the "Salim Group" which he built, prospered in Suharto's New Order, receiving state monopolies over the import of cloves and flour milling and gradually building multinational interests that spanned, before the crash, agribusiness, cement, property and banking (Backman, 2001; Vatikiotis, 2004; Studwell, 2007, loc. 3826–3831).

A similar pattern is apparent in the rise of Thailand's Charoen Pokphand (CP) Group, owned by the Cheeravanont family. Established by two Chinese migrants who built strong personal connections with Thailand's military elites of the 1950s and 1960s, this Thai version of the Asian family business model likewise laid its foundations under a protective state umbrella. Technical skills and intellectual property were channelled into the company's agribusiness enterprises through joint-venture arrangements that gradually increased the Group's international competitiveness (Pananond, 2009). All Asian conglomerates had to change their strategies in the wake of the 1997 financial crisis, but in Thailand the CP Group remains one of the country's most powerful business houses and, through CEO Dhanin Cheeravanont, closely aligned with the Shinawatra family, another family business headed by former prime minister Police Lieutenant Colonel Thaksin Shinawatra, architect of Thailand's largest telecommunications corporation, the Shin Corporation (Shin Corp) (McCargo and Pathmanand, 2005).

China's largest corporations are either wholly state-owned or share common interests with state-owned counterparts and implement strategies aligned with China's energy and food security priorities. The privately owned New Hope Group, the state-owned China National Cereals, Oils and Foodstuffs Corporation (COFCO) and the state-owned Beidahuang Group share an interest in agricultural market liberalization in China, and each pursues an ambitious global agenda of overseas expansion to reap grains for the voracious China market (Lawrence, 2011; Grain.org, 2012). Reflecting the hybrid nature of China's market economy, state-controlled businesses operate alongside private firms, which are increasingly subject to "rational–legal" regulation, and through which the Chinese state, and the Chinese Communist Party, seeks to retain its paramount position (Guthrie, 2009, pp. 101–105). This strengthening of national business regulation is not as paradoxical as it might at first seem, given the common intellectual origins of classical and Marxian economics. Neither is there an anomaly in the use of market principles to break down personalized and particularistic *guangxi* networks, and with this potential future sources of opposition to the axial networks of the one-party state.

At issue here is not whether we can read the formulation of a "transnational capitalist class" (Sklair, 2003) amidst this global diversity. Rather, the preceding analysis suggests that the disaggregation and re-aggregation of corporate connections reflects a systemic logic that accommodates the appearance of contradictory patterns. Efficiency and opportunity drive the search for new network relations. Control is however the imperative driving the micromanagement of "corporatized" organizations – as it is in authoritarian states – but evident too is the enduring drive to circumvent national and international rules. A further example, TNCs are moving away from direct ownership of offshore operations towards alliances with in-country partners and increasingly to non-equity relationships with suppliers. These non-equity relationships or "modes" give greater flexibility to transnationals to select production locations and shift assets across geographical space in pursuit of greatest investment returns – without protracted stakeholder negotiations (Dicken, 2011; UNCTAD, 2011, pp. 160–161).

The largest corporations seek to transcend states, and yet states remain critical to the exercise of corporate power. Global economic history exposes patterns of competition between capital and state alliances in the formation and interpretation of global trade rules. As Europe laid the foundations of its single market in the 1990s, US-based tropical food companies Chiquita, Del Monte and Dole successfully lobbied for an end to Europe's preferential treatment of agricultural imports from former European colonies in the Caribbean and Africa under the Lomé Convention. The Convention, introduced in 1973 by the then European Community, exemplified the interventionist social market orientation of European economic policy. The US and the governments of Latin American "banana republics," in which US tropical fruit companies were major investors, argued successfully that the Lomé "banana protocol" breached the General Agreement on Tariffs and Trade (GATT)/World Trade organization (WTO) rules because it, and the Convention in general, inhibited global free trade, a victory which translated into a significant loss of market share and opportunity for smallholder producers in African and Caribbean countries, but not for Del Monte and Dole which, tellingly, and cynically, were also investors in African banana producing countries which benefitted from the scheme (Myers, 2004). As with environmental protections discussed in Chapter 2, social and economic development partnerships, created promote a measure of economic justice, can perversely be subject to adverse interpretation and be deemed as unlawful under international trade law.

The competitive imperative

As with the rise of the networked state, the emergence of networked corporate entity signals changes in the ways in which power is exercised in the global system. Concentration of influence and control through mergers and acquisitions are a feature of the resources sector where the costs of resource extraction have escalated as new unconventional and marginal energy mineral deposits are "recovered" from more technically and financially challenging locations – as with deep-water offshore exploration and drilling and onshore shale oil and gas (UNCTAD, 2012b; Loder, 2013; Price Waterhouse Coopers, 2013; Rigzone, 2013). That global vertical integration in oil and gas might lead to a reduction in energy costs over the long term, as foreshadowed by many resource economists, challenges Smithian assumptions about the inevitable drift towards monopolistic practices in industries dominated by an increasingly narrow group of interests. Indeed, Smith assumed that the "natural" tendency of "merchants and manufacturers" was to seek monopolistic rents (Smith, 1790, p. 705). The global price of oil is, however, set not by state intervention but by global market dynamics. Here is the conundrum of the global oil price, which, despite lower production costs among Middle Eastern, African and Asian oil exporting countries, tracks the price of Brent Crude and West Texas Intermediate Crude, set by the world's highest cost oil producers, and not by the restriction of supply relative to global demand by the Organization of Petroleum Exporting Countries (OPEC) (Bina, 2013, p. 127; EIA, 2013). The much vaunted "shale oil revolution" could, if anything, enhance the price advantage of US oil and gas, and potentially lower prices in the medium term, but unconventional "tight" oil and gas reserves are costly to exploit and are rapidly depleted. The logical upshot of these pressures is the pursuit of ever-tighter, more technologically demanding and costlier reserves, and greater concentrations of capital to meet these costs, with all the attendant environmental risks that on past experience this will necessarily entail.

So we have evident patterns of increasing depth and variability in global economic interconnections parallel to significant power concentrations. Power matters in the contemporary global economy, and economic or market power is both structural and relational. There are many dangers or risks in this new hypersensitive global system that are systemic in nature. Not least is the growing appetite among the "super rich" for wealth inequality and their alarming detachment from and disinterest in the lives, aspirations and expectations of the vast majority of the world's population (Freeland, 2012). Global policymakers assert that rates of poverty are declining globally, but the gulf is still widening between those at the top of the global wealth pyramid and those at the bottom. It is also the case, counting from the 1980s to the present day, that the actual numbers of people living in near and absolute poverty, as measured by the World Bank, have remained static at around two billion (WDI, 2012, p. 71). The very urgency with which poverty and inequality became the primary policy concern for global policy elites at the UN and the World Bank in the 1990s reflects deep misgivings as to the consequences of severe economic imbalances for global political stability in key world regions, and the legitimacy of the liberal global system (Sklair, 2002, pp. 51–55). Despite significant gains in meeting human quality of life targets set by the UN's Millennium Development Goals (MDGs), inequality, it seems, is emerging as the greater political challenge worldwide (Ferguson, 2012; Freeland, 2012). Historically, countries and corporate entities have not climbed up the ladder of development through playing by anything like the competition rules set by today's global technocratic elites.

Conservative historian Niall Fergusson lays much of the blame for the Global Financial Crisis (GFC) at the feet of governments and their poor record of financial market regulation (Ferguson, 2012). For capitalism's supporters, like Hernando De Soto, corruption, oppression and inefficient regulation – not capitalism *per se* – are fundamentally responsible for the impoverishment of peoples (De Soto, 2001, p.194). Once celebrated for underpinning the rise of Asia in the late twentieth century, the "Asian Way" became the subject of derision following the 1997 Asian Financial Crisis. A decade later in the world's largest and arguably most competitive economy, with advanced economic governance processes and a democratic system of government, a real estate scam involving some of the world's most well-known and trusted financial institutions brought the global economy to the brink of collapse. Writing after the 1997 Asian Financial Crisis, when international anti-corruption rhetoric reached a crescendo, Francois Godement dared to remind us that moral compromise was once an acceptable price for Western investors seeking a share of Southeast Asia's economic boom (Godement, 1999, pp. 55–56, 132).

Explanations for catastrophes all too readily point to individual error, governmental weaknesses or to rogue "bad apples." Scapegoating hides or denies our limited capacity to predict the future, a reality highlighted repeatedly by periodic financial crises which, when they strike, threaten to severely undermine the stability of the global system. Securitization in financial markets is meant to spread risk and offer greater surety to investors and yet these markets, or, more to the point, those who trade in mortgage-backed securities, fail to adequately price risk – as far as risk can be priced given that the future is unknowable. Sophisticated risk mitigation strategies give the sense that deft management can pre-empt all possible negative eventualities. But while routine predictions of market movements can be framed within "normal" parameters or "tolerable" bandwidths of variability, the likelihood of exceptional occurrences sparking financial chaos is regularly underestimated – often because important variables are ignored or simply not "known" – including the potential impact of irrational or fraudulent dealings by highly educated, influential and normally law-abiding finance professionals (Haldane and Alessandri, 2009).

Destabilized exchange rates and depressed economies are among many damaging impacts of financial crimes according to the Financial Action Task Force (IMF, 2011a, p. 67). Yet, the underregulated but legal global trade in high-risk mortgage-backed securities or derivatives, traded by legal financial actors, led to a global financial crisis that caused bank asset devaluations totalling US$4 trillion by early 2009 – roughly equal to the earlier stated annual value of global money laundering (IMF, 2011b, p. 70). The GFC and Eurozone crisis were caused not by conventional transnational criminals but by "respectable" global risk managers, behaving with criminal irresponsibility. Asset inflation and the inadequate pricing of risk for certain derivatives based upon US "subprime" mortgage-backed securities were the result of chains of human decisions, guided by financial self-interest, not impersonal market forces or any single person or institution.

The securitization of finance brings informal economies under the scrutiny of global regulators. From Chinese *guangxi* to South Asian *havala* networks, these informal remittance systems are being slowly criminalized to render the global financial system more transparent and calculable and, therefore, more governable (IMF, 2011b, x). The global Anti-Money Laundering/Transnational Crime and Terror Finance regime is driven principally by the urgency of the so-called "War on Terror" with the justification that opportunities for circulation of criminal funds and terror finance have to be curtailed. The US Patriot Act requires all banks with US operations to keep records of all customers and all financial transactions, including records of customers/clients that benefit from correspondent account transactions in the US – whether they are US residents/citizens or not even domiciled in the US (DoT, 2011). Yet, hypercompetition, and the stratospheric wealth gains open to those who play the system to greatest effect, engenders the deliberate and systematic avoidance of regulatory scrutiny and financial obligations, alluded to in Chapter 1.

Informal or "shadow" banking constitutes a major investment pool in China, estimated to be worth US$3.2 trillion in 2012 (Rabinovich, 2013). Yet, while informal and illicit financial "freedoms" are increasingly circumscribed as governments seek to foreclose alternatives and further *informationalize* global finance through tax data sharing, secrecy is still permitted for approved legal persons seeking to avoid tax obligations. Tax "planning" for tax avoidance is widespread and, according to senior political leaders and bureaucrats in the UK, the US and Australia legitimate – but the distinction between avoidance and evasion is highly nuanced (Murphy, 2011, p. 21). Concern among G20 countries over the profit-shifting activities of global technology companies like Google and Apple is driven in large part by concerns over falling government revenues, not by any genuine wish to end tax havens once and for all (OECD, 2013; Rawnsley, 2013). Technology companies minimize tax in one jurisdiction by charging local affiliates royalties on the intellectual property bound up in technology software and hardware. This is akin to *transfer pricing*, another transnational business practice that can be legal and illegal depending upon the degree of price variability and tax reduction achieved. Simply, goods manufactured for export in Country A are sold to a parent or affiliate company in Country B at a vastly reduced price thereby minimizing tax paid in Country A. This is a routine business activity, which is only rendered illegal where the transfer price is "fixed" at a point lower than the market value of the traded good. Where this affects the tax revenues of small countries struggling with high debts and desperate for finance to build schools and hospitals or roads and railways the consequences for human security can be far-reaching. "Poor governance" is regarded as a primary cause of collapsing governmental authority in "fragile" and "failing" states, but transnational tax evasion imposes costs upon heavily indebted countries in particular by eroding state income, and thus denuding poor states of vital means with which to build a viable social base (Christian Aid, 2009; Lawrence, 2009; Tax Justice Network, 2011).

Regulation avoidance by otherwise lawful persons and entities is not purely a matter of evading governmental financial oversight but also a form of financial risk minimization. Light-footedness and evasiveness is evident in practices designed to circumvent labour standards and environmental regulations by investing in countries with limited regulatory capacity. This was again brought to light in 2013 with the entirely avoidable deaths of 114 female textile factory workers in Bangladesh's capital, Dhaka, an industry integral to global supply chains for major retailers and fashion brands. The tragedy and travesty is underscored by the fact that this was not an isolated case in Bangladesh's textiles industry (Burke, 2013; *SMH*, December 22, 2013). Foreign investors escape the legal consequences of these human tragedies because of the complex ways in which global capital is compartmentalized, and shareholder interests firewalled against litigation. Bangladesh textiles producers contract to supply global retailers who hold no equity in any factory enterprise, which means all financial risk is borne by the contractor. As said, this arrangement is one of the appeals of increasingly popular non-equity finance relationships between global companies and local affiliates. Legal differentiation between parent companies and foreign affiliates works according to a similar logic but with affiliates, and their investors, which usually include some parent company shareholders, bearing local legal liability.

Global companies advocate for global trade rules but not for global legal jurisdiction with the attendant risks of a sovereign international humanitarian law. The Union Carbide Company (UCC) deftly exploited jurisdictional anomalies to minimize shareholder liability for the Bhopal catastrophe, in which as many as 8,000 people were killed directly by a toxic cloud of methyl isocyanate that leaked from its Indian subsidiary's chemical pesticide factory in December 1984. UCC argued successfully that Union Carbide India, in which UCC held a 50.9 per cent stake, bore primary responsibility for the disaster and that litigation should be channelled through India's legal system and not through US courts (ICFTU-ICEF, 1985). UCC then agreed to a very favourable and "grossly inadequate" US$470 million out-of-court compensation settlement (Lakhani, 2009). With people still reportedly dying from the toxic effects of the leak, Dow Chemicals, which acquired UCC in 2001, rejects any legal responsibility for allegedly substantial intergenerational consequences of UCC's past actions (ICFTU-ICEF, 1985; Lakhani, 2009). National jurisdictions create a convenient global chequerboard or chessboard upon which only the deft and the well-resourced have any chance of winning – "on balance."

The celebrated "Trafigura Case" has become emblematic of the worst abuses of maritime and environmental law by European shipping and trading companies in Africa. Trafigura Beheer, a London-based commodity trader from the Netherlands, disposed of 530 tons of poisonous sludge from the Panamanian-flagged *Probo Koala*, under lease to Trafigura, at waste dumps around Abidjan, the former capital of Côte d'Ivoire, in August 2006. The waste contaminated groundwater water supplies used by communities living close to the dump sites resulting in at least 16 deaths and the severe poisoning of another 105,000 people – a statistic likely to increase over time given the incapacity of city authorities to decontaminate polluted areas. The *Probo Koala* had sought to discharge the waste at the port of Amsterdam, but Trafigura, having first attempted to offload without informing port authorities of the waste's hazardous nature, refused to pay the cost of decontamination when caught. Instead, Trafigura deliberately sought out a port where disposal costs would be much cheaper. In this instance, however, litigation was initiated successfully through British and Dutch courts and the company found financially liable for both the environmental and human impacts, although for only a fraction of the actual harm done (White, 2008, pp. 118–119; Monbiot, 2009; Cox, 2010, pp. 273–275; Leigh, 2010).

The limitation of legal liability is a risk mitigation strategy employed by all private entities across all business sectors. All forms of economic endeavour, be they capitalist or socialist, entail acceptance or tolerance of a large degree and range of risk, provided this risk is widely distributed – or socialized – and legal liability either *individuated* as much as possible or eliminated altogether. Intergovernmental efforts to create a new regulatory framework to govern financial risk struggle against this imperative, while banking representatives strive to assert it. Loose local and international lending practices are regarded as one of the main contributors to the GFC. To guard against a repeat chain reaction of exposed bad debts creating a fresh global liquidity crisis, the Bank of International Settlements (BIS), through the Basel Committee on Banking Supervision (BCBS), proposed higher asset ratios to encourage "micro-prudential" behaviours conducive to "transparency" and global financial stability under a new Basel III accord (BCBS, 2011, p. 2). Arguments against stricter capital base requirements from within the global banking industry claim restrictions on lending practices impede growth and are counter-productive. The Organisation for Economic Co-operation and

Development's (OECD) Patrick Slovik asserts that stricter oversight only serves to "increase the incentives of banks to bypass the regulatory framework" (Slovik, 2012, p. 10). Lobbying by industry leaders succeeded in softening the impact of Basel III while, lending weight to Slovik's analysis, there is a significant increase in "off-exchange" share trades through anonymous "dark pools" (Cave, 2013; Poljak, 2013). "Micro-imprudent" and clandestine trading practices have returned at Goldman Sachs through its Multi Strategy Investing Group (Abelson, 2013). Clearly, "systemically significant" interests are gaming the system to maximize returns on capital invested, regardless of the risks, or at least where risk is defrayed and thus calculated out of consideration. The question of whether or not this gaming is justifiable or unconscionable is a debatable matter perhaps. But the "downside" risks of this behaviour represent major threats to political order and the rule of law in those countries most severely damaged and least able to bear the impacts of economic crisis.

Human capacities for collective irrationality and individual criminality, writ large in each successive financial crisis of recent decades, persist as threats to global financial stability but this capacity is shared among policymakers and the assemblages of financial market actors that comprise the global financial community (Shiller, 2000). Globalization, especially FDG, entails the unrelenting increase in the number of economic transactions and decisions necessary to keep the global system running. Hence, logically, this witnesses a parallel increase in the potential for illegal actions – from simple inadvertent rule infringements to deliberate law breaking. But the highly complex methods by which global business is transacted place much corporate behaviour substantially beyond the purview of state regulatory authorities. Cases brought by the US Department of Justice (DoJ) against major global banks for violations of US sanctions against Iran, HSBC in 2012 being the most high profile, and for criminal fraud concerning the manipulation of interbank lending rates by Barclays Bank, also in 2012, highlight a growing appetite for stricter corporate regulation by governments and the general public. However, global capital markets have become nationally ungovernable pillars of a financially interdependent global economy, and global financiers seem determined and "hell bent" on gambling vast sums far from public scrutiny.

High-frequency risk

The US Senate's Permanent Subcommittee of Investigation's inquiry into London-based HSBC revealed a litany of regulatory failings internal to the bank, leading to the charge of complicity with money laundering and violation of US sanctions against Iran. Importantly, these were not the actions of a few "rogue" bank employees but systemic failings attributable to decisions taken at the highest levels of HSBC Group management (US Senate, 2012). While falling short of accusing the Group, and its US affiliate HSBC US (HBUS), of complicity in terrorism by materially aiding the circulation of "terror finance," the implications of the Subcommittee's findings could have led in this direction. Strict anti-money laundering provisions were enacted under the umbrella of the Patriot Act (2002) to block financial transactions that directly or indirectly benefit "prohibited persons and countries," that is, individuals and countries designated as threats to US security by virtue of their known or suspected connections to named terrorist groups listed in Executive Order 13224. In addition to al-Qaeda and its financiers, as discussed in the previous chapter, anti money-laundering measures were also targeted at Iran. Whether or not the targeting of Iran is justified, or the securitization of finance the most effective way to address terrorism, US security strategy, and by implication international efforts to promote global security through the UN and the global financial system, was undermined by corporate entities aggressively and unlawfully pursuing their commercial self-interest.

The Senate inquiry was unequivocal in its condemnation of HBUS and HSBC for gross and "systematic" concealment, or criminal fraud, on a global scale (US Senate, 2012, pp. 5, 113; DoT OFAC, n/d). Taking the definition of transnational organized crime advanced in the UN Convention against Transnational Organized Crime (CTOC) Convention, suspect HSBC transactions were "transnational" in scope, "organized" to the extent that they involved more than one bank employee, and judged "criminal" under US law. The scale of criminality is found in not only the value but also the sheer volume of suspect dealings. Federal investigators forensically uncovered some 25,000 *unreported* (emphasis added) transactions that were, in some way, connected to Iran. Valued at US$19.4 billion, these dealings occurred over a five-year time period from 2002 to 2007, and, because of the persons and entities involved, were potentially "transactions of interest," that is, of potential interest to criminal investigators (US Senate, 2012, pp. 5–6, 113–114). "Negligence" also resulted in US$881 million in "drug money" being laundered through the US from HSBC Mexico to the benefit of Mexican and Columbian drug traffickers. Compliance violations extended to transactions that also violated US sanctions against Sudan, Burma and Libya, and violations of the Trading with the Enemy Act through banking transactions with clients in Cuba (*USA v. HSBC and HBUS*, Case 1:12, cr763, 1–3, 2012). Crucially, under US corporate law, the definition of "knowing" involvement in financial fraud, and hence criminal culpability, is very broad, and ignorance or negligence is no defence. Whether or not HSBC and HBUS executives did or did not know of these transgressions, the point is there is a reasonable expectation that they should have known.

Central to investigations was the management of "correspondent" banking services. Correspondent accounts are local accounts opened on behalf of foreign affiliates and other institutions to facilitate bulk finance transfers in foreign and US currency. The potential for these transactions to be used for illicit transfers makes correspondent accounts of particular interest to US regulators and, yet, HSBC affiliates in the US, Europe and Middle East were found to have deliberately masked the identities of "persons of interest" by moving funds "automatically" through HBUS transaction accounting systems – a virtual spin cycle analogous to and suggestive of laundering. Communication and transaction monitoring settings on DoJ filters were reset to screen out what were thought to be low-risk transfers, although HBUS was evidently ill equipped to judge the nature or level of national security risk to which it was exposed and to which it exposed US citizens (*USA v. HSBC and HBUS*, Case 1:12, cr763, 3, 2012).

At HSBC suspicious offshore transactions were routinely overlooked and valuable clients appeased. HBUS was found to have ignored regular large volume conversions of US dollar travellers' checks by the Hokuriku Bank in Japan on behalf of Russian customers through the accounts of Japanese clients of questionable authenticity (Levin, 2012; US Senate, 2012, p. 7). The Group's management of its relationship with the Saudi Arabian Al Rajhi Bank further exemplifies the commercial incentives and pressures to sidestep legal obligation and broader social and national security responsibilities. Correspondent banking services for Al Rajhi were suspended in 2005 because its founder and some family members were linked by the CIA to the proscribed al-Haramain Foundation and Islamic Relief Organization, both Islamic NGOs suspected of being financial conduits for al-Qaeda. Regardless of the accuracy of CIA intelligence, HSBC decision-makers either did not appreciate the significance of the alleged link or else judged US national security a second-order issue. When the Al Rajhi Bank's Saudi owners threatened to close their account altogether unless allowed to once again trade in US currency, commercial considerations outweighed legal obligations and HSBC bowed to client demand, even though this implicated the Group in dealings that might be construed as "trading with the enemy" (Levin, 2012; US Senate, 2012, p. 210).

Global security risk and US law were insufficient disincentives for this major global institution to establish and maintain strict prudential oversight of its banking interests in the new lucrative world of Islamic finance. Evidently, senior decision-makers considered the risks of investigation, and no doubt the risks to US national security, to be outweighed by potential commercial gains. Instructively, this is not an isolated case. The Investigator's Report detailed a track record of sanctions and Banking Act violations involving Credit Suisse, Lloyd's Bank, ABN Amro and ING Bank. Senior decision-makers in many of the world's major banks either deliberately ignored, or, by virtue of their disinterest, or contempt, encouraged violations of US law, for the sake, it would seem, if we take HSBC actions as a guide, of maximizing their customer base (US Senate, 2012, pp.5–6, 118). When considered alongside the efforts undertaken to deceive regulators and evade scrutiny, negligence appears to be a very weak and forgiving term with which to characterize HSBC's global practices.

This case cannot be attributed to poorly conceived regulation, and the deficiencies exposed can be interpreted as further evidence of an alarmingly cavalier business culture within large and outwardly prudential banking corporations. The value of laundered funds circulating through HSBC affiliates was never formally quantified but the sheer volume and value of suspect transactions suggests that the amount was substantial (Levin, 2012). HSBC Holdings and HBUS accepted criminally liability, yet, penalties incurred amounted to a mere US$1.26 billion "forfeited" to the US DoJ, with an additional US$665 million in fines for various civil offences (DoJ, 2012a). Perhaps, given the scale and complexity of global banking, discrepancies are to be expected as an inevitable and even tolerable "margin of error." The number of persons named on the US Office of Foreign Assets Control (OFAC)-prohibited list equates to a miniscule fraction of the HSBC's 89-million-person global customer base (2011), and the total value of suspect transactions a drop in the ocean when compared to HSBC's global assets, valued at US$2.5 trillion (2011). Anyone can make a mistake!

Given the scope of operations, the fact that HSBC affiliates were demonstrably understaffed points to a pivotal dysfunction that opens a window on to more fundamental flaws in the global system. The incessant drive for cost minimization invites the prioritization of efficiency and profitability over broader social and political considerations, and precipitates unlawful behaviour, be this deliberate or the consequence of human indecision or error. In the worst cases, these pressures culminate in gross fraud or human, industrial and environmental catastrophe.

Responsibility and profitability need not be mutually exclusive ends, but frequently – too frequently – they are manifestly so in practice, even where eloquent company codes and prudential checklists suggest otherwise.

The behaviour of HSBC and others fell within the purview of US homeland security because money laundering is signalled as a national security threat in the dominant transnational organized crime–terror narrative. Yet, the potential global harm inflicted by financial market failures, measured against the GFC, is of a much greater order of magnitude. Moreover, as said, such failures are caused not by criminal or terrorist entities but, to labour the point, otherwise law-abiding bank employees exploiting irresistible opportunities to manufacture yield for their employers and shareholders – and themselves. In global capital markets valued at over US$1,000 trillion in 2011 (including market capitalization, bond and share trading, and derivatives trading), interest rate movements of a fraction of one per cent up or down can either gain or cost a trader and institution potentially billions of dollars (Accenture, 2012, p. 3). Wilful and extensive manipulation of indicators critical to the calculation of financial risk in the global economy came to light during US DoJ investigations into rate-setting practices at Barclays Bank (DoJ, 2012b). The London Interbank Offered Rate (LIBOR) and the European equivalent, Euro Interbank Offered Rate (EURIBOR), are calculated daily, at a set time, and determine the interest rate payable at the settlement of derivatives and currency swap contracts in the world's major financial centres. These contracts are slices of time covering trades spanning a matter of hours to one-year agreements involving multiple parties ranging from central banks to commercial traders and private investors. Panels of leading commercial banks submit daily individual estimates of the cost of interbank borrowing, which are then used to calculate an average interest rate, which becomes the global "benchmark rate" for derivatives markets and an authoritative indicator of rates for "systemically significant" retail banking services. The British Banker's Association (BBA) has traditionally set LIBOR, but because this rate also affects other global currencies, including the US dollar, sterling and Japanese yen, and because British-based global banks like Barclays operate in multiple jurisdictions, LIBOR and BBA members are subject to regulatory oversight in the US and elsewhere (CTCT, 2012; DoJ, 2012c). But it is in the US where regulatory interventionism is at its most vigorous (Garrett, 2011).

The rate-setting process is, however, described within the banking industry as a "fix" because arbitrary parameters are applied to calculate of the final rate, "rounded" to fractions of a decimal point. To guard this hair-trigger setting, impartial arm's-length management and trading practices are essential. "Submitters" must be institutionally separate from and must not communicate with or give consideration to the professional self-interest of derivatives and currency traders working in the same bank. Further, there should be no collusion between BBA Panel members or with other banks to set favourable rates. Quoted email communications between Barclays' "submitters" and traders give insight into the expressed state of mind of persons under enormous pressure to secure stellar investment returns from booming (and then crashing) derivatives and currency markets. Colloquialisms such as getting "killed" or "I'm a dead man" are figures of speech that capture the daily normality of high stress, which in turn reflect upon the stakes involved in currency dealing (DoJ, 2012c, pp. 6, 11). Light was also shed upon the dynamics surrounding the representation of interbank rates, especially the implications of estimates for market impressions of bank commercial viability (DoJ, 2012c, pp. 10–13). Barclays admitted that "certain members of management" urged submission of "improperly lower" US dollar rates to give an inflated impression of solvency at the outset of the GFC. The play, designed to silence media speculation, was a deliberate strategy to manage reputational risk at a critical time for the bank and the entire global financial system (DoJ, 2012c, pp. 15–18).

The actions undertaken in the name of, and therefore legally by Barclays Bank, were clearly fraudulent but the DoJ pulled its punches. "Dirty" rate fixing within Barclays and by Barclays in collusion with other banks also arguably violated "conspiracy," "restraint of trade" and "monopoly" clauses in the Sherman Antitrust Act (USC, Title 15, Ch. 1.1; Henning, 2012). The DoJ findings, accepted by Barclays Bank, detail misdemeanours including "deceptive conduct" and "false and misleading" submissions, and can be interpreted conveniently as just the behaviour of some "rotten fruit," or they can be read as a systemic weakness in the private administration of global capitalism. At an individual level, people, be they bank employees or mining engineers, are expected to dissociate themselves from their immediate personal financial concerns, and the "organic social whole" of their corporation, to serve the abstract and remote end of systemic integrity. While adherence to codes of professional conduct is essential to routine system maintenance, individual decisions under pressure do not conform to the ideal of uniform human rationality. Notably, however, investigations into Barclays covered a period that spanned the immediate pre- and post-GFC years, and while decisions taken during 2007 and after can be understood as the actions of responsible people working under enormous pressure to preserve their company and their careers, pre-2007 dirty fixes are symptomatic of a different set of human impulses. On an organizational level, as with BP and *Deepwater Horizon*, this was not Barclays Bank's first and only "offence" under US law. The company was found guilty and fined US$298 million in 2010 for sanctions violations (Clark, 2010). Nor were criminal charges and penalties confined to the US. In the UK, Barclays and its coconspirator UBS accepted fines for fraudulent rate fixing. Criminalization, rationalizations of process and automation are the means by which governments propose to minimize future rate fraud, which only means that the next major financial crisis will likely be triggered from some other corner of the global system – perhaps in those secret spaces where regulators cannot peer.

Limited liabilities

The threat of criminal proceedings to an extent mitigates the risk of corporate crime, but there is a limit to the appetite for corporate law enforcement, even in the US (Henning, 2012; Smallberg, 2013). For Barclays, HSBC and others, criminal penalties in the US were either diminished or converted to civil fines in return for cooperation and contrition. There is an apparent overriding concern not to antagonize potential major investors with increased litigation risk or deter US overseas investment by widening the extraterritorial reach and scope of US law (Garrett, 2011, p. 1783). This inclination became transparent in 2013 with the US Supreme Court's rejection of an Alien Torts case brought by the Ogoni people of the Niger Delta against Royal Dutch Petroleum, or Shell as the company is commonly known. The Alien Torts Statute is actually a section of the Judiciary Act of 1789 that grants US district courts power to hear cases on criminal matters concerning acts "committed within their respective districts, or upon the high seas" and to grant "alien" persons the right to pursue a civil law suit for "violation of the law of nations or a treaty of the United States" (*Annals of Congress*, 1789, pp. 2242–2243; USC Title 28, Pt. IV, Ch. 85, 1350). The expansive interpretation of this law permits cases to be heard on treaty violations by US juristic persons committed outside the US in foreign sovereign jurisdictions. The narrower view, confirmed by the Supreme Court in *Kiobel v. Royal Dutch Petroleum*, is that district courts do not, and should not, have the legal competence to apply US laws extraterritorially, and that the Statute was never meant to be applied to all cases of crime and treaty violations anywhere (569 US, 2013, pp. 1–3).

As discussed, there are many legal, political and systemic threads to the issue of corporate responsibility for, and complicity in, unlawful acts that occasion harm, financial, physical and environmental. Disputes over resources rights, including both above- and below-ground resources, have major political ramifications in developing states, especially where government legitimacy is weak or land ownership laws are ambiguous or non-existent. Court cases brought in the US against multinational corporations for alleged violations on international and US law foreground the fine line that many companies (and their employees) tread between the protection of corporate interests and "self-regulation" with regard to their normative and legal obligations. Resources companies are exposed to extreme financial and legal risk because many operations depend on access to contested territory, which necessitates cooperation with national governments, whatever the methods used by state security forces to "secure" governmental control and public acquiescence. Alien Torts claims concerning the resources companies Rio Tinto in Papua New Guinea, Unocal in Burma, Exxon-Mobil in Indonesia and Shell in Nigeria illustrate not just the repugnance of some corporate practices to international humanitarian law but also the ethical limits of corporate responsibility. To put it another way, the scope for ethical and lawful practice is constrained the closer corporations operate to the frontiers of globalization.

Compliance with the requirements of local governmental and business practices is a matter of necessity for resources companies. Dependence upon local authorities to smooth legal processes necessary to gain access to minerals and for protection of assets entails uncomfortable and potentially damaging compromises. The case of Bougainville Copper in the now autonomous PNG province of Bougainville is instructive. Bougainville Copper Limited (BCL), a subsidiary of Conzinc Rio Tinto Australia (CRA), now Rio Tinto, began working copper deposits at Panguna on the island of Bougainville in the 1970s creating a local "boomtown" economy and society common in areas of rapid and lucrative mining development. Local objections to the environmental and social impacts of the mine added to the sense of grievance on the part of local landowners who claimed they were not satisfactorily compensated for the use of their land by BCL, legal though this appropriation was under PNG law. Such objections and grievances are common enough in mining and other resource industries but when combined with radicalized secessionist sentiment, as was the case on Bougainville in the 1980s, the consequences can be far-reaching. A civil war burst open long-standing social divisions on Bougainville between 1988 and 1997, and only concluded when agreement was reached to move the island towards full independence from PNG – an agreement that has yet to be honoured (McIntosh, 1990, pp. 18–22; Regan, 2010, pp. 12–24).

Bougainville Island residents in 2002 filed the first of four Alien Torts cases against Rio Tinto in *Sarai v. Rio Tinto PLC*, for complicity in "genocide, war crimes and crimes against humanity" allegedly perpetrated by Papua New Guinea soldiers during the Bougainville conflict (*Sarei v. Rio Tinto*, 2011). A common feature of "virtue-less" corporate–state–society relations in areas of extreme societal tension, the PNG government used troops to guard BCL-CRA assets at Panguna against the real threat of destruction by the Bougainville Revolutionary Army (BRA). "Protection" quickly escalated into "counterinsurgency" that inflamed anti-state and anti-company sentiment amongst the local population and precipitated a cycle of violence in which crimes were perpetrated by both the Papua New Guinea Defence Forces and BRA (O'Callaghan, 2002, pp. 9–10). Litigation is only one of the more visible legacies of the human traumas caused by the conflict. Damage to surrounding ecosystems arising from the leaching of toxic waste from mine tailings, during the period of operation (1972–1989) and as a result of neglect over the next 24 years, are, by all accounts (save those of Rio Tinto), substantial (Pain 2007, p. 256). The Sarei case was drawn out over a decade, as often happens with Alien Torts suits, and international crimes allegations were eventually withdrawn, leaving only environmental damages claims outstanding. "Lawfare" is the norm in the mining industry where the size of returns on an investment can hinge upon securing and defending title claims over rich mineral deposits against competitors, and/or fending off contractual claims by disappointed venture partners. As with compliance battles against government taxes and regulations, "title fights" are just another area of routine litigation that requires deft legal handling. Thus, while US torts cases and the like add to the legal burdens of corporate operations, they are, despite their high public profile, marginal if irritating distractions – until, that is, the risk of an adverse judicial finding increases.

Bougainville is an extreme exemplar of investment and human security risk, but there are many potentially destructive land and environmental disputes involving mining companies, both in developed and in developing countries. It is not as if there is any shortage of advice and guidance on how to proceed with investments in circumstances of high risk, financial and human. The *OECD Guidelines for Multinational Companies*, first issued in the 1970s, sets out a template for prudential governance of international business activities. The pre-2011 versions of these Guidelines were, however, reticent on the issue of human rights, specifying merely the importance of "trust" and the need to "respect the human rights of those affected by their activities," shortcomings identified by the UK Joint Committee on Human Rights (OECD, 2008, p. 14; UK JCHR, 2010). The OECD's Investment Committee furnished the global corporate sector with "risk awareness" tools for operations in "weak governance zones," which it defines as countries where governments "cannot or will not" govern according to their sovereign obligations (OECD, 2006, p. 11). Movement towards recognition of non-commercial responsibilities was also under way in some of the world's largest and, because of the nature of their core business, most invasive corporations.

Undoubtedly motivated by its experiences in Bougainville, Rio Tinto published its *Human Rights Guidance* as a supplement to its corporate code to stress the human rights obligations of the company and its employees (Rio Tinto, 2003). As is the nature of such "guidelines," responsibilities to "consult," "respect," "acknowledge," "protect" and "know" are stressed repeatedly in relation to "local cultures," "indigenous rights" and "local peoples." These responsibilities are balanced against the Company's "limited ability to influence" (Rio Tinto, 2003, p. 3). Despite the extensive evidence of and much propaganda about corporate power over developing country governments, the global reality is that in the intense competition for precious mineral resources, tolerance levels for state crimes are necessarily flexible. There is an uncomfortable "bite point" between good intentions and operational realities with which all resources corporations struggle. Simply, if one company makes too many demands upon a government, well, there are many more competitors only too willing to take its place. For these reasons, resources corporations, in particular, are keen to narrow the scope of the legal definition of complicity so as to evade accusations of guilt by implication and association.

A case can be made for private companies to be considered part of any "security assemblage" beyond those private security actors attached to military operations and their actions made subject to greater public scrutiny. Corporations seek security or control over their strategic assets – property, resources and supply lines, especially pipelines – to ensure operational viability and minimize shareholder exposure to loss (Rio Tinto, 2003). Given the value of capital risked in an overseas mining venture, it is understandable that mining corporations will seek to minimize risk by cooperating with the government of the country in which they operate – at all levels. Corporate entities in "frontier" areas thereby stray close to the edge of legal tolerances. Subsidizing paramilitary security guards to protect oil and gas pipelines in Latin America, Africa and Asia, for example, directly implicates a company in the actions of these paramilitary forces, even if the company exerts no direct control over them. Resources company employees are thus often placed in an invidious position. Operational and company imperatives can lead key decision-makers into unlawful territory and force uncomfortable choices upon individuals often ill-equipped to make ethical decisions under pressure in "far away" places, with no clear knowledge of local conditions or of how their actions appear when viewed through the lens of international criminal law. Inexperience does not, however, explain senior management behaviour in countries with which companies are very familiar by virtue of long-term investments and close relationships to local political elites.

"Successful" Torts cases can only result in civil penalties and not criminal conviction for violations of international criminal law. In 2009, Shell paid US$15.5 million to Nigerian plaintiffs to mitigate claims lodged for Shell's alleged complicity in the execution of Nigerian rights campaigner and writer Ken Saro-Wiwa by the Nigerian military government of Sony Abacha in 1995. This was an out-of-court settlement that reflected a "compromise" between Shell and the plaintiffs, which included the son of Ken Saro-Wiwa, one of the nine leaders of the Ogoni people's campaign against oil operations in the southeastern Niger Delta province of Ogoniland (Statement of Agreement, *Wiwa v. Shell*, 2009; *Wiwa v. Anderson*, 2009). The Ogoni people's struggle against the Nigerian state and foreign oil companies sprung from justifiable economic and environmental grievances relating to the benefits and impacts of oil exploration. Inevitably, given the nature of Nigeria's kleptocratic military leaders in the closing decades of the twentieth century, the Delta's indigenous peoples did not receive nor were they offered a share of oil returns, while drilling and exploration left pollution trails across the region, with Ogoniland one of the worst affected (Campbell, 2011; UNEP, 2011, pp. 24–26). Saro-Wiwa and his compatriots were denied procedural justice and executed for allegedly "inciting" the murder of four political opponents. It is maintained by the families of those unlawfully killed that Shell was complicit in the deaths by virtue of its lobbying the Abacha government, against which there ranged a host of allegations of human rights abuses that were perpetrated by the military against the peoples of the Niger Delta, which gave rise to the southern "oil insurgency," in which Shell and other oil companies were materially implicated.

The Delta region was at the time on the cusp of a fresh oil investment boom, and the Ogoni people presented an obstacle to potentially spectacular returns on investment for oil companies and the Nigerian state. In the context of regular lobbying of government ministers, which is the norm for oil companies with extensive vested interests to protect, there is every reason to assume that frustrations with Saro-Wiwa's Movement for the Survival of the Ogoni People were aired by foreign oil interests. There is also every reason to assume that the Abacha government required no foreign advice or prompting in its determination to break the movement. Shell is on record as having pleaded directly with Abacha for clemency for all charged (Shell, n/d). Under an expansive interpretation of complicity in criminal law, however, any adverse intimation that might influence the decision-making processes of the perpetrator/s of a crime can potentially be construed as collusion. Accordingly, the plaintiffs' deposition asserted full, that is knowing, complicity by Shell in crimes perpetrated against the Ogoni and the killing of Saro-Wiwa. It was alleged that

> [t]he executions of Ken Saro-Wiwa, John Kpunia, Saturday Doobee, Felix Nuate, Daniel Gbokoo, and Dr. Barinam Kiobel and the imprisonment and torture of Michael Tema Vizor by the Nigerian Military junta and the campaign to falsely accuse them were carried out with the knowledge, consent, and/or support of Defendant Brian Anderson, then Managing Director of the Nigerian subsidiary of Royal Dutch Petroleum Company and Shell Transport and Trading Company, p.l.c., ("Royal Dutch Shell") as part of a pattern of collaboration and/or conspiracy between Royal Dutch/Shell and the military junta of Nigeria to violently and ruthlessly suppress any opposition to Royal Dutch/Shell's conduct in its exploitation of oil and natural gas resources in Ogoni and the Niger Delta (*Wiwa v. Anderson*, 2003, p. 1).

This was only one of a number of alien tort cases before US courts since the mid to late 1990s. Preceding Shell, Unocal (Chevron) opted in 2007 for an out-of-court settlement with a group of 15 Burmese villagers who claimed the company was complicit in their forced labour on Unocal's Yadana gas pipeline – a joint project with the French company Total and the Burmese military government. Evidence that the Burmese state used slave labour to help lay the pipeline brought international condemnation of Unocal, strong denials of any wrongdoing by the company and the embarrassment of having to account for how and why it could cooperate with and trust a demonstrably venal regime (*Doe v. Unocal*, 2002, pp. 1495–1496). The company strategy extinguished the court case as a public issue but, crucially, allowed Unocal to maintain its defence.

More important, by avoiding the possibility of an adverse finding, Unocal ensured the issue did not become the subject of a judicial decision, thereby blocking the creation of a potentially more costly legal precedent. Settlements are few, however, although the documentation generated reveals further the scope for unlawful action by companies active in politically contested and heavily militarized "business contexts." Clearly, the threat of adverse legal judgement is sufficient to force companies to look to their moral obligations under international law (Battersby et al., 2011).

Cases of suspected malpractice involving US companies operating in Colombia were discussed in a specially convened House of Representatives joint committee in 2007 – such was the level of public concern over allegations of US company complicity in political violence in Colombia. To date no foreign resources company operating in Colombia has been prosecuted for complicity in murder, but Chiquita International, formerly the United Fruit Company, pleaded guilty in the US District Court of Columbia to making payments to the designated terrorist organization the Autodefensas Unidas de Colombia or United Self-Defence Forces of Colombia (AUC) in return for protection of its plantations. Chiquita, as United Fruit, was largely responsible for globalizing the Central and South American banana trade in the early twentieth century and, in the process, mastered the art of "doing business internationally" using their market power to extract generous land concessions from accommodating governments, to restrict the growth of labour unions and, later, to stymie the spread communist ideology (Wiley, 2008).

The available evidence strongly suggests that many resources companies are predisposed to pay whomsoever is available and able to protect assets, regardless of their affiliations. Chiquita paid the Fuerzas Armadas Revolucionarias de Colombia or Revolutionary Armed Forces of Colombia (FARC) for protection; then, when AUC paramilitary groups appeared near its plantations, it seized the opportunity to reduce its security by paying a lower rate of protection to paramilitaries (*USA v. Chiquita*, 2007). BP is said to have used a private security firm, Defence Systems Limited, to protect its assets in the Antioquia and Magdalena Medio departments, which included liaison with paramilitaries linked to the Colombian army and the alleged supply of advanced military equipment to the notorious 14th Brigade. Scandals associated with the protection of oil pipeline assets extend to the US. Occidental Petroleum is also implicated in the sponsorship of paramilitary units responsible for war crimes in the same conflict-prone regions of Colombia as BP (House, 2007a). Risk management calculations by mining companies lean heavily towards asset protection and compliance with the wishes of capricious governments. This is simply the principle of amorality at work however we might weigh the moral rights of and obligations to shareholders and employees (Battersby et al., 2011).

US-registered mining, food and beverage companies are said to have gone beyond payment for protection, to engage in contracted killings of union organizers. While estimates vary, since the mid 1980s between 3,000 and 4,000 Colombian trade unionists have died at the hands of paramilitaries, the Colombian army and FARC/ Ejército de Liberación Nacional or National Liberation Army (ELN) guerrillas – mainly paramilitaries. Citing a culture of impunity extending to the highest levels of government, Human Rights Watch and trade unionists in Colombia and the US argue that these murders were in fact assassinations designed to limit the unionization of mine, pipeline and plantation workers, hence limiting the possibility of union action in pursuit of higher pay and better working conditions (House, 2007a). If this was the case, then these targeted killings served their purpose as labour unionization shrank to a mere four per cent of Colombia's workforce by 2013 (Franklin, 2013). The pursuit of economic gains at the global edge can be both brutal and brutalizing.

In *Juan Aquas Romero v. Drummond Company* 2008 and *Jane Doe et al. v. Drummond Company* 2010, the American mining company Drummond Coal was accused of complicity in the murder of three Sintramienergetica union officials at its La Loma mine by AUC paramilitaries in 2001 (*Romero et al. v. Drummond*, 2008; *Doe v. Drummond*, 2010). The case against Drummond states that the company's director, Augusto Jiminez, paid protection money to the AUC and that the AUC unit responsible for the murders, the Juan Andres Alvarez Front, was allowed to camp on Drummond property. If true, the company is likewise in violation of US anti-terror legislation but also potentially guilty of a war crime against civilian trade unionists (*Doe v. Drummond*, 2010). Alien tort cases brought by foreign plaintiffs against US companies endure a long deliberative process and, despite some major victories, tend not to succeed. Ironically, the Bush Administration tried and failed to restrict alien tort claims by foreign nationals but, in the case of Chiquita, found the district court process a useful supplement to its war against terror. While much of the evidence against companies like Drummond is cited before the US Congress and published by human rights NGOs, it has not been proved in a court of law. Eliot Engel, chair of the House of Representatives Subcommittee on the Western Hemisphere, acknowledges, however, that these are "credible allegations" (House, 2007a, p. 52). Official recognition of systemic labour abuse in Colombia by the Obama Administration is arguably one of the beneficial upshots of torts litigation in the late 2000s, but the violence against Colombian trades unionists has only partly subsided. Death threats and other forms of intimidation remains widespread, and elements within the US conservative establishment still regard union movements across Latin America as seedbeds of organized crime and terrorism (House, 2007a; Biron, 2012; Purdue, 2012; Franklin, 2013).

Where claims of human rights violations or worse become drawn into legal battles involving rival companies, the risks of legal and reputational damage are greatly increased. A dispute between Drummond Coal and the Dutch company Llanos Oil over a Colombian oil concession, developed by Llanos and then controversially transferred by the Colombian government to Drummond, led to court action against Drummond in the Netherlands. Llanos Oil developed a special interest in the alien tort claims against Drummond in 2007. The 2010 court proceedings were used by Llanos to reflect upon the character of Drummond in support of its contention of unlawful collusion between the company and the Colombian government (Battersby et al., 2011, p. 165). The lawsuit against Drummond in the Netherlands exemplifies the potential for a matrix of international legal cases to accumulate around contentious issues involving commercial and human rights claims. The danger of increasingly complex cross-cutting international law suits raises the stakes for smaller resources companies especially including the costs of litigation, potential fines and potential seizure of assets. Drummond's international reputation has been irreparably harmed, and its future business ventures are likely to come under even more intense scrutiny from international trade unionists. Yet, all the companies facing Alien Torts litigation received a *carte blanche* reprieve from the US Supreme Court in 2013.

Alien torts cases are, as said, drawn-out affairs and, hence, prohibitively costly. They are also limited in effectiveness to companies with registered assets in the US, where judicial attitudes towards torts suits have shifted appreciably over the past decade. Indicative of a new conservative mood within the US Supreme Court, judicial interpretation of the Alien Torts Statute has narrowed to knock out compensation claims lodged against U.S. companies for alleged treaty violations in foreign countries. In April 2013 the Court found against the Ogoni plaintiffs, who were prosecuting a claim against Shell for more extensive complicity in Nigerian international human rights violations in Ogoniland in *Kiobel vs. Royal Dutch Petroleum* (Wuerth, 2013). Following closely on this decision, the U.S. Ninth Circuit Court of Appeals in June 2013 dismissed the plaintiffs' case in *Sarei v. Rio Tinto* and the District Court of Alabama dismissed the case against *Drummond,* citing *Kiobel* but also finding against the plaintiffs on the grounds of inadmissible evidence (*Giraldo v. Drummond,* 2013). As said, these pivotal decisions are based primarily upon a legal technicality: that the Alien Torts Statute does not apply to acts committed outside the U.S. The Supreme Court determined that extraterritorial application of U.S. law was not the express intent of the Statute's drafters, not whether any violations of international law actually occurred as claimed (*Kiobel v. Royal Dutch Petroleum,* 2013, pp. 11–13). One aspect of the *Sarei v. Rio Tinto* case worthy of consideration in light of the expansive interpretation of criminal responsibility applied to HSBC and Barclays Bank appears in a brief brought before the Supreme Court by the National Foreign Trade Council seeking legal clarification in *Rio Tinto v. Sarei* (2012) – one of several filed in tandem. The document explicitly separated complicity and consequence, detaching the notion of "aiding and abetting" from mere proximity to a crime, to focus exclusively upon the much higher standard of demonstrable intent, "purpose" or *mens rea* (*Rio Tinto v. Sarei,* 2012, p. 12). The extent to which this reasoning swayed the Court's later decision to uphold the Circuit Court's finding in favour of Rio or helped to clear the way for *Kiobel* cannot be known. Still, the directions issued by the Supreme Court appear to run counter to the growing extraterritorial activism of US legislators and law enforcement agencies on matters of national security and national economic interest.

A global collusion curse

Foreign investment can bring development gains to underdeveloped countries, not least employment-generating projects critical to the establishment of social order and political stability. Yet, investment and economic growth without consideration for legitimacy and lawfulness can, as discussed, exacerbate societal chaos. The public perception of corporate malpractice, whether proven in a court of law or not, weakens the rule of law nationally and internationally. When the activities of some corporations demonstrably undermine UN sanctions, subvert humanitarian aid schemes for private ends or disregard international conventions, not only do they contravene international law but they also undermine human and global security. Many reputable TNCs trade profitably with, or under the auspices of, authoritarian governments in Africa, Asia and Latin America with poor human rights records and operate in zones of conflict or extreme societal distress where they risk transgressing international human rights laws and the laws of war. With regard to the torts cases discussed above, criminality or liability is contestable. With regard to major international corruption cases, however, allegations are frequently irrefutable.

The UN Oil-for-Food Programme is a celebrated instance of UN failure and incompetence, but the programme's shortcomings are in large part attributable to the willingness of many aberrant well-known (and some less well-known) corporations to subvert sanctions and breach international law. The programme's structure presented strong incentives for the Iraqi regime of Saddam Hussein to collude with US, Australian, British, Russian, French, German and Swiss businesses and business people to subvert UN sanctions. Evidence before the Independent Committee of Inquiry chaired by Paul Volcker, established to investigate systemic malfeasance in the programme, drew attention to the elaborate labyrinthine transactions by which reputable companies distance themselves from their illicit activities and gains. Iraq, or more specifically, the Iraqi regime of Saddam Hussein, was allowed a role in the negotiation of oil contracts and humanitarian aid purchases, a loophole that allowed it to earn US$1.8 billion in illegal payments from the sale of trading rights to foreign oil, agricultural and manufacturing interests during the life of the programme (1995–2002). In return, colluding companies received a share of the US$64.2 billion in Iraqi oil sales and the US$34.5 billion in food and other essential humanitarian supplies sold to Iraq (Volcker, 2005, pp. 21, 252). The worst offenders included Trafigura Berheer, the commodities company implicated in toxic-waste dumping in Côte d'Ivoire, and the Australian wheat marketer AWB Ltd. Interestingly, AWB executives escaped the scandal without charge, despite protracted Australian federal government investigations into illegal AWB payments to Iraq (Battersby and Siracusa, 2009).

For the many structural reasons outlined above, the prudential regulation of global business remains largely a matter of self-regulation. Anti-corruption efforts face similar limitations, even though the scope of the global anti-corruption norm has widened appreciably. The institutional infrastructure of the anti-corruption norm is today extensive, including the World Bank, Transparency International, formed by former Bank executives, United Nations Office on Drugs and Crime (UNODC), OECD, and national-level anti-corruption agencies. The regime's formation reflects globalization of production and investment and the evolution of networked forms of business which requires an internationally coordinated governance response. The 1999 OECD Convention against the

Bribery of Foreign Officials (38 ratifications) and the UN's Convention against Corruption (2005) (169 states party to it, as of 2013) represent the main legal instruments through which the global anti-corruption norm is asserted. Corruption is criminalized as bribery, defined under Australian criminal law, for example, as the direct or indirect provision of a "benefit" to a "foreign public official" to "obtain a business advantage" (Criminal Code Act, 1995, Ch. 4. 70.2). This law applies to the criminal conduct of Australian legal persons, subject to specific criteria, "whether or not the conduct constituting the alleged offence occurs in Australia" and "whether or not a result of the conduct constituting the alleged offence occurs in Australia" (Criminal Code Amendment Act, 2000, Ch. 2, Pt. 2.7, 15.3). That the clauses are necessary is a reflection on both the ongoing transnationalization of Australian business enterprises and the reality that corruption occurs in every country, and not just in developing Asia or Africa. To reiterate a point, historically, private companies from Western countries have been widely complicit in the corruption of governments in the industrialized and developing worlds before the term and the crime of "corruption" was legally defined, and private companies, through their actions, affect the climate of governance in the country in which they operate. But enforcement of this, as with all other international norms, requires broad international commitment at the governmental level as well as acceptance by "trend-setting" corporate entities.

As indicated in Chapter 3 with regard to strategic cash transfers by US forces operating in Afghanistan, objections to commercially suspect practices can be waived in the name of national security. The US-registered and largely American-owned PMSC, Blackwater (Xe), received extensive public attention for the scale of its contractual relations with the US government and its operational behaviour in Iraq. From 2001 to the end of 2006, the company earned US$1.024 billion in US government contracts to provide security for US diplomatic staff and land and air support to US operations in Iraq and central Asia, with US$945 million of this earned during 2005–2006 alone. This company, it was alleged before Congress, received a substantial proportion of its income from US government sources through uncompetitive "no-bid" processes, contradicting the market-efficiency logic used to justify outsourcing by Republican and Democrat administrations alike. Veiled allegations of mercenary profiteering were levelled at former US Navy SEAL Erik Prince, the US$1-billion-a-year owner of Prince Group Holdings, of which Blackwater (Xe) is a part. Congressional concerns were raised over apparent differences between contract pricing schedules and the actual wages paid to company field operatives, suggesting a substantial profit to the company and its owner (House, 2007b, pp. 2, 80, 89, 178; Battersby et al., 2011).

Is the global anti-corruption norm, therefore, a convenient principle to be applied or set aside as required in state or corporate realpolitik? Enforcement of Iranian sanctions under the US Patriot Act, as said, demonstrates the potential for anti-money laundering provisions to be used for more traditional geostrategic security aims. Corruption is also expressly stated as a US and a global security issue on the grounds that corruption is a facilitator of transnational crime and by implication terrorism (DoJ, 2012d, 2). Bribery and other forms of business–government associations that impede the spread of market globalism are the principal targets of the US Foreign Corrupt Practices Act (FCPA), and market globalism is the *raison d'être* for the US- and World Bank-sponsored global anti-corruption campaign. Looking from a geostrategic standpoint, the largest Chinese state-owned corporations are challenging US competitiveness in key global industries, oil and gas, agriculture and telecommunications, making the elimination of all aspects of the "Asian Way" a key US economic priority. This is nothing new. Informal "understandings" between Asian government officials, Asian political leaders and US economic competitors, principally the British Empire, and British and Australian capital, were a major source of annoyance to Washington before and after World War II (Battersby, 2007). Today, however, this objective is pursued through an international regime. With the spread of Chinese corporate and state political influence into Africa, non-market ties built upon transnational family networks, "personal understandings" and a sense of mutuality of political interest challenge the impersonal market idealism of US regulators, and frustrate the ambitions of corporate America.

A quixotic or purely selective and punitive norm of "absolute integrity" is becoming globalized, backed by an "ever-expanding view of US jurisdiction" (Freshfields et al., 2012, p. 2). There are many ways to pay a bribe or to earn the gratitude of people in key decision-making positions. For Western mining companies seeking access to mineral resources in Thailand during the early decades of the twentieth century, donations to local public works were looked upon favourably, what today might be classified as corporate philanthropy, and paid a political dividend because such gestures were received as demonstrations of respect and a willingness to "do business." The appointment of the relatives of local dignitaries to boards of directors of mining companies was commonplace (Battersby, 2007). To capture these relationships requires an expansive definition of bribery, such as is evolving under the FCPA.

As the text of the Act states, a bribe can be construed as "an offer, payment, promise to pay, or authorization of the payment of any money, or offer, gift, promise to give, or authorization of the giving of anything of value" (USC, Title 15, Ch. 2B, Sect. 78.1 b2B).

In 2013, the Australian–South African mining giant BHP-Billiton came under investigation by the US DoJ and the Australian Federal Police for suspected "irregular" payments to the politically influential and well-connected Beijing Olympic Committee prior to the 2008 Olympics. Official scrutiny is homing in on payments for a "sponsorship deal and hospitality package," made at arm's-length through a US consulting firm. In what emerges as common a pattern in DoJ investigations, BHP-Billiton was, like HSBC and Barclays, reportedly in the habit of keeping audit trails to a minimum on sensitive financial matters, in this case on donations and benefits paid out in advantageous directions (McKenzie et al., 2013; Wyld, 2013). US anti-corruption law expects both paper compliance and evidence of the mindful anticipation of exposure to corruption risk (USC Title 15, Ch. 2B, Sect. 78, b2A; Freshfields et al., 2012). This is a much trickier hurdle to navigate, where operating in a high-risk country involves constant risk. The manager of Rio Tinto's Shanghai office, Stern Hu, was sentenced in 2010 to ten years in a Chinese prison for industrial espionage and bribery involving Chinese steel mills. Newspaper coverage in Australia and China raised unanswered questions as to whether or not Hu's behaviour, and that of his accomplices, was an isolated case (Zhang and Tong, 2009; Garnaut, 2010).

Corruption, fraud and market manipulation are global security issues because of the increasing systemic implications of corporate unlawfulness. This is not, however, solely for the reasons outlined by US regulators, or for that matter *just* because market failure in a globalized economy threatens the integrity of the entire global system. There can be no end to the "war against corruption" simply because what is deemed corrupt in a legal sense incorporates so many dimensions of routine human interaction, and because of the ever-present commercial imperative to maximize competitive in a hypercompetitive global system. There is also a question as to the intent of anti-corruption agitation, by the US in particular. The forced adoption of anti-corruption and trade liberalization rules by finically weakened governments in Asia in the wake of the 1997 Asian Financial Crisis invites the conclusion that an extensive global political agenda attaches to the global policing of corporate crime. China and many of its Southeast Asian neighbours have acceded to the UN corruption convention, but this is a precondition for international acceptance in a global economy still largely predicated upon broadly liberal market principles. Yet, cooperation between businesses and the protective state is a feature both of Asian developmentalism and of the "infant industry" or "strategic trade" model of statist economic development. Collusion was and remains a rational strategy pursued by corporate entities under conditions of unequal global competition and local political pressure and opportunity.

Nowhere is this better exemplified than in the treatment of the Chinese information systems company, Huawei Technologies, in the US and by key US allies, the UK and Australia. The list of US concerns about Huawei's growing global reach is extensive. The US Select Committee on Intelligence maintains that Huawei most likely trades with persons and entities proscribed under the Iranian sanctions regime, is subsidized by the Chinese state and aids the Chinese military in its intelligence-gathering activities against the US and its allies. Technology sourced directly or indirectly from Huawei is, thus, according to the Committee, likely to pose a risk to US security because of the potential for strategic components to be doctored with malware to create a back door into critical US information systems (Rogers and Ruppersberger, 2012, pp. 3, 7–8, 32; House, 2011). The Committee's warnings are lent credibility by Mandiant, a US-based Internet security software company, which claims a "solid connection" to China, and by inference the Chinese state, for frequently attempted and successful cyber intrusions into public and private information infrastructure in the US. At issue are alleged connections between Huawei's founder, Reng Zhengfei, and the intelligence wing of China's People's Liberation Army, for which Reng supposedly worked before embarking upon a business career. Mandiant designates one PLA unit, Unit 61398, located in Shanghai, as an Advanced Persistent Threat (Rogers and Ruppersberger, 2012, pp. 13–14; House, 2011; Mandiant, 2013). Yet, the Intelligence Committee report also indicts China's opaque state capitalist system, and the undefined but presumably substantial power of the Chinese state to command obedience from private companies (Rogers and Ruppersberger, 2012, p. 10; House, 2011).

In the domain of global technology relations, convergence between strategic security and commercial concerns presents a major systemic challenge because emerging rivalries, if they are to be "managed," require an impossible compromise. For reasons that mirror US misgivings, the Australian government excluded Huawei from tendering for contracts related to the National Broadband Network, and explains why the UK government, at the end of 2012, initiated a review of Huawei's role in the refurbishment of Britain's phone system in a government-approved joint venture with British Telecom (BT) (UK ISC, 2013). The international security dimension to this commercial arrangement is that the UK and Australia are part of a long-standing intelligence-sharing partnership with the US that dates from World War II, and upon which each relies if not for hard intelligence then for the sake of shared global and regional geostrategic commitments. Huawei's blanket assurances and those of its overseas partners and affiliate directors, including many prominent former politicians, are insufficient to negate the security anxieties of globally networked and exposed states, or at least their security establishments, that view China as a global antagonist if not a direct military threat. The truth with which the UK and Australia have to grapple is that any commercial dealings with Huawei that expose national security infrastructure to even the remotest suggestion of "foreign" espionage risk will be read as disloyalty by Washington and conceivably lead to a severance of UK–US–Australian intelligence ties.

Either there is a complete lack of reflective capacity within the US security establishment or US–Chinese commercial rivalry speaks to a more fundamental divide. US privacy laws acknowledge the right of security and law enforcement authorities to access private communications data, including actual transcripts or digital record of conversations, without a specific warrant. If we accept that the sequestering or surrender of private data without legal warrant is a violation of a fundamental human right, and a transgression against the laws of nations, then in what category of crime do we put the actions of the National Security Agency (NSA) or the UK's equivalent, GCHQ? As was recognized in the case of Yahoo Hong Kong's surrender of personal electronic communications by Chinese dissident Wang Xiaoning to Chinese government authorities in 2002, on the global plane of interstate relations, legal and non-state market actors are often willingly or unwittingly compromised but, nonetheless, complicit in violations of international law and humanitarian principle. Wang was imprisoned in China for his dissent, and Yahoo was the subject of Alien Torts litigation by Wang's family who claimed successfully that Yahoo violated US international human rights obligations. The difference between US-style regulation and Chinese-style corporatism is surely much subtler today than any ideological divide between capitalism and communism. The Chinese state asserted its national security prerogatives as it is entitled to do under Chinese law, just as the US asserts its sovereign prerogative over Western telecommunications companies in the US. This dyadic rivalry, played out across many domains of global relations, is a rivalry forged in the world of contemporary networked realpolitik.

The state of global business regulation

It is both fashionable and standard practice to treat politics and commerce as discrete areas of human endeavour and scholarly inquiry. The political economy approach to international relations has struggled for relevance since the demise of communism and, yet, the issues discussed above demand a new synthesis, one not driven by ideology or disciplinary prejudice as much as by the complex realities of network integration and globalization. It is through business regulation that international norms are most aggressively promoted at the national and international levels. Market globalism is a form of cosmopolitanism and the extension of regulatory powers can be read as the globalization of some cosmopolitan values. As with the governance of global political relations, there are limits to the regulation of global capital. Corporate criminality is systemic to the extent that commercial practices judged or defined as criminal in some jurisdictions are tolerated and practised in all jurisdictions, including, it would seem, by agents and agencies acting with tacit governmental authorization. International "benchmarks" of legitimate and responsible corporate practice are, thus, set only at a price that the market will bear.

Concern for corporate governance and CSR is read, cynically, as but the latest in a long history of strategic ripostes by business and the liberal state to placate disaffected "losers" from globalization, and disguise, as Sklair argues, a deepening "crisis of capitalism" (Sklair, 2002). To dismiss CSR as little more than shallow public relations is, however, to grossly oversimplify a very diverse and evolving field of corporate social practice. Within the continental European sphere, and distinct from the Anglo-American sphere, countries still evidence a social market orientation in their economic policies and the European Union's key treaties reflect this "European way." Dubbed the "Rhenish" or "Rhineland" model, social objectives are given equal weighting with economic objectives, which, in the microcosm of the European corporation, means that the power of shareholders and the interests of investors are balanced with the needs of the organization as a whole. In contrast to the individualistic competition valourized in North America, European governments and businesses accept, in the ideal if not in practice, a greater degree of social responsibility, towards their workforces and towards society as a whole (Hutton, 2003; Hix and Hoyland, 2011, p. 202; Dicken, 2011). There is mounting evidence that corporations are, despite their primary profit orientation, able to engage in "norm-governed behaviour," beyond minimal compliance with financial reporting standards and conditions of credit or equity finance (Bull and McNeill, 2007, p. 164). CSR advocates argue that corporate actors and corporate philanthropists provide income-generating opportunities and, through innovative community engagement initiatives, stimulate tangible "human quality of life" improvements. (Davis, 2005; Blowfield and Murray, 2008). Many companies strive to accommodate humanitarian and international obligations through cooperation with international NGOs and a range of "stakeholders." The provision of mobile communications technologies by leading companies like the Norwegian IT giant, Nokia, to people in developing countries, helps close the "digital divide" while also extending the global market for technology products (Nokia, 2011).

The idea that the interests of business can be balanced with the global public interest is popular among advocates of embedded liberalism like John Gerard Ruggie. The eighth and least often noted of the UN MDGs specifies a role for business in global social development, and stresses the urgency with which businesses of all kinds should engage with the MDG agenda. Business "enlistment" is facilitated at the global level through the UN Global Compact, the brainchild of John Ruggie, which is designed to promote voluntary "compliance" with international norms in all facets of business practice (UN Global Compact, n/d). The Global Compact is predicated on the assumption that private companies and business people can be persuaded to act for the common good beyond creating profits and employment. The considerable human and financial resources of transnational corporate actors and their undoubted political influence can, so it is thought, be harnessed and directed towards the achievement of MDG objectives.

The promotion of positive compliance with international laws, standards and protocols, meaning compliance with the spirit and intention of rights and standards and not merely the letter of the law, goes hand in glove with negative compliance, meaning fear of litigation. New management technologies, including performance metrics and company audits, offer scope for closer policing of corporate practice but only where companies are willing to calculate their "bottom line" in other than purely financial terms. However, Daniel Kaufmann warns against "over-regulation" in campaigns against corruption advocating instead a focus upon individual "integrity," rather than legal compliance alone (Kaufmann, 2005 pp. 83–88). This values-based approach to persuasion and education as a means to counter the abuse of power is constructivist in orientation but emerges from the reality that there are limits to what can be achieved by the enforcement of compliance. The pursuit of absolutes, be it moral integrity, financial transparency or even optimal economic efficiency, can erode the very social capital upon which human societies depend. As Frank Anechiarico and James B. Jacobs conclude from their 1990s study of corruption in New York City, "corruption is a socio-political fact of life" (Anechiarico and Jacobs, 1996, p. 191). Yet, they argue, the determination to eliminate corruption, paradoxically, generates an anti-corruption "pathology" fuelled by the increasing power of technology to gather information and compile data on all aspects of government. Placing government employees down to the most minor official "on notice" that their every movement is being monitored, they claim, works counter to the objective of corruption control by instilling and perpetuating a culture of fear and evasion at all levels of an organization (Anechiarico and Jacobs, 1996, p. 194).

Conclusion

Moral perfection is an elusive quality and one that is not encouraged by the demand pressures or imperatives of a global system in which the frontiers of legality and criminality are shifting rapidly. Self-regulation alone cannot guarantee that there will be no repeat of the environmental catastrophe in the Gulf of Mexico, that some large and politically influential corporate actors will not wilfully disregard international human rights conventions or undermine international security regimes. As Michael Edwards writes, "if business wants to save the world, there are plenty of opportunities . . . pay your taxes . . . pay decent wages . . . don't subvert politics . . . obey regulations" (Edwards, 2010, p. 31). But companies, large corporations, business associations and lobbyists will not accept these obligations if compliance is deemed contrary to the interests of "business" conflated with the public interest at large.

If global governance were simply a matter of technocratic measurement, organization and "performance" control through the mechanisms of self-regulated liberal markets politics might well be negated as a factor of production and exchange. But liberal or market globalism and the assertion of liberal globalizing norms generates opposition because, as argued in this book and by authorities on complexity and complex systems, normative uniformity is an unnatural condition into which to force complex human societies. More important, the pursuit of moral perfection and the expectation of universal compliance with absolutist ideals run contrary to fundamental principles of democracy and enlarge the scope for "organized hypocrisy" beyond the sphere of government and into the corporate boardroom.

5 Invidious Choices: Humanitarianism on the Edge

"Civil society" is no less fraught with moral and legal complexities than the society of states or the commercial world of Transnational Corporations (TNC). Populated by globally minded not-for-profit organizations, civic groups, moral entrepreneurs, voluntary associations and the increasingly vocal digital populace, local and global civic space is heterogeneous and fractious. We see civil society, of which NGOs are usually read as a significant constituent element, as a space of progressive social engagement, independent from government, and where people pursue social objectives, not commercial profit (Anheier, 2012a). As with narratives of terror and transnational crime convergence, or the supposed convergence of economic relations towards a single global market, claims of a nascent or convergent "global civil society" do not reflect complex reality. The global civilities, which cosmopolitans see as harbingers of a fabulous cosmopolis are, as Albert Drainville asserts, possibly little more than "ghosts" and "spectres" of a possible future as yet unrealized (Drainville, 2004, p. 10).

NGOs, and Civil Society Organizations (CSOs) more broadly, are of necessity political actors, to the extent that they articulate norms and demand adherence to legal and moral standards at whichever level they operate. The neutrality of humanitarian space and the impartiality of civic advocacy are but two areas of sustained controversy. The boundaries between civic action and the pursuit of power and commercial return were never unbreachable and are increasingly permeable in today's hypercompetitive global system. In their multifarious ways, civil society actors, International NGOs (INGOs) especially, are co-producers of the integrated and integrating circuits of coded protocols through which globalization is governed, and consequently many are complicit in the systemic irregularities explored in the preceding chapters. As registered organizations, they are subject to laws of incorporation, accountable for their expenditures and practices and are criminally liable for their actions where these violate national and international criminal codes. Within organized civil society we find multitudes of code makers, code switchers and code breakers, and wherein even the best intentioned find that the moral high ground does not always sit clearly above the water line of unlawfulness.

CSOs by name and number

The precise scale of organized civil society is impossible to calculate with any degree of precision. Registration requirements make it somewhat easier to gauge the number of non-governmental entities, but even here the numbers are, to say the least, "impressionistic." Paralleling the definition of the TNC, an INGO is any not-for-profit organization active in two or more countries. INGOs numbered a mere 176 in 1909, rising over the next 84 years to 28,900 in 1993, and an estimated 40,000 by the late 1990s (Commission on Global Governance, 1996, p. 82; Anheier, 2001, pp. 221–226; Kovach et al., 2003, p. 1). If we take as a reasonable starting point the global TNC–affiliate ratio of roughly 1:10, acknowledging that by no means are all NGOs are INGO affiliates, there would be as many as 400,000 NGOs across all world regions, and likely many more CSOs. Whatever their accurate number, these actors have, in the areas of development assistance, won increased credence at the UN and other multilateral institutions that today rely upon international- and national-level non-governmental networks to implement development projects at the local level. In addition to this service delivery role, NGOs are "informational" and accountability actors gathering data on social need and evaluating social, economic and environmental impacts arising from development programmes, government policies and corporate practices (DeMars, 2005).

The non-governmental "sector" is vast and populated by a disorienting array of large and small organizations, some involved in specific and locally focused programmes drawing a handful of volunteers and others belonging to global federations and engaged in multi-issue "programmatic" campaigns. Among the most well-known are, Cooperative for Assistance and Relief Everywhere (CARE), Save the Children Fund, Greenpeace, Amnesty International (AI), Oxfam, World Vision and the Friends of the Earth. However, within the "civil society" space we find philanthropic actors, often linked with former Western political leaders and prominent business people, who are an increasingly visible source of strategic aid. From the long-standing Ford Foundation, established by Henry Ford's son, Edsel, in 1936, to the more recent Bill and Melinda Gates Foundation, the Clinton Foundation and Clinton Global Initiative, and George Soros's Open Society Foundations, they represent the "business end" of the philanthropic sector through direct engagement with social development projects (Ford Foundation, 2014).

There are multiple imperatives that define NGO strategies and practices and the frequently "uncomfortable" and ambiguous spaces that these actors or entities inhabit in the global system. The National Endowment for Democracy is a useful case in point, founded by an act of US Congress as a "bipartisan" non-government agency tasked with the promotion of democracy around the world; the organization claims non-government, non-profit status and yet receives the bulk of its funding from and is subject to review by Congress (Reagan, 1983). More complicated is the International Committee of the Red Cross (ICRC) which derives funding from member governments paid through national Red Cross societies. Governed by a committee of private Swiss citizens, the ICRC qualifies as an "independent" humanitarian organization. The terms "organization," "foundation" and "committee" imply formal managerial control that troubles those who favour more "spontaneous" forms of civic engagement. Committed to grass-roots democratization of the counter-hegemonic variety, the World Social Forum (WSF), formed in the early 2000s as a global counterpoint to the World Economic Forum (WEF), and the so-called "Occupy" movement that emerged in the wake of the Global Financial Crisis (GFC) fulfil accountability roles to the extent that they are collections of many civic groups committed to global "transformation" through awareness-raising public dialogue and demonstrations.

Growth in the INGO sector, the so-called NGO "bloom" (DeMars, 2005, p. 34), reflects broader processes or patterns of globalization and social change. The increasing density and speed of communications has enabled more people to connect across the global social plane and to find common interests and causes. Global consciousness or awareness – globality – emerges, according to neo-Marxist interpretations, through the production of global consumer products which create the psychological space for transnational social consciousness to emerge as the locus of "counter power" to global capitalism and the capitalist state (Beck, 2005, pp. 236–240). Global telecommunications renders audible the myriad human fears about nuclear power and the power of nuclear weapons, the fate of the natural environment, insecurity of employment in a volatile global economy, food security and safety. Such risk sensitivity is propelling the formation of a "world risk society" (Beck, 1999) or "global civil society" (Falk, 1999) with transnational organizations and movements at the vanguard (Beck, 1999, pp. 13–15). The larger INGOs are global agenda shapers and norm changers and, thus, influential actors in an evolving and multi-layered "system" of global governance cohering around a shared *mentalité* of global risk (Beck, 1999; Falk, 1999; Hall and Biersteker, 2002; Held, 2010, pp. 31–33).

Civil society is thus cast as a counter-hegemonic entity with the potential to overturn or at least undermine a state–capital "nexus" which legitimates the "culture ideology" of the free market and the corporation (Sklair, 2001). This is a revolutionary development and Beck assumes that the Global South, comprising civil society actors, community representatives and intellectuals from developing countries all buttressed by community representatives, organizations and intellectuals on the left of politics in the North, or the developed world, will eventually cohere to generate an unstoppable momentum against the excesses of global capital. Of course Beck's characterization, as with that of Falk and Castells, assumes that civil society entities are invested with a common political sociality, and politicizes global social practice in ways that are problematic for "professional" aid and development organizations – including intergovernmental and governmental agencies.

The historical trajectory of civil society formation presents a much more multi-layered and nuanced picture. Religious orders provided some of the earliest conceptions of world society, in St. Augustine's *City of God*, for example, and cosmopolitan imaginings are traced back to the Stoic philosophers of classical Greece. Missionary societies operated at and beyond the edge of empires seeking converts and proclaiming the superiority of Western civilization. Evangelism and imperialism were in many ways complementary phenomena, in British India, for example, but anti-slavery advocates were motivated by a humanistic ethic, which accommodated notions of a common humanity, if not human equality, as it is understood today. Modern humanitarianism emerged parallel to the rise of Christian evangelism, which, as with the anti-slavery movement of William Wilberforce, engendered a recognizably if not consciously global mood (Keck and Sikkink, 1998, pp. 41–51; DeMars, 2005; Barnett, 2011).

Humanitarian activism evidences more than mere "bourgeois pity" for the poorer orders. Without the rise of the industrial bourgeoisie, the ICRC could not exist. It was Swiss businessman Henri Dunant's humanitarian diplomacy and personal fortune that bankrolled the ICRC and persuaded European governments to accept the principle that there are moral constraints on the use of military force. The Geneva Conventions established that the ICRC should be granted access to war zones, where staff could provide medical aid to wounded soldiers on all sides – in effect codifying the principle of neutrality to the benefit of future generations of aid workers (Battersby and Siracusa, 2009; Barnett, 2011). Nineteenth-century "organized compassion," as Michael Barnett defines it, was a Western middle-class phenomenon that speaks to a sense of civilizational optimism and arrogance, but also a sense that the worst effects of industrialization had to be ameliorated, including the industrialization of warfare (Barnett, 2011, p. 50). Civil society movements defined many international social norms, like the Woman's Christian Temperance Union (WCTU), for example, which campaigned successfully for the state-level criminalization of opium in the US and which lit the political fuse for international opium control. The movement's evangelical social reform agenda encompassed women's suffrage and alcohol prohibition, which it took to the global stage from the late nineteenth century (Tyrell, 1991; Okrent, 2011). Its considerable successes reflected a general pattern of normative globalization, whereby certain social or commercial values are "selected" and then codified at a national level before being distributed globally through transnational and international networks of power. For the WCTU these networks were imperial (Tyrell, 1991); for their twentieth-century secular counterparts, economic globalization and the institutionalization of global governance defined new vectors for transnational dissemination and engagement.

The expansion of NGO influence in the latter half of the twentieth century is in part explained by the adoption of an institutionalized international development agenda post-World War II through the UN and the Bretton Woods Institutions. Decolonization contributed to the proliferation of issues of established humanitarian concern, and the identification of new grounds for social intervention, namely, poverty, food security, public health, education, population control and natural disaster. The institutions, under the UN umbrella of dedicated funds to address specific development issues, created specialist areas of humanitarian action on a globalizing and secular development agenda. Development-oriented non-government actors carved out significant roles filling the ballooning welfare service gaps or "unmet" social "demand." Increased funds available to NGOs – from intergovernmental and governmental sources – but also from public donations from increasingly affluent industrialized nations, generated by media-driven campaigns to raise public awareness of famines and wars across the "Third World," enabled the expansion and multiplication of development actors (Lindenberg and

Bryant, 2001, pp. 3, 10; Barnett, 2011; Barnett and Weiss, 2011). The connection between the institutionalized non-government "sector," the state and transnational capital is historically, especially when viewed from a system-level perspective, much closer than latter-day champions of civil society care to admit.

Stressing the deliberative dimension of global governance, Wayne Sandholtz argues that normative globalization is the "product of the constant interplay between rules and behaviour" but the outcomes of this interplay are subject to an array of different and competing pressures (Sandholtz, 2009, p. 6). Network power is highly context sensitive. Development organizations like CARE, Oxfam and World Vision are more dependent upon "target" country governments for their "licence to operate." As with TNCs, without governmental approval NGO resources cannot be deployed and projects implemented with minimal risk to development workers. For the global environmental campaigner Greenpeace, confrontation with governments and private companies is integral to its campaign to bring political pressure to bear. Similarly, advocacy organizations can be more outspokenly "interventionist" and campaign for institutional change within target countries. In addition to the high-profile AI and Human Rights Watch (HRW), there is a range of smaller advocacy INGOs pursuing more narrowly defined aims, which seek to influence governmental decision-making patterns. For example, Penal Reform International (PRI), a medium-scale internationalist humanitarian organization based in the Netherlands, declares its strategic intent "to create a climate for [criminal justice] reform by lobbying, public education, persuasion and international pressure." Its network power as such depends upon its capacity to influence government and governmental authorities in post-authoritarian states and build the capacities of CSOs supportive of its agenda (PRI, 2006).

The relative independence of NGOs derives from either their determination to function without major sponsorship or their capacity to mobilize substantial financial or human resources. Both options depend upon the capacity to generate and draw strength from relational power dynamics – that is, the power of networks, and as the scale of operations increases so distanciated interdependencies become more important and problematic. INGOs occupy "nodal points" in interlocking matrices of local and transnational social capital – and larger circuits of global finance capital. Strategic positing is critical for the accumulation and distribution of finance, information and human capital along lengthy humanitarian supply chains. Command power of parent bodies over national affiliates varies between organizations and, unlike many internal arrangements within TNCs, national branches enjoy substantial autonomy to the point that they can compete against each other internationally for donor funds. Coordination between INGOs, even within INGO "families," is often stymied by intense competition for scarce funds, exposing the civil society sector as a whole to ridicule (Cooley and Ron, 2004, pp. 488–489). Corporate authority and "network cohesion" therefore rests on head office control over branding, message and strategy which in turn depends upon organizational impact – measured as income, viability of projects and programmes and influence over the formulation and reformulation of international norms (DeMars, 2005; Lake and Wong, 2009; Keck and Sikkink, 1998).

Sustained social and political impact is directly linked to an organization's ability to grow its market share in the production and transfer of humanitarian "goods." Compassion is a multimillion-dollar industry, and the larger INGOs are, because of the incomes they generate and the staff and volunteers they employ, significant economic actors in their own right. AI is a modern global federation of 80 national branches. It distinguishes between financial members and "supporters" and claims a combined global AI "movement" of 4.6 million people who cohere around a shared commitment to the advancement of human rights, and exemplifies the normative power that can be generated by effectively coordinated transnational social capital (DeMars, 2005; Lake and Wong, 2009, pp. 140–149). AI's International Secretariat is, on its own, a medium-sized business enterprise with income in excess of £50 million (AI, 2012a). Globally, revenues for the AI network of country branches exceeded US$250 million (€202 million) in 2009 (AI, n/d). The Secretariat follows a corporate strategic plan replete with the jargon of modern organizational management, "accountability," "effectiveness," "leverage," "solutions" and, crucially, "brand" (AI, 2010; AI, 2014). Established to campaign for the release of prisoners of conscience, AI's global agenda has expanded to encompass advocacy actions on all forms of human rights abuse – a move designed to increase scale and impact, but also to maximize its potential membership base (Gosh, 2013). It is an entity of genuinely global "reach" (Shetty, 2014), which is becoming either increasingly mobile or globally "footloose."

It is not, therefore, only at the intersections between international humanitarian law and national practice that organizations like AI must operate. As a corporate entity, AI, like its counterparts, must also respond to market disciplines and navigate the regulatory hurdles of the modern state, in the manner of a private transnational organization if not corporation. Even though income from government grants accounts for a tiny fraction of AI Ltd's funds, AI's independence is contingent upon broad political acceptance of its operations. In liberal democratic states, generally, NGOs are allowed to operate freely, to campaign, protest, make public statements and generally enjoy the right to free speech. But there are constraints. Laws of incorporation also apply to not-for-profit organizations or, as under the UK Companies Act, "community interest companies" (2006, Ch. 46, Pt. 1, 6, p. 3). This imposes legal obligations to be accountable for financial management, and accountable to government for the disbursement and use of government funds. Incorporation is not, however, simply a matter of prudential oversight. At the national and intergovernmental levels, registration is the means by which the actions of CSOs are regulated.

Beginning in the late 1980s, NGOs became legitimized participants in UN consultative processes. Organizations seeking affiliation register with the UN Economic and Social Committee (ECOSOC) and receive "consultative status" in return for meeting strict criteria, including "conformity with the spirit, purposes and principles of the Charter of the United Nations" and the pursuit of aims that "reflect in a balanced way the major viewpoints or interests in these fields in all areas and regions of the world" (UN ECOSOC Resolution, 1996/31, July 25, 1996). Registered entities are "guests" at the UN and are only admitted into the circle by virtue of their willing compliance with UN requirements and missions. Clearly, NGOs are expected to serve the UN and their worth to the organization is measured by their capacity to materially aid UN objectives. According to the Committee, 3,912 NGOs held UN consultative status as of September 1, 2013, of which 154 were under temporary suspension for failure to comply with reporting obligations (UN ECOSOC, 2013). This elevated status is given to larger, well-organized and well-funded organizations capable of meeting bureaucratic requirements, but a further 31,000 NGOs assist the UN in its various missions as project partners (UN ECOSOC, 2014). Viewed in a sympathetic light, INGO–UN consultations represent a limited form of democratic engagement between the "global executive" and "global public." The process is an endorsement of the representative legitimacy of those INGOs accorded consultative status. Viewed negatively, however, it is a form of co-option.

Registration and regulation at the national level reflect similar concern to place limits on the operations of some transnational networks through the "power of the purse." In the Australian context, NGOs that wish to tender for government overseas development funding must register with the Australian Agency for International Development (AusAID). The government-aid sector partnership agreement acknowledges the

Australian Council for International Development (ACFID) as the peak body representing Australian non-governmental development organizations and accepts ACFID's "right to comment on government policy and advocate for policy change," in return for submitting to the standard liberal governance values of "accountability," "evaluation," "development effectiveness" and "transparency," and accepting the theoretical nexus between "stability" and "prosperity" (AusAID–ACFID, 2009; AusAID, 2011, p. 6). The brute reality is that registration privileges, including government funding, will not flow to organizations that pursue aggressive political campaigns against the government of the day or which subvert Australian foreign policy aims overseas. Even if transgression of these principles does not constitute a crime in a legal–technical sense, exclusion, rejection, suspension or delisting can imply something more than bureaucratic displeasure.

Critical junctures

The most politically active NGOs assume a "presumptive legitimacy" to operate in public space, to persuade, lobby and mobilize public opinion in pursuit of normative goals (DeMars, 2005, p. 170). But inclusion, albeit at the fringe of international deliberation, through affiliation with governments and intergovernmental institutions, also implicates NGO actors in global strategies to promote a liberal development agenda. Taking a critical view, the relative ease with which AI and other Western rights and development organizations consult with the UN is a reflection of a common cultural and political origin. For this reason, Western INGOs are often caricatured as imperialist or capitalist agents by activists engaged in "grass-roots" social campaigns to mitigate the deleterious effects of liberal development programmes upon communities in the Global South (Rajagopal, 2004; Hardt and Negri, 2009). Disaster intervention, for example, has become big business for relief organizations because substantial development aid runs in the direction of the latest natural or human-induced humanitarian catastrophe, meaning that the search for long-term sustainable development is often deferred or ignored elsewhere (Cooley and Ron, 2004, pp. 488–489). INGOs follow operational priorities and pursue strategies that can be interpreted critically as "predatory"; for example, AI's decision to move the locus of its enterprise to the "Global South and East" in response to the emergence of new global centres of power and wealth in Brazil, Russia, India and China (BRIC), although Russia and China are off-limits (Shetty, 2014). There is clearly a difference in more of thought governing the operations of "organizations" and "movements" for global change.

Financial considerations are important for any NGO but *financialization* imposes greater financial strictures affecting organizational decisions of larger NGOs. AI's "downsizing" of its global workforce in 2011 reflects its weakened financial position post the GFC – juxtaposed, with much irony, against a severance payment of £533,103 for former director Irene Khan in 2009 (Young, 2011; Cohen, 2012). AI, like any large employer, has financial responsibilities towards its full-time employees, including a defined benefit pension programme that requires the "preservation" of a proportion of annual donations to cover future financial obligations. Income declines post-GFC are attributed to prudential "revaluation" of liabilities and reduced transfers from national-level organizations which too have suffered declining returns on investment (AI, 2012a, p. 7). These fiscal realities are easily ignored or simply unrecognized because of the redistributive missions of humanitarian organizations. Given AI's public image and the antagonistic nature of its work, every criticism that could conceivably be made of its financial affairs has been made, particularly from the Israeli NGO Monitor, but also from former senior directors who allege a growing primacy of monetary considerations in AI's global push (Gosh, 2013).

As NGO budgets become larger and as donors demand greater financial accountability, so NGOs have had to adopt modern management practices and develop organizational structures that mirror the private sector. Those who urge greater professionalism and greater concern for efficiency and accountability in the non-governmental sector welcome this convergence (Lindenberg and Bryant, 2001). Others are concerned that donor influence and contractual requirements generate an incremental process of "isomorphic" change in which NGOs become corporatized and co-opted to serve the purposes of those governments and business organizations from which they derive essential funding. Academics and NGO professionals voice concern over the adoption of business models that, while applicable in the commercial sphere, sit uncomfortably with the humanitarian orientations of much NGO work, and which corrode the foundations of altruism upon which organizations are built (Hopgood, 2008; Edwards, 2010). Moral principle is no justification for inadequacy, profligacy and failure to deliver on obligations to donors or intended beneficiaries. Then again, in shifting the terms of engagement with social issues from the pursuit of justice to the delivery of services and efficiencies, neo-liberal economic principles are privileged over counter-narratives asserting the illegitimacy of liberal capitalism.

There is, thus, a major tension in the process of civil society formation – between market pressures on the one hand and the pressing need for international cooperation to address development challenges on the other. One key point of difference between the worlds of INGO "professionals" and of transnational social movements is the latter's allegedly spontaneous rejection of liberal developmentalism and the principles of organization that this entails. Popular outpourings of anti-capitalist sentiment such as the Occupy movement of 2011 or the street protests at the WEF meeting in Seattle in 2000 are the visible manifestations of a widespread popular sense that liberal international institutions, and liberal–capitalist governments in the North and South suffocate rather than advance democracy. Derided in the liberal media for naïveté, or ideological incoherence, or both, these movements are more evolutionary than revolutionary, and represent a different dynamic of mobilization. For Manuel Castells, the Occupy movement, which sprang to world attention with street protests against corporate greed centred on Wall Street in New York, signalled a global "rhizomatic" convergence of "outrage and hope" reaching across 82 countries and 952 cities at its zenith (Castells, 2012, pp. 3, 110). It was, he writes, an effervescent social phenomenon where communications networks patched together the frustrations of millions, channelling the energy of the so-called "Arab Spring" into a wider global movement (Castells, 2012, pp. 7, 31).

Mass protests appear disparate and uncoordinated on account of their heterogeneity and fall into a social category that Michael Hardt and Antonio Negri term the "multitude" (Hardt and Negri, 2005). This they define as "an irreducible multiplicity" cohering through the progressive elimination of political "division" though not, as they are at pains to say, the elimination of cultural diversity (Hardt and Negri, 2005, pp. 112, 129). Within this social crowd is to be found the germ of creativity, which, if allowed to flourish untainted by association with the corrupting influences of capital and institutionalized political power, can give rise to a new form of politics. Viewed from this vantage point, social movements are the genesis or the ignition point for a creative movement for change independent of the organizational priorities and reformist political objectives of northern NGOs. They are the epitome of "self-organization" – or *autopoeisis* – rather than hierarchical organization, of confluence rather than control. Unity, such as it is, stems from a collective refusal to accept injustice, which is as much a consequence of harsh lessons and bitter experience than any attachment to anti-capitalist ideology *per se* (Hardt and Negri, 2005, p. 129; Castells, 2012, pp. 31, 119). A central claim of the "Occupiers" was that the movement represented an experiment in genuine, un-orchestrated, social democracy, designed to demonstrate alternative possibilities (Occupy Together, 2014). As Douglas Rushkoff, of Occupy Wall Street, explained,

> The occupiers are actually forging a robust micro-society of working groups, each one developing new approaches – or reviving old approaches – to long-running problems. In just one example, Occupy's General Assembly is a new, highly flexible approach to group discussion and consensus building. Unlike parliamentary rules that promote debate, difference and decision, the General Assembly forges consensus by "stacking" ideas and objections much in the fashion that computer programmers "stack" features. The whole thing is orchestrated through simple hand gestures (think commodities exchange). Elements in the stack are prioritized, and everyone gets a chance to speak. Even after votes, exceptions and objections are incorporated as amendments (Rushkoff, 2011).

The "Movement" attracted a heterogenous body of participants, and advocates, including many working in senior roles within mainstream INGOs. It was both an above-ground campaign to capture public attention by seizing public spaces, which each protest entity did for a short while before being forcibly dissolved by the intervention of law enforcement authorities, and remains an underground movement harnessing the anonymity of the Internet's Tor networks to exchange information and intelligence, and share ideas and strategies (Occupy.Network, 2014). As a global phenomenon, it survives as an idea shared by a claimed 3,050 "Occupy Together communities" (Occupy Together, 2014). The movement exemplifies what network analysts describe as a "scale-free network" where each node is able to operate independently of other nodes – to self-organize – and to spawn new centres which can then form into new nodes in an ever-expanding, self-replicating and spaceless sociopolitical "organism." Its legitimacy and appeal issue both from its proclaimed spontaneity and from its claims to speak for the "99 per cent" against the 1 per cent of people who control the vast bulk of global wealth. Pivotal to this assertion, dressed in modern network and communications theory, is the neo-Marxist idea that all politics eventually coheres around shared economic class interests.

The quantification of representativeness claims is difficult in social entities antithetical to the notion of membership. Available measures, such as they are, suggest a significant but relatively small number of core adherents for the Occupy movement. The mobile messaging service,

Twitter, registers 194,312 "followers" for Occupy Wall Street, while #OccupyTogether records 230,000 Facebook likes! By comparison, the popular commercial music artist and "teen idol", Justin Bieber, attracts a 48-million-plus Twitter following (Occupy Together, 2014; Twitter.com, 2014a, 2014b). This undoubtedly reflects the marketing power of the global pop industry, but also the unpopularity of "difficult" decisions and the ephemerality of "clicktivism." Since the GFC, electoral politics in many Western democracies has returned right of centre governments committed to pro-business agendas, including trade liberalization. Clearly, there is no global consensus on the evils of capitalism. Divergent economic interest among the "99 per cent" is neither the sole nor indeed the most significant line of division within global civil society space.

The global fault line between secularism and religious belief is arguably more salient and fiercely contested. Justice globalists claim universal principles applicable to all societies irrespective of religion or ideology. Assertions of the "indivisibility" of rights carry the implicit message that all societies, irrespective of religion, language and tradition, share certain basic human values and ideals. Universalists like Robert E. Goodin claim an objective "universal morality" – arising from a "convergence" of solutions to common human problems (Goodin, 2003, p. 72). The idea of a universal moral order is not peculiar or specific to the Western Judeo-Christian tradition. Each of the world's other major universal religions – Islam, Hinduism, Buddhism, Taoism and the philosophical teachings of Confucius – assumes a higher authority to the state. While the language of rights evolved in the West, parallel ideas to the principles upon which Western rights thinking evolved can be traced through the Qur'an, the Bhagavad Gita and the teachings of various ancient Chinese sages. For example, Confucius's *The Analects* contains many specific recommendations against the arbitrary exercise of power, and Confucius enjoins those in authority to cultivate their humanity, which, it is asserted, is the source of durable political legitimacy (Leys, 1997, pp. 58–59). Such cosmic concerns have a contemporary and cosmopolitan ring but they do not patch over the obvious fractures with and between religious communities, and between the religious and the secular.

Members of deeply religious communities are opposed to, indeed "offended" by, secularism and secularization. Manfred Steger distinguishes dyadic contests between forward-looking "market globalism" and "justice globalism" on the one hand and the backward-looking, possibly millennial, "imperial globalism" and "religious globalisms" on the other, each battling for the ideological high ground at all levels of global society (Steger, 2009; Steger et al., 2013). Islamist jihadism is a reaction to adopted secularism and the pervasiveness of Western culture, international institutions and the larger non-governmental development agencies. The paradox here is that the act of resistance itself generates alternate forms of globalization – "alter globalizations" – cohering around oppositional ideologies and practices (Steger et al., 2013).

Efforts to integrate human rights into Islamic practice are further proof of the evolutionary nature of human rights and of the potential for constructive dialogue to overcome cultural differences. The Organization of the Islamic Conference, an intergovernmental organization of 56 Islamic countries from Africa, the Middle East and Asia, developed the Cairo Declaration on Human Rights in Islam in 1990. Premised upon natural rights as revealed in Islamic teaching, the declaration is in many ways complementary to international human rights law and the law of war. Article 1 of the declaration recognizes rights as derived from "basic human dignity" and proscribes "discrimination on the basis of race, colour, language, belief, sex, religion, political affiliation, social status or other considerations" (OIC, 1990, Art. 1a). The document includes sections specifying the crime of genocide, the rights of prisoners of war and the rights of civilians in conflict. However, women's rights are differentiated from the rights enjoyed by men.

The Cairo Declaration assigns a specific gender-based role towards women, which for women's rights advocates is repugnant to the UN Convention on the Elimination of Discrimination against Women (CEDAW), the INGO that oversees implementation of CEDAW. Specifically, CEDAW is premised on the idea that the gender-based differentiation of social roles encourages discrimination and violence against women. It thus calls for an end to the denial of basic rights and freedoms to half the world's population. In many Islamic societies, women are subject to discrimination on the basis of their gender – from repressive dress codes to restrictions on freedom of movement and the denial of the right to tertiary education or even the right to sign a bank cheque. Such discrimination constitutes a form of oppression that is not sanctioned by the Qur'an or the Cairo Declaration, which upholds the right to reject and to speak out against injustice which is, nonetheless, tolerable within the boundaries of propriety established by the Declaration (OIC, 1990, Art. 22a; Freeman, 2007 pp. 112–113). The "gap" between the Declaration and CEDAW is epitomized in Article 5a of the UN Convention which calls on state parties to "modify the social and cultural patterns of conduct of men and women, with a view to achieving the elimination of prejudices and customary and all other practices which are based on the idea of the inferiority or the superiority of either of the sexes or on stereotyped roles for men and women" (CEDAW, 1979). Islamic states have ratified CEDAW but with the reservation that where international law and Islamic *Sharia* law conflict, principles set out in the latter religious code are given greatest weight (CEDAW, 2006).

Yet, one crucial point that Western secular INGOs overlook at their peril is the lived reality of religious belief among Muslim women who do not identify with global feminism (Rashid, 2006, pp. 9–10). It is not the case that religious and secular principles are incommensurable, but, if we are to respect people's rights to their cultural traditions, agreement needs to be reached upon the meaning or boundaries of acceptable cultural tradition for each culture and each social group. Islamic women's organizations campaign for women's rights, often at great risk to individual activists who run the gauntlet of political persecution and, in countries like Afghanistan and Pakistan especially, threats of terror violence. The orthodox–progressive divide is not limited to Islam. When AI first adopted an explicit pro-abortion agenda in 2007, strongest condemnation arose from within the Catholic Church, which maintains the strictest of religious injunction against abortion (Khorfan and Padela, 2010). AI's stance is not out of step with Islamic scholarly opinion in pressing for decriminalization of abortion, and appropriate medical care for women who become pregnant through "rape, sexual assault or incest, or whose lives or health are at grave risk due to pregnancy" (Amnesty, 2007; Khorfan and Padela, 2010, pp. 103–104). Given the increasing signs of civil society formation around the issues of sexual rights, including gay, lesbian and transgender rights in the 2000s, AI's strategic shift made both political and commercial good sense. AI's global membership base has not declined and, if anything, sits at record levels.

That said, there are many points of disagreement between faith-based NGOs and secular observers. Part of the growth of INGOs in the last quarter of the twentieth century, religious development organizations, like the Seattle-based World Vision Inc. and the worldwide World Vision federation of affiliate branches, dwarf AI Ltd and the AI global network, in terms of income (US$ 2 billion in 2012–2013) and scale of operations (WVI, 2014, p. 4). It exports an explicitly Christian agenda through "secular" development programmes that address education, poverty alleviation, disaster relief, housing and clean water. The terms of its Christian "ambassadorship" are carefully worded to deflect criticism of proselytization, but the organization exudes Christian values through its management practices and project activities, including a publicly stated requirement for employees to submit to Christian principles (Kapralos, 2010; WV Inc., 2014). Religious rhetoric is toned down by affiliated World Vision Australia, for example, but acceptance of "Christian values" likewise remains a prerequisite to employment and career progression (WVA, 2014). Organizational rules and regulations ensure that a Christian message seeps through into the communities in which World Vision works. This is proselytization by osmosis, difficult to define in religious or civil law.

Religiosity is pervasive and suspect from a secular humanitarian perspective, but not so, paradoxically, from a multi-faith standpoint (Hammond, 2008). The view among many faith-based development organizations is that "interfaith cooperation and understanding" is not just possible but essential for the effectiveness of their humanitarian programmes (Kessler and Arkush, 2009; Tadros, 2010). Some religious belief is evidently preferable to no religious values at all. But the surge, or resurgence, of faith-based social activism reflects and is affected by deeper fault lines in global society that opened up after September 11. In practice, Islamic NGOs and INGOs are a focus of instinctive suspicion and surveillance for connections with global circuits of terror finance.

CSOs and criminal liability

As argued in this book, *unlawfulness* is not a concept defined in order to provide clearer demarcations between legality and criminality. All civil society actors are subject to contrary pressures arising from the nature of their diverse objectives and the different sociopolitical contexts in which these are pursued. Development practitioners and rights advocates play an active part in defining, through practice and debate, not only international rules governing aid allocations and human rights norms, but also armed humanitarian interventions and the management of liberal globalization. As David Kennedy argues, advocating for military intervention to prevent genocide and crimes against humanity, for example, involves humanitarian organizations and advocates in the co-creation of normative limits for acceptable killing (Kennedy, 2004). CSOs also challenge norms and defy law in the pursuit of normative change, and, consequently, often feel the weight of law used to silence them. In authoritarian and post-authoritarian democracies, NGO protest is frequently read as anti-state agitation and so activists endure an often antagonistic relationship with governments, officials and politicians. Greenpeace, as do many other politically oriented INGOs, relies upon bold public statements to draw attention to state environmental crimes. International passengers and the crew of Greenpeace vessel *Arctic Sunrise*, the so-called "Arctic 30," were arrested by armed Russian coastguards and charged with piracy for attempting to stage a protest against the Russian oil company Gazprom on one of their drilling platforms in the Barents Sea in September 2013. Their purpose was to draw world attention to Russian oil exploration in the Arctic, which, from Greenpeace's standpoint, is an environmental crime (*SMH*, December 25, 2013).

The Russian state is adopting its own version of "lawfare" to discourage political interventions such as that by Greenpeace. Amendments to Russia's criminal code and Non-Commercial Organization Law introduced since 2006 brings activism, especially, within the purview of the crimes of espionage and defamation, and subjects all protest actions to a "threat to the interests of Russia" test (ICNL, 2013a). Political activities are permitted, although this reflects the fact that the Russian state has entered civil society space by providing support for the "Nashi" youth movement that espouses a brand of Russian conservatism consistent with Putin's national agenda. Legal prohibitions and mountainous regulatory requirements are designed to restrict the scope and capacity for civic action and ban any organization with financial or personal connection to US NGOs, activists or the US state. Most contentious is the designation of foreign NGOs as "foreign agents," which merely intensifies the climate of official hostility to perceived outside interference within Russia's new "security state" (Soldatov and Borogan, 2010; ICNL, 2013a). AI's strategic aim to influence policy decisions affecting human rights in Russia, to say nothing of China, appears "aspirational" at best.

NGOs and their employees can be held criminally liable for the crimes that they commit in the name of global justice. Transparency International is an anti-corruption INGO, based in Berlin, Germany, and organized as a global network of national branches. A "liberal" organization founded by former World Bank executives, it finds current government tolerances, in developed and developing countries alike, for corrupt practices at the very least untenable, if not unconscionable. The organization defines its role as monitor, networker and agent of policy reform but, like its more radical or religious counterparts, exports norms supportive of one particular view of global normative order. The criminal liabilities of corporations operating corruptly as defined by the UN Anti-Corruption Convention has parallels in the INGO sphere, because INGOs must also operate in politically and legally ambiguous contexts, and, because of power asymmetries, are vulnerable to the demands of corrupt government officials. Concern over exposure to corruption litigation at home forces aid agencies to be vigilant in business transactions in humanitarian aid projects – as best they can – so as to avoid even the faintest whiff of bribery.

Political realities impose compromises upon even the most steadfast humanitarian NGO workers. Operational imperatives, and what Nicholas Stockton describes as a "culture of urgency," lead many organizations to stray into moral quagmires and forced compromises (Stockton, 2005). Parallel to the corporate world, relations between even the largest NGOs and host governments are asymmetrical, and usually favour the latter at great risk to NGO reputations and capacity to operate. As developing countries crave Foreign Direct Investment (FDI), so investors are forced to acclimatize to local political conditions and, as discussed above, comply with sovereign authority – even where, as in the case of land and mineral rights, the exercise of this authority is often disputed. Political leaders and government officials in disaster- or conflict-riven countries likewise seek foreign aid, but aid suppliers are similarly forced to submit to local political conditions once inside a country and, as one Australian Broadcasting Corporation (ABC) journalist put it, with regard to post-tsunami relief efforts in the Indonesian province of Aceh, to simply "bend with the wind" when pressured (ABC, 2005). In addition to a widespread "allergy to accountability," non-governmental actors are often insufficiently equipped with experienced professional management staff able to resist pressure to conform to local political exigencies (Stern, 2008, p. 129; Stockton, 2005).

In responding to humanitarian disasters, be they environmental and natural or caused by human conflict, NGOs enter countries or parts of countries where political order has temporarily collapsed and where social order has disintegrated. Or, they can choose to operate "behind enemy lines" to provide assistance to people in rebel territories in violation of the state sovereignty norm and in violation of the laws of the divided, but still sovereign, nation-state in which they intervene. In either circumstance, humanitarian workers are demonstrably not in control but are, nonetheless, "there" because assistance is required. Hostage to circumstance and exposed to the changing moods of those with whom they must deal, compromise on matters of international principle can be a matter of life and death, both for those in need and for the relief workers themselves. Bribery of border guards or army commanders can be the price of access to wounded and sick civilians and non-combatants. But such acts are effectively criminalized in countries where northern NGOs are headquartered, and from where the extending arm of extraterritorial law brushes up against international humanitarian practice (Ewins et al., 2006).

Cash payments are often required for safe passage through zones where central authority is weak or non-existent, and there are grounds for debating whether or not payments made to someone with no official authority constitutes bribery under the terms of the UN corruption convention and CTOC, or national-level anti-corruption laws. Cooperation with corrupt officials potentially places any organization at risk. In post-disaster or post-conflict circumstances the imperative to aid and rebuild as quickly as possible while meeting strict donor funding schedules creates irresistible external pressures to compromise. Despite extensive research into and monitoring of aid flows, the issue of corruption dogs relief efforts, and, because of the potential legal liabilities created, renders those closest to the cutting edge of aid delivery reluctant to openly discuss practices that are now effectively criminalized in the Global North where larger interventionist INGOs are based.

Neutrality is meant to be the shield behind which humanitarian workers can protect themselves and conduct their operations. Neutrality is critical to the provision of humanitarian protection under the Geneva conventions. It means that in principle, in conflict zones especially, the wounded and the sick of all conflict parties are entitled to medical treatment and respect for their fundamental human rights. In practice, ICRC medical centres or UNHCR (United Nations High Commissioner for Refugees) refugee camps can become havens for guerrilla fighters and, hence, a source of material support for one or more party. Humanitarian assistance and neutrality are elastic terms that can be stretched to accommodate partisan behaviour on the part of large aid organizations and "guerrilla humanitarians" operating on the edge of national and international laws. Acquiring information and evidence "in-country," which is critical of the government, in violation of visa restrictions, is a violation of law in countries where free speech is heavily circumscribed. The smuggling of documentary evidence of human rights violations through customs or transmitting damning images through the Internet is likewise regarded as a violation of law in authoritarian and post-authoritarian states. Distributing information critical of a regime, or promoting ideas and values that challenge the basis of authoritarian control or communicating with criminal, anti-state, rebel or otherwise proscribed groups, are likewise activities that are likely to result in imprisonment or deportation. Such actions are justified by appeals to a higher moral authority or principle, but at the level of national law enforcement they can be judged criminal offences.

AI distinguishes between the rights and political views of prisoners of conscience, asserting the lawful entitlements of people to protection and justice regardless of their ideological leanings (AI, 2014). This necessarily entails upholding the rights to a fair trial and lawful, humane detention for those who may or may not have committed international crimes or crimes against a state. Advocating rights for persons belonging to a designated terrorist organization, advocating for their release, and for respect for their rights under civilian as opposed to military law, as with Islamist fighters and suspected terrorists held at Guantanamo Bay in Cuba, creates tension between rights groups and the security establishment. Within authoritarian states, however, advocacy in support of political prisoners is not accepted and cannot be conceived as neutral. In China, criticism of the state must be proven accurate to be lawful under Article 41 of the Constitution of the People's Republic of China (PRC, 1982). Even though civil society space is growing rapidly, the state restricts the scope for advocacy NGOs to operate within the law, under which criticism of socialism, and indeed the very principle of the one-party socialist state, is effectively criminalized (ICNL, 2013b; see Ch. 2).

It is often said that people break laws every day of the week without realizing it. Indeed, it is not hard to break the law when law becomes so all-encompassing, where so many everyday actions and circumstances are subject to one or more rules, codes and potential legal liabilities. The scope for laws to be framed and invoked to catch the unwitting or to slowly undermine basic rights is limitless, even in democratic societies, especially when security is invoked as the prime reason. The global anti-terror regime and the national-level laws upon which it depends expand the notion of criminal complicity to incorporate the indirect provision of "material assistance" to terrorists. The International Convention for the Suppression of the Financing of Terrorism, 1999, clearly states that financial support for terrorism must be intentionally given and "in the knowledge that they are to be used, in full or in part, in order to carry out [a criminal act] intended to cause death or serious bodily injury to a civilian, or to any other person not taking an active part in the hostilities in a situation of armed conflict" (Art. 2b). It is clear, however, in the construction of the US Patriot Act, that an action that unknowingly or negligently and only potentially offers avenues for terrorist groups to access and circulate finance is sufficient to warrant criminal investigation (House, 2001). The law powers might be latent but they, nonetheless, hang as a threat over the operations of "neutral INGOs."

The actions of the Hong Kong and Shanghai Banking Corporation (HSBC), with regard to the Al Rajhi Bank, fall within the scope of Articles 2.1 and 2.3 of the terror finance convention, as did the Patriot Act, but what of the disbursement of development finance? Much financial aid is handed out in very large and very small amounts to persons in "jurisdictions of interest," like Gaza, for example. Harakat al-Muqawama al-Islamiyya (the Islamic Resistance Movement), or Hamas for short, is an Islamic NGO and also the ruling party, but has been designated a terrorist organization by the US, which potentially implicates in crimes of terror any organization or person providing or allowing material assistance to flow to members or followers of Hamas or their families (Slim, 2009). Hamas is committed to the eradication of the state of Israel and prosecutes this mission through its armed militant wing, the Izz a-Din al-Qassam Brigades. Despite ambiguously stepping back from this position after winning power in the Palestinian elections in 2006, Hamas remains linked to Islamist militants and to suicide and rocket attacks against Israeli civilians (Knudsen, 2005, p. 1384; CFR, 2007). The US government, like most Western governments and many secular and faith-based aid organizations, provides substantial aid to the Palestinian Territories but with strict accounting controls to "ensure" that funds do not materially assist terrorism, meaning that aid must not be paid directly to anyone associated with Hamas (Zanotti, 2013).

NGOs in the Palestinian territories must, therefore, walk a very narrow tightrope, with fewer staff available to maintain records and meet the strict reporting requirements necessary to receive US aid funding and to avoid Department of Justice scrutiny. Amendments to the US Code under the Patriot Act require organizations engaged in making or facilitating the transfer of money to keep records on "the identity and address of the participants in a transaction or relationship, including the identity of the originator of any funds transfer" (House, 2001, Sec. 311: p. 29). Application appears selective, where records of payments by the US military to Private Military and Security Contractors (PMSCs) and to Afghan tribal leaders are concerned, for example, but not for Gaza. And, as in Afghanistan and Iraq, US aid money is used to achieve key foreign policy aims, which also raises questions as to the neutrality of those aid NGOs that apply for and then redistribute US aid money in countries of intense US strategic interest.

The "business end" of global justice

Local NGOs and INGOs that work across battle lines are uniquely positioned to act as brokers between conflict parties and to assist in seeking resolutions to persistent intrasocietal conflict. The organization Geneva Call, for example, works to persuade rebel groups to recognize and comply with the Geneva conventions and serves as a conduit for two-way communications between rebels and the state forces against whom they fight. Its mission statement declares its neutrality and primary concern with respect for the laws of war and international humanitarian law by all conflict parties but specifically "armed non-state actors." In pursuit of its agenda, the organization inevitably treads gingerly along a legal tightrope between higher moral principle and compliance with increasingly proscriptive state-level anti-terror laws and policies that narrow the "space" for lawful humanitarian action (Geneva Call, 2010, pp. 2, 13). Neutrality in practice is, however, hostage to directional pressures from materially interested parties, including but not confined to allies of the belligerent entities.

As discussed, there is a strong moral case for aiding civilians on either side of the military front line but political realities and realpolitik can conspire against the realization of humanitarian aims. Rainer Baudendistel's study, *Between Bombs and Good Intentions: The Red Cross and the Italo-Ethiopian War, 1935–1936* (2006), offers an invaluable historical perspective on the political dynamics that can undermine the neutrality of humanitarian organizations during armed conflict. The ICRC, partly because of the divided nature of the Red Cross movement and its financial dependence upon national Red Cross societies and their respective governments, faced the self-appointed diplomatic challenge of ensuring Italy's engagement with the ICRC while also providing humanitarian assistance to Ethiopia. To maintain balance or impartiality the ICRC perplexingly, but not inexplicably, refused to take action to uphold the principles of the Geneva conventions (Baudendistel, 2006, p. 194; Barnett, 2011, pp. 92–93) Even though the ICRC had full knowledge of Italian violations, which included air force bombing raids on Red Cross medical stations in Ethiopia and the use of mustard gas, in his attempts to formulate an effective response, Committee president, Max Huber, refused to denounce fascist Italy. As a consequence, writes Baudendistel, the Committee "unwittingly became an instrument of Italian policy, facilitated in a subtle way by its own sympathies for Mussolini" (2006, pp. 213, 289). NGOs and humanitarian workers do not operate in a political vacuum and, whether they like it or not, are part of the political dynamic of complex humanitarian crises.

The ICRC and other organizations that operate extensively in conflict zones, like Médecins Sans Frontières (MSF), trade on their reputation for neutrality to gain access to victims of conflict. But neutrality is not the same as impartiality and, further, neither neutrality nor ignorance constitutes a defence against complicity in international treaty violations – at least not according to current thinking about corporate criminal liability for transgressions of the US Patriot Act and FCPA.

If the pursuit of justice is treated as a zero-sum game, then the provision of relief at the front line is a "no win" situation for the organizations involved. In his scathing critique of the failures and moral compromises of African food aid in the 1990s, Alex de Waal condemned well-known aid organizations for complicity in the inhumanity of dictators and warlords, citing the example of Ethiopia under Colonel Mengistu Haile Mariam in the 1980s. There, international aid agencies were perversely complicit in aiding Mengistu's prosecution of war in Tigray province and by implication the consequential famine that claimed an estimated 400,000 lives (De Waal, 1997, pp. 106–112). De Waal's case rests on the strategies widely used by dictatorial regimes engaged in the suppression of armed insurgency or just "routine" repression. International aid helps to discount the cost of emergency health services and food supplies for civilian populations, and thereby increases the amount of state food and medical assistance available for reallocation to front-line government troops, or for conversion into cash to line the pockets of the government and its supporters (De Waal, 1997; Terry, 2002; Duffield, 2007). Such resource transfers from donors through INGO in-country operations are "indirect" but they, nonetheless, impact upon the prosecution of wars, including the perpetration of rights abuses against insurgents and civilians in rebel-controlled areas.

MSF's disaster relief operation following the 2005 Pakistan earthquake in Kashmir entailed close cooperation with both government forces and civilian elements linked to the Pakistani Taliban (Brauman and Vidal, 2011). The Pakistani military was responsible for the governance of Azad Kashmir, where the earthquake hit, over which it maintained a regime of routine political oppression that intensified during the relief operation, and which it exploited to impose even tighter controls on the local population in prosecution of its counter-insurgency campaign (HRW, 2006). Yet, MSF's mission is to provide medical assistance to people in need and not to campaign against human rights violations or speak out about war crimes. Marc Le Pape takes on criticism of "selective humanity" making the case for pragmatic flexibility, and for case-by-case treatment of the moral challenge of dealing with brutal authoritarian and totalitarian regimes. MSF entered Myanmar in the 1990s where cooperation with the military junta, including an agreement for MSF in-country staff not to speak out against the regime, was, Le Pape argues, a "realistic" solution to the challenge of providing medical aid to Burmese people (Le Pape, 2011, pp. 239–240). From a pragmatic view, the fact that some assistance can get through the walls of menacing indifference is sufficient justification for humanitarian organizations like MSF to risk both reputation and, it should not be forgotten, the lives of relief staff. Former MSF research director Fiona Terry, who takes a very critical view of the record of humanitarian relief work, acknowledges that the various MSF country groups which "played golf" with the regime, were, nonetheless, able to slowly push out from the capital Yangon and into provincial and sensitive border areas to provide critical medical care (Terry, 2011, pp. 112–120). Compromise is arguably necessary, unavoidable and common, but also a secondary consideration to the primary aim of delivering urgent medical assistance to people in need. For de Waal, however, such "moral elasticity" is unconscionable and tantamount to complicity in international crime (De Waal, p. 147).

Not speaking out is not the same, however, as not seeking to influence international opinion against a pariah government. Relief workers are especially well placed to obtain first-hand intelligence about possible or actual war crimes, the location of evidence and the names of witnesses. Information filters out and up through the internal structures of an organization and can be, and indeed is, forwarded to those in a position to take action, be they investigators or advocates engaged in international tribunals, as with the International Criminal Tribunal for the former Yugoslavia (DeMars, 2005, pp. 125–134). The reality is that NGOs are part of the global information economy, operating as collection and transmission points for information and, indeed, "intelligence" across the vast global information grid. For MSF units operating in rebel-controlled areas of Syria, the appearance of neutrality is critical to the lives of MSF staff on the ground, and yet the demands of the 24/7 information economy requires extreme care in how operational reports from the field are handled. MSF entered the conflict zone without authorization from the Syrian government. Tackling the question of legal ambiguity head on by appealing to a higher moral principle, one MSF worker on the ground stressed the standard neutrality principle asserting, "we make no distinction between supporters and opponents of the regime in administering care" (MSF, 2012). Yet, MSF was the agency to which the international community and the international media looked for evidence of chemical weapons use against rebel fighters and civilians in August 2013 – and it obliged. Even without any attribution, or, indeed, confirmation that chemical weapons had been deployed, MSF's acknowledgement that it had first-hand evidence of the administering of medical aid to people in Damascus presenting with "neurotoxic symptoms" was sufficient to add momentum to the US diplomatic campaign against Assad, Iran and Russia (BBC, August 24, 2013; MSF, 2013). The organization was subject to the moral compulsion to assist in the investigation of a war crime and, at the same time, was denounced for politically assisting Syrian rebels (Cartalucci, 2013).

Expropriation of aid supplies, food and medicines is part of the price that aid organizations are often willing to pay in return for a limited licence to operate. Like de Waal, Fiona Terry and journalists David Rieff and Linda Polman have written at length about how and why in many instances NGOs veer dangerously close to complicity in international crime (De Waal, 1997; Terry, 2002; Rieff, 2003; Polman, 2010). It seems that every decade yields a fresh humanitarian challenge and with this many bitter lessons on the limits of humanitarianism. In the 1990s it was the wars that accompanied the disintegration of the former Yugoslavia that generated the most sustained reflection on the nature of humanitarian assistance and many prescient and scathing critiques of humanitarian practice. But in conflict situations how is crucial aid to be delivered, and assistance rendered to the sick and the wounded, without at some point compromising with the demands of armed combatants, desensitized by war, to the finer points of international law?

Established after the 2004 Indian Ocean Tsunami, World Vision refuges, or "temporary living centres" in Aceh, Indonesia, had the potential, according to an ABC Four Corners report, to assist the Indonesian military's counter-insurgency against the Gerakan Aceh Merdeka or Free Aceh Movement (GAM) by helping to concentrate the local population and thereby assist in surveillance. By necessity established under the supervision of the Indonesian Army, temporary accommodation built by World Vision Australia (WVA) and other aid agencies, it was alleged, could be used by the Indonesian Armed Forces or Tentara Nasional Indonesia (TNI) for population control, potentially implicating aid workers and their employers in crimes against humanity (ABC, 2005). INGO coordination staff negotiating with Indonesian authorities recognized that the TNI's *relokasi pengungsi* programme was legally suspect, from an international law perspective, and feared that "humanitarian space" could be compromised (*Inside Indonesia*, 2005). A ceasefire between GAM and the Indonesian state in August 2005 relieved political tensions in Aceh to a degree, but also minimized the potential reputational risk to INGOs cooperating with the Indonesian state to find shelter for hundreds of thousands of displaced persons (WV Asia Pacific, 2007). But the reconstruction programme in Aceh was also subject to corrupt practices on the part of government officials who colluded with local building contractors to winnow away substantial amounts of aid money. The construction, and subsequent destruction, of shoddily built and unsafe emergency housing, funded by donations to Oxfam and Save the Children

Fund, is but one well-reported case in point. Given the high levels of commercial corruption risk in Indonesia, and the reputation for venality of local officials overseeing the allocation of building and supply contracts in Aceh, this was either a case of inadvertence due to inexperience or otherwise negligence on the part of the staff involved (Guerin, 2006).

Much effort is invested in addressing the risks of corruption in humanitarian aid but, perversely, the elevated risk of corruption litigation could well have some unintended consequences. The international response to the Haiti earthquake of 2010 sparked the perennial criticisms of the injustices of aid spending, manifest in the image of the wealthy Western aid professional ministering to the destitute from the comfort of a brand new turbo-diesel four-wheel drive. The pattern of aid flows to aid agencies and the salaries and benefits paid to agency staff relative to affected populations entrench suspicions of legalized sequestration or lawful malfeasance in the aid and development "industry" (Weisbrot, 2011). This might, however, partially and paradoxically, also reflect the effectiveness of anti-corruption legislation and the countless conferences, training programmes, guidelines and training materials generated in the global anti-corruption effort, by raising the spectre of criminal liability, and the stakes, for complicity in corruption and money laundering. Risk is reduced if development funds remain directly controlled by the aid agencies involved, state and non-state, rather than released into open circulation. Litigation risk is reduced – in theory – if construction contracts are given to foreign companies based in countries with robust anti-corruption laws (though not necessarily the graver risks and injustices of bribery, favouritism, misappropriation or profiteering by subcontractors).

Whether they accept the nomenclature or not, relief NGOs are security actors and their actions shape security space in greater or lesser ways. This is, as Mark Duffield asserts, merely confirmation of the securitization of development (Duffield, 2007). Any international assistance operation attracts an army of civilian development workers and spawns a community of NGOs – ranging from the well-credentialed big players to relatively unknown local organizations – and this inevitably arouses the suspicion of security agencies. The relationship between NGOs and military and law enforcement agencies is fraught with tensions in operational areas, arising in part from different organizational cultures but also from different modes of operation. A joint report by the European Network of NGOs in Afghanistan (ENNA) and the British Agencies Afghanistan Group (BAAG) alleges cultural insensitivity on the part of the International Security Assistance Force and criticizes inappropriate relationships and reliance on unaccountable agencies and companies in the provision of reconstruction and development assistance. This is but one more non-government agency reporting on alleged favouritism towards private contractors by Western militaries (ENNA–BAAG, 2009, p. 9). It also, however, includes accusations of harassment of some NGOs by military personnel and the failure of military–NGO consultative mechanisms to ensure an adequate flow of information. There are many potential and evident points of tension between civilian and military organizations, one of which concerns the thorny question of NGO "neutrality," suggesting that from a military perspective, some NGOs, at least, might not be considered to be on the same side (McAvoy and Chamy, 2013). Soldiers, police and security contractors are bound to disciplinary and legal obligations, whereas NGOs can operate with greater independence – and, indeed, need to for their own protection – and make freelance contact with "the enemy" (ENNA–BAAG, 2009, p. 5). NGOs are natural conduits for information and secrecy is increasingly guarded and justified as critical to the informational dimension of military intervention. As a consequence of the rise of the security state, there is a tendency for Western militaries and governments to declare all operational details, however minor, "security in confidence."

The pursuit of humanitarian aims can take organizations or groups of humanitarian activists deep into unlawful territory, both figuratively speaking and in reality. Writing of the "honesty" of those prepared to make the moral choice to work with rebels, de Waal argues for the security-enhancing virtues of abandoning neutrality and operating in rebel-controlled areas within states riven by conflict. Reflecting upon the lessons of the 1983–1985 Ethiopian famine, the effective protection of civilians in rebel-controlled areas in Tigray and Eritrea was only achieved when some aid agencies decided to direct to the rebel Tigrayan People's Liberation Front (TPLF) and Eritrean People's Liberation Front (EPLF) – which proved to be more effective providers of "governance" and more inclined to prioritize human security (De Waal, 1997, pp. 130–131; Duffield, 2007, pp. 73–75). This occurred, however, with the assistance of the US and other Western donor governments, which viewed the conflict through the usual Cold War lens but which warmed to the anti-Mogadishu, and thus anti-Soviet, rebel cause at a time when Soviet communism was teetering (Duffield, 2007, p. 73). At the opposite extreme of the Indonesian Archipelago in West Papua, secular humanitarian agencies and faith-based organizations consciously work against the Indonesian state in advocating for Papuan independence – to the frustration of the Indonesian government and Australia's security policy community. Operating with no pretension of neutrality, and appealing to a higher standard of global justice, such non-state actors enable separatism by, at the very least, serving as messengers to the outside world, although the extent to which they might be complicit in emboldening insurgents is open to debate (Suter, 2006, p. 23). Geopolitical context clearly determines the "legitimacy" of unlawful humanitarian action.

The appeal of "direct action" to alleviate human suffering is obvious. Direct action offers a way for people to express their frustration at the glacial pace of global policy action and take bold steps to "correct" perceived intergovernmental failings. But direct international "humanitarian" action is a form of international political action that eliminates distinctions between aid and activism – and, potentially, activism and transnational crime, if not international crime, if we take the notion of complicity to the extreme. However admirable it might be to place oneself in harm's way, unarmed, in the name of a higher moral purpose, such actions can have unintended deleterious consequences. The "Freedom Flotilla" dispatched by an international coalition of civil society groups in May 2010 aimed to breach an Israeli blockade of Gaza, a step that logically entailed confrontation with Israeli authorities. Ostensibly an aid delivery exercise, its political purpose is undeniable and the deaths, at the hands of Israeli naval counter-terrorism commandos, of nine passengers on board one of the six vessels involved provoked international outrage and condemnation (Palmer, 2011). The action led to pressure on Israel from the UN to permit more aid into Gaza and this might be claimed as a positive outcome of a bold initiative. But the Flotilla led to the deaths of civilians, reinforced Israel's siege mentality and, by feeding what Gahssan Hage terms the "narcissism of victimhood," cut further away at the prospects of sustainable peace in the Middle East (Hage, 2010).

Code switchers

This chapter is not concerned purely with the moral dilemmas faced by NGOs and their staff, but also the unlawful dimensions to civil society space. Civil society groups, be they humanitarian organizations or "transformative" entities, shape international debate about law, justice and the use of force. Transnational movements are fluid, inchoate, volatile in the sense that they ebb and flow with shifting priorities of those who organize them – and we should not forget that movements, however spontaneous they appear, need organizers skilled in the art of social and political mobilization (Costoya, 2007, pp. 19–12). If we at least acknowledge grand theories of civil society formation, civil society space is where disparate and divergent groups and individuals cohere, if not converge, on issues of broad concern. Taking the Occupy movement as an example, "respectable" humanitarians gathered with activists and more radical groups, including those who publicly sought association with the hacktivist entity "Anonymous," by wearing the distinctive Fawkesian "V" mask, or identified with the iconic image of Argentinian revolutionary Che Guevara, the epitome of counter-cultural affectation and chic (Heath and Potter, 2004). Gandhi, Guevara, Guy Fawkes, all are exhumed and "accessorized" to rebellion in the ideologically hybrid space of civil protest and disobedience.

The celebration of the Occupiers' network connectivity invites critical reconsideration of the liberating potential of the Internet, and of the democratic potential of cyber space. The Internet enlarges the scope for political mobilization and non-violent protest but even in "virtual" space, the dividing line between protest and violence is blurred. The phenomenon of online or Internet activism includes actions by many smaller groups that extend across national borders and that engage in actions directed against the perceived enemies of global democracy and justice. In the Western sphere, the "hacktivist" group "Anonymous" is gaining a reputation for incisive cyber activism in pursuit of what Coleman and Golub argue are largely liberal values (Coleman and Golub, 2008). Such groups demonstrate the speed and fluency with which the Internet can be used as a tool to mobilize transnational political protest but also to coordinate acts of sabotage that are both unlawful and, in the evolving discourses of cyber warfare, arguably violent. Violence is understood as an act or actions intended to inflict physical harm on another human being but the meaning of the word extends to threats of harm, aggression and the destruction of property. Information systems hacking and Distributed Denial-of-Service attacks (DDoS) are just two of the means employed by online hacktivists, who might easily be regarded as cyber insurgents or bandits. Their techniques are becoming weapons in the cyber armouries of nation-states, which therefore conceivably strips these practices of their non-violent pretensions.

Cyber infiltrations by activist groups like Anonymous target perceived sources of global injustice, the Pentagon, CIA and the US security studies community and global banking institutions. Designed to harry, annoy and draw public attention to questions of democracy, hacktivism is a form of unilateral intervention and, where attacks violate the privacy and reputations of private individuals, cause criminal damage. Digital utopians portray the Internet as a vast space for democratic and radical action where like-minded people can collaborate to remake the world.

But utopianisms contain inbuilt contradictions forgotten in the pursuit of mass mobilization (Berenskoetter, 2011). Belief in the perfectibility of human society provides convenient dispensation for the violation of human rights through extrajudicial sanction and summary justice delivered by virtual means but with enduring "real" impacts on those upon whom sentence is passed. In the utopian assertion that "the internet puts the multitude in touch with itself" can also be found the seeds of irrationality that Arendt warned was the consequence of radicalism pushed to the extreme (Ray, 2007, p. 7; Arendt, 1970). The Internet fragments identities and communities as much as it creates distanciated unanimities for positive change. Notions of "selfhood" for the global multitude could be just one more rhetorical relic of a bygone technological age.

How revolutionary, then, is the Internet? The American and French Revolutions occurred without the aid of online social media but, nonetheless, made use of the social media of the day to communicate and to organize. The Internet adds an element of rapidity to the process of local political change as it does to the processes of global economic exchange. Analysis of rapidly escalating popular protests in Egypt, Tunisia, Libya and Syria points to the extensive use of Facebook by protest organizers to coordinate demonstrations, refine tactics and negotiate common aims (Choucri, 2012). Revolutionary sentiment spread quickly across the Maghreb making this an international phenomenon with global ramifications for great power strategies. Less attention is given, however, to the conditions that spurred these events, not least rising food prices and food shortages that increased the daily hardships faced by silent majorities. The Internet is not an axiomatic or quintessential democratic space but one populated by all kinds of social actors pursuing profit by lawful or unlawful means, or spreading messages of hate, and it is open to manipulation by governments and powerful corporations to market their messages. Therefore, it should not be romanticized as the catalyst or the venue for some future global rebellion.

Hacktivism is a crime against the laws of most states, save where the state is the hacker and where law is contorted or convoluted in ways that attenuate privacy. Anonymous "cadres" have been apprehended, charged and gaoled in the US where the tide of law and regulation is moving most swiftly against the right of anonymity. The tide has also turned against the duty to speak out against international crimes, established under the Nuremberg Principles, as indeed it has against many principles institutionalized at the end of World War II, including the rights of refugees. Just as the trial and sentencing of Bradley Manning gave the journalistic community pause for thought, the ongoing pursuit of Julian Assange by the US government, despite the soap operatic farce of his pursuit, and many official denials, is the exemplar of how network insecurities drive litigation diplomacy and indicates, alarmingly, just how far the US security state has evolved.

Manning provided Assange and WikiLeaks with roughly 720,000 classified documents, including Army and State Department records detailing military operations in Iraq and Afghanistan, standard diplomatic duplicity and torture (Barnes, 2013; Simpson and Roshan, 2013; Sledge, 2013). An expansive interpretation of the 1917 US Espionage Act in conjunction with the Patriot Act gives licence to the public branding of Julian Assange as a spy and an enemy of the state. The law can be massaged to imply that WikiLeaks is, if not a terrorist organization, then one indirectly responsible for providing information to the "enemy." Endangering human life clauses written into the Espionage Act and Patriot Act can be given alarmingly wide interpretation. Leaked information implicated in the death of a US citizen transforms the act of whistle-blowing into a capital offence. Publication of official secrets giving any advantage to a terrorist group is potentially an act of espionage and terrorism, and, if linked to the deaths of US citizens at the hands of a terrorist group, is also potentially a capital offence (US Code, Title 18 Pt. 1, Ch. 113B, 2331:1–3).

Many bytes have been chewed off in the pursuit of Assange and the denunciation of WikiLeaks. Information was not relayed directly by Manning or Assange to any proscribed organization or foreign power, but Snowden's sojourn as a "guest" of the Russian state associates his whistle-blowing circumstantially but visibly and directly with a "foreign power" and, thus, squarely within the scope of the Espionage Act. On the available evidence, WikiLeaks, Manning, Anonymous and Snowden have not killed or physically harmed a single human being. Prosecutors in the Manning trial were forced to acknowledge that no US deaths could be linked to Manning's leaks. But they are an annoyance and an embarrassment – and a hindrance to US diplomacy and that of its closest allies. Cyber activist groups are conflated with criminal entities and spoken of in the same breath as traffickers and terrorists, with no differentiation between them with regard to political and criminal motives. The direction of counter-terrorism and information security in the US, UK and other democratic states is towards less privacy and, paradoxically, less accountability – all in the name of national security. And, all the while, right-wing extremists groups, many openly bearing arms under the guise of sport or self-defence, gather global momentum (Bob, 2012).

Movements against allegedly unjust government or simply against perceived injustice usually begin with non-violent opposition, although, as discussed in Chapter 2, this was not the case with the Libyan uprising. But an espoused ideology of non-violence is not in itself a guarantor that opposition will remain peaceable. In practical terms, the transitions occasioned by the collapse or sudden departure of an illegitimate regime can be socially catastrophic, as was the case in India at the time of partition. Public opposition to British rule in India was strengthened by Gandhi's campaign of non-violence against the Raj, as was the moral authority of the Indian nationalist cause. Yet Gandhi's political doctrine contained many anomalies. Not least, Gandhi's injunction against violence was conditional rather than absolute, leaving scope for individuals to justifiably abandon non-violence in the face of unconscionable brutality. As there were limits to one's right to express dissent and to pursue non-cooperation, so were there limits to non-violence, and, where pushed to the extreme, "it is better to be violent, if there is violence in our hearts" (Gandhi, 2007, p. 51).

This statement provides a rationale for violence that political radicals, including right-wing vigilantes, of a violent persuasion can seize upon to justify the escalation from passive to armed "resistance." Indeed, the language of non-violent activism leaves room for creative and selective interpretation when the laws and institutions, as much as the practices of brutal suppression by the state, constitute a form of violence (Arendt, 1972, p. 160). Ironically, such elasticity of meaning leaves the exercise of counter-power through mass mobilization, political pressure, disruption and the like open to the criticism that the opposition is likewise violent – in intent if not action. When political tensions reach a crescendo, and political leadership disintegrates or becomes dysfunctional, the risk of violence increases and, warns Arendt, so too does the risk of irrationality (Arendt, 1972, p. 161). Pacifist ideals are frequently subverted to justify not merely resistance but the use of force to attack the sources of perceived injustice. Militant and militarist sentiment can likewise be ignited to pursue campaigns against injustice, defined by an alternate vision of right.

Mark Kurlansky, in his study of non-violence, stresses the attractiveness of non-violent causes to the violently inclined. Revolutionary transformations led by fanatical "fantasists" – as Paul Berman points out in his extended essay, *Power and the Idealists* (2005) – can culminate in a cycle of violence and repression as radicals seize the power of the state to make inroads into all facets of public and private life. When revolutionary idealists become Berman's "fantasists," driven by visions of a perfectible future, political violence becomes justified to achieve utopian ends, and opponents can be hurt or killed. Where ideological extremists achieve control over the state, warns Berman, people die in large numbers in the name of the revolution or justice or God. Power can be a catalyst for an uncertain chain of political reactions, and peace might be the least likely outcome from the violent pursuit of ideological ends (Berman, 2005, p. 181).

Arendt gave similar warning in *In Crises of the Republic* where she writes, "to tear the mask of hypocrisy from the face of the enemy, to unmask him and the devious machinations and manipulations that permit him to rule without using violent means . . . these are still among the strongest motives in today's violence on the campuses and in the streets" (Arendt, 1972, p. 162). Such "radical transparency" is precisely the aim of Assange and WikiLeaks, which, however simplistic, enjoys mass appeal. But in the process of radicalizing society against the hypocrisy of the governing classes, radicals risk creating the circumstances in which political and criminal violence flourish in the name of revenge masked as "restorative justice" or restitution. Here is her definitive paradox of political action. To rage against intolerable injustice was essential for the regeneration of democratic society but in this rage lay the germ of irrationality and the risk of even greater suffering as an unintended consequence of democratization (Arendt, 1972, pp. 160–161). This is precisely because the radical, of whichever persuasion or wing, cannot accept that any other set of ideas or beliefs can or should enjoy the same level of popular support.

The organizational skills of oppositional groups, and the interests that surround and exploit them, are highly advanced today. Techniques of asymmetric struggle of armed revolts against the state have been honed over the past century and summarized in the doctrines of counter-insurgency or "fourth generation warfare." Sufficient moral power must be mobilized by the weaker party if it is to bring about the desired political or revolutionary change; state crimes, especially murders or atrocities, give oxygen to popular anti-government sentiment and help spread the wildfires of unrest. The language of non-violence or violence, justice or injustice, victimhood and the rhetoric of democracy provide sufficient ideological cohesion to subordinate or mask ideological differences in the short term. Such is the level of understanding of the mechanics of protest and rebellion that the boundaries between orchestration and prefabrication can become blurred, leading to allegations that some supposed "grass-roots" movements are in fact little more than "astroturf" campaigns (Monbiot, 2010b; Waites, 2011).

Three recent cases in point are the right-wing Tea Party in the US and the Red and Yellow Shirt movements in Thailand. Each allegedly serves wealthy business interests who invest in anti-government agitation by the more vociferous elements of the "precariat" (Standing, 2011), namely, the economically marginalized and those of the affluent middle classes who cling precariously to the soft edges of economic security in an unstable global economy (Monbiot, 2010a; Battersby et al., 2011, pp. 103–111; Waites, 2011). Perhaps there is good reason to be suspicious when political protest appears to imitate the sleek, manufactured and superficially inclusive consumerism of capitalist "culture ideology" (Monbiot, 2010b; Sklair, 2002). But the public anger displayed by divergent "people's" movements in Thailand reflects deep and long-running grievances against and within the country's power elites (Battersby et al., 2011). The irony is that the outcome of such left–right/right–left and elite/precariat combinations can be a more precarious future for those who take to the streets – or to the *maquis*. This assumes of course that there can be no accommodation or tolerable and therefore durable *status quo* between class interests.

Working with corporations

Is it possible to set aside ideology in pursuit of narrower pragmatic development gains? The preceding discussion is intended as another and differently directed brake on convergent thinking. Value conflicts between different categories of non-state actors – humanitarian, business and those in between – are an inevitable consequence of divergent thinking and priorities, but the coordinated search for some common ground, or some comparable principles, at least offers the possibility of a viable pragmatic prescription with which to advance the cause of peace and human enablement both regionally and globally. Given that governments have thus far failed to meet a global commitment to set aside 0.7 per cent of GDP each year for Overseas Development Assistance (ODA), there is logic in tapping into the vast resources of the global corporate sector. One reliable indicator of social giving by leading corporations in the US, the Committee Encouraging Corporate Philanthropy (CECP), reported cash and in-kind social development contributions of, at the very minimum, US$19.9 billion in 2011 (CECP, 2012, p. 4). As touched upon in Chapter 4, there is evidence to suggest that NGO–business cooperation, however tenuous, can effect positive, practical social change and alter corporate culture (Rivera-Santos and Rufin, 2010; Overbeek and Harms, 2011). Even Leslie Sklair, acknowledges that benefits can ensue from "Corporate Social Responsibility" (CSR) projects, even if these schemes are intended to advance the commercial interests of those businesses involved and humanize their corporate image and feed the "culture ideology" of capitalism (Sklair, 2001, p. 151). Non-governmental actors can choose to attack the image or find means to modify corporate practice.

The history of confrontation between business and civil society groups reflects deeper "disagreement" between market and justice globalisms, as much as different organizational aims and governance practices. Greenpeace, for example, is a "direct action" political organization that, since its formation in 1971, has been at the forefront of environmental campaigns to lift public awareness of environmental issues and force governments and companies to be more environmentally responsible in policy and practice. It galvanized global opinion against French nuclear testing in the South Pacific, for which the organization's flagship, the *Rainbow Warrior*, was sabotaged and sunk by French intelligence operatives in Auckland, New Zealand, in 1985. Greenpeace's confrontational approach draws inevitable condemnation and refutation from governments and corporations targeted in its campaigns. However, Greenpeace is on record as having deliberately massaged evidence for political advantage in one celebrated case involving a decommissioned Shell-owned drilling platform, Brent Spar, which was to be scuttled in deep water off the east coast of Scotland in 1995. Greenpeace claimed, falsely, that this would release 5,500 tons of crude oil stored on board into the North Sea. Launching a major and effective consumer boycott of Shell products, Greenpeace forced Shell into a humiliating backdown (Kellow, 1999; Mosch, 2005; Kuszewski and Crowther, 2010). Whether because of a crisis of self-confidence sparked by this campaign, or, as Leslie Sklair argues, a deeper "crisis of capitalism" emerging in the 1990s, resources companies made a concerted effort to develop "green credentials" and to manage public opinion on resource-related issues (Sklair, 2001, p. 151, 2002, p. 53; Kuszewski and Crowther, 2010).

None of this discounts the reality that companies will invest time and resources in protecting their financial bottom line, even where this means undermining the pursuit of a social good or a fundamental human right. Advocacy campaigns designed to reshape corporate practices require long lead times between commencement and actual impact upon the global regulatory environment. "Lawfare" of a different form to that fought over alien torts litigation in the US ensues in the face of efforts by rights or environmental groups to introduce or change legislation to make companies more accountable to international standards of "best practice." Resistance can be fierce and the protracted struggle that led to the International Code for the Marketing of Breast-Milk Substitutes began in the 1960s with attempts to regulate the promotion of infant formula in developing countries on account of its detrimental impacts on maternal and infant health. The introduction of the Code in the 1980s was challenged by food companies (and their legal legions) across multiple national jurisdictions in order to influence the stringency of regulations at the national level. The slow pace of ratifications through the 1990s reflects the reluctance of many states to enforce regulation on a very large and increasingly footloose industry sector (Richter, 2001, pp. 77–78). Similar tales abound with regard to pharmaceutical company patent rights and the provision of life-preserving medications for HIV/AIDS sufferers in Africa and South Asia, and the efforts of economic and political conservative forces to stymie global action on climate change.

Sponsorship of "grass-roots" social entrepreneurship and social enterprise formation too is lauded and applauded by development organizations as a means of empowering disadvantaged peoples and communities (McWade, 2012). Stripping away the ideological element to cross-sectoral antagonisms, Miguel Rivera-Santos and Carlos Rufin explore the organizational dimensions of alliance relations, concentrating on supposedly neutral measures: "aims," "objectives," "trust" and "interests". A strong dose of pragmatism can result in mutual, if geographically limited, gains for companies and humanitarian NGOs through tactical cooperative engagement at strategic points on the global social plane (Rivera-Santos and Rufin, 2010, p. 65). In a different dimension and on a smaller, less-visible scale, ethical investing profits from the growth of ethical consumption in this emerging field of CSR. Humanitarian NGOs play a prominent intermediary role in creating market incentives and adding market value by certifying products as ethically, meaning sustainably, produced or sourced (Miyata, 2007). For NGOs, alliances with business increase the flow of resources, financial and human, in the direction of social or environmental need. This, however, raises related questions about the relative impacts of cooperation on organizational structures and mission, and the degree to which there exists a genuine "harmony of interest" between humanitarian NGOs and corporations or just a pragmatic *modus vivendi*.

Acknowledgement of social responsibility by businesses is conditioned by the strength of regulatory pressures: legal, moral, political, social, and subject to changing corporate imperatives. For liberal progressives and radicals alike, solutions to global justice challenges can be found in rights-based approaches to development, and by reconciling humanitarian values with the technocratic "classificatory" approach to development and global governance (Sklair, 2002, p. 22). But this also requires the conception of social "responsibility" in terms that resonate with the all-pervasive language and practices of modern organizational and strategic management, negating or at least deflecting alternative interpretations that foreground the gendered nature of capitalism, the masculinism embedded in the notion of aggressive individualism and the violence which both critical and conservative scholars argue is engendered by the very nature of capitalist competition.

Laws of revolution and evolution

If civil society space is so widely populated and beset by relational tensions and value conflicts, on what grounds can civil society actors reasonably claim to have any significant or lasting social impact? Greenpeace can lay claim to having changed corporate practice through its Brent Spar campaign against Shell and the actions of organizations like Greenpeace have shaped the global environment agenda. "Aid effectiveness" can be assessed at the micro level by measuring internal project performance indicators, where the emphasis is placed upon the efficient management of "performance targets." AI, for example, subjected selected programmes to qualitative project evaluations to help mark its fiftieth anniversary. With advocacy organizations like AI, media exposure, including social media engagement, is an additional important and quantifiable measure, which can at the very least indicate reach and receptivity (Amnesty, 2012b). In development projects, participants can be evaluated for their experiences, how project activities helped to improve amenities, skills or opportunities at a localized level, and the available data can give a very favourable impression (Riddell, 2007, pp. 179–181). The larger question of how effective aid and development programmes are at a systemic level in changing macroeconomic and macropolitical conditions and dynamics is much harder to establish. Pro-aid macroeconomists stress a positive correlation between aid flows and economic development, but aid has proven to also lead to dependency, and much aid has been misspent (Collier, 2008, pp. 100–102; Banerjee and Duflo, 2011; Karlan and Appel, 2011). Establishing a statistical link between aid and the enjoyment of subjective rights is even more problematic, and most probably impossible. Civic space is growing in authoritarian China, and the state is striving to establish control over this space, using the social development capacities of local NGOs while at the same time strictly regulating them to restrict their political influence.

The spread of both the hardware and software of Internet-mediated communications has expanded the scope for non-state transnational and global engagement. Undoubtedly, global society is more extensive and complex, and more open even if this openness is challenged on many fronts.

For liberal modernizers, the realization of political rights is an evolutionary process. The world has acquired a growing corpus of international humanitarian law, and this, it can be argued, is a consequence of increasing sophistication and interdependence. At the national level it is possible to plot a trajectory of gradual recognition of rights: political, economic, social and cultural. The collapse of communism in Eastern Europe was replicated in lesser ways by the demise of military-controlled regimes in Asia and Latin America. William DeMars questions whether advocacy organizations had any net effect on human rights violations in Argentina under military rule (DeMars, 2005, p. 110). Democratization, when it occurred across Latin America, reflected more complex combinations of shifting public sentiment and changed international economic conditions brought about by the historic shifts in global geopolitics that also hastened democratic transitions in Asia, in Thailand and South Korea. The rule of Chile's General Augusto Pinochet, from 1973 to 1989, is characteristic of Latin America's era of military dictatorship from the 1960s to the 1980s. Pinochet came to power in a military coup in 1973 and immediately suspended parliamentary government and banned political parties. Opposition activists were imprisoned, and many were "disappeared" – a euphemism for political execution. But the Pinochet regime could not survive the end to Cold War, and Pinochet eventually succumbed to international pressure, including pressure from the US, to restore democratic rule (Skidmore and Smith, 2005, pp. 133–137). As in neighbouring Argentina, parliamentary democracy resumed and with it greater recognition and respect for civil and political rights (Eakin, 2007, p. 270).

This turn towards democracy is attributed by Fukuyama to late twentieth-century globalization of liberal capitalist values, in effect, a reassertion of Rostow's liberal modernization thesis. In this regard, at the macropolitical level, NGOs, both advocacy and developmental, have most evidently played a part in shaping international norms and the climate of international opinion, but change comes, and indeed must come, from within societies (DeMars, 2005). In China, the world's largest totalitarian state, ordinary people are challenging the system. Since the late 1980s, China has pursued a strategy of economic modernization that entailed opening the economy to Western investment and to capitalist enterprise. The change was in part driven by demands from the country's urban middle classes for greater political freedom, which led to the Tiananmen Square protests and massacre in June 1989. Economic modernization offered a release valve for social pressure for political change, but the stresses created in Chinese society by rapid modernization have merely highlighted structural weaknesses within the state. Economic development and democratization might well be complementary processes, but neither occurs automatically as a consequence of the other, and it is possible for countries such as China to maintain high rates of economic growth while severely restricting or even curtailing political participation. The question for Western analysts is how long authoritarian regimes can maintain a vicelike grip on the reins of power, and yet there are suggestions that China's next generation is less concerned with democratic reforms and is content to increase material consumption and accumulate wealth (Kaplan, 1997; Ma, 2013).

Aid and development NGOs alone cannot make substantial impacts on key macrolevel indicators of socioeconomic progress, including democratization. And, as argued, the degree of international investment – not necessarily in dollars – that is required to make a difference has yet to be achieved, even if the monetary allocations involved appear large (Riddell, 2007, pp. 254, 266). The direction of development dollars has also been heavily and unjustifiably skewed towards grand schemes of economic development at the expense of social objectives (Banerjee and Duflo, 2011). After their formation, the UN and the World Bank Group pursued divergent paths to development accompanied by divergent conceptions of how development was to be achieved. The UN, epitomized by the work of UN Development Programme (UNDP) and of the UN Conference on Trade and Development (UNCTAD) under Raul Prebisch, pursued a social development objective, while the World Bank pursued orthodox liberal modernization advocating free markets, privatization and FDI to aid recipients. Greater financial resources were made available to the latter, and to the International Monetary Fund (IMF), which sharpened institutional rivalries (Kennedy, P., 2006, pp. 114–117). UN practitioners have learned, slowly, that sustainable development necessitates greater emphasis upon human development measured not in gross financial returns but levels of human security (Chapter 2). Also, development practitioners in the government and non-government fields are increasingly averse to measuring aid effectiveness in purely dollar terms because, philosophically, the purpose of aid is, or should be, to develop people first (Riddell, 2007, pp. 262–266).

Development discourse has expanded to encompass a much broader range of concerns, including human rights. Following Amartya Sen's logic, development is a question of freedom, and freedom is an inalienable right, not a consumable good (Sen,1999). The notion of Asian human rights competes against the idea and idealization of Asian economic developmentalism. One of the "authors" of the "Asian values" debate, Singapore's former prime minister and "elder statesman" Lee Kuan Yew, argued that in "Eastern societies" the rights of community come before the rights of the individual. Setting forth an organic view of society he asserted, in a 1994 interview that, "In the East the main object is to have a well-ordered society so that everybody can have maximum enjoyment of his freedoms. This freedom can only exist in an ordered state and not in a natural state of contention and anarchy" (Zakaria, 1994, p. 111). Speaking in defence of the suppression of democracy protesters at Tiananmen Square, Lee Kuan Yew suggested that the alternative was cataclysmic political disorder (Zakaria, 1994, pp. 122–123). The irony here is that China remains best by extensive civic disorder, with recorded public protests, large and small, reaching 230,000 incidents for 2010 (Göbel and Ong, 2012, p. 8).

The moral rejoinder to the cultural relativist critique of human rights comes from Sen, who, like Fukuyama, stresses the diversity of intellectual traditions within "Western" and "Asian" cultures. Asian essentialism or "exceptionalism" stands on shaky historical and moral ground, not least because, it is argued, respect for rights does not impede the development to which Asian modernizers aspire. To these cultural arguments must be added the political reality that Asian governments have endorsed international human rights law and hence enjoy the rights and privileges of members of the international community, which in turn incur obligations (Twiss, 1998, p. 30). Asian human rights scholars emphasize the principle of reciprocal obligation in Confucian thought. Students of Chinese philosophy emphasize the humanism implicit in the writings of Confucius and the injunctions for superiors to remember their obligations to their subordinates (Chang, 1998). The proliferation of Asian human rights NGOs is further evidence that humanitarian values are not "un-Asian." Then again, aid spending by multilateral banks and the UN was, from the early 1990s, increasingly tied to both trade liberalization and democratization under the umbrella concept of "good governance." However, questions remain as to the efficacy of agitation by rights campaigners in authoritarian states.

Rights, and the laws that enshrine and uphold them, have increasing practical utility in an increasingly complex world. Denial of basic civil and political rights, argues Sen, inhibits the achievement of basic enabling economic and social rights and, consequently, could be perceived as a drain on a country's economic growth rather than a prerequisite for social stability (Sen, 1999, p. 15). Did recognition of this argument influence the dramatic change in direction by the Burmese junta in 2010 when Myanmar held its first democratic general election for more than two decades? Following the switch from military dictatorship to authoritarian democracy, rapprochement with the West has yielded substantial financial dividends for former military rulers and the state elites who positioned themselves to gain the greatest benefit from the country's slow and spasmodic opening up to the outside world. Space for democratic action has enlarged, Aung San Suu Kyi is no longer under house arrest and her National League for Democracy is allowed to campaign. Yet, this transformation did not stem directly from the protests of INGOs. Instead, change arose through accommodations sought and found between Myanmar and the Association of Southeast Asian Nations (ASEAN). Intra-ASEAN commercial interests played a significant role behind the scenes, and limited democratization spiced with greater economic openness is sufficient to satisfy Western governments that Myanmar is on the right track.

Conclusion

For Asian human rights groups, there can be no genuine democratization without greater regard for social justice and ASEAN governments display limited regard for both, which are subordinated to national economic goals and of course "stability" (ICNL, 2013c). For movements seeking to transform the global system, there must be no concession to the realities of international politics, because, as De Mars asserts, rights advocates and organizations "cannot acknowledge the political constraints facing actors without undermining their own recommendations" (DeMars, 2005, p. 55). Could this inflexibility be a weakness? With more engaged organizations, groups, and persons more attentive to the world around them and more concerned about a common future, civil society can, in an ideal sense, act to restrain the arbitrary exercise of power. The complexities of globalization are such that more radical solutions risk multiplying the injustices against which movements for change coalesce or organize. Arguably, the best defences against arbitrary power are to be found in the complexities of a plural global society with a multiplicity of actors and interests. Complexity and diversity are essential to system maintenance, be this human or ecological, and within complex ecologies, elements or agents can accumulate greater or lesser gravitational pull and drag interwoven matrices or "webs" in favourable directions (Urry, 2003, pp. 139–140). Taking a constructivist view, this is one possible "critical path" towards the creative recoding of global relations.

6
Amorality, Complexity and Cosmopolitan Code

That transnational crime, conventionally defined, is increasing in scale and value is not in dispute. So why take a study of crime and security to such lofty heights as complexity theory and meta-governance? Debate about the plurality of international actors or the liberal theory of markets seems, at first glance, far removed from illegal logging in the rainforests of Brazil or Indonesia! Yet this book was never designed to be a narrative of crime and criminality or of rebellions and counterinsurgencies and counterterrorism operations. From the outset, the aim was to locate crime and security within wider systems of law and governance practice and to explore the systemic nature of transgression, or *unlawfulness*. The identification of criminals and security threats is, on one level, a matter of detecting criminal enterprise, identifying criminal suspects, apprehending and then punishing those who violate codified law. Within sovereign legal systems this can be relatively as straightforward as catching drug traffickers or persons guilty of murder, theft and a whole raft of objectively defined offences. Here, however, this exploration is concerned with the shifting boundaries of crime and criminality and the contested nature of security space. Crime and security are increasingly interwoven but the *mentalité* of crime control complements a conservative strain of non-traditional security defined as control or threat disablement. Prone to the simplistic attractions of convergent thinking, responses to real global challenges are consequently unbalanced.

The preceding chapters characterize the global system as unpredictable, chaotic, and complex – though not disordered. Patterns of convergence and divergence are equally discernible in the social, economic and political spheres – as far as it is meaningful to treat these as separate domains. This is a necessary position from which to engage in a discussion of normative structures and issues in global affairs. To explore the nature of *unlawfulness*, analysis needs to be anchored in some notion of material reality – or materiality. Likewise, to explore the nature of law from an international or global systemic perspective requires that we step outside the theory of law, and outside philosophical idealism, to examine how laws are made, broken and altered in practice. The globe is not and cannot be "one big courtroom" or a juridified whole any more than it is a hopelessly disordered and ungovernable place, and the globe has become a place in the public imagination. Within this global place, social relations are ordered by unique sets of cosmopolitan code, many of which sit incongruently alongside the "base" settings of the global system. Unlike its previous conceptual incarnations, as Niebuhr's immoral society or Bull's anarchical society of states, in the unlawful society, the globe is indeed an intricately governed space in which a vast constellation of actors and entities interact and where the basic operating codes are arbitrary, indifferent, agnostic and amoral.

Code is cracking everywhere

The global crime–security nexus is a conjuncture of multidimensional and cross-cutting issues that defy simplistic binary distinctions between legal and criminal, right and wrong, good and evil. By exploring this nexus through the concept of *unlawfulness*, it is possible to "capture" a multi-layered space of unlawful human action populated by a diverse assemblage of actors or entities that operate on or across the bright lines or the dull edge of law. There is messiness in globalization that renders modernist means inadequate to achieve security or negate all forms of harmful human action. Governance is not simply a matter of "closing the gaps" between law and practice, because these "gaps" are contested spaces, generated by the interaction dynamics of a complex of systems within which humans do not behave according to any uniform model of rational individuality. There are observable traces, however, of resistance to control and to law across state, security, corporate and humanitarian dimensions of globalization.

The multiplicity of legal jurisdictions and the reality that laws are often incongruent does not explain all cases of unlawful practice. In short order, states have need of laws and yet transgress the laws of nations as a matter of routine, usually for reasons of national security or economic welfare but also for reasons of private interest; corporate actors seek to modify the regulatory environments in which they operate, to exploit the spaces between regulatory regimes, and leverage political influence; and in the civil society space, agents of social change likewise seek to alter the legal landscape and to test the edge of law or otherwise cross deliberately into outlaw territory.

Globalization opens new vistas for criminal endeavour as it does for endeavours yet to be criminalized. But globalization also opens new frontiers for the extension of laws, through extraterritorial legislation and enforcement, to the formation of new global norms and regimes. Whatever the jurisdictional variations in degree, principle and purpose across the global patchwork of sovereign states, the overwhelming directional shift is towards greater state control over society through increased surveillance or additional regulatory constraint. The so-called Global War on Terror is the catalyst for the globalization of anti-terror laws, the codification of corporate crimes and the extension of state controls over transnational and global finance. This law revolution occurs along the multi-purpose switch-tracks of global regulation.

Taking the global anti-corruption norm as an exemplar, we can interpret this as an instrument that erodes avenues for elite social coalitions to control the organs of state power to their financial advantage, to undermine global counter-terrorism or counter-narcotics efforts and to disregard international human rights. Limiting or eliminating the power of corrupt dictators or venal regimes is a global good in anybody's book – save for those who lose out. Anti-corruption laws are, however, primarily designed to eliminate the impact of crude collusion on market processes and thereby, in aggregate terms, maximize economic performance, growth and wealth treated as both public and private goods. In combination with the national subscription to market competition norms, they further encode the global system in ways that undermine the autonomy of states and which thereby regulate authentic democratic politics to satisfy market expectations. Anti-corruption and anti-competitiveness are separate but complementary areas of business regulation which in combination break down obstacles to the freer movement of capital at the state level and free up the global plane to the operations of the largest, most flexible, self-organizing and largely amoral corporate networks.

Base code is amoral but codified laws embody, as Antonio Cassese writes, commonly held values inscribed into objective statements of normative principle (Cassese, 2008, p. 11). Built to reconfigure international relations at this syntactic level, the superstructures of global governance, however, remain part of and subject to the influence of reticulated globalized power networks (Simpson, 2007). Consequently, there remain many avenues and incentives to legally disrupt and circumvent codified law and legal principle – and to recode law to suit pressing circumstances. International or global society has built-in tolerances for deception, evasion and destruction; the universality of spying is evidence enough of this, as it is for organized violence, human rights abuses, environmental harm and the infiltration and immobilization information networks. This *unlawfulness* is encoded into the operating protocols of the global overworld. It reaches far beyond money laundering, illegal trafficking and credit card fraud into practices that are at once legal but unconscionable – or illegal yet justifiable. It draws in every government of every country that spies on its enemies and friends, forges identities, deceives and steals or trades in contraband goods. It involves every non-state actor that subverts law to serve commercial or humanitarian ends. It spans every revolutionary movement, rebel force, paramilitary outfit and terrorist cell, and all those who protect and trade with them. The connections between this overworld and the global underworld are much closer than anyone cares to admit, in public at least. But this is not a convergent danger or some nascent evil empire rising up to threaten the world.

The loci of global *unlawfulness* are not confined to the global "badlands" even if profiles of global criminality direct attention towards "jurisdictions of concern" in the Global South and the Global East. Terror and transnational criminals stalk the imagination and the fear generated by these spectral figures can only be allayed through the rapid identification and interception of imminent threats, before any crimes are committed. In spite of a generation of institutionalized campaigns against racism and ethnocentrism, biometric information technologies harden racial stereotypes of "persons of interest" of "Asian" or "Middle Eastern" appearance, because, according to unspoken security code, crime and terror are social phenomena with racial or "ethnic" as well as political characteristics. Meta-data and personal information are processed with algorithms of criminality and political extremism inferred from "baselines" derived through the analysis of every scrap of available information on every known "deviant," criminal or otherwise (Magnet, 2011). Stereotypes of deviance are no longer simply matters of race, class or political prejudice to be tackled through education, training and professionalization. They are instead indispensable to the practices of crime and security risk control.

States are caught in an unending race against crime, continually struggling to keep pace with social change and technological innovation while struggling to abide by laws that they create. States fill lawless voids with new categories of crime that become outmoded the moment they are written into law. But states also delay the passage or adoption of laws deemed central to the global common good but detrimental to national interests – often, in practice, the interests of elite groups. International regimes exist because there are sufficient incentives for them to be formed and observed, but the order achieved is only partial. This is the paradox of governance in the twenty-first century. Negating *unlawfulness* is not simply a matter of stricter policing of norms and the enforcement of law because the inflexible rule of law can encourage abuse of power and privilege and entrench social division.

Laws define values and establish frameworks within which human actions can be judged and, if need be, lawfully punished. But law and law enforcement are only aspects not the entirety of governance at any level. This realization is emerging across many fields. Enhanced technical expertise in the fields of international law, business and political negotiation, health care and scientific research permits the definition of new global "problems" rendering them "governable" through international or global policy presided over by courts or "dispute resolution mechanisms" of many kinds. Gerry Simpson questions whether this "juridification" of international politics merely enlarges the schedule of work for international jurists without delivering any enlargement of the scope of justice in practice. War crimes trials are, he argues, "selective" and outcomes largely predetermined. Celebrity criminals are paraded in public view, their crimes known in advance, and the trial itself is merely a confirmation that defendants are indeed guilty and liable for legal retribution. This might have some cathartic effect but the deterrence value is debatable (Simpson, 2007, pp. 14–19, 35, 108). As Janine Clark makes clear in her analysis of Rwandan war crimes prosecutions, the sheer volume of international criminal law violations is inestimable and quite evidently beyond the capacity of international, and indeed national, court systems to accommodate (Clark, 2009, pp. 13–14). Principles of restorative justice, she argues, affirm law and justice because they allow for the perpetrators of even the most heinous crimes to be more than just rehabilitated but drawn back into society. If, as with Clark's analysis, legal scholars can argue for judicial acknowledgement of human complexity and the need to understand the sociopolitical contexts of criminal acts, then similar restorative considerations can or should apply also to greater and lesser crimes under national and international law, and to the cultivation of regard for social codes that counter tendencies towards crime and criminal violence. Parallels can be drawn with the evolving peace process in Colombia between the state and the Fuerzas Armadas Revolucionarias de Colombia (FARC); or to the resolution of Thailand's insurgency of the 1970s and 1980s which saw communist cadres, many quite possibly guilty of war crimes, and all certainly guilty of crimes under Thai law, amnestied and admitted back into civilian life. For some, such accommodations are unconscionable, if lawful, but the historical evidence is that they can also be law affirming by at least establishing the social conditions of durable peace.

Complex systems cannot be governed solely through the strict application and enforcement of codified law but the notion of self-organization raises as many, if different, concerns. Market globalists place enormous faith in the power of market forces and political rationality to restrain the use of force and promote international cooperation. The pacifying qualities of affluence are read in the evidence of declines in the incidence of organized violence since the end of the Cold War in the 1990s, linked in part to rising per capita incomes and democratization (Pinker, 2011, pp. 297–305). Extreme market globalists go so far as to argue that markets, if permitted to operate without any government intervention whatsoever, are sufficient for the ordering of global economic relations and, one can infer, all global relations (Pauly, 2002). Self-organizing mercantile courts created an early form of international commercial law – the medieval *ius mercatoria*, which provided the confidence necessary for the growth of Europe's transnational economy. But markets are indifferent to anything that does not serve the market, and without conscious effort to encode market relations with cosmopolitan norms, evolutionary trajectories can veer sharply away from the kinds of moral community envisaged by founding liberal political economists, including Smith.

Prediction, predestination, pre-emption

Complexity, scale and volume are governed through numbers and lists but indices are prescriptive tools that reflect the predilections of those who determine them. Applied superficially, criteria and checklists encourage cultures of conformity and compliance and negate avenues for deliberation. Quantified governance indicators represent a narrowing of political debate over the nature and purpose of government within limits imposed by a falsely assumed consensus on the superiority of neoliberal market ideology, which, at the very least, constrains an important deliberative element of the democratic process because it denies absolutely that there is any viable or justifiable alternative. The idea that the future can be calculated exercises a powerful hold over the human imagination. The art of politics is in many ways the art of representing the present and future in ways that appeal to popular expectations, as it is of explaining, convincingly, failure to meet these expectations. Routine predictions for everyday happenings are usually framed within "tolerable" parameters or "bandwidths" of risk but the likelihood of the exceptional occurrence that triggers catastrophe is regularly underestimated – often because critical interrelationships, human and systemic, are ignored, deliberately set aside or, more to the point, simply incalculable.

The consequences of social action in this "chaotic" society are never certain, for which reason attempts to construct certainty or control "outcomes" will always generate unanticipated and unintended results. Recognition of global complexity and non-linearity is an apposite baseline from which to construct a more reflexive approach to the governance of global crime and security. At the very least, recognition of the complex nature of reality would be a useful antidote to the preponderance of convergence analysis and convergent analy*ses* of global change. Control regimes are at best two-dimensional technologies for a four-dimensional world where the present is imperfect and the future "best-guessable" but unpredictable. Tracking, profiling, interdiction and sanction are among the standard functions of security control systems the world over, but where security and justice are construed too narrowly and conventionally as the apprehension of criminals and the enforcement of law, subtler yet critical questions of legitimacy and lawfulness are swept aside or overlooked, until, that is, shortcomings are exposed in the sudden eruption of complex international crises. The desire for omniscience is manifest in the preponderant governmentalities of security, from the notion of the "failed state" and its voluminous statistical validations to the avid accumulation of information or data on every detectable human interaction. This is but a contemporary materialization of a perennial political concern over the relative merits of liberty versus security defined as order (Skinner, 1979, pp. 23–28; Bauman, 2001, pp. 41–56). Only today, belief in the need for a powerful sovereign is buttressed with the techniques and knowledge claims of risk managers replete with an armoury of statistical measures, correlated predispositions, vectors and trends, all of which supposedly render the future knowable and, thus, mutable through pre-emptive interventions (Bernstein, 1998). The irony is that such interventions prevent only what might never have happened from actually happening, while also "manufacturing" a new set of reactions requiring fresh calculations, recalibrations and interventions (Giddens, 1990; Beck, 1999).

The global transnational organized crime–terror narrative establishes casual relationships between decontextualized indicators of threat, money laundering and other conventional financial crimes, trafficking, and crime–terror network formations, weak law enforcement regimes and "captured" states. Governance indicators suggest a strong correlation between democratic systems, the rule of law and high levels of economic prosperity, and encourage the conclusion that the greatest criminal threats are to be found among the world's poorer nations. So, we have statistical evidence to hand that the risks of terrorism and transnational organized crime have their locus within the Global South, among conflict-prone states with high levels of political dissonance, endemic corruption and low levels of integration with the global licit economy while at the same time being woven into global networks of illicit trade. And we have the global prescription – liberal democracy and free markets. Predestination is making a comeback, stripped of any theological considerations, and recast as predeterminism.

Rationality is a much used and abused word. Modern market globalism is a form of capitalism stripped clean of Adam Smith's requirement for economic calculations to be balanced against moral considerations (Smith, 1759, pp. 207–208). This is not the same as arguing that there are no moral compulsions to which corporate entities must submit, simply that amorality is the norm. Concern for Corporate Social Responsibility (CSR) can be interpreted as a reflexive response to both the depredations of excoriating capitalistic competition and the expansion of legal constraints imposed on corporate behaviour by nation states. Market globalists regard free markets for trade and investment as the *sine qua non* of global capitalism without which there could be no spreading of prosperity. But the "movement" of global trade and finance does not follow the "clockwork" logic of individual, self-interested economic maximization. Notions of "the market" privilege only certain aspects of human psychology: the individualistic, self-interested, acquisitive and the competitive (Polanyi, 2001). Human beings are, after all, complex systems existing within larger social complexes where actions and consequences are neither predetermined nor random. This variability in human rationalizations of self-interest is of central concern to behavioural economists who struggle to assimilate this into a general predictive theory (Loewenstein, 2004, loc. 17074–17075). Clearly, there are many human "variables" at play in a global economic system that is increasingly volatile, regularly defies prediction and, yet, continues to grow rapidly in size and value.

Within this chaotic complex of contradictory impulses, it is material power and not scientific "truth" which is decisive. Otherwise, how are we to accommodate the reality that the greatest challenges to global security, measured in terms of economic devastation, political manipulation, violation of international law or military interventionism, have emanated from within those countries that direct the global economy and govern global security affairs?

As Matt Andrews suggests, there is a wide gap between political reality and the "script" or *mentalité* of governance as represented by global policy elites (Andrews, 2012). At issue here is not whether it is a good idea to develop models of democracy that can help persuade liberals and all the rest that liberalism is good. The representativeness, and with it the legitimacy of the "global executive" – namely, the elites that govern the UN and Bretton Woods Institutions – is questioned widely on the grounds that they are "undemocratic" in inclination and out of touch (Weiss, 2000; Stiglitz, 2002; Chang, 2007; Held, 2010). "Reform" of this system from a legitimacy standpoint requires more engagement with, and inclusion of, the global populous, or "multitude," to establish some popular connection with what are often distant and seemingly impenetrable monoliths (Hardt and Negri, 2009; Held, 2010). Liberalism is not a universal ideology and there are strong objections to liberal governance prescriptions handed down "from above," especially from deep within the Global South (Rajagopal, 2004; Hardt and Negri, 2009). Either these objections can be considered in the light of illiberal interventionism or they can be dismissed as the rants of criminals and terrorists.

There is ever more reason to argue that the base code for global society is amoral. When attempts to build a cosmopolitan order come to grief, the system switches to default settings and order is restored by whatever methods are considered necessary by those with the means. In an amoral system, all actions are validated or invalidated arbitrarily by the extent to which they ensure systemic survival and the nature of such systems need not be liberal or democratic (Moeller, 2006; Luhmann, 2013). To put it another way, self-organizing or *autopoeitic* systems are indifferent – what progressive liberals of the radical and market variety consider "perfect." It is likely, however, that the world is gravitating towards an inflection point that could trigger a catastrophic regression. There is therefore an urgent need to revisit the work of Arendt to remind ourselves that the most insidious threats to democracy come from within, and not from some alien, immigrant fifth column, or a subterranean terror network, but the very institutions through which democratic states are governed and government legitimated.

Diffusion, collision, reaction

The advent of the Internet and cyberspace adds a fresh layer of complexity to models of complex interdependence. One advantage to this theorization of cyberspace is the illumination of the coded dimensions of human interaction and the connection between legal codification and networked power. Once, philosophers referred to humans in a "state of nature" to represent theoretical principles of order. Today, theories of biological and systemic complexity provide a new set of referents and coordinates. Digitopianism has, however, one great disadvantage, this being the attendant mistaken belief that digital encoding increases system plasticity and opens the door to the normative reconfiguration of global politics. *Informationalization* is, if anything, enhancing to the power of state institutions tasked with societal control.

The globalization of transnational criminal law paradoxically sharpens borderlines and toughens border regimes. This should be of no surprise because globalization, in spite of the popular rhetoric of borderlessness, and the libertarian idealism of market and justice globalists, entails the contrapuntal hardening of physical frontiers and the terrestrial extension of state powers (Battersby, 1998–1999). The scale, velocity and invasiveness of globalization means that responses to perceived and real global security challenges are more extensive, faster and more invasive than in the past. This makes governments, and indeed any kind of organization, concerned for the integrity of informational systems and more inclined to seek tighter regulation over what can be controlled. For these reasons the Internet is demonstrably less free than when it was first touted as the agent of global openness, transparency and democracy (Brevini and Murdoch, 2013).

The state is not dead, nor dying, and for realists peace, the corollary of security, still ensues from an orderly system or society of sovereign nation-states where security is synonymous with stability and is to be preserved by overlapping and often interlocking global and regional power balances of limited durability (Waltz, 1979, p. 112; Mearsheimer, 2001; Gilpin, 2003). Political realism, in its most traditionalist form, treats the growing density of global–local linkages as mere ripples on the surface of international affairs. If anything, writes John Mearsheimer, increasing global complexity renders the world less amendable to governance through international institutions and institutionalized market exchange (Mearsheimer, 2001, p. 504). Such arguments rest on psychological assumptions about human nature and, allegedly, constant human tendencies – such as the drive for security through power and basic human self-interest – that give rise to power politics. From this standpoint, while we can appreciate the cooperative spirit in which international institutions are formed, they exist only because cooperation increases opportunities for the self-interested pursuit of state priorities (Hasenclever et al., 2002).

Yet this "mental model" of order, as with all "imaginaries," offers or generates prescriptions riddled with error and risk, because default settings are reconfigurable (Denzau et al., 2007; Steger, 2009). There are many realisms and Mearsheimer's "offensive realism," for example, should be considered alongside Charles Glaser's "defensive realism" thesis that states engage in the self-interested pursuit of peace through cooperation. This subtle semantic shift invites the conclusion that international cooperation can succeed when powers, both rising and declining, eliminate uncertainty about each other's intentions and signal their desire for the peaceful resolution of disputes (Glaser, 2010, pp. 272–273). Absolute transparency is, however, a radical principle, and one that can serve the interests of state security agencies, financial criminals, embodied information snatchers and organic meta-data harvesters, as much it might further the aspirations of peacemakers and digitopian rebels.

The proliferation of systems integrating technologies and practices through the global economy in telecommunications, transport, defence information and financial services generates new vistas of globality and new spectra of vulnerability (Klibi and Martel, 2012; Ghadge et al., 2013). This can be interpreted as the continuation of the "time–space compression" and "world systems" formation that define the integrative dynamics and tendencies of the modern global system (Harvey, 1991; Wallerstein, 2004; Curran, 2008). A countermovement is, however, discernible in the firewalling national communications systems, a form of digital ring fencing or fence building buttressed by increasingly invasive state surveillance. Given the Internet's dependence upon physical infrastructure, "balkanization" is a possibility insofar as *de facto* "nationalization" is a reality in China (Brown, 2013; Schmidt and Cohen, 2013). And terrestrial and digital borders are policed and defended by whatever means, with threats of attack or retaliation for incursion, and through the sponsorship of rebel forces. Crime remains a vital strategy and tool in states' armouries of security practice but this has grave systemic implications in today's hyper-networked world.

The historical record of conflicts past indicates a clear danger that the sensitivities generated by the pursuit of a competitive edge in cyber offence elevates the risk of systemic destabilization by heightening interstate tension. Any technological innovation is potentially highly disruptive and thus likely to cause anxiety as much as it provides opportunity for disruption. Contributing to this state of affairs, the human condition is today characterized by a reflexive relationship with risk at the individual, state and global levels (Beck, 1994; Beck, 1999; Giddens, 1994; Giddens, 1999). The transition from hierarchically structured industrial societies to more fluid or "liquid" post-Fordist societies has increased human sensitivity to uncertainty, as it has increased the uncertainties of everyday life (Baumann, 2000; Castells, 2000). These social transformations filter through into the security domain in many different ways to "produce" reflexive responses to actual and perceived risks.

System maintenance is threatened by new ideologies and new techniques of control. There is a danger that in policing an increasingly complex world through a war and law enforcement paradigm rather than a governance paradigm, we risk losing whatever integrity there is in the current global system established at the end of World War II, along with the credibility of institutions designed to promote international peace and security. In a highly volatile, interconnected global system, the consequences of rapid shifts at any level can produce system-wide catastrophic effects, hence the need to find frameworks and governance principles that can limit oscillations between war and peace, criminality and compliance, prosperity and poverty, order and societal chaos. Multipolar world systems can function under conditions of mutual gain among core powers and their affiliates but, as technologies transform capabilities, economic and strategic interests can radically diverge and political tensions can evolve along disturbing trajectories – especially when former leading states struggle to keep up with rising powers (Gilpin, 2003; Wallerstein, 2011).

The number and scope of global Internet-mediated activities and the potential for harm arising from nefarious Internet use points to a need for globally coordinated oversight. But while intergovernmental regulation is possible, governments are far from unanimous, perhaps for good reason, in supporting a norm of global Internet control. In a global system constituted from a plurality of actors, governance might best be conceived, therefore, as a set of practices that seek balance and conciliation, and where no single policy prescription, law or institution can achieve an even global distribution of opportunities or outcomes. Yet, the codes of the Internet are being rewritten not to eliminate multiplicity or create a convergent global society, but to differentiate between trusted and distrusted, to exclude and to preclude.

Cosmopolitan code

Cosmopolitan code is everywhere; in the languages people use to communicate across cultural boundaries, in the ideation of global justice and a just system of global governance. Charles Taylor writes of the "social imaginary" as "the ways people imagine their social existence, how they fit together with others [. . .] the expectations that are normally met, and the deeper normative notions and images that underlie these expectations" (Taylor, 2007, p. 23). Manfred Steger's concept of the "global imaginary" closes the circle – but not the book – on the evolution of global consciousness*es* and global ideologies (Steger, 2009). This imagining and articulation of global norms is likewise a systemic process, part of the encoding of global relations. To even conceive of something like "globalization," one must first imagine the globe and acknowledge *de facto* membership of a globally connected populace (Lefebvre, 1991, p. 365; Robertson, 1992, p. 2). But the emergent global mind is not accompanied by a parallel universal agreement on the nature of global justice or security.

International law is a contested domain of cosmopolitan practice as much because international laws unsettle realist defaults as because people dispute which norms should be internationalized. In principle, international laws provide essential anchors to which governance platforms can be attached, from which global relations can be ordered, and power politics rendered more complicated and restrained. If the kind of cosmopolitan orders that Bull, Niebuhr and other philosophers of realism believe are possible, then global amorality has to be challenged somewhere, somehow, and these challenges need sufficient institutional weight to have any impact whatsoever. And it is the case that these institutions are battlegrounds for competing state and private interests, which is one reason as to why they are imperfect. Global action on climate change fails to materialize not because the science of climate change is wrong – that is neither here nor there – but because rules envisaged with which to address climate change threaten the utility of markets, defined in purely economistic terms.

The issue, however, is not that globalization is contested, but rather that one day it might not be contested at all. Market universalism is perhaps a form of cosmopolitan code but one that requires acceptance of a world of indifference. There is no moral equivalent because moral universalism is itself destructive of local identities, traditional social relations and practices. For justice globalists, the failures of governments to look beyond the reasons of state are merely further evidence of the need for a new conception of global order in which the state is no longer the central actor. Neither perspective satisfactorily acknowledges the role of power, greed, indifference and malice in global and national affairs. Periodic financial crises demonstrate that markets can fail, and fail spectacularly, yet government interventions to control market forces can also be catastrophic. In a world abundant with rules and regulatory institutions, agreement as to the meaning of governance remains elusive and global government by an enlightened executive an illusory ideal (Held, 2010; Whitman, 2005). Likewise, the idea of a universal cosmopolitan formula, a kind of computational model into which complex questions are fed and from which simplified answers are drawn, is a mirage that many have chased to no avail. The Western mind requires a reconciliation, a balance, an equation or a synthesis, but dialectical principles cannot accommodate the reality of contradiction, perplexity or complexity. Utopias are idealized syntheses that can sanction intractability and lead either to complete withdrawal into alternative social worlds or, more dangerously, to extremism and revolutionary violence. There cannot be, and from an Arendtian viewpoint, indeed, should not be, any end to political vitality, contestation and struggle however – provided this does not degenerate into violence.

Systems integrity hinges upon the quality of decision-making from a command down to an operational level. In surveillance and enforcement systems, operatives require the facility to make judgements conscious of general principles of justice. In a more risk-averse world, random and disparate issues are even more likely to be interpreted through "trusted" or established models of human behaviour than through an unorthodox "global" frame that accommodates a broad interdisciplinary spectrum of concepts and approaches. There is no single theoretical model that can adequately explain international or global relations; thus, the most fruitful line of inquiry into any international or global phenomenon requires an intuitive and reflexive theoretical framework that draws upon a range of available explanatory ideas (Strange, 1994; Rosecrance, 1999; Wendt, 1999; Barkin, 2010).

Without this built-in element of reflexive discernment, systems can quickly become control regimes and turned to serve the interests of those who have learned how to monopolize them. And the evidence is that this is indeed what is happening as organizations seek ways to minimize risk in a world of increasing complexity. Rule making, compliance and rule enforcement must, however, go hand in hand with responsiveness to real and perceived injustices; otherwise, there can be no basis upon which to build a legitimate and durable system of government or durable order in an increasingly complex world. Addressing complexity and the need for a set of governing values that enable people to accept and deal with uncertainty, Emilian Kavalski argues for "resilience" derived from value-guided action rather than rigid adherence to any single ideology of right action or law (Kavalski, 2008). David Held's cosmopolitanism requires acceptance of difference and the formulation of communicative codes that cross cultural frontiers without dissolving cultural identities (Held, 2010). Resilience and acceptance are fundamental principles complemented by awareness of the need for restraint that arises from recognition that absolute perfection is as much an undesirable goal as it is an unattainable one. This is the argument of this book, written mindful of the hazardous terrain upon which it stands.

Bibliography

Aas, K. F. (2007) *Globalization and Crime*. London: SAGE.

Abbott, J. P. (2001) "Democracy@internet.asia? The Challenges to the Emancipatory Potential of the Net: Lessons from China and Malaysia." *Third World Quarterly*. 22(1): pp. 99–114.

(ABC) Australian Broadcasting Corporation (February 7, 2005) Transcript, ABC Four Corners, *After the Tsunami*. http://www.abc.net.au/4corners/content/2005/s1297976.htm (Accessed February 15, 2012).

Abelson, M. (2013) "Secret Goldman Team Still on the Punt." *Australian Financial Review*. January 9. http://www.afr.com/p/world/secret_goldman_team_still_on_the_3YDpLfuBfciNXJf8hQcO3J (Accessed January 10, 2013).

Abizadeh, A. (2011) "Hobbes on the Causes of War: A Disagreement Theory." *American Political Science Review*. 105(2): pp. 298–315.

Abrahamsen, R. and Williams, M. C. (2011) *Security Beyond the State: Private Security in International Politics*. Cambridge: Cambridge University Press.

(ACC) Australian Crime Commission (2011) "Organized Crime in Australia," 2011. http://www.crimecommission.gov.au/publications/organised-crime-australia/organised-crime-australia-2011-report (Accessed February 7, 2012).

Accenture (2012) *Capital Markets: Key Facts 2012, "Know Your Numbers."* http://www.accenture.com/SiteCollectionDocuments/PDF/Accenture-CM-Key-Facts-Sept-2012.pdf (Accessed February 12, 2014).

(ACFID) Australian Council for International Development (2014) "Our Members." http://www.acfid.asn.au/membership/our-members (Accessed January 19, 2014).

(ADMA) Asian Digital Marketing Association (2012) *Asia Pacific Digital Marketing Yearbook, 2012*. http://www.asiadigitalmarketingyearbook.com/ (Accessed December 1, 2013).

(AfDB) African Development Bank Group (2013a) Federal Republic of Nigeria: Country Strategy Paper, 2013–2017. ORWA, 2013. http://www.afdb.org/fileadmin/uploads/afdb/Documents/Project-and-Operations/Nigeria%20-%202013-2017%20-%20Country%20Strategy%20Paper.pdf (Accessed November 11, 2013).

(AfDB) African Development Bank Group (2013b) *African Economic Outlook 2013 (Pocket Edition)*. African Development Bank Group, Organization for Economic Cooperation and Development, United Nations Development Programme and Economic Commission for Africa. http://www.africaneconomicoutlook.org/fileadmin/uploads/aeo/PDF/Pocket%20Edition%20AEO2013-EN.web.pdf (Accessed December 3, 2013).

(AFP) Agence France-Presse (2011) "France Confirms Arms Drops to Rebels." *Defense News*. June 29, 2011. http://www.defensenews.com/story.php?i=6953105 (Accessed November 6, 2011).

Agnew, D. J., Pearce, J., Pramod, G., Peatman, T., Watson, R., Beddington, J. R., and Pitcher, T. J. (2009) "Estimating the Worldwide Extent of Illegal Fishing." *PLoS ONE*. 4(2): e4570. doi:10.1371/journal.pone.000457.

Aldrich, R. (2006) *The Faraway War: Personal Diaries of The Second World War in Asia and the Pacific*. London: Corgi.

(AI) Amnesty International (2014) "Who We Are." Amnesty International Website. http://amnesty.org/en/who-we-are/about-amnesty-international (Accessed January 12, 2014).

(AI) Amnesty International (2012a) *Amnesty International Report, 2012, State of the World's Human Rights*. London: Amnesty International.

(AI) Amnesty International (2012b) "AI@50 Global Project Evaluation." http://www.amnesty.org/en/who-we-are/accountability/impact (Accessed November 3, 2013).

(AI) Amnesty International (2010) *Amnesty International's Integrated Strategic Plan, 2010 to 2016*. London: Amnesty International Website. http://www.amnesty.org/sites/impact.amnesty.org/files/POL%2050_002_2010%20Public%20ISP.pdf (Accessed January 12, 2014).

(AI) Amnesty International (2007) "Protecting the Rights of Women: Kate Gilmore Speaks." August 9. http://www.amnesty.org.au/svaw/comments/2420/ (Accessed October 8, 2013).

(AI) Amnesty International (n/d) "Amnesty International 50th Anniversary: Facts and Figures." http://static.amnesty.org/ai50/ai50-facts-and-figures.pdf (Accessed November 12, 2013).

(AI USA) Amnesty International USA (2009) *Carnage and Despair: Iraq Five Years On*. New York. NY: Amnesty International USA. http://www.amnesty.org/en/news-and-updates/report/carnage-and-despair-iraq-20080317 (Accessed May 31, 2010).

Al-Rodhan, N. R. F. (2008) *Emotional Moral Egoism: A Neurophilosophical Theory of Human Nature and its Universal Security Implications*. Lit: Zurich.

Al-Sishani, M. B. (2014) "From Chechen Mafia to the Islamic Emirate of the Caucasus: The Changing Faces of the Insurgency-Organized Crime Nexus." In Cornell, S. and Jonsson, M. (ed.) *Conflict, Crime and the State in Postcommunist Eurasia*. Philadelphia. PA: University of Pennsylvania Press. pp. 83–102.

Alford, P. (2012) "Bill on Illegal Logging Could Trigger Trade Dispute with Jakarta." *Australian*. March 12. http://www.theaustralian.com.au/opinion/columnists/bill-on-illegal-logging-could-trigger-trade-dispute-with-jakarta/story-e6frg78x-1226296353818 (Accessed October 17, 2013).

Aljeffri, S. Z. (2003) "Islam and the Status of Women." Address to the Hawke Centre, University of South Australia, May 1. www.unisa.edu.au/hawkecentre/events/2003events/islam_transcript.asp (Accessed April 28, 2008).

Alpers, P. and Twyford, C. (2003) "Small Arms in the Pacific." Occasional Paper No. 8, Small Arms Survey. http://www.smallarmssurvey.org/publications/by-type/occasional-papers.html (Accessed March 2, 2012).

Andreas, P. (2011) "Illicit Globalization: Myths, Misconceptions, and Historical Lessons." *Political Science Quarterly*. 126(6) Fall: pp. 403–425.

Andreas, P. and Nadelmann, E. (2006) *Policing the Globe: Criminalization and Crime Control in International Relations*. Oxford: Oxford University Press.

Andrews, M. (2012) "Good Governance Scripts: Will Compliance Improve Form or Functionality?" In Jomo, K. S. and Chowdhury, A. (ed.) *Is Good Governance Good for Development?* London: Bloomsbury. pp. 97–113.

Anechiarico, F. and Jacobs, J. B. (1996) *The Pursuit of Absolute Integrity*. Chicago: University of Chicago Press.

Anheier, H. K. (2012a) "Civil Society, Global." In Annheier, H. K. and Juergensmeyer, M. (ed.) *Encyclopedia of Global Studies* (Volume 1) Thousand Oaks: SAGE. pp. 198–205.

Anheier, H. K. (2012b) "Revolutions." In Annheier, H. K. and Juergensmeyer, M. (ed.) *Encyclopedia of Global Studies*.(Volume 4). Thousand Oaks: SAGE. pp. 1486–1490.

Anheier, H. K. (2001) "Measuring Global Civil Society." In Anhier, H. K., Glasius, M., and Kaldor, M. (ed.) *Global Civil Society*. Oxford: Oxford University Press. pp. 221–230.

Aning, K. (2007) "Are There Emerging West African Criminal Networks? The Case of Ghana." *Global Crime*. 8(3): pp. 193–212.

Annals of Congress, 1789. Library of Congress. http://memory.loc.gov/ammem/amlaw/lwac.html (Accessed November 12, 2013).

Annan, K. (2000) *We the Peoples: The Role of the United Nations in the 21st Century*. New York, NY: United Nations.

Antolini, D. E. (2009) "National Park Law in the U.S.: Conservation, Conflict, and Centennial Values." *William & Mary Environmental Law & Policy Review*. 33(3): pp. 851–921, 851. http://scholarship.law.wm.edu/wmelpr/vol33/iss3/5 (Accessed July 7, 2013).

Anton, D. K. (2011) *Public International Law and International Civil Litigation: From Ecuador to the United States and Back (Twice) – Chevron v. Donziger*, November 11, Precedent, Forthcoming. http://ssrn.com/abstract=1960251 (Accessed July 27, 2013).

Anyadike, O. (2013) "Colombia's Internally Displaced People Caught in a Corridor of Instability," *Guardian*, August 12. http://www.theguardian.com/global-development/2013/aug/12/colombia-internally-displaced-people-instability (Accessed December 4, 2013).

Arendt, H. (2000a) "The Perplexities of the Rights of Man." In Baher, P. (ed.) *The Portable Hannah Arendt*. London: Penguin. pp. 31–45.

Arendt, H. (2000b) "The Revolutionary Tradition and its Lost Treasure." In Baher, P. (ed.) *The Portable Hannah Arendt*. London: Penguin. pp. 508–544.

Arendt, H. (1972) *Crises of the Republic*. New York. NY: Harcourt and Brace.

Arendt, H. (1970) *On Violence*. New York. NY: Houghton Miflin Harcourt.

Arendt, H. (1958) *The Origins of Totalitarianism* (2nd Edition). New York. NY: Harcourt Brace.

Arnold, G. (2005) *The International Drug Trade*. New York. NY: Routledge.

Ashton, C. (2013) *Cybersecurity Strategy for the European Union*. High Representative of the European Union for Foreign Affairs and Security in Conjunction with the European Commission, JOIN (2013). http://eeas.europa.eu/policies/eu-cyber-security/cybsec_comm_en.pdf (Accessed October 14, 2013).

(ATT) *Arms Trade Treaty* (2013) http://www.un.org/disarmament/ATT/ (Accessed November 10, 2013).

(AusAID) Australian Agency for International Development (2013) "List of Accredited Non-government Organizations (NGOs)." http://aid.dfat.gov.au/ngos/Pages/accredited.aspx (Accessed January 12, 2014).

(AusAID) Australian Agency for International Development (2011) *Humanitarian Action Policy 2011*. Canberra: Commonwealth of Australia.

(AusAID) Australian Agency for International Development and Australian Council for International Development (ACFID) (2009) "Partnership Agreement

Between the Commonwealth of Australia (AusAID) and the Australian Council for International Development (ACFID)." March 24, 2009. http://www.ausaid.gov.au/publications/pubout.cfm?ID=331_8701_2438_4818_2680 (Accessed January 27, 2012).

(AusAID) Australian Agency for International Development (2000) *Good Governance: Guiding Principles for Implementation*. Canberra: Commonwealth of Australia.

Aviles, W. (2006) *Global Capitalism, Democracy, and Civil-Military Relations in Colombia*. Albany. NY: State University of New York Press.

Ba, A. D. (2009) *Region, Regionalism, and the Association of Southeast Asian Nations*. Stanford. CA: Stanford University Press.

(BAAG-ENNA) British Agencies Afghanistan Group and European Network of NGOs in Afghanistan. (2009) *Aid and Civil-Military Relations in Afghanistan*. BAAG and ENNA Policy Briefing Paper. http://www.baag.org.uk (Accessed September 21, 2009).

Backman, M. (2001) *Asian Eclipse: Exposing the Dark Side of Business in Asia*. New York. NY: John Wiley.

Baird, R. (2004) "Illegal, Unreported and Unregulated Fishing: An Analysis of the Legal, Economic and Historical Factors Relevant to its Development and Persistence." *Melbourne Journal of International Law*. 5(2): pp. 1–36.

Baker, C. D. (2003) "Tolerance of International Espionage: A Functional Approach." *American University International Law Review*. 19(5): pp. 1091–1113.

Ball, D. and Mathieson, S. (2007) *Militia Redux: Or Sor and the Revival of Paramilitarism in Thailand*. Bangkok: White Lotus.

Ban, Ki-moon (2011) SG/SM13535, May 2, United Nations. http://www.un.org/News/Press/docs/2011/sgsm13535.doc.htm (Accessed May 5, 2013).

Banerjee, A. V. and Duflo, E. (2011) *Poor Economics: A Radical Rethinking of the Way to Fight Poverty*. New York: Public Affairs.

Bangalore, S. and Messerli, F. H. (2013) "Gun Ownership and Firearm-related Deaths." *American Journal of Medicine*. 126(10): pp. 873–876.

Baragona, S. (2010) "US Farmers Depend on Illegal Immigrants." *Voice of America*, August 11. http://www.voanews.com/content/usfarmersdependonillegalimmigrants100541644/162082.html (Accessed July 17, 2013).

Barber, B. (2003) *Jihad Vs McWorld*. London: Corgi.

Bargent, J. (2013) "Report Traces How FARC Wages War While it Talks Peace," *Insight Crime*, December 19. http://www.insightcrime.org/news-briefs/report-traces-how-farc-wages-war-while-it-talks-peace (Accessed January 3, 2014).

Barkin, J. S. (2010) *Realist Constructivism: Rethinking International Relations Theory*. Cambridge: Cambridge University Press.

Barnes, J. E. (2013) "What Bradley Manning Leaked." *Washington Wire* (Wall Street Journal) August 21. http://blogs.wsj.com/washwire/2013/08/21/what-bradley-manning-leaked/ (Accessed December 3, 2013).

Barnett, M. (2011) *Empire of Humanity: A History of Humanitarianism*. Ithaca. NY: Cornell University Press.

Barnett, M. and Weiss, T. (2011) *Humanitarianism Contested: Where Angels Fear to Tread*. Abingdon: Routledge.

Barnett, M. and Finnemore, M. (2004) *Rules for the World: International Organizations and World Politics*. Ithaca. NY: Cornell University Press.

Barry, J. A. (2008) "Covert Action Can Be Just." In Johnson, L. K. and Wirtz, J. J. (ed.) *Intelligence and National Security: The Secret World of Spies* (2nd edition) New York: Oxford University Press, pp. 286–294.

Barry, N. (2003) "The Theory of the Corporation." *Ideas on Liberty*. 53: pp. 22–26. http://www.fee.org/files/docLib/feat5.pdf (Accessed June 21, 2010).

Basel Committee on Banking Supervision (BCBS) (2011) *Basel III: A Global regulatory Framework for More resilient Banks and Banking Systems*. Basel: Bank for International Settlements Communication.

Bassiouni, M. C. (2011) "Introduction: Crimes of States and Other Forms of Collective Group Violence by Nonstate Actors." In Rothe, D. L. and Mullins, C. W. (ed.) *State Crime: Current Perspectives*. New Brunswick. NJ: Rutgers University Press. pp. 80–541.

Battersby, P. (2012a) "Geneva Conventions." In Jurgensmeyer M. and Anheier, H. K. (ed.) *Encyclopedia of Global Studies*, (Volume 2). Thousand Oaks. CA: SAGE. pp. 621–625.

Battersby, P. (2012b) "World War." In Juergensmeyer M. and Anheier, H. K. (ed.) *Encyclopedia of Global Studies* (Volume 4) Thousand Oaks. CA: SAGE. pp. 1768–1771.

Battersby, P. (2007) *To the Islands: White Australians and the Malay Archipelago*. Lanham. MD: Lexington Books.

Battersby, P. (1998–1999) "Border Politics and the Broader Politics of Thailand's International Relations: from Communism to Capitalism." *Pacific Affairs*. 71(4): pp. 473–488.

Battersby, P. and Siracusa, J. M. (2009) *Globalization and Human Security*. Lanham. MD: Rowman and Littlefield.

Battersby, P., Siracusa, J. M., and Ripiloski, S. (2011) *Crime Wars: the Global Intersection of Crime, Political Violence and International Law*. Santa Barbara. CA: Praeger.

Baudendistel, R. (2006) *Between Bombs and Good Intentions: The Red Cross and the Italo-Ethiopian War*. New York. NY: Berghan Books.

Bauman, Z. (2001) *The Individualized Society*. Cambridge: Polity.

Bauman, Z. (2000) *Liquid Modernity*. Cambridge: Polity.

Bavier, J. (2012) "Who are Boko Haram and Why are They Terrorizing Nigerian Christians? *Atlantic*. January 24. http://www.theatlantic.com/international/archive/2012/01/whoarebokoharamandwhyaretheyterrorizingnigerianchristians/251729/ (Accessed November 5, 2013).

Bayley, D. H. (2006) *Changing the Guard: Developing Democratic Police Abroad*. New York: Oxford.

BBC (2013) "MSF-Backed Hospitals Treated Syria 'Chemical Victims.'" *BBC News*. August 24. http://www.bbc.co.uk/news/world-middle-east-23827950 (Accessed October 12, 2013).

(BDS) Bureau of Diplomatic Security (2007) US Embassy, Baghdad, September 16, Spot Report 091607-01.

Beck, U. (2005) *Power in the Global Age*. Cambridge: Polity.

Beck, U. (1999) *World Risk Society*. Cambridge: Polity.

Beck, U. (1994) "The Reinvention of Politics: Towards a Theory of Reflexive Modernization." In Beck, U., Giddens, A., and Lash, S. (ed.) *Reflexive Modernization: Politics, Tradition and Aesthetics in the Modern Social Order*. Stanford. CA: Stanford University Press, pp. 1–55.

Beith, M. (2013) "After Six Years of Bloodshed, Mexico's Drug Wars Shows Little Sign of Waning." *Atlantic*. June 4. http://www.theatlantic.com/international/archive/2013/06/after-six-years-of-bloodshed-mexicos-drug-war-shows-little-sign-of-waning/276533/ (Accessed June 27, 2013).

Beittel, J. S. (2009) *Mexico's Drug-Related Violence*. Congressional Research Service, May 27. www.fas.org/sgp/crs/row/R40582.pdf (Accessed February 12, 2012).

Bellamy, C. (2007) *Absolute War: Soviet Russia in the Second World War*. New York. NY: Vintage.

Berenskoetter, F. (2011) "Reclaiming the Vision Thing: Constructivists as Students of the Future." *International Studies Quarterly*. 55(3): pp. 647–668.

Berman, P. (2005) *Power and the Idealists*. New York: W. W. Norton.

Bernstein, P. L. (1998) *Against the Gods: The Remarkable Story of Risk*. New York. NY: John Wiley.

Bharadwaj, A. (2002) "Man, State and the Myth of Democratic Peace." *Strategic Analysis*. 26(2): pp. 305–315.

Bina, C. (2013) *A Prelude to the Foundation of Political Economy: Oil, War and Global Polity*. New York. NY: Palgrave Macmillan.

Bird, R. J. (2003) *Chaos and Life: Complexity and Order in Evolution and Thought*. New York. NY: Columbia University Press.

Biron, C. (2012) "Assault on Colombian Trade Unions Continues." *Al Jazeera*. August 5. http://www.aljazeera.com/indepth/features/2012/07/201273175715676335.html (Accessed December 30, 2013).

Bishop, M. and O'Goldman, E. (2003) "The Strategy and Tactics of Information Warfare." *Contemporary Security Policy*. 24(1): pp. 113–139.

Blimes, L. (2013) "The Financial Legacy of Iraq and Afghanistan: How Wartime Spending Decisions Will Constrain Future National Security Budgets." HKS Faculty Research Working Paper Series, RWP13-006, March 2013.

Blok, A. (2011) "War of the Whales: Post-Sovereign Science and Agonistic Cosmopolitics in Japanese Global Whaling Assemblages." *Science, Technology, Human Values*. 36(1): pp. 55–81.

Bloomfield, S. (2008) "The Thin Blue Line." *Melbourne Age*. June 17.

Blowfield, M. and Murray, A. (2008) *Corporate Responsibility: A Critical Introduction*. Oxford: Oxford University Press.

Blyth, M. (2013) *Austerity: The History of a Dangerous Idea*. Oxford: Oxford University Press.

Boas, M. (2009) "Terminology Associated with Political Violence and Asymmetric Warfare." In Okumu, W. and Botha, A. (ed.) *Domestic Terrorism in Africa: Defining, Addressing and Understanding its Impact on Human Security*. Pretoria: Institute for Security Studies, pp. 7–13. http://www.iss.co.za/uploads/TERRORISMREPORT (Accessed May 8, 2010).

Bob, C. (2012) *The Global Right Wing and the Clash of World Politics*. New York. NY: Cambridge.

Boot, M. and Kirkpatrick, J. (2004) "Think Again Neocons." *Foreign Policy*. January/February. http://www.foreignpolicy.com/articles/2004/01/01/think_again_neocons (Accessed July 16, 2013).

Bourke, J. (1999) *An Intimate History of Killing: Face to Face Combat in 20th Century Warfare*. London: Basic Books.

Boutros-Ghali, B. (1992) *An Agenda for Peace: Preventive Diplomacy, Peace-Making and Peace-Building*. Report of the Secretary-General, United Nations, A/47/277-S/24111, June 17. www.un.org/docs/SG/agpeace.html (Accessed January 21, 2008).

Borch, F. L. (2001) *Judge Advocates in Combat: Army Lawyers in Military Operations from Vietnam to Haiti*. Washington. DC: US Army.

Bowden, M. (2012) *The Finish: The Killing of Osama Bin Laden*. London: Grove.

Brack, D. (2013) "Combating Illegal Logging: Interaction with WTO Rules." Chatham House Briefing Paper, EER BP 2013/01, May. http://www.chathamhouse.org/sites/default/files/public/Research/Energy,%20Environment%20and%20Development/0513bp_brack.pdf (Accessed February 4, 2014).

Brack, D. (2009) "Combatting Illegal Logging: Interaction with WTO Rules." Chatham House Briefing Paper. http://www.chathamhouse.org/publications/papers/view/109079 (Accessed June 12, 2011).

Bradbury, S. (2005) "Memorandum for John A. Rizzo, Senior Deputy General Counsel, Central Intelligence Agency." May 10, 2005, US Department of Justice. http://ccrjustice.org/newsroom/press-releases/ccr-decries-immunity-torture%2C-secrecy (Accessed December 4, 2013).

Braithwaite, J. and Drahos, P. (2000) *Global Business Regulation*. Cambridge: Cambridge University Press.

Brauman, R. and Vidal, C. (2011) "Natural Disasters: 'Do Something!'" In Magone, C., Neuman, M., and Weissman, T. (ed.) *Humanitarian Negotiations Revealed: The MSF Experience*. New York. NY: Columbia University Press. pp. 219–236.

Bremmer, I. (2010) *The End of the Free Market: Who Wins the War Between States and Corporation*. London: Portfolio.

Brevini, B. and Murdock, G. (2013) "Following the Money: WikiLeaks and the Political Economy of Disclosure." In Brevini, B., Hintz, A., and McCurdy, P. (ed.) *Beyond WikiLeaks: Implications for the Future of Communications, Journalism and Society*. Houndmills: Palgrave Macmillan, pp. 1071–1479.

Bricknell, S. (2010) *Environmental Crime in Australia*. Canberra: Australian Institute of Criminology.

British American Tobacco (2011) *Annual Report 2011*. www.bat.com/ar2011 (Accessed December 12, 2013).

Broad, W. J., Markoff, J., and Sanger, D. E. (2011) "Israeli Test on Worm Crucial in Iran Nuclear Delay." New York Times, January 15. http://www.nytimes.com/2011/01/16/world/middleeast/16stuxnet.html?pagewanted=all (Accessed January 10, 2012).

Brodzinsky, S. (2013) "FARC Rebels and Colombian Government Reach Deal over Political Participation." *Guardian*. November 7. http://www.theguardian.com/world/2013/nov/06/farc-rebels-deal-political-participation (Accessed December 2, 2013).

Brown, I. (2013) "Will NSA Revelations Lead to the Balkanisation of the Internet?" *Guardian*, November 2. http://www.theguardian.com/world/2013/nov/01/nsa-revelations-balkanisation-internet (Accessed November 29, 2013).

Brownlee, J. (2007) *Authoritarianism in an Age of Democratization*. New York. NY: Cambridge.

Brunk, D. (2008) "Dissecting Darfur: Anatomy of a Genocide Debate." *International Relations*. 22: pp. 25–44.

Bull, B. and McNeill, D. (2007) *Development Issues in Global Governance: Public-Private Partnerships and Market Multilateralism*. London: Routledge.

Bull, H. (2002) *The Anarchical Society: A Study of Order in World Politics* (3rd edition). New York. NY: Columbia University Press.

Burke, J. (2013) "Bangladesh Factory Fires: Fashion Industry's Latest Crisis." *Guardian*, December 9. http://www.theguardian.com/world/2013/dec/08/bangladesh-factory-fires-fashion-latest-crisis (Accessed December 31, 2013).

Burns, R. D., Siracusa, J. M., and Flanagan, J. (2013) *American Foreign Relations since Independence*. Santa Barbara, CA: Praeger.

Bush, G. W. (2006) "Address to the UN General Assembly: A More Hopeful World Beyond Terror and Extremism." www.whitehouse.gov/news/releases/2006/09/20060919-4.html (Accessed June 30, 2008).

Bush, G. W. (2004) *National Drug Control Strategy*. Washington: Office of National Drug Control Policy, 2004.

Buzan, B. (1983) *People, States and Fear: The National Security Question in International Relations*. London: Wheatsheaf.

Buzan, B. and Waever, O. (2007) *Regions and Powers: The Structure of International Security*. Cambridge: Cambridge University Press.

Buzan, B., Waever, O., and de Wilde, J. (1998) *Security: A New Framework of Analysis*. London: Lynne Rienner.

Bybee, J. S. (2002) "Memorandum for John A. Rizzo, Acting General Counsel of the Central Intelligence Agency: Interrogation of al Qaeda Operative." US Department of Justice, August 1, 2002. http://ccrjustice.org/newsroom/press-releases/ccr-decries-immunity-torture%2C-secrecy (Accessed December 2, 2013).

Byman, D. (2013) "Why Drones Work: The Case for Washington's Weapon of Choice." *Foreign Affairs*. 92(4) July/August: pp. 32–43.

Campbell, D. F. J., Pölzlbauer, P., Barth, T. D., and Polzlbauer, G. (2012) Democracy Rankings, 2012. http://www.democracyranking.org/downloads/2012/Scores_of_the_Democracy_Ranking_2012-A4.pdf (Accessed April 23, 2012).

Campbell, J. (2013) "Should U.S. Fear Boko Haram?" CNN.com. http://edition.cnn.com/2013/10/01/opinion/campbell-boko-haram/index.html (Accessed December 3, 2013).

Campbell, J. (2011) *Nigeria: Dancing on the Brink*. Lanham. MD: Rowman and Littlefield.

Carafano, J. J. (2012) *Wiki at War: Conflict in a Socially Networked World*. College Station. TX: Texas A&M University Press.

Carafano, J. J. (2008) *Private Sector, Public Wars: Contractors in Combat—Afghanistan, Iraq, and Future Conflicts*. Westport. CT: Praeger Security International.

Cartalucci, T. (2013) "Doctors' Behind Syrian Chemical Weapons Claims Are Aiding Terrorists." *Global Research*. August 25. http://www.globalresearch.ca/doctors-behind-syrian-chemical-weapons-claims-are-aiding-terrorists/5346870 (Accessed October 14, 2013).

Carter L., Burnett D., Drew S., Marle G., Hagadorn L., Bartlett-McNeil, D., and Irvine, N. (2009) "Submarine Cables and the Oceans – Connecting the World." UNEP-WCMC Biodiversity Series No. 31. ICPC/UNEP/UNEP-WCMC. http://www.iscpc.org/publications/ICPC-UNEP_Report.pdf (Accessed November 1, 2013).

Carthew, A. (2010) "Thaksin's Twitter revolution – How the red shirts' protests increase the use of social media in Thailand." In Behnke, P. (ed.) *Social Media and Politics: Online Social Networking and Political Communication in Asia*. Singapore: Konrad Adenaur Stiftung, pp. 23–38.

Case, D. (2010) "Inside the Faith-based Discrimination Controversy." *Global Post*. January 27. http://www.globalpost.com/passport/correspondent-call/100127/inside-the-faith-based-discrimination-controversy (Accessed January 20, 2014).

Casey, J. (2010) *Policing the World: The Practice of International and Transnational Policing*. Durham. NC: Carolina University Press.

Cassese, A. (2008) International Criminal Law (2nd edition). Oxford: Oxford University Press.

Castells, M. (2012) *Networks of Outrage and Hope: Social Movements in the Internet Age*. Cambridge: Polity.

Castells, M. (2011) *The Information Age: Economy, Society and Culture, Volume II, The Power of Identity* (2nd Edition). Oxford: Blackwell.

Castells, M. (2009) *The Information Age: Economy, Society and Culture, Volume I, The Rise of the Network Society* (2nd Edition). Oxford: Blackwell.

Castells, M. (2000) *The Information Age, Economy, Society and Culture: The Rise of the Network Society* (Volume I) (2nd Edition). Oxford: Blackwell.

Caulkins, J. P., Kulick, J. D., and Kleiman, M. A. R. (2011) "Think Again: The Afghan Drug Trade." *Foreign Policy*. April 1. http://www.foreignpolicy.com/articles/2011/04/01/think_again_the_afghan_drug_trade (Accessed February 10, 2012).

Cave, T. (2013) "Equity Trading Lifts and Big Players Return." *Financial News*. December 29. http://www.efinancialnews.com/story/2013-12-16/equity-trading-lifts-off-in-europe-big-players-return?ea9c8a2de0ee111045601ab04d673622 (Accessed December 30, 2013).

(CBD) Convention on Biological Diversity (1992) United Nations Treaty Series, I-30619, entered into force December 29. 1993. http://www.cbd.int/ (Accessed July 5, 2003).

(CECP) Committee Encouraging Corporate Philanthropy (2012) *Giving in Numbers, 2012 Edition*. New York. NY: CECP. http://cecp.co/research/benchmarking-reports/giving-in-numbers.html (Accessed April 5, 2013).

(CEDAW) (2006) Declarations, Reservations, Objections and Notifications of Withdrawal of Reservations Relating to the Convention on the Elimination of All Forms of Discrimination against Women CEDAW/SP/2006/2. http://daccess-dds-ny.un.org/doc/UNDOC/GEN/N06/309/97/PDF/N0630997.pdf?OpenElement (Accessed July 8, 2012).

(CEDAW) *Convention on the Elimination of All Forms of Discrimination Against Women* (1979) http://www.un.org/womenwatch/daw/cedaw/cedaw.htm (Accessed February 2007).

(CFR) Council on Foreign Relations (2007) "Hamas." *Backgrounder*. June 8. www.cfr.org/publication/8968/ (Accessed March 15, 2008).

(CGC) Commission on Global Governance (1996) *Our Global Neighborhood: The Report of the Commission on Global Governance*. Oxford: Oxford University Press.

Chalk, P. (2008) *The Malay Muslim Insurgency in Southern Thailand: Understanding the Conflict's Evolving Dynamic*. Santa Monica, CA: RAND Corporation.

Chambers, R. (n/d) "The Unocal Settlement: Implications for the Developing Law on Corporate Complicity in Human Rights Abuses." http://www.wcl.american.edu/hrbrief/13/unocal.pdf?rd=1 (Accessed October 3, 2009).

Chang, I. (1997) *The Rape of Nanking: The Forgotten Holocaust of World War II*. London: Penguin.

Chang, Ha-Joon (2007) *Bad Samaritans: Rich Nations, Poor Policies and the Threat to the Developing World*. London: Random House.

Chang, W. (1998) "Confucian Theory of Norms and Human Rights." In De Barry, W. T. and Weiming, T. (ed.) *Confucianism and Human Rights*. New York. NY: Columbia University Press. pp. 116–125.

Chernick, M. (2005) "Economic Resources and Internal Armed Conflicts: Lessons from the Colombian Case." In Arnson, C. and Zartman, I. W. (ed.) *Rethinking the Economics of War: The Intersection of Need, Creed and Greed*. Baltimore: Johns Hopkins University Press. pp. 178–205.

Chiarugi, M. and Archibugi, D. (2009) "Piracy Challenges Global Governance." *Open Democracy*. April 9. http://www.opendemocracy.net/article/piracy-challenges-global-governance (Accessed April 9, 2009).

Chief Counsel's Report (2011) *Macondo: The Gulf Oil Disaster*. National Commission on the BP Deepwater Horizon Oil Spill and Offshore Drilling. www.oilspillcommission.gov (Accessed August 12, 2013).

Chin, Ko-Lin (2009) *The Golden Triangle: Inside Southeast Asia's Drug Trade*. Ithaca. NY: Cornell University Press.

Chinwo, E. (2013) "Nigeria: MEND Claims Responsibility for Niger Delta Oil Spills." *AllAfrica.com*, October 21. http://allafrica.com/stories/201310210942.html (Accessed November 7, 2013).

Chivvis, C. S. and Liepman, A. (2013) *North Africa's Menace: AQIM's Evolution and the U.S. Policy Response*. RAND Corporation, RR415. http://www.rand.org/content/dam/rand/pubs/research_reports/RR400/RR415/RAND_RR415.pdf (Accessed October 5, 2013).

Chomsky, N. (2003) "Terror and Just Response." In Sterba, J. P. (ed.) *Terrorism and International Justice*. Oxford: Oxford University Press. pp. 69–87.

Choucri, N. (2012) *Cyberpolitics in International Relations*. Cambridge. MA: MIT Press.

Christian Aid (2009) "False Profits: Robbing the Poor to Keep the Rich Tax Free." March. http://www.christianaid.org.uk/Images/false-profits.pdf (Accessed October 4, 2009).

Cisco Systems (2013) *Cisco Virtual Network Index: Forecast and Methodology, 2012–2017*. May 29. San Jose. CA: Cisco Systems Inc. http://www.cisco.com/en/US/solutions/collateral/ns341/ns525/ns537/ns705/ns827/white_paper_c11-481360_ns827_Networking_Solutions_White_Paper.html (Accessed September 23, 2013).

Clapper, J. A. (2013) *Worldwide Threat Assessment of the US Intelligence Community*. Statement for the Record, Senate Select Committee on Intelligence, March 12, 2013. http://www.dni.gov/files/documents/Intelligence%20Reports/2013%20ATA%20SFR%20for%20SSCI%2012%20Mar%202013.pdf (Accessed October 4, 2013).

Clark, J. (2009) "Learning from the Past: Three Lessons from the Rwandan Genocide." *African Studies*. 68(1): pp. 1–28.

Clark, T. (2003) *Canadian Mining Companies in Latin America: Community Rights and Corporate Responsibility*. Centre for Research on Latin America and the Caribbean (CERLAC) and MiningWatch, Colloquia Papers Series. http://www.yorku.ca/cerlac/documents/Mining-report.pdf (Accessed May 25, 2008).

Clark, W. K. and Levin, P. L. (2009) "Securing the Information Highway." *Foreign Affairs*. 88(6): pp. 2–10.

Clarke, R. A. and Knake, R. K. (2010) *Cyber War: The Next Threat to National Security and What to Do About It.* Harper Collins e-books.

Clauzewitz, C., Von. (1982) *On War.* London: Penguin.

Coady, T. (2009) *Morality and Political Violence.* New York. NY: Cambridge University Press.

Cohen, M. A. (1992) "Environmental Crime and Punishment: Legal/Economic Theory and Empirical Evidence on Enforcement of Federal Environmental Statutes." *Journal of Criminal Law and Criminology.* 82(4): pp. 1056–1108.

Cohen, N. (2012) "Is Amnesty Still Fit to Fight on Anyone's Behalf?" *Guardian.* November 11. http://www.theguardian.com/commentisfree/2012/nov/11/nick-cohen-is-amnesty-fit-fight (Accessed November 30, 2013).

Coleman, G. (2013) *Coding Freedom: The Ethics and Aesthetics of Hacking.* Princeton. NJ: Princeton University Press.

Coleman, G. and Golub, A. (2008) "Hacker Practice: Moral Genres and the Cultural Articulation of Liberalism." *Anthropological Theory.* 8(3): pp. 255–77.

Coll, S. (2005) *Ghost Wars: The Secret History of the CIA, Afghanistan and Bin Laden, from the Soviet Invasion to September 10, 2001.* London: Penguin.

Collier, P. (2008) *The Bottom Billion: Why the Poorest Countries Are Failing and What Can Be Done About It.* New York. NY: Oxford University Press.

Constantin, L. (2011) "Anonymous' Robin Hood Credit Card Fraud Campaign Could Hurt More Than Just Banks." *PC World.* November 30. http://www.pcworld.idg.com.au/article/408925/anonymous_robin_hood_credit_card_fraud_campaign_could_hurt_more_than_just_banks/ (Accessed November 12, 2013).

Convention on the Prohibition of the Development, Production and Stockpiling of Bacteriological (Biological) and Toxin Weapons and their Destruction, 1972. http://www.opbw.org/convention (Accessed March 3, 2010).

Cooley, A. and Ron, J. (2004) "The NGO Scramble: Organizational Insecurity and the Political Economy of Transnational Action." In Brown, M. E., Cote, O. R. Jr., Lynn-Jones, S. M., and Miller, S. E. (ed.) *New Global Dangers: Changing Dimensions of International Security.* Cambridge. MA: MIT Press. pp. 477–511.

Corkill, E. (2011) "Ex-Tokyo Cop Speaks Out on a Life Fighting Gangs — and What You Can Do." *Japan Times.* November 6. http://www.japantimes.co.jp/print/fl20111106x2.html (Accessed February 17, 2012).

Cornell, S. and Jonsson, M. (2014) "The Nexus of Crime and Conflict." In Cornell, S. and Jonsson, M. (ed.) *Conflict Crime and the State in Postcommunist Eurasia.* Philadelphia. PA: University of Pennsylvania Press. pp. 1–22.

Costoya, M. M. (2007) *Toward a Typology of Civil Society Actors: The Case of the Movement to Change International Trade Rules and Barriers.* Civil Society and Social Movements Programme Paper No. 30, United Nations Research Institute for Social Development, 2007. http://www.unrisd.org/.

Council of Europe (2011) *Convention on Cybercrime.* Budapest, November 23. http://conventions.coe.int/treaty/en/treaties/html/185.htm (Accessed February 12, 2012).

Cox, G. (2010) "The Trafigura Case and the System of Prior Informed Consent Under the Basel Convention – A Broken System?" *Law, Environment and Development Journal.* 6(3): pp. 263–283. http://www.lead-journal.org/content/10263.pdf (Accessed May 6, 2013).

Cox, N. J. C. (2001) "The Ministry of Economic Warfare And Britain's Conduct of Economic Warfare, 1939 – 1945." PhD Diss. London: King's College London.

Cribb, J. (2010) *The Coming Famine: The Global Food Crisis and What We Can do to Avoid It*. Berkeley. CA: University of California Press.

Criminal Code Act (1995) Australia. http://www.opbw.org/nat_imp/leg_reg/australia/crimcode.pdf (Accessed January 1, 2014).

Cronin, A. K. (2013) "Why Drones Fail: When Tactics Drive Strategy." *Foreign Affairs*. 92(4) July/August: pp. 44–54.

Cronin, A. K. (2009) *How Terrorism Ends: Understanding the Decline and Demise of Terrorist Campaigns*. Princeton. NJ: Princeton University Press.

(CSBR) Coalition for Sexual and Bodily Rights in Muslim Societies "Sexuality and Human Rights in Muslim Societies." http://www.csbronline.org/about-csbr/sexuality-and-human-rights-in-muslim-societies/ (Accessed January 20, 2014).

(CSIS) Center for Strategic and International Studies (2010) "Conference Report: The Dynamics of North African Terrorism." http://csis.org/files/attachments/100216_NorthAfricaConferenceReport.pdf (Accessed October 20, 2013).

(CTFC) Commodity Futures Trading Commission (2012) "CFTC Orders Barclays to Pay $200 Million." Press release, PR: 6289-12, June 27. http://www.cftc.gov/PressRoom/PressReleases/pr6289-12 (Accessed May 3, 2013)

Cullen, P. M. (2008) "The Role of Targeted Killing in the Campaign against Terror." *Joint Forces Quarterly*. 48 (1): pp. 22–29.

Curran, S. (2008) "The Global Complexity Framework." *Globalizations*. 5(2): pp. 107–109.

Daadler, I. and Stavridis, J. (2012) "NATO's Triumph in Libya." *Foreign Affairs*. 91(2): pp. 2–7.

Daddis, G. A. (2012) "The Problem of Metrics: Assessing Progress and Effectiveness in the Vietnam War." *War in History*. 19(1): pp. 73–98.

Daly, M. W. (2007) *Darfur's Sorrow: A History of Destruction and Genocide*. Cambridge: Cambridge University Press.

Dando, M. (2009) "Biologists Napping While Work Militarized." *Nature*. 460(20): pp. 950–951.

Dauvergne, P. (2001) *Loggers and Degradation in the Asia-Pacific: Corruption and Environmental Management*. Cambridge: Cambridge University Press.

Dauvergne, P. (1997) *Shadows in the Forest: Japan and the Politics of Timber in Southeast Asia*. Cambridge. MA: MIT Press.

Dauvergne, P. and Lister, J. (2011) *Timber*. Cambridge: Polity.

Davis I. (2005) "The Biggest Contract." *Economist*. May 26. http://www.economist.com/node/4008642 (Accessed 12 December 2012).

DeFronzo, J. (2011) *Revolutions and Revolutionary Movements* (4th edition). Boulder. CO: Westview.

DeMars, W. E. (2005) *NGOs and Transnational Networks: Wild Cards in World Politics*. London: Pluto.

De Montclos, Pérouse, M-A. (2008) "Conversion to Islam and Modernity in Nigeria: A View from the Underworld." *Africa Today*. 54(4): pp. 71–87.

De Nevers, R. (2006) "The Geneva Conventions and New Wars." *Political Science Quarterly*. 121: pp. 369–71.

De Soto, H. (2001) *The Mystery of Capital: Why Capitalism Triumphs in the West and Fails Everywhere Else*. London: Black Swan.

De Waal, A. (2007) "Darfur and the Failure of the Responsibility to Protect." *International Affairs*. 83(6): pp. 1039–1054.

De Waal, A. (2004) "The Politics of Destabilization in the Horn, 1989–2001." In De Waal, A. (ed.) *Islam and Its Enemies in the Horn of Africa*. Bloomington. IN: Indiana University Press, pp. 182–230.

De Waal, A. (1997) *Famine Crimes: Politics and the Disaster Relief Industry in Africa*. Oxford: James Currey.

De Waal, A. and Abdel Salam, A. H. (2004) "Islamism, State Power and Jihad in Sudan." In De Waal, A. (ed.) *Islam and Its Enemies in the Horn of Africa*. Bloomington. IN: Indiana University Press, pp. 71–113.

Dean, M. (2000) "Risk, Calculable and Incalculable." In Lupton, D. (ed.) *Risk and Sociocultural Theory: New Directions and Perspectives*. Cambridge: Cambridge University Press, pp. 131–159.

Deen, E. S. (2013) *AFRICOM: Protecting US Interests Disguised as 'Military Partnerships.'* Al Jazeera Centre for Studies. http://studies.aljazeera.net/ResourceGallery/media/Documents/2013/5/21/2013521134923251734AFRICOM%20Protecting%20US%20interests.pdf (Accessed November 6, 2013).

Defense News (October 21, 2011) http://www.defensenews.com/article/20111021/DEFSECT02/110210305/Libya-Arms-Threaten-Infiltrate-Africa-Conflicts (Accessed February 10, 2012).

Deibert, R. J. (2013) *Black Code: Inside the Battle for Cyberspace*. Toronto: McClelland and Stewart.

Deibert, R. J. and Rohozinski, R. (2010) "Under Cover of the Net: The Hidden Governance Mechanisms of Cyberspace." In Clunan, A. L. and Trinkunas, H. A. (ed.) *Ungoverned Spaces: Alternatives to State Authority in an Era of Softened Sovereignty*. Stanford. CA: Stanford University Press. pp. 255–272.

Democracyranking.org. (2012) "Global Quality Indicators, 2007–2008 and 2010–2011." http://www.democracyranking.org/downloads/2012/Democracy-Ranking-2012_List%20of%20indicators.htm (Accessed April 23, 2012).

Denzau, A. T., North, C. D., and Roy, R. K. (2007) "Shared Mental Models: A Postscript." In Roy, R. K., Denzau, A. T., and Willets, T. D. (ed.) *Neoliberalism: National and Regional Experiments with Global Ideas*. New York. NY: Routledge. pp. 14–25.

Der Derian, J. (2001) *Virtuous War: Mapping the Military-Industrial-Media-Entertainment Network*. Boulder. CO: Westview.

Deutsche Weller (2013) "Mali's Tuareg Rebels Suspend Peace Talks with Government." September 27. www.dw.de/malis-tuareg-rebels-suspend-peace-talks-with-government/a-17118174 (Accessed September 28, 2013).

(DFTAT) Department of Foreign Affairs and Trade (2003) *Advancing the National Interest: Australia's Foreign and Trade Policy White Paper*. Canberra: Commonwealth of Australia.

Dicken, P. (2011) *Global Shift: Mapping the Changing Contours of the World Economy* (6th edition). London: SAGE.

Dinar, S. (2011) "Resource Scarcity and Environmental Degradation: Analyzing International Conflict and Cooperation." In Dinar, S. (ed.) *Beyond Resource Wars: Scarcity, Environmental Degradation and International Cooperation*. Cambridge. MS: MIT Press. pp. 14–53.

Docker, J. (2008) *The Origins of Violence: Religion, History and Genocide*. Sydney: University of New South Wales Press.

(DoD) US Department of Defense (2011) *Cyberspace Policy Report: A Report to Congress Pursuant to the National Defense Authorization Act for Fiscal Year 2011*.

Section 934, November 2011. www.defense.gov/home/features/2011/0411_cyberstrategy/docs/NDAA%20Section%20934%20Report_For%20webpage.pdf (Accessed February 12, 2012).

Doe I v Unocal Corp, Opinion, U.S. 395 F.3d 932 (9th Circuit), 2002. http://www.escr-net.org/docs/i/1054008 (Accessed July 2, 2009).

Doe, J et al. v Drummond Company PLC, 2: 09 CV01041-RDP (Alabama District Court) 2010.

(DoJ) US Department of Justice (2012a) "Press Release" (Relating to the HSBC settlement), December 11. http://www.justice.gov/opa/pr/2012/December/12-crm-1478.html (Accessed July 3, 2013).

(DoJ) US Department of Justice (2012b) "Agreement" (with Barclays Bank PLC) June 26. http://www.justice.gov/iso/opa/resources/337201271017335469822.pdf.

(DoJ) US Department of Justice (2012c) "Appendix A: Statement of Facts" (with Barclays Bank PLC). http://www.justice.gov/iso/opa/resources/9312012710173426365941.pdf (Accessed September 2, 2012).

(DoJ) US Department of Justice (2012d) *A Resource Guide to the U.S. Foreign Corrupt Practices Act*. November 14. www.justice.gov/criminal/fraud/fcpa and www.sec.gov/spotlight/fcpa.shtml (Accessed December 20, 2013).

Donadio, R. (2012) "Brother, Can You Spare $6 Trillion?" *New York Times*. February 17. http://www.nytimes.com/2012/02/18/world/europe/italy-arrests-8-in-fake-us-treasury-bonds-scam.html (Accessed February 18, 2012).

Donohue, L. K. (2008) *The Cost of Counterterrorism: Power, Politics, and Liberty*. Cambridge. NY: Cambridge University Press.

(DoS) US Department of State (2013) *Trafficking in Persons Report, 2012*. http://www.state.gov/j/tip/rls/tiprpt/2012/ (Accessed June 23, 2013).

(DoT) US Department of Treasury (2011) "Financial Crimes Enforcement Network: Amendment to the Bank Security Regulation – Imposition of Special Measure Against the Islamic Republic of Iran as a Jurisdiction of Primary Money Laundering Concern." US Federal Register, Vol. 76, No. 228, Monday, November 28, 2011, 72878–72885m. http://www.fincen.gov/statutes_regs/patriot/section311.html (Accessed March 18, 2012).

(DoT) US Department of Treasury (2010) *CISADA: The New U.S. Sanctions on Iran*. http://www.treasury.gov/resource-center/sanctions/Programs/Documents/CISADA_english.pdf (Accessed August 31, 2012).

(DoT) US Department of Treasury Office of Foreign Asset Control (OFAC) (n/d) *An Overview of O.F.A.C. Regulations Concerning Sanctions Against Iran*. http://www.treas.gov/ofac (Accessed August 31, 2012).

Dower, J. W. (1986) *War Without Mercy: Race and Power in the Pacific War*. New York. NY: Pantheon Books.

Downs, E. and Maloney, S. (2011) "Getting China to Sanction Iran." *Foreign Affairs*. 90(2): pp. 15–21.

Du Rausas, M. P., Manyika, J., Hazan, E., Bughin, J., Chui, M., and Said, R. (2011) *Internet Matters: The Net's Sweeping Impact on Growth, Jobs, and Prosperity*. McKinsey Global Institute, McKinsey and Company. http://www.mckinsey.com/features/sizing_the_internet_economy (Accessed October 20, 2013).

Duffield, M. (2010) "The Liberal Way of Development and the Development-Security Impasse: Exploring the Global Life-Chance Divide." *Security Dialogue*. 41(1): pp. 53–76.

Duffield, M. (2007) *Development, Security and Unending War: Governing the World of Peoples*. Cambridge: Polity.

Drainville, A. C. (2004) *Contesting Globalization: Space and Place in the World Economy*. London: Routledge.

Dunant, H. (1986) *A Memory of Solferino*. Geneva: International Committee of the Red Cross.

Dwoskin, E. (2013) "Undocumented Workers Would Get a Fast Track to Citizenship. Why?" *Businessweek*. June 13. http://www.businessweek.com/printer/articles/125234-undocumented-farmworkers-would-get-a-fast-track-to-citizenship-dot-why (Accessed October 16, 2013).

Eakin, M. C. (2007) *The History of Latin America: Collision of Cultures*. New York: Palgrave.

(EC) European Commission (2011) *Annual Report on the European Union's Development and External Assistance Policies and their Implementation in 2011*. Brussels: European Union.

(EC) European Commission (2009) Commission Regulation No. 1010/2009, October 22, *Official Journal of the European Union*, October 27. http://eur-lex.europa.eu/LexUriServ/LexUriServ.do?uri=CELEX:32009R1010:en:NOT (Accessed November 28, 2013).

Economist (December 14, 2012) http://www.economist.com/blogs/babbage/2012/12/internet-regulation (Accessed November 29, 2013).

Edwards, M. (2010) *Small Change: Why Business Won't Save the World*. San Francisco. CA: Berrett-Koehler.

(EIA) Energy Information Administration (2013) *Annual Energy Outlook 2013*. http://www.eia.gov/forecasts/archive/aeo13/source_oil_all.cfm#oil_price (Accessed November 2, 2013).

(EIU) Economic Intelligence Unit (2012) *Democracy Index 2012: Democracy at a Standstill*. http://www.eiu.com/Handlers/WhitepaperHandler.ashx?fi=Democracy-Index-2012.pdf&mode=wp&campaignid=DemocracyIndex12 (Accessed April 2, 2013).

Elliott, L. (2007) "Transnational Environmental Crime in the Asia Pacific: An 'Un(der)securitized' Security Problem?" *Pacific Review*. 20(4): pp. 499–522.

Ellis, S. (2011) "West Africa's International Drug Trade." In Gilman, N., Goldhammer, J., and Weber, S. (ed.) *Deviant Globalization: Black Market Economy in the 21st Century*. New York. NY: Continuum. pp. 114–138.

Elmer, G. (2012) "Panopticon – Discipline – Control." In Ball, K., Haggerty, K. D., and Lyon, D. (ed.) *Routledge Handbook of Surveillance Studies*. New York. NY: Routledge. pp. 21–29.

Endeshaw, A. (2004) "Internet Regulation in China: The Never-ending Cat and Mouse Game." *Information & Communications Technology Law*. 13(1): pp. 41–57.

Engvall J. (2014) "Tajikistan: From Drug Insurgency to Drug-State Nexus." In Cornell, S. and Jonsson, M. (ed.) *Conflict, Crime and the State in Postcommunist Eurasia*. Philadelphia. PA: University of Pennsylvania Press, pp. 49–67.

Escobar, A. (1995) *Encountering Development: The Making and Unmaking of the Third World*. Princeton. NJ: Princeton University Press.

(ESINA) European Union Agency for Network and Information Security (n/d) "National Cyber Security Strategies in the World." http://www.enisa.europa.eu/

activities/Resilience-and-CIIP/national-cyber-security-strategies-ncsss/national-cyber-security-strategies-in-the-world (Accessed December 17, 2013).

Espionage Act of 1917, U.S. Code 794, Title 19, Part 1, Chapter 37.

Esty, D., Goldstone J. A., Gurr, T. R., Harff, B., Levy M., Dabelko, G. D., Surko, P., and Unger, A. N. (1998) *State Failure Task Force Report: Phase II Findings*. McLean. VA: Science Applications International Corporation.

(EU) European Union (2003) *A Secure Europe in a better World: European Security Strategy*. European External Action Service. http://www.eeas.europa.eu/csdp/about-csdp/european-security-strategy/ (Accessed April 25, 2014).

(EU ISS) European Union Institute for Security Studies (2012) *Global Trends 2030: Citizens in an Interconnected and Polycentric World*. Paris: European Policy and Strategy Analysis System (EPAS). http://www.iss.europa.eu/publications/detail/article/espas-report-global-trends-2030-citizens-in-an-interconnected-and-polycentric-world/.

Evans, G. (2011) "Ending Mass Atrocity Crimes: The Responsibility to Protect Balance Sheet After Libya." Second Renate Kamener Oration, Melbourne, July 31, 2011. http://www.gevans.org/speeches/speech443.html (Accessed November 1, 2011).

Evans, G. (1989) *Australia's Regional Security*. Ministerial Statement by the Senator the Hon. Gareth Evans QC, Minister for Foreign Affairs and Trade, Canberra: Commonwealth of Australia.

Ewins, P., Harvey, P., Savag, K., and Jacobs, A. (2006) *Mapping the Risks of Corruption in Humanitarian Action*. London: Overseas Development Institute.

Executive Order 12957, March 17, 1995, "Prohibiting Certain Transactions with Respect to the Development of Iranian Petroleum Resources." Federal Register. Vol. 60, No. 52, March 17, 1995, pp. 14615–14616. https://www.federalregister.gov/articles/1995/03/17/95-6849/prohibiting-certain-transactions-with-respect-to-the-development-of-iranian-petroleum-resources (Accessed January 2, 2013).

Faber, E. M. H. (2013) "Grand Strategy and Human Thinking." In Ronis, S. R. (ed.) *Forging an American Grand Strategy: Securing a Path Through a Complex Future (Selected Presentations From A Symposium at the National Defense University)*. Strategic Studies Institute and US Army War College Press. http://www.StrategicStudiesInstitute.army.mil/ (Accessed October 31, 2013).

Falk, R. (1999) *Predatory Globalization: A Critique*. Cambridge: Polity.

(FAO) Food and Agriculture Organization of the United Nations (2012) *State of the World's Fisheries*. 2012. Rome: FAO.

(FAO) Food and Agriculture Organization of the United Nations (2010) *State of the World's Fisheries. 2010*. Rome: FAO.

Farah, D. (2013) *Transnational Organized Crime, Terrorism, and Criminalized States in Latin America: An Emerging Tier-One National Security Priority, Drug Trafficking, FARC, Hugo Chavez, FMLN, Liberia*. Progressive Management e-book.

FARC-EP/Colombia. Official Website. http://farc-epeace.org/ (Accessed January 24, 2014).

Farrell, H. and Finemore, M. (2013) "The End of Hypocrisy: American Foreign Policy in the Age of Leaks." *Foreign Affairs*. 92(6): pp. 22–26.

Feinstein, A. (2011a) *The Shadow World: Inside the Global Arms Trade*. London: Hamish Hamilton.

Feinstein, A. (2011b) "Where Is Gaddafi's Vast Arms Stockpile?" *Guardian*. October 26. http://www.guardian.co.uk/world/2011/oct/26/gadaffis-arms-stockpile (Accessed February 10, 2012).

Ferguson, N. (2012) *The Great Degeneration: How Institutions Decay and Economies Die*. London: Allen Lane.

Ferguson, W. (2013) *Collective Action and Exchange: A Game-Theoretic Approach to Contemporary Political Economy*. Stanford. CA: Stanford University Press.

Feyerabend, P. (1991) *Against Method* (2nd edition). New Left Books: London.

Fisher, M. (2012) "A Land Without Guns: How Japan Has Virtually Eliminated Shooting Deaths." *Atlantic*. July 23. http://www.theatlantic.com/international/archive/2012/07/a-land-without-guns-how-japanhas-virtually-eliminated-shooting-deaths/260189/ (Accessed October 24, 2013).

Fisk, R. (2011) "America's Secret Plan to Arm Libya's Rebels." *Independent*. March 7. http://www.independent.co.uk/news/world/middle-east/americas-secret-plan-to-arm-libyas-rebels-2234227.html# (Accessed November 6, 2011).

Flint, J. (2009) *Beyond "Janjaweed": Understanding the Militias of Darfur*. Geneva: Small Arms Survey, Graduate Institute of International and Development Studies. http://citeseerx.ist.psu.edu/viewdoc/download?doi=10.1.1.168.4626&rep=rep1&type=pdf (Accessed July 5, 2012).

Ford Foundation (2014) "History: Overview." http://www.fordfoundation.org/about-us/history (Accessed January 12, 2014).

Forland, T. F. (1993) "The History of Economic Warfare: International Law, Effectiveness, Strategies." *Journal of Peace Research*. 30(2): 151–162.

Foucault, M. (1994) "Governmentality." In Faubion, J. D. (ed.) *Michel Foucault: Power, Essential Works of Foucault, 1954–1984*. London: Penguin. pp. 201–222.

Franklin, S. (2013) "A Daughter's Quest for Justice in Colombia." Pulitzer Center on Crisis Reporting. November 5. http://pulitzercenter.org/reporting/south-america-colombia-labor-unions-activists-murder-government-politics-poverty (Accessed January 2, 2014).

Freeland, C. (2012) *Plutocrats: The Rise of the New Global Super-Rich and the Fall of Everyone Else*. London: Allen Lane.

Freeman, M. (2007) *Human Rights: An Interdisciplinary Approach*. Cambridge: Polity.

Freshfields Bruckhaus Deringer (2012) *Briefing: U.S. Foreign Corrupt Practices Act – Guidelines Published by the U.S. Government*. www.freshfields.com (Accessed April 6, 2013).

Friedman, M. (1970) "The Social Responsibility of Business is to Increase Profits." *New York Times Magazine*, September 13. http://www.umich.edu (Accessed March 23, 2012).

Fukuyama, F. (2007) *After the Neocons: America at the Crossroads*. London: Profile.

Fukuyama, F. (1992) *The End of History and the Last Man*. London: Penguin.

Gagnon, V. P. (2004) *The Myth of Ethnic War: Serbia and Croatia in the 1990s*. Ithaca, NY: Cornell University Press.

Galeotti, M. (2004a) "Introduction: Global Crime Today." *Global Crime*. 6(1): pp. 1–7.

Galeotti, M. (2004b) "The Russian 'Mafiya': Consolidation and Globalization." *Global Crime*. 6(1): pp. 54–69.

Gandhi, M. K. (2007) "Extract I-240." In Merton, T. (ed.) *Gandhi on Non-Violence*. New York. NY: New Directions, p. 51.

Gardner, T. and Hampton, R. (2012) "US Extends Waivers on Iran Sanctions to China and India." Reuters, December 7. http://www.reuters.com/article/2012/12/07/us-usa-iran-sanctons-idUSBRE8B615M20121207 (Accessed January 2, 2012).

Garfinkel, S. (2000) *Database Nation: The Death of Privacy in the 21st Century*. Sebastopol. CA: O'Reilly.

Garnaut, J. (2010) "Bribery Rife in Rio Tinto China Operation: Court." *Age*. April 17. http://www.theage.com.au/business/bribery-rife-in-rio-tinto-china-operation-court-20100416-skmr.html (Accessed January 3, 2012).

Garrett, B. L. (2011) "Globalized Corporate Prosecutions." *Virginia Law Review*. 97(8): pp. 1775–1875.

Garson, G. D. (2006) "Securing the Virtual State Recent Developments in Privacy and Security." *Social Science Computer Review*. 24(4): pp. 489–496.

Gellman, B. and Blake, A. (2013) "Edward Snowden Identified as Source of NSA Leaks." *Washington Post*. June 10 (iPad edition).

Gellman, B. and Nakashima, E. (2013) "U.S. Spy Agencies Mounted 231 Offensive Cyber-operations in 2011, Documents Show." *Washington Post*. August 30 (iPad edition).

Geneva Call (2010) *Annual Report 2010*. http://www.genevacall.org/resources/annual-reports/annual-reports.php (Accessed February 10, 2012).

Geneva Declaration Secretariat (2011) *Global Burden of Armed Violence*. Geneva declaration.http://www.genevadeclaration.org/measurability/global-burden-of-armed-violence/global-burden-of-armed-violence-2011.html (Accessed April 7, 2013).

Geneva Declaration Secretariat (2008) *Global Burden of Armed Violence*. Geneva: Geneva Declaration.

Gerlach, M. L. (1992) *Alliance Capitalism: The Social Organization of Japanese Business*. Berkeley. CA: University of California Press.

Ghadge, A., Dani, S., Chester, M., and Kalawsky, R. (2013) "A Systems Approach for Modelling Supply Chain Risks." *Supply Chain Management: An International Journal*. 18(5): pp. 523–538.

Ghani, G. and Lockhart, C. (2009) *Fixing Failed States: A Framework for Rebuilding a Fractured World*. Oxford: Oxford University Press.

Ghosh, P. (2013) "Amnesty International: The High Cost of Human Rights Activism and Charity." *International Business Times*. June 12. http://www.ibtimes.com/amnesty-international-high-cost-human-rights-activism-charity-1301765 (Accessed October 14, 2013).

Gibson, R. M. (2011) *The Secret Army: Chiang Kai-shek and the Drug Warlords of the Golden Triangle*. Singapore: John Wiley.

Giddens, A. (1999) *Runaway World: How Globalization is Reshaping Our Lives*. London: Profile Books.

Giddens, A. (1994) "Living in a Post-Traditional Society." In Beck, U., Giddens, A., and Lash, S. (ed.) *Reflexive Modernization: Politics, Tradition and Aesthetics in the Modern Social Order*. Stanford. CA: Stanford University Press. pp. 56–109.

Giddens, A. (1990) *The Consequences of Modernity*. Stanford. CA: Stanford University Press.

Gilbert, A. (1978) "Marx on Internationalism and War." *Philosophy and Public Affairs*. 7(4): pp. 346–369.

Gilpin, R. (2003) *Global Political Economy: Understanding the International Economic Order*. Hyderabad: Orient Longman.

Giraldo et al. v Drummond et. al. 2:09-cv-01041-RDP. 25 July 2013. http://www.lawfareblog.com/wp-content/uploads/2013/07/455_Order-granting-SJ-for-DCI-and-DLTD.pdf (Accessed January 2, 2014).

Gladstone, R. and Kushkush, I. (2013) "U.S. is Asked to Hold Sudan Leader if he Visits UN." *New York Times*. September 18. http://www.nytimes.com/2013/09/19/world/africa/united-nations.html?_r=0 (Accessed November 8, 2013).

Glaser, C. L. (2010) *Rational Theory of International Politics: The Logic of Competition and Cooperation*. Princeton. NJ: Princeton University Press.

Glenn, R. W. (2000) "Introduction." In Marshall, S. L. A. (ed.) *Men against Fire: The Problem of Battlefield Command*. Norman. OK: University of Oklahoma Press.

Global Peace Index (n/d) http://www.visionofhumanity.org/gpi-data/#/2011/scor (Accessed January 4, 2012).

Godement, F. (1999) *The Downsizing of Asia*. London: Routledge.

Goodin, R. (2003) "Globalising Justice." In Held, D. and Koenig-Archibugi, M. (ed.) *Taming Globalization: New Frontiers of Governance*. Cambridge: Polity, pp. 68–92.

Gorman, S. and Valentino-Devries, J. (2013) "New Details Show Broader NSA Surveillance Reach." *Wall Street Journal*. August 30. http://online.wsj.com/news/articles/SB10001424127887324108204579022874091732470 (Accessed November 21, 2013).

Goswami, N. (2013) "Tracking the Source of 'Weapon Providers' for NE Rebels." *IDSA Comment*, Institute for Defence Studies and Analysis, November 7. http://www.idsa.in/idsacomments/TrackingthesourceofWeaponProvidersforNERebels_ngoswami_071113#footnote1_ehpyjfl (Accessed November 30, 2013).

Göbel, C., and Ong, L. H. (2012) *Social Unrest in China*. London: Europe China Research and Advice Network. http://www.euecran.eu/Long%20Papers/ECRAN%20Social%20Unrest%20in%20China_%20Christian%20Gobel%20and%20Lynette%20H.%20Ong.pdf (Accessed March 10, 2014).

Grain.org (2012) "Who Will Feed China: Agribusiness or its Own Farmers? Decisions in Beijing Echo Around the World." *Against the Grain*. August 4. http://www.grain.org/article/categories/13-against-the-grain (Accessed February 21, 2013).

Griffiths, H. and Jenks, M. (2012) *Maritime Transport and Destabilizing Commodity Flows*. SIPRI Policy Paper 32, Solna: Stokholm International Peace research Institute.

Gross, M. (2010) *Moral Dilemmas of Modern War: Torture, Assassination, and Blackmail in an Age of Asymmetric Conflict*. New York. NY: Cambridge.

Grossman, D. (1995) *On Killing: The Psychological Cost of Learning to Kill in War and Society*. Boston: Little, Brown and Company.

Guaquetta, A. (2003) "The Colombian Conflict: Political and Economic Dimensions." In Ballentine, K. and Sherman, J. (ed.) *The Political Economy of Armed Conflict: Beyond Greed and Grievance*. Boulder. CO: Lynne Rienner. pp. 73–106.

Guerin, B. (2006) "After the Tsunami, Waves of Corruption." *Asia Times Online*, September 20. http://www.atimes.com/atimes/Southeast_Asia/HI20Ae01.html (Accessed January 2, 2014).

Guilherme, L. (2011) "Preserving the Millennium: The 'Impossible Possibility' of the World Community in Reinhold Niebuhr." Paper for the Third Global International Studies Conference, WISC 2011, University of Porto, Porto. http://www.wiscnetwork.org/porto2011/papers/WISC_2011-756.pdf (Accessed November 30, 2011).

Gunaratna, R. (2009) "The Threat to the Maritime Domain: How Real is the Terrorist Threat." In Norwitz, J. H. (ed.) *Pirates, Terrorists and Warlords: The History, Influence, and Future of Armed Groups Around the World*. New York. NY: Skyhorse Publishing. pp. 87–96.

Guthrie, D. (2009) *China and Globalization: The Social, Economic and Political Transformation of Chinese Society*. New York. NY: Routledge.

Hage, G. (2010) "On Narcissistic Victimhood." In Gaita, R. (ed.) *Gaza: Morality, Law and Politics*. Crawley. Western Australia: University of Western Australia. pp. 101–126.

Hague Convention (IV) Respecting the Laws and Customs of War on Land and Its Annex: Regulations Concerning the Laws and Customs of War on Land, October 18, 1907. http://www.refworld.org/docid/4374cae64.html (Accessed December 4, 2013).

Haldane, A. G. and Alessandri, P. (2009) "Banking on the State." paper by Haldane, A. G., Executive Director, Financial Stability, Bank of England, based on a presentation delivered at the Federal Reserve Bank of Chicago Twelfth Annual International Banking Conference on "The International Financial Crisis: Have the Rules of Finance Changed?" Chicago, September 25. http://www.bis.org/review/r091111e.pdf (Accessed November 10, 2011).

Hall, R. B. and Biersteker, T. J. (2002) "Private Authority as Global Governance." In Hall, R. B. and Biersteker, T. J. (ed.) *The Emergence of Private Authority in Global Governance*. Cambridge: Cambridge University Press, pp. 203–222.

Halliday, F. (2005) *The Middle East in International Relations: Power, Politics and Ideology*. Cambridge: Cambridge University Press.

Halperin, M. H. and Blair, K. M. (2012) "The Need to Protect Democracy in Mali." *Huffington Post*. April 2. http://www.huffingtonpost.com/morton-h-halperin/mali-coup_b_1392491.html (Accessed October 4, 2013).

Hammes, T. (2008) "War Evolves into the Fourth Generation." In Terriff, T., Karp, A., and Karp, R. (ed.) *Global Insurgency and the Future of Armed Conflict: Debating Fourth Generation Warfare*. London: Routledge. pp. 21–44.

Hammes, T. (2006) *The Sling and the Stone: On War in the 21st Century*. Minneapolis. MN: Zenith.

Hammond, L. (2008) "The Power of Holding Humanitarianism Hostage and the Myth of Protective Principles." In Barnett, M. and Weiss, T. G. (ed.) *Humanitarianism in Question: Politics, Power, Ethics*. Ithaca. NY: Cornell University Press. pp. 173–195.

Hammond, P. (2013) "New Cyber Reserve Unit Created." UK Government, September 29. https://www.gov.uk/government/news/reserves-head-up-new-cyber-unit (Accessed December 17, 2013).

Hanlon, Q. H. (2009) "Globalization and the Transformation of Armed Groups." In Norwitz, J. H. (ed.) *Pirates, Terrorists and Warlords: The History, Influence, and Future of Armed Groups Around the World*. New York. NY: Skyhorse. pp. 124–134.

Hanrahan, C. E. (2001) *The U.S.–European Union Banana Dispute*. CRS, Library of Congress, United States, RS21030, December 11. http://assets.opencrs.com/rpts/RS20130_20011211.pdf (Accessed February 23, 2013).

Hanson, S. (2008) "Colombia's Right-Wing Paramilitaries and Splinter Groups." *Backgrounder.* January 11. http://www.cfr.org/publication/15239 (Accessed March 31, 2008).

Harden, M. (2005) "Still No Regrets For Frail Enola Gay Pilot (Col. Paul Tibbets)." *Free Republic*. August 6. http://www.freerepublic.com/focus/f-news/1458133/posts (Accessed November 10, 2012).

Hardt, M. and Negri, A. (2009) *Commonwealth*. Cambridge. MA: Harvard University Press.

Hardt, M. and Negri, A. (2005) *Multitude*. New York. NY: Penguin.

Hardt, M. and Negri, A. (2000) *Empire*. Cambridge. MA: Harvard University Press.

Harff, B. and Gurr, T. R. (2004) *Ethnic Conflict in World Politics* (2nd edition). Boulder. CO: Westview.

Harris, T. (n/d) "Settling a Corporate Accountability Lawsuit Without Sacrificing Human Rights: Wang Xiaoning v. Yahoo." *Human Rights Brief*. http://www.wcl.american.edu/hrbrief/15/2harris.pdf (Accessed July 21, 2013).

Harvey, D. (1991) *The Condition of Postmodernity*. Oxford: Blackwell.

Hasenclever, A., Mayer, P., and Ritterberger, V. (2002) *Theories of International Regimes*. Cambridge: Cambridge University Press.

Hashim, A. S. (2013) *When Counterinsurgency Wins: Sri Lanka's Defeat of the Tamil Tigers*. Philadelphia. PA: University of Philadelphia Press.

Hayden, P. (2009) *Political Evil in a Global Age: Hannah Arendt and International Theory*. London: Routledge.

Heath, J. and Potter, A. (2004) *Nation of Rebels: Why Counterculture Became Consumer Culture*. New York. NY: Harper Collins.

Hedahl, M. (2009) "Blood and Blackwaters: A Call to Arms for the Profession of Arms." *Journal of Military Ethics*. 8(9): pp. 19–33.

Hedge, C. (2008) *American Fascists: The Christian Right and the War on America*. London: Vintage.

Held, D. (2010) *Cosmopolitanism: Ideals and Realities*. Cambridge: Polity.

Held, D. (2003) "From Executive to Cosmopolitan Multilateralism." In Held, D. and Koenig-Archibugi, M. (ed.) *Taming Globalization: Frontiers of Governance*. Cambridge: Polity. pp. 160–186.

Held, D., McGrew, A., Goldblatt, D., and Perraton, J. (2000) *Global Transformations: Politics, Economics and Culture*. Cambridge: Polity.

Henning, P. J. (2012) "What the Barclays Settlement Means for Other Banks." *New York Times*. July 3. http://dealbook.nytimes.com/2012/07/03/whats-next-after-the-barclays-settlement/ (Accessed September 2, 2012).

"Henry Dunant-Biographical 1901." In Haberman, F. W. (ed.) (1972) Nobel Lectures: Peace 1901–1925, Amsterdam: Elsevier Publishing Company, Amsterdam. http://nobelprize.org/nobel_prizes/peace/laureates/1901/dunant-bio.html (Accessed June 28, 2008).

Henry, N. (2011) *War and Rape: Law, Memory and Justice*. Abingdon: Routledge.

Herbst, J. (2000) *States and Power in Africa: Comparative Lessons in Authority and Control*. Princeton. NJ: Princeton University Press.

Hersh, S. (1972) "C.I.A. Aides Assail Asia Drug Charge: Agency Fights Reports That It Ignored Heroin Traffic Among Allies of U.S. C.I.A. Aides Fight Reports That Agency Ignored Southeast Asian Heroin Traffic," *New York Times*, July 22. http://query.nytimes.com/mem/archive/pdf?res=F10D12F9345A137B93C0AB178CD85F468785F9 (Accessed March 24, 2014).

Hill, P. (2003) "Heisei Yakuza: Burst Bubble and Botaiho." *Social Science Japan Journal*. 6(1): pp. 1–18.

Hirsch, A. (2012) "Mali's Conflict and a 'War Over Skin Colour." *Guardian*. July 7. www.theguardian.com/commentisfree/2012/jul/06/mali-war-over-skin-colour/ (Accessed July 19, 2013).

Hirschman, A. O. (1991) *The Rhetoric of Reaction: Perversity, Futility, Jeopardy*. Cambridge. MA: Belknap.

Hirschman, A. O. (1978) "Exit, Voice and the State." *World Politics*. 31(1): 90–107.

Hirschman, A. O. (1970) *Exit, Voice and Loyalty: Responses to Decline in Firms, Organizations and States*. Cambridge. MA: Belknap.

Hix, S. and Hoyland, B. (2011) *The Political System of the European Union*. Basingstoke. UK: Palgrave Macmillan.

Holzgrefe, J. L. (2003) "The Humanitarian Intervention Debate." In Holzgrefe, J. L. and Keohane, R. (ed.) *Humanitarian Intervention: Ethical, Legal and Political Dilemmas*. Cambridge: Cambridge University Press. pp. 36–43.

Homer Dixon, T. F. (1999) *Environment, Scarcity, and Violence*. Princeton. NJ: Princeton University Press.

Hooper, R. (2013) "In Science Terms Japan Has no Need at all to Kill Whales." *Japan Times*, August 10. http://www.japantimes.co.jp/news/2013/08/10/national/in-science-terms-japan-has-no-need-at-all-to-kill-whales/#.Ulo-7mT-Jc8 (Accessed October 14, 2013).

Hopgood, S. (2008) "Saying 'No' to Walmart: Money and Morality in Professional Humanitarianism." In Barnett, M. and Weiss, T. G. (ed.) *Humanitarianism in Question: Politics, Power, Ethics*. New York. NY: Cornell University Press. pp. 98–123.

Hopkins, N. (2011) "UK Military Steps up Plans for an Iran Attack Amid New Nuclear Fears." *Guardian*. November 2. http://www.guardian.co.uk/world/2011/nov/02/uk-military-iran-attack-nuclear.

Howard, P. N., Duffy, A., Freelon, D., Hussain, M., Mari, W., and Mazaid, M. (2011) *Opening Closed Regimes: What was the Role of Social Media During the Arab Spring?* Project on Information Technology and Political Islam. Seattle. WA: University of Washington.

(HRW) Human Rights Watch (2010) *Colombia: Paramilitaries' Heirs, the New Face of Violence in Colombia*. New York. NY: Human Rights Watch.

(HRW) Human Rights Watch (2006) *With Friends Like These: Human Rights Violations in Azad Kashmir*. September, volume 16(6). http://www.hrw.org/reports/2006/pakistan0906/pakistan0906webwcover.pdf (Accessed January 12, 2012).

(HRW) Human Rights Watch (2000) "Update on Human Rights Violations in the Niger Delta." hrw.org/backgrounder/africa/nigeriabkg1214.htm (Accessed December 18, 2007).

(HRW) Human Rights Watch (1999) *The Price of Oil: Corporate responsibility and Human Rights Violations in Nigeria's Oil Producing Communities*. www.hrw.org/reports/1999/nigeria/Nigew991-01.htm (Accessed December 18, 2007).

Human Rights First (2008) *Private Security Contractors and War: Ending the Impunity*. New York. NY: Human Rights First.

Huntington, S. P. (2006) *Political Order in Changing Societies* (2nd edition). New Haven. CT: Yale University Press.

Huntington, S. P. (1993) *The Third Wave: Democratization in the Late Twentieth Century*. Norman. OK: University of Oklahoma Press.

Hutchinson, S. and O'Malley, P. (2007) "A Crime-Terror Nexus? Thinking on Links Between Terrorism and Criminality." *Studies in Conflict and Terrorism*. 30(12): pp. 1095–1107.

Hutton, W. (2003) *The World We're In*. London: Abacus.

Ibeanu, O. (2009) *Report of the Special Rapporteur on the Adverse Effects of the Movement and Dumping of Toxic and Dangerous Products and Wastes on the Enjoyment of Human Rights*. United Nations General Assembly, Human Rights Council, September 3, A/HRC/12/26/Add.2. http://www.un.org (Accessed June 26, 2010).

(ICEM) International Federation of Engineering, Chemical, Mine and General Workers Union (2007) "Trial Begins in US on Drummond Coal's Alleged Murders of Colombian Trade Unionists" July 16. http://www.icem.org/en/78-ICEM-InBrief/2331-Trial-Begins-in-US-on-Drummond-Coal%E2%80%99s-Alleged-Murders-of-Colombian-Trade-Unionists (Accessed May 19, 2010).

(ICFTU-ICEF) International Confederation of Trades Unions-International Federation of Chemical, Energy, and General Workers Unions (1985) *The Report of the ICFTU-ICEF Mission to Study the Causes and Effects of the Methyl Isocyanate Gas Leak at the Union Carbide Pesticide Plant in Bhopal, India on December 2/3rd, 1984*. www.bhopal.net/oldsite/documentlibrary/unionreport 1985.html (Accessed July 9, 2013).

(ICG) International Crisis Group (2011) *Aid and Conflict in Afghanistan*. Crisis Group Asia Report No. 2010, August 4. http://www.crisisgroup.org/~/media/Files/asia/south-asia/afghanistan/210-%20Aid%20and%20Conflict%20in%20 Afghanistan.pdf (Accessed June 4, 2012).

(ICG) International Crisis Group (2009a) Guinea-Bissau: Beyond Rule of the Gun, Policy Briefing no. 61, June 25. http://www.crisisgroup.org/~/media/Files/africa/west-africa/guinea-bissau/B061%20Guinea-Bissau%20Beyond%20 Rule%20of%20the%20Gun.pdf (Accessed May 23, 2010).

(ICG) International Crisis Group (2009b) Somalia: The Trouble with Puntland, Policy Briefing no. 64, August 12. http://www.somaliawatch.org/archive-jun09/090815601.pdf (Accessed August 2, 2010).

(ICG) International Crisis Group (2008) "Executive Summary." *Latin American Drugs 1: Losing the Fight*. Latin America Report No. 25, March 14.

(ICG) International Crisis Group (2007a) *Darfur's New Security Reality*. Africa Report No. 134, November 26.

(ICG) International Crisis Group (2007b) *Colombia: Moving Forward with the ELN*, Latin American Briefing No. 16, Bogota/Brussels, October 11, 2007, 2–5. http://www.crisisgroup.org/en/regions/latin-america-caribbean/andes/colombia/b016-colombia-moving-forward-with-the-eln.aspx (Accessed April 4, 2009).

(ICISS) International Commission on Intervention and State Sovereignty (2001) *The Responsibility to Protect: Research, Bibliography, Background*. Canada: International Development Research Centre. www.idrc.ca/openebooks/963-1/#page_7 (Accessed January 20, 2008).

(ICJ) International Court of Justice (2014) *Whaling in the Antarctic* (*Australia v. Japan: New Zealand Intervening*), March 31. http://www.icj-cij.org/docket/files/148/18136.pdf (Accessed April 6, 2014).

(ICNL) International Center for Not-for-Profit Law (2013a) *NGO Law Monitor: China*. June 6. http://www.icnl.org/research/monitor/china.pdf (Accessed January 12, 2014).

(ICNL) International Center for Not-for-Profit Law (2013b) *NGO Law Monitor: Russia*. August 20. http://www.icnl.org/research/monitor/russia.html (Accessed January 12, 2014).

(ICNL) International Center for Not-for-Profit Law (2013c) *NGO Law Monitor: Association of Southeast Asian Nations*. August 20. http://www.icnl.org/research/monitor/asean.html (Accessed January 12, 2014).

(ICRC) International Committee of the Red Cross (1949) *Geneva Convention Relative to the Protection of Civilian Persons in Time of War* (Fourth Geneva Convention), August 12, 75 UNTS 287. http://www.refworld.org/docid/3ae6b36d2.html (Accessed December 4, 2013).

(ICTSD) International Centre for Trade and Sustainable Development (2012) "Indonesian Diplomat Speaks Out Against Australia's Illegal Logging Bill." October 1. http://ictsd.org/i/press/ictsd-in-the-news/146261/ (Accessed October 17, 2013).

(IEP) Institute for Economics and Peace (2011) *Structures of Peace: Identifying What Leads to Peaceful Societies, Institute for Economics and Peace, 2011*. http://www.visionofhumanity.org/info-center/structures-of-peace-2/ (Accessed January 4, 2012).

(IISS) International Institute for Strategic Studies (2007) "Contractors in War: Blackwater Case Will Test Regulation." *Strategic Comments*. 13(9): pp. 1–2.

(ILO) International Labour Office (2008) *ILO Action against Trafficking in Human Beings*. Geneva: International Labour Organization.

(IMF) International Monetary Fund (2011a). *Anti-Money Laundering and Combating the Financing of Terror (AML/CFT): Report on the Review of the Effectiveness of the Program*. http://www.imf.org/external/np/pp/eng/2011/051111.pdf (Accessed May 2, 2012).

(IMF) International Monetary Fund (2011b) *Global Financial Stability Report: Grappling with Crisis Legacies, September 2011*. Summary Version, Washington. DC: IMF. http://www.imf.org/External/Pubs/FT/GFSR/2011/02/index.htm (Accessed January 6, 2012).

(IMF) International Monetary Fund (2009) *Global Financial Stability Report: Responding to the Financial Crisis and Measuring Systemic Risks, April 2009*. Washington. DC: IMF. http://www.imf.org/external/pubs/ft/gfsr/2009/01/index.htm (Accessed January 6, 2012).

(IMF) International Monetary Fund Legal Department (2011) *Anti-Money Laundering and Combating the Financing of Terror (AML/CFT): Report on the Review of the Effectiveness of the Program*. Washington. DC: International Monetary Fund, May 11. http://www.imf.org/external/np/sec/pn/2011/pn1174.htm (Accessed January 6, 2011).

Immigration and Refugee Board of Canada (2008), *Colombia: the Recruitment Methods of the Revolutionary Armed forces of Colombia (Fuerzas Armadas Revolucionarias de Colombia, FARC) and Government Measures to Help FARC Members*

Reintegrate into Civilian Society (2005–2008), April 14, COL102787.FE. http://www.unhcr.org/refworld/docid/4829b55c23.html (Accessed June 30, 2010).

(IMO) International Maritime Organization (2013) *Reports on Acts of Piracy and Armed Robbery Against Ships, Annual Report, 2012*. MSC.4/circ.193, April 2. http://www.imo.org/OurWork/Security/SecDocs/Documents/PiracyReports/193_Annual2012.pdf (Accessed November 11, 2013).

(IMO) International Maritime Organization (2011) *Reports on Acts of Piracy and Armed Robbery Against Ships, Annual Report, 2010*. MSC.4/Cic.169, April 1, 2011. http://www.imo.org/OurWork/Security/SecDocs/Documents/PiracyReports/169_Annual2010.pdf (Accessed November 11, 2013).

(IMO) International Maritime Organization (2009) *Reports on Acts of Piracy and Armed Robbery Against Ships, Annual Report 2008*. MSC.7–9.4/circ.133, March 19. http://www.imo.org/OurWork/Security/PiracyArmedRobbery/Pages/PirateReports.aspx (Accessed May 30, 2009).

(IMO) International Maritime Organization (2007) *Reports on Acts of Piracy and Armed Robbery Against Ships, Annual Report 2006*. MSC.4/circ.98, April 13. http://www5.imo.org/SharePoint/blastDataHelper.asp/data_id%3D18566/98.pdf (Accessed May 30, 2009).

Inglehardt, R. and Welzel, C. (2012) "The WVS Cultural Map of the World." World Values Survey. http://www.worldvaluessurvey.org/wvs/articles/folder_published/article_base_54 (Accessed April 23, 2013).

(INLEA) International Narcotics and Law Enforcement Affairs Bureau (2013) *International Narcotics Control Strategy Report, Volume II, Money Laundering and Financial Crimes*. United States Department of State. http://www.state.gov/p/inl/rls/nrcrpt/ (Accessed November 21, 2013).

(INLEA) International Narcotics and Law Enforcement Affairs Bureau (2011) *International Narcotics Control Strategy Report, Volume II, Money Laundering and Financial Crimes*. United States Department of State. http://www.state.gov/p/inl/rls/nrcrpt/ (Accessed July 21, 2011).

(INLEA) International Narcotics and Law Enforcement Affairs Bureau (2008) *International Narcotics Control Strategy Report, Volume II, Money Laundering and Financial Crimes*. United States Department of State. http://www.state.gov/p/inl/rls/nrcrpt/ (Accessed July 21, 2011).

Inside Indonesia (2005) "Aceh After the Tsunami: Interview with Cornelia Lennenberg." October 3, 84. http://www.insideindonesia.org/edition-84-oct-dec-2005/aceh-after-the-tsunami-2207132 (Accessed March 29, 2012).

Institute for Economics and Peace (n/d) Global Peace Index. http://economicsandpeace. org/research/iep-indices-data/global-peace-index (Accessed April 2, 2013).

International Commission of Jurists (2008) *Corporate Complicity and Legal Accountability Volume 3*. Geneva: International Commission of Jurists.

International Conferences (The Hague) (1907) *Hague Convention (IV) Respecting the Laws and Customs of War on Land and Its Annex: Regulations Concerning the Laws and Customs of War on Land*, October 18, 1907. http://www.refworld.org/docid/4374cae64.html (Accessed December 4, 2013).

International Convention against the Recruitment, Use, Financing and Training of Mercenaries (1989) http://www.un.org/documents/ga/res/44/a44r034.htm (Accessed June 4, 2010).

International Rivers (2012a) "Three Gorges Dam: A Model of the Past." Fact Sheet. Berkeley. CA: International Rivers. http://www.internationalrivers.org/resources/three-gorges-dam-a-model-of-the-past-3512 (Accessed June 10, 2013).

International Rivers (2012b) *The New Great Walls: A Guide to China's Overseas Dam Industry*. Berkeley. CA: International Rivers. http://www.internationalrivers.org/resources/the-new-great-walls-a-guide-to-china%E2%80%99s-overseas-dam-industry-3962 (Accessed June 4, 2013).

Internet World Stats (2013) http://www.internetworldstats.com/stats.htm (Accessed December 3, 2013).

(IOM) International Organization for Migration (2011) *World Migration Report, 2011*. Geneva: IOM.

Iraq Body Count (n/d) http://www.iraqbodycount.org/ (Accessed November 27, 2013).

(ISC) Intelligence and Security Committee (2013) *Foreign Involvement in the Critical National Infrastructure: The Implications for National Security*. UK Parliament, https://www.gov.uk/government/uploads/system/uploads/attachment_data/file/205680/ISC-Report-Foreign-Investment-in-the-Critical-National-Infrastructure.pdf (Accessed December 1, 2013).

(ITU) International Telecommunication Union (2012) *Measuring the Information Society, 2012*. Geneva: ITU.

(IWM) Information Warfare Monitor and Shadowserver Foundation (2010) *Shadows in the Cloud: Investigating Cyber Espionage 2.0*, April 6. http://shadows-in-the-cloud.net (Accessed April 20, 2010).

Jacinto, L. (2013) "What's in a Name? Boko Haram Gets a New Terror Title." *France 24 International News*. November 11. http://www.france24.com/en/20131115-nigeria-boko-haram-terrorist-group-usa-implicationsdesignation (Accessed December 1, 2013).

Jackson, P. (2010) *Politics, Religion and the Lord's Resistance Army in Northern Uganda*. Religions and Development Programme. Working Paper 43-2010. University of Birmingham. http://www.rad.bham.ac.uk (Accessed December 15, 2013).

Jervis, R. (1976) *Perception and Misperception in International Politics*. Princeton. NJ: Princeton University Press.

Johnson, D. H. (2004) *The Root Causes of Sudan's Civil Wars*. Oxford: James Currey.

Jones, D. M. (2012) "Terrorism." In Annheier, H. K. and Juergensmeyer, M. (ed.) *Encyclopedia of Global Studies*. Volume 4, Thousand Oaks: SAGE. pp. 1638–1642.

Juergensmeyer, M. (2008) *Global Rebellion: Religious Challenges to the Secular State, from Christian Militias to Al Qaeda*. Berkeley: University of California Press.

Junger, S. (2011) "Blood Oil." In Gilman, N., Goldhammer, J., and Weber, S. (ed.) *Deviant Globalization: Black Market Economy in the 21st Century*. New York. NY: Continuum. pp. 197–214.

Kabbashi M. Suliman and Ahmed A. A. Badawi (2010) "An Assessment of the Impact of China's Investments in Sudan." Africa Portal, African Economic Research Consortium. http://www.africaportal.org/dspace/articles/assessment-impact-china%E2%80%99s-investments-sudan (Accessed January 28, 2014).

Kagan, R. (2008) "Neocon Nation: Neoconservatism c. 1776." *World Affairs Journal*. Spring. http://www.worldaffairsjournal.org/article/neocon-nation-neo-conservatism-c-1776 (Accessed June 10, 2012).

Kahler, M. (2013) "Economic Crisis and Global Governance: The Stability of a Globalized World." In Kahler, M. and Lake, D. A. (ed.) *Politics in the New Hard Times: The Great Recession in Comparative Perspective*. Ithaca. NY: Cornell University Press. pp. 43–73.

Kahler, M. (2009) "Collective Action and Clandestine Networks: The Case of Al Qaeda." In Kahler, M. (ed.) *Networked Politics: Agency, Power and Governance*. Ithaca. NY: Cornell University Press. pp. 103–124.

Kahn, R. and Kellner, D. (2004) "New Media and Internet Activism: From the 'Battle for Seattle' to Blogging." *New Media and Society*. 6(1): pp. 87–95.

Kaldor, M. (2001) *New Wars and Old Wars: Organized Violence in a Global Era*. Cambridge.UK: Polity.

Kant, I. (1804) *The Metaphysical Elements of Ethics*. Public Domain e-Book. Abbott, T. K. (trans.).

Kant, I. (1804) *Fundamental Principles of the Metaphysics of Morals*. Public Domain e-Book. Abbott, T. K. (trans.).

Kant, I. (1804) *The Critique of Pure Reason*. Public Domain e-Book. Abbott, T. K. (trans.).

Kant, I. (1788) *The Critique of Practical Reason*. Public Domain e-book. Abbott, T. K. (trans.).

Kaplan, D. E. and Dubro, A. (2003) *Yakuza: Japan's Criminal Underground*. Berkeley. CA: University of California Press.

Kaplan, R. D. (1997) "Was Democracy Just a Moment?" *Atlantic*. December 1. http://www.theatlantic.com/magazine/archive/1997/12/was-democracy-just-a-moment/306022/ (Accessed December 3, 2013).

Kapralos, K. J. (2010) "Non-Christians Need Not Apply." *Global Post*. January 11. http://www.globalpost.com/dispatch/ngos/100110/world-vision-religion-foreign-aid (Accessed January 20, 2014).

Karlan, D. and Appel, J. (2011) *More Than Good Intentions: How Economics is Helping to Solve Global Poverty*. New York. NY: Penguin.

Kaspersky Lab (2013) *Kaspersky Security Bulletin 2012: The Overall Statistics for 2012 – Securelist*. http://www.securelist.com/en/analysis/204792255/ (Accessed September 29, 2013).

Katchadourian, R. (2011) "The Stolen Forests: Inside the Covert War on Illegal Logging." In Gilman, N., Goldhammer, J., and Weber, S. (ed.) *Deviant Globalization: Black Market Economy in the 21st Century*. New York. NY: Continuum. pp. 180–196.

Kaufmann, D. (2005) "Myths and Realities of Governance and Corruption." In World Economic Forum (WEF) *The Global Competitiveness Report, 2005–2006*. Basingstoke: Palgrave Macmillan. pp. 81–98.

Kavalski, E. (2008) "The Complexity of Global Security Governance: An Analytical Overview." *Global Society*. 22(4): pp. 423–443.

Kavalsky, B. (2005) "Pictures and Lessons of Development Practice." In Indermit S., Gill, I. S., and Pugatch, T. (ed.) *At the Frontlines of Development: Reflections from the World Bank*. Washington: The World Bank. pp. 19–45.

Keay, A. (2007) "Tackling the Issue of the Corporate Objective: An Analysis of the United Kingdom's 'Enlightened Shareholder Value Approach'." *Sydney Law Review*. 29: pp. 577–612.

Keck, M. E., and Sikkink, K. (1998) *Activists Beyond Borders*. Ithaca. NY: Cornell University Press.

Keegan, J. (1993) *A History of Warfare*. London: Hutchinson.

Kelle, A., Nixdorff, K., and Dando, M. (2006) *Controlling Biochemical Weapons: Adapting Multilateral Arms Control for the 21st Century*. Houndmills: Palgrave.

Kellow, A. (1999) *International Toxic Risk Management: Ideals, Interests and Implementation*. Cambridge: Cambridge University Press.

Kelsay, J. (2003) "Al-Shaybani and the Islamic Law of War." *Journal of Military Ethics*. 2(1): pp. 63–75.

Kennedy, D. (2006) *On War and Law*. Princeton. NJ: Princeton University Press.

Kennedy, D. (2004) *The Dark Sides of Virtue: Reassessing International Humanitarianism*. Princeton. NJ: Princeton University Press.

Kennedy, P. (2006) *The Parliament of Man: The United Nations and the Quest for World Government*. London: Penguin.

Kennedy, P. (1990) *The Rise and Fall of the Great Powers: Economic Change and Military Conflict from 1500–2000*. London: Unwin Hyman.

Kenney, M. (2009) "Turning to the 'Dark Side': Coordination, Exchange, and Learning in Criminal Networks." In Kahler, M. (ed.) *Networked Politics: Agency, Power and Governance*. Ithaca. NY: Cornell University Press. pp. 79–102.

Kenney, M. (2007a) *From Pablo to Osama: Trafficking and Terrorist Networks, Government Bureaucracies, and Competitive Adaptation*. University Park. PA: Pennsylvania University Press.

Kenney, M. (2007b) "The Architecture of Drug Trafficking: Network Forms of Organization in the Colombian Cocaine Trade." *Global Crime*. 8(3): pp. 233–259.

Keohane, R. O. (2005) *After Hegemony: Cooperation and Discord in the World Political Economy* (2nd edition). Princeton. NJ: Princeton University Press.

Keohane, R. O. and Nye, J. S. (2012) *Power and Interdependence* (4th edition). Boston. CT: Longman.

Kessler, E. and Arkush, M. (2009) *Keeping Faith in Development: The Significance of Interfaith Relations in the Work of Humanitarian Aid and International Development Organizations*. Cambridge: Woolf Institute of Abrahamic Studies. http://www.religion-and-development.nl/documentation-centre/2889/keeping-faith-in-development-the-significance-of-interfaith-relations-in-the-work-of-humanitarian-aid-and-international-development-organisations (Accessed November 7, 2013).

Khorfan, R. and Padela, A. I. (2010) "The Bioethical Concept of Life for Life in Judaism, Catholicism, and Islam: Abortion When the Mother's Life is in Danger." *Journal of the Islamic Medical Association*. 42: pp. 99–105.

Kilcullen, D. (2010) *Counter Insurgency*. Melbourne: Scribe.

Kilcullen, D. (2009) *The Accidental Guerrilla: Fighting Small Wars in the Midst of a Big One*. Melbourne: Scribe.

Kindiki, K. (2007) *Intervention to Protect Civilians in Darfur: Legal Dilemmas and Policy Imperatives*. ISS Monograph Series No. 131. Pretoria: Institute for Security Studies.

Kinloch, S. P. (1996) "Utopian or Pragmatic? A UN Permanent Military Volunteer Force." *International Peacekeeping*. 3(4): pp. 166–190.

Kinsey, C. P. Hansen, S. J. and Franklin, G. (2009) "The Impact of Private Security Companies on Somalia's Governance Networks." *Cambridge Review of International Affairs*. 22(1): pp. 147–161.

Kiobel v. Royal Dutch Petroleum Co., 569 U.S._(2013), US Supreme Court, October Term 2012: 3. http://www.supremecourt.gov/opinions/12pdf/10-1491_l6gn.pdf (Accessed June 30, 2013).

Kishiro, T. (2012) "Japan. Progress report on small cetacean research, April 2011 to March 2012, with statistical data for the calendar year 2011." Ministry of Agriculture, Forestry and Fisheries, Government of Japan, SM/2012. http://www.jfa.maff.go.jp/j/whale/w_document/pdf/130531_progress_report.pdf (Accessed October 17, 2013).

Klausner, M. (2006) "The Contractarian Theory of Corporate Law: A Generation Later." *Journal of Corporate Law*. 31: pp. 780–797. http://lawnotes4.law.virginia.edu/pdf/olin/conf07/klausner.pdf (Accessed July 12, 2012).

Klibi, N. and Martel, A. (2013) "Scenario-based Supply Chain Network Risk Modelling." *European Journal of Operational Research*. 223: pp. 644–658.

Klomegah, K. N. (2013) "Russia Eyes Africa to Boost Arms Sales." *Guardian*. April 5. http://www.theguardian.com/world/2013/apr/04/arms-trade-africa (Accessed June 25, 2013).

Knudsen, A. (2005) "Crescent and Sword: The Hamas Enigma." *Third World Quarterly*. 26(8): pp. 1373–1388.

Kovach, H., Neligan, C., and Burall, S. (2003) *Global Accountability Report, 2003: Power Without Accountability?* One World Trust. http://www.oneworldtrust.org/publications/cat_view/64-publications-by-project/65-global-accountability-report/85-2003-global-accountability-report (Accessed February 2, 2012).

KPMG LLP (2013) *Illicit Tobacco in Australia*. London: KPMG LLP. http://www.bata.com.au/group/sites/bat_7wykg8.nsf/vwPagesWebLive/DO9879X3/$FILE/medMD9D4L6C.pdf?openelement (Accessed January 28, 2014).

Kranser, S. (1999) *Sovereignty: Organized Hypocrisy*. Princeton. NJ: Princeton University Press.

Kuperman, A. J. (2013) "A Model Intervention? Reassessing NATO's Libya Campaign." *International Security*. 38(1): pp. 105–136.

Kurlansky, M. (2007) *Non-Violence: The History of a Dangerous Idea*. London: Vintage.

Kuszewski, J. and Crowther, Y. (2010) "Brent Spar: Battle that Launched Modern Activism." Ethical Corporation: Business Strategy. May 5. http://www.ethicalcorp.com/communications-reporting/brent-spar-battle-launched-modern-activism (Accessed June 12, 2013).

Kuzmarov, J. (2009) *The Myth of the Addicted Army: Vietnam and the Modern War on Drugs*. Amherst. MA: University of Massachusetts Press.

Lachmann, R. (2010) *States and Power*. Cambridge: Polity.

Laessing, U. (2013) "Sudan's Darfur Gold Rush Brings Death and Displacement to Jebel Amer," *Guardian*, October 15. http://www.theguardian.com/global-development/2013/oct/15/sudan-darfur-gold-rush-jebel-amer (Accessed December 4, 2013).

Lake, D. A. and Wong, W. H. (2009) "The Politics of networks: Interests, Power, and Human Rights Norms." In Kahler, M. (ed.) *Networked Politics: Agency, Power and Governance*. Ithaca. NY: Cornell University Press, pp. 127–150.

Lakhani, N. (2009) "Bhopal: The Victims are Still Being Born." *Independent*. November 29. http://www.independent.co.uk/news/world/asia/bhopal-the-victims-are-still-being-born-1830516.html (Accessed November 12, 2012).

Lambach, D. (2006) "Security, Development and the Australian Discourse about Development." *Australian Journal of Political Science*. 41(3): pp. 407–418.

Lambert, N. (2012) *Planning Armageddon: British Economic Warfare and the First World War*. Cambridge. MA: Harvard University Press.

Lawrence, F. (2011) "Global Food Crisis: China Land deal Causes Unease in Argentina." *Guardian*. June 1. http://www.theguardian.com/global-development/2011/jun/01/china-land-deal-unease-argentina-agribusiness (Accessed August 7, 2013).

Lawrence, F. (2009) "The Brand New freezers that Cost 18p Each ... and Other Ways to Avoid Tax." *Guardian*. March 26. http://www.guardian.co.uk/business/2009/mar/26/taxavoidance-internationaltrade (Accessed October 4, 2009).

Lawson, S. and MacFaul, L. (2010) *Illegal Logging and Related Trade: Indicators of a Global Response*. London: Chatham House.

Le Pape, M. (2011) "Epilogue in the Name of Emergency: How MSF Adapts and Justifies its Choices." In Magone, C., Neuman, M., and Weissman, T. (ed.) *Humanitarian Negotiations Revealed: The MSF Experience*. New York. NY: Columbia University Press. pp. 237–250.

Lee, M. (2011) *Trafficking and Global Crime Control*. London: SAGE.

Lee, R. E. (2011) "The Modern World System: Its Structures, Its Geoculture, Its Crisis and Transformation." In Palumbo-Liu, D., Robbins, B., and Tanoukhi, N. (ed.) *Immanuel Wallerstein and the Problem of the World*. Durham. NC: Duke University Press. pp. 45–67.

Lefebvre, H. (1991) *The Production of Space*. Nicholson-Smith, D. (trans.).Oxford: Blackwell.

Leigh, D. (2010) "Trafigura Faces Criminal Charges over Attempt to Offload Toxic Waste." *Guardian*. June 1. http://guardian.co.uk (Accessed June 25, 2010).

Lenin, V. I. (1994) "Socialism and War." In Freedman, L. (ed.) *War*. Oxford: Oxford University Press, pp. 95–98.

Leonardsen, D. (2010) *Crime in Japan: Paradise Lost?* Houndmills: Palgrave Macmillan.

Lessig, L. (2006) *Code Version 2.0*. New York. NY: Basic Books.

Levin, C. (2012) "U.S. Vulnerabilities to Money Laundering, Drugs and Terrorist Financing: HSBC Case History." U.S. Senate Permanent Subcommittee on Investigations. July 17. http://www.levin.senate.gov/newsroom/speeches/speech/levin-opening-statement-us-vulnerabilities-to-money-laundering-drugs-and-terrorist-financing-hsbc-case-history#sthash.4nRE2F6T.dpuf (Accessed October 2, 2013).

Lewis, P., Borger, J., and McCarthy, R. (2013) "Dubai Murder: Fake Identities, Disguised Faces and a Clinical Assassination." *Guardian*. February 17. http://www.theguardian.com/world/2010/feb/16/dubai-murder-fake-identities-hamas (Accessed November 4, 2012).

Libicki, M. C. (2009) *Cyber-deterrence and Cyberwar*. Santa Monica. CA: Rand Corporation.

Lieven, A. and Hulsman, J. (2006) *Ethical Realism: A Vision for America's Role in the World*. New York. NY: Vintage.

Lind, W. S., Nightengale, K., Schmitt, J. F., Sutton, J. W., and Wilson, G. I. (1989) "The Changing Face of War: Into the Fourth Generation." *Marine Corps Gazette*. October. http://www.mca-marines.org/files/The%20Changing%20Face%20of%20War%20-%20Into%20the%20Fourth%20Generation.pdf (Accessed January 7, 2012).

Lindenberg, M., and Bryant, C. (2001) *Going Global: Transforming Relief and Development NGOs*. Bloomfield. CA: Kumarian Press.

Linklater, A. (2011) *The Problem of Harm in World Politics: Theoretical Investigations*. Cambridge: Cambridge University Press.

Lobasz, J. K. (2009) "Beyond Border Security: Feminist Approaches to Human Trafficking." *Security Studies*. 18: pp. 319–344.

Loder, A. (2013) "U.S. Shale Oil Boom May Not Last as Fracking Wells Lack Staying Power." *Businessweek*. October 10. http://www.businessweek.com/articles/2013-10-10/u-dot-s-dot-shale-oil-boom-may-not-last-as-fracking-wells-lack-staying-power (Accessed December 3, 2013).

Loewenstein, G. (2004) "Out of Control: Visceral Influences on Behaviour." In Camerer, C. F., Loewenstein, G., and Rabin, M. (ed.) *Advances in Behavioural Economics*. Princeton. NJ: Princeton University Press. pp. 17058–17927.

Lorenz, E. N. (2004) *The Essence of Chaos*. Taylor and Francis e-Library.

Lovink, G. (2011) *Networks Without a Cause: A Critique of Social Media*. Cambridge: Polity.

Luhmann, N. (2013) *Theory of Society, Volume 2 (Cultural Memory in the Present)*. Barrett, R. (trans.) Stanford. CA: Stanford University Press.

Luhmann, N. (1986) "The Autopoiesis of Social Systems." In Geyer, F. and van der Zouwen, J. (ed.) *Sociobiological Paradoxes: Observation, Control and Evolution of Self-Steering Systems*. London: SAGE. pp. 172–192.

Lynn, J. (2009) "US rejects Biological Weapons Checks." *Reuters*. December 9. http://www.reuters.com/article/2009/12/09/us-arms-biological-idUS-TRE5B82DG20091209 (Accessed July 5, 2012).

Ma, D. (2013) "Young Chinese People May Just Not Be That Into Western-Style Democracy." *Atlantic*. July 18. http://www.theatlantic.com/china/archive/2013/07/young-chinese-people-may-just-not-be-that-into-western-style-democracy/277885/ (Accessed December 7, 2013).

MacKinnon, M. (2014) "Gazprom's Spire a Market for Putin's Power." *Globe and Mail*. January 19. http://www.theglobeandmail.com/news/world/gaz-prom-spire-a-marker-for-putins-power/article16402618/ (Accessed January 22, 2014).

Maga, T. (2001) "'Away from Tokyo': The Pacific Islands War Crimes Trials, 1945–1949." *The Journal of Pacific History*. 36(1): pp. 37–50.

Magnet, S. A. (2011) *When Biometrics Fail: Gender, Race and the Technology of Identity*. Durham. NC: Duke University Press.

Makarenko, T. (2004) "The Crime-Terror Continuum: Tracing the Interplay between Transnational Organised Crime and Terrorism." *Global Crime*. 6(1): pp. 129–145.

Malesevic, S. (2010) *The Sociology of War and Violence*. Cambridge: Cambridge University Press.

Mandel, R. (2011) *Dark Logic: Transnational Criminal Tactics and Global Security*. Stanford. CA: Stanford University Press.

Mandiant (2013) *APT1: Exposing One of China's Cyber Espionage Units*. http://intel-report.mandiant.com/ (Accessed February 27, 2013).

Mann, A. (2013) "US Bikie Gang, Mongols, Will Cause Havoc in Australia," *ABC News*. http://www.abc.net.au/news/2013-10-16/warning-mongol-bikie-gang-will-cause-havoc-in-australia/5027198 (Accessed January 12, 2014).

Marald, E. (2001) "The BT Kemi Scandal and the Establishment of the Environmental Crime Concept." *Journal of Scandinavian Studies in Criminology and Crime Prevention*. 2: pp. 149–170.

Marshall, S. L. A. (1947) *Men Against Fire: The Problem of Battle Command*. Norman. OK: University of Oklahoma Press.

Martell, L. (2007) "The Third Wave in Globalization Theory." *International Studies Review*. 9(2): pp. 173–196.

Marx, K. (1990) *Capital: A Critique of Political Economy, Volume 1*. London: Penguin.

Marx, K. and Engels, F. (2012) *The Communist Manifesto*. NP: Ngims Publishing.

Masters, J. (2013) "Al Qaeda in the Islamic Maghreb." *CFR Backgrounder*. http://www.cfr.org/world/al-qaeda-islamic-maghreb-aqim/p12717 (Accessed October 23, 2013).

Mathiesen, T. (2013) *Towards a Surveillant Society: The Rise of Surveillance Systems in Europe*. Sherfield on Loddon Hook: Waterside Press.

Matthews, C. (2013) "Why the FBI Can't Get its Hands on Silk Road Kingpin's $80 Million Hoard." *Time Magazine*. October 11. http://business.time.com/2013/10/11/why-the-fbi-cant-get-its-hands-on-silk-road-kingpins-80-million-hoard/ (Accessed November 12, 2013).

Mazzetti, M., Chivers, C. J., and Schmitt, E. (2013) "Taking Outsize Role in Syria, Qatar Funnels Arms to Rebels." *New York Times*. June 29. http://www.nytimes.com/2013/06/30/world/middleeast/sending-missiles-to-syrian-rebels-qatar-muscles-in.html (Accessed July 7, 2013).

McAvoy, J. and Charny, J. R. (2013) "Civil-Military relations and the US Armed Forces." *Humanitarian Exchange Magazine*. 56, January. http://www.odihpn.org/humanitarian-exchange-magazine/issue-56/civil%E2%80%93military-relations-and-the-us-armed-forces (Accessed January 12, 2014).

McCargo, D. and Pathmanand, U. (2005) *The Thaksinization of Thailand*. Copenhagen: Nordic Institute of Asian Studies Press.

McCarthy, D. M. P. (2011) *An Economic History of Organized Crime: A National and Transnational Approach*. Abingdon: Routledge.

McCoy, A. W. (2003) *The Politics of Heroin: CIA Complicity in the Global Drug Trade*. Chicago. IL: Lawrence Hill.

McElroy, D. (2013) "Al Qaeda's Scathing Letter to Troublesome Employee Mokhtar Belmokhtar Reveals Inner Workings of Terrorist Group," *Telegraph*, May 29. http://www.telegraph.co.uk/news/worldnews/al-qaeda/10085716/Al-Qaedas-scathing-letter-to-troublesome-employee-Mokhtar-Belmokhtar-reveals-inner-workings-of-terrorist-group.html (Accessed January 12, 2014).

McIntosh, A. (1990) "The Bougainville Crisis: A Southern Crofters' War." *Radical Scotland*. 44: pp. 18–22.

McKenzie, N., Baker, R., and Garnaut, J. (2013) "BHP Gamed the Games." *Australian Financial Review*. March 13. http://www.afr.com/p/national/bhp_gamed_the_games_cWTZjePY4oF7Z84jCs5jWM (Accessed March 13, 2013).

McLuhan, M. (1994) *Understanding Media: The Extension of Man*. Cambridge. MA: MIT Press.

McNeill, J. R. and McNeill, W. (2003) *The Human Web*. New York. NY: Norton.

McNeish, H. (2013) "Over 200 Wounded in South Sudan Clashes: UN." Relief Web July 14. http://reliefweb.int/report/south-sudan-republic/over-200-wounded-south-sudan-clashes-un (Accessed October 24, 2013).

McWade, W. (2012) "The Role of Social Enterprises and Social Investors in the Development Struggle." *Journal of Social Entrepreneurship*. 3(1): pp. 96–112.

Meadows, D. H., Meadows, D. L., Randers, J., and Behrens, W. (1972) *The Limits to Growth*. New York. NY: Universe Books.

Mearsheimer, J. (2001) *The Tragedy of Great Power Politics*. New York. NY: WW Norton.

Melvin, N. J. (2007) *Conflict in Southern Thailand: Islamism, Violence and the State in Patani*. Stockholm: SIPRI.

Mendlesohn, R. (2011) "Climate Change, Cooperation, and Resource Scarcity." In Dinar, S. (ed.) *Beyond Resource Wars: Scarcity, Environmental Degradation and International Cooperation*. Cambridge. MS: MIT Press. pp. 55–84.

Mengisteab, K. (2013) "Poverty, Inequality, State Identity and Chronic Inter-State Conflicts in the Horn of Africa." In Bereketab, R. (ed.) *The Horn of Africa: Intra-State and Inter-State Conflicts and Security*. London: Pluto Press. pp. 711–943.

Meredith, M. (2005) *The State of Africa: A History of the Continent Since Independence*. New York. NY: Free Press.

Meron, T. (2009) "The Geneva Conventions and Public International Law." *International Review of the Red Cross*. 91 (875), September. http://www.icrc.org/eng/resources/documents/article/review/review-875-p619.htm (Accessed November 10, 2012).

Merton, T. (ed.) (2007) *Gandhi on Non-Violence, Selected Texts from Mohandas K. Gandhi's Non-Violence in Peace and War*. New York. NY: New Directions.

Meyer, J. A. and Califano, M. G. (2006) *Good Intentions Corrupted: The Oil-for-Food Scandal and the Threat to the UN*. New York. NY: Public Affairs Reports.

Midlarsky, M. I. (2011) *Origins of Political Extremism: Mass Violence in the Twentieth Century and Beyond*. Cambridge: Cambridge University Press.

Miller, S. and Selgelid, M. J. (2007) "Ethical and Philosophical Considerations of the Dual-use Dilemma in the Biological Sciences." *Science and Engineering Ethics*. 13, pp. 533–580.

Mitchell, M. (2009) *Complexity: A Guided Tour*. Oxford: Oxford University Press.

Miyata, Y. (2007) "Markets for Biodiversity." *Journal of Sustainable Forestry*. 25(3–4): pp. 281–307.

Modelski, G. (2012) "Kondratieff (K-) Waves in the Modern World System." In Grinin, L., Tesselano, D., and Korotayev, A. (ed.) *Kondratieff Waves: Dimensions, and Prospects at the Dawn of the 21st Century*. Volgograd: 'Uchitel' Publishing House, pp. 65–76.

Modelski, G. and Thompson, W. R. (1999) "The Long and the Short of Global Politics in the Twenty-First Century: An Evolutionary Approach." *International Studies Review*. 1:2, Summer, 1999, pp. 109–140.

Moeller, H. G. (2006) *Luhmann Explained: From Souls to Systems*. Chicago. IL: Open Court.

Mohamedou, M. O. (2011) *The Many Faces of Al Qaeda in the Islamic Maghreb*. GCSP Policy Paper No. 15. http://www.gcsp.ch/Regional-Capacity-Development/Publications/GCSP-Publications/Policy-Papers/The-Many-Faces-of-Al-Qaeda-in-the-Islamic-Maghreb (Accessed October 20, 2013).

Monbiot, G. (2010a) "The Tea Party Movement: Deluded and Inspired by Billionaires." *Guardian*. October 26.

Monbiot, G. (2010b) "These Astroturf Libertarians are the Real Threat to Internet Democracy." *Guardian*. December 14. http://www.theguardian.com/commentisfree/libertycentral/2010/dec/13/astroturf-libertarians-internet-democracy (Accessed April 30, 2014).

Monbiot, G. (2009) "From Toxic Waste to Toxic Assets, The Same People Always Get Dumped On." *Guardian*. September 21. http://guardian.co.uk (Accessed June 25, 2010).

Morozov, E. (2011) *The Net Delusion: How Not to Liberate the World*. London: Penguin.

Mosch, T. (2005) "Brent Spar, 10 Years On," *Deutsche-Welle World*. June 20. http://www.dw-world.de/dw/article/0,2144,1621883,00.html (Accessed June 12, 2013).

MRAG (2009) *Illegal, Unreported and Unregulated Fishing*. Policy Brief, No. 8. London: MRAG. http://www.m2cms.com.au/uploaded/5/MRAG%20UK%20 Policy%20Brief_IUU.pdf (Accessed June 12, 2012).

MRAG and Fisheries Ecosystems Restoration and Research Centre (2008) *The Global Extent of Illegal Fishing*. University of British Colombia (UBC). http://www.docstoc.com/docs/68042250/The-Global-Extent-of-Illegal-Fishing (Accessed July 14, 2010).

(MSF) Médecins Sans Frontières (2013) "Syria: Thousands Suffering Neurotoxic Symptoms Treated in Hospitals Supported by MSF." Press Release, August 24. http://www.doctorswithoutborders.org/press/release.cfm?id=7029 (Accessed November 12, 2013).

(MSF) Médecins Sans Frontières (2012) "Inside Syria: Two Months of Surgical Interventions." Press Release, August 22. http://www.msf.org.au/media-room/press-releases/press-release/article/inside-syria-two-months-of-surgical-interventions.html (Accessed August 29, 2012).

Mueller, R. S. (2011) "Statement Before the House Committee on Appropriations, Subcommittee on Commerce, Justice, Science, and Related Agencies," Washington. D.C. April 06. http://www.fbi.gov/news/testimony/fbi-budget-for-fiscal-year-2012 (Accessed February 4, 2011).

Murphy, R. (2011) "Out of Sight," *London Review of Books*, 33(8): April 21. http://www.lrb.co.uk/v33/n08/richard-murphy-ii/out-of-sight (Accessed January 7, 2012).

Myers, G. (2004) *Banana Wars-The Price of Free Trade: A Caribbean Perspective*. London: Zed Books.

Nagl, J. A. (2002) *Learning to Eat Soup with a Knife: Counterinsurgency Lessons from Malaya and Vietnam*. Chicago: University of Chicago Press.

Naim, M. (2005) *Illicit: How Smugglers, Traffickers, and Copycats are Hijacking the Global Economy*. New York: Doubleday.

Naqvi, Y. (2003) "Amnesty for War Crimes: Defining the Limits of International Recognition." *International Review of the Red Cross*. 851. www.icrc.org/Web/eng/siteeng0.nsf/htmlall/5SSDUX/$File/irrc_851_Naqvi.pdf (Accessed June 27, 2008).

Nassar, J. R. (2005) *Globalization and Terrorism: The Migration of Dreams and Nightmares*. Lanham. MD: Rowman and Littlefield.

Nasu, H. (2013) "The Future of Nanotechnology in Warfare," *Global Journal*. July 4. https://law.anu.edu.au/sites/all/files/coast/the_future_of_nanotechnology_in_warfare_the_global_journal.pdf (Accessed November 4, 2013).

Nesvetailova, A. and Belli, C. (2013) "Global Financial Governance: Taming Financial Innovation." In Harman, S. and Williams, M. (ed.) *Governing the World? Cases in Global Governance*. London: Routledge, pp. 46–61.

Newman, E. (2004) "The 'New Wars' Debate: A Historical Perspective Is Needed." *Security Dialogue*. 35(2): pp. 173–189.

(NIC) National Intelligence Council (2012) "Global Trends 2030: Alternative Worlds," Washington: Directorate of National Intelligence. http://publicintelligence.net/global-trends-2030/ (Accessed June 12, 2013).

Nicks, D. (2012) *Private Bradley Manning, Wikileaks and the Biggest Exposure of Official Secrets in American History*. Chicago: Chicago Review Press.

Niebuhr, R. (1934) *Moral Man and Immoral Society: A Study in Ethics and Politics*. New York. NY: Charles Scribner's Sons.

Nitobe, I. (2007) *Bushido: the Soul of Japan*. Alcester, UK: Read Books.

Nokia (2011) *Nokia Sustainability Report, 2011*. http://i.nokia.com/blob/view//1449730/data/2/-/nokia-sustainability-report-2011-pdf.pdf (Accessed January 4, 2014).

Nordstrom, C. (2007) *Global Outlaws: Crime, Money, and Power in the Contemporary World*. Berkeley: University of California Press.

Norland, R. (2010) "U.S. Turns a Blind Eye to Opium in Afghan Town." *New York Times*. March 20. http://www.nytimes.com/2010/03/21/world/asia/21marja.html?pagewanted=all (Accessed February 10, 2012).

Nossal Institute for Global Health (2010) "Dependent on Development: The Interrelationships between Illicit Drugs and Socio-economic Development," December 2010. http://www.soros.org/initiatives/drugpolicy/articles_publications/publications/dependent-development-20110313 (Accessed February 4, 2012).

Nuruzzaman, M. (2006) "Paradigms in Conflict: The Contested Claims of Human Security, Critical Theory and Feminism." *Cooperation and Conflict*. 41(3): pp. 285–303.

O'Callaghan, M-L. (2002) "Weaving Consensus: The Papua New Guinea-Bougainville Peace Process." Conciliation Resources. http://www.c-r.org/sites/default/files/Accord%2012_3The%20origins%20of%20the%20conflict_2002_ENG.pdf (Accessed February 3, 2014).

O'Harrow, R. (2009) *No Place to Hide*. London: Penguin, 2006.

Obama, B. (2013) "Text of Obama's Speech at the U.N." *New York Times*. September 24. http://www.nytimes.com/2013/09/25/us/politics/text-of-obamas-speech-at-the-un.html (Accessed October 28, 2013).

Obama, B. (2011) *International Strategy for Cyberspace: Prosperity, Security and Openness in a Networked World*. http://www.whitehouse.gov/sites/default/files/rss_viewer/internationalstrategy_cyberspace.pdf (Accessed September 29, 2013).

Obama, B. (2010) *Cyberspace Policy Review: Assuring a Trusted and Resilient Communications Infrastructure*. www.whitehouse.gov/assets/.../Cyberspace_Policy_Review_final.pdf (Accessed September 12, 2010).

Occupy.Network (2014) Official Website. http://www.occupy.net/ (Accessed May 1, 2014).

Occupy Together (2014) Official Website. http://www.meetup.com/occupytogether/ (Accessed May 1, 2014).

(OECD) Organization of Economic Cooperation and Development (2013) *OECD Secretary General Report to the G20 Finance Ministers*. http://www.oecd.org/tax/2013-OECD-SG-Report-to-G20-Heads-of-Government.pdf (Accessed June 30, 2013).

(OECD) Organization for Economic Cooperation and Development (2011) *OECD Guidelines for Multinational Enterprises*. Paris: OECD Publishing. http://dx.doi.org/10.1787/9789264115415-en (Accessed January 2, 2014).

(OECD) Organization for Economic Cooperation and Development (2008) *OECD Guidelines for Multinational Enterprises*. Paris: OECD Publishing. http://www.oecd.org/investment/mne/1922428.pdf (Accessed January 2, 2014).

(OECD) Organization for Economic Cooperation and Development (2006) *OECD Risk Awareness Tool for Multinational Enterprises in Weak Governance Zones*. Paris: OECD. http://www.oecd.org/daf/inv/corporateresponsibility/36885821.pdf (Accessed March 4, 2013).

Ohmae, K. (1996) *The End of the Nation State*. London: Harper Collins.

(OIC) Organization of the Islamic Conference (1990) *Cairo Declaration on Human Rights in Islam*. August 5. www1.umn.edu/humanrts/instree/cairodeclaration.html (Accessed April 28, 2008).

(Oil Spill Commission) National Commission on the BP Deepwater Horizon Oil Spill and Offshore Drilling (2011) "Deepwater: The Gulf Oil Disaster and the Future of Offshore Drilling," Report to the President. www.oilspillcommission.gov (Accessed August 12, 2013).

Okrent, D. (2011) *Last Call: The Rise and Fall of Prohibition*. New York. NY: Scribner.

(ONDCP) Office of National Drug Control Policy (2013) *National Drug Control Strategy, FY 2013 Budget Performance Summary*. http://www.whitehouse.gov/ondcp (Accessed October 12, 2013).

Oosterveld, V. (2012) "Gender and the Charles Taylor Case at the Special Court for Sierra Leone." *William & Mary Journal of Women and the Law*. 19(1) pp. 7–33.

(OPA) Office of Public Affairs, December 11, 2012. http://www.justice.gov/opa/pr/2012/December/12-crm-1478.html (Accessed December 26, 2012).

Oreskes, N. and Conway, E. M. (2011) *Merchants of Doubt: How a Handful of Scientists Obscured the Truth on Issues from Tobacco Smoke to Global Warming*. London: Bloomsbury.

Oshita, O. O. (2009) "Domestic Terrorism in Africa: Ontology of an Old War in New Trenches." In Okumu, W. and Botha, A. (ed.) *Domestic Terrorism in Africa: Defining, Addressing and Understanding its Impact on Human Security*. Pretoria. South Africa: Institute for Security Studies, pp. 27–40.

(OSJI) Open Society Justice Initiative (2013) *Globalizing Torture: CIA Secret Detention and Extraordinary Rendition*. New York. NY: Open Society Foundations. http://www.opensocietyfoundations.org/reports/globalizing-torture-cia-secret-detention-and-extraordinary-rendition (Accessed June 30, 2013).

Osuji, O. (2011) "Fluidity of Regulation-CSR Nexus: The Multinational Corruption Example." *Journal of Business Ethics*. 103, pp. 31–57.

Overbeek, G. and Harms, B. (2011) "From Sponsor to Partner: Business Alliances that Support Nature Conservation in the Netherlands." *Journal of Integrative Environmental Sciences*. 8(4): pp. 253–266.

Pachio, E. (2011) "Cyber Crime: Big But Not Bigger Than Drugs." *Insight*. September 13. http://insightcrime.org/insight-latest-news/item/1554-cyber-crime-big-but-not-bigger-than-drugs (Accessed February 18, 2012).

Pain, N. (2007) "Access to Environmental Justice in the South West Pacific." In Harding, A. (ed.) *Access to Environmental Justice: A Comparative Study*. Leiden: Brill, pp. 237–270.

Palmer, G. (2011) *Report of the Secretary-General's Panel of Inquiry on the 31 May 2010 Flotilla Incident*. United Nations. www.un.org/News/dh/infocus/.../Gaza_Flotilla_Panel_Report.pdf (Accessed February 16, 2012).

Pananond, P. (2009) "Thai Multinationals Entering the Big League." In Ramamurti, R., and Singh, J. V. (ed.) *Emerging Multinationals in Emerging Markets*. Cambridge: Cambridge University Press. loc. 5810–6523.

Passel, J. S., Cohn, D., and Gonzalez-Barrera, A. (2013) *Population Decline of Unauthorised Immigrants Stalls, May Have Reversed*. Washington. DC: Pew Research Center. http://www.pewhispanic.org/files/2013/09/Unauthorized-Sept-2013-FINAL.pdf (Accessed November 28, 2013).

Patrick, S. M. (2012) "(Almost) Everyone Agrees: The U.S. Should Ratify the Law of the Sea Treaty." *Atlantic*. June 10. http://www.theatlantic.com/international/archive/2012/06/-almost-everyone-agrees-the-us-should-ratify-the-law-of-the-sea-treaty/258301/ (Accessed June 10, 2013).

Pauly, L. W. (2002) "Global Finance, Political Authority, and the Problem of Legitimation." In Hall, R. B. and Biersteker, T. J. (eds) *The Emergence of Private Authority in Global Governance*. Cambridge: Cambridge University Press, pp. 76–90.

Peel, M. (2009) *A Swamp Full of Dollars: Pipelines and Paramilitaries at Nigeria's Oil Frontier*. London: I.B. Tauris.

Peimani, H. (2009) *Conflict and Security in Central Asia and the Caucasus*. Santa Barbara. CA: ABC-CLIO.

Pelissie du Rausas, M., Manyika, J., Hazan, E., Bughin, J., Chui, M., and Said, R. (2011) *Internet Matters: The Net's Sweeping Impact on Growth, Jobs and Prosperity*. May. McKinsey Global Institute. http://www.mckinsey.com/insights/high_tech_telecoms_internet/internet_matters (Accessed June 7, 2013).

Perl, R. F. (2004) "State Crime: The North Korean Drug Trade." *Global Crime*. 6(1): pp. 117–128.

Pettis, M. (2013) *The Great Rebalancing: Trade, Conflict, and the Perilous Road Ahead for the Global Economy*. Princeton. NJ: Princeton University Press.

Picciotto, S. (2011) *Regulating Global Corporate Capitalism*. Cambridge: Cambridge University Press.

Pieth, M. and Ivory, R. (2011) "Corporate Criminal Liability: Emergence, Convergence, and Risk." In Pieth, M. and Ivory, R. (ed.) *Corporate Criminal Liability: Emergence, Convergence, and Risk*. Ius Gentium: Comparative Perspectives on Law and Justice 9, Heidelberg: Springer, pp. 2–63.

Pillsbury, Winthrop, Shaw and Pittman and Proviti Inc. (2010) *The Global Privacy and Information Security Landscape: Frequently Asked Questions*. http://www.protiviti.com.au/en-US/Documents/Resource-Guides/Information-Security-Privacy-FAQs-Pillsbury-Protiviti.pdf (Accessed June 8, 2013).

Pinker, S. (2011) *The Better Angels of Our Nature: Why Violence Has Declined*. New York. NY: Penguin Viking.

Ploch, L. (2011) *Africa Command: U.S. Strategic Interests and the Role of the U.S. Military in Africa*. Congressional Research Service, CRS Report RL34003. http://www.fas.org/sgp/crs/natsec/RL34003.pdf (Accessed October 30, 2013).

Ploch, L., Blanchard, C. M., O'Rourke, R., and Mason, C. R. (2010) *Piracy on the Horn of Africa*. Congressional Research Service, CRS Report, RL0528. http://www.fas.org/sgp/crs/row/R40528.pdf (Accessed January 1, 2011).

Polanyi, K. (2001) *The Great Transformation: The Political and Economic Origins of Our Time*. Boston: Beacon.

Poljak, V. (2013) "Ceasefire in the War on Evil Banks." *Australian Financial Review*. January 12 (ipad edition).

Pollard, N. A. (2002) "Globalization's Bastards: Illegitimate Non-State Actors in International Law." *Low Intensity Conflict & Law Enforcement*. 11(2–3): pp. 210–238

Polman, L. (2010) *The Crisis Caravan: What's Wrong with Humanitarian Aid*. New York. NY: Metropolitan Books.

Postman, N. (1993) *Technopoly: The Surrender of Culture to Technology*. London: Vintage.

(PRC) People's Republic of China (1982) *Constitution of the People's Republic of China*. http://english.people.com.cn/constitution/constitution.html (Accessed September 14, 2013).

Prebisch, R. (1971) *Change and Development-Latin America's Great Task, Report Submitted to the Inter-American Development Bank*. New York. NY: Praeger.

(PRI) Penal Reform International (2006) "Developing and Implementing Standards," http://www.penalreform.org/english/frset_activ_en.htm (Accessed May 1, 2006) (web page inactive).

Price Warterhouse Coopers (2013) *Shale Oil: The Next Energy Revolution*. February. www.pwc.co.uk (Accessed March 24, 2013).

(Protocol I) Protocol Additional to the Geneva Conventions of 12 August 1949, and relating to the Protection of Victims of International Armed Conflicts, June 8, 1977, International Committee of the Red Cross. Geneva, 1977, pp. 3–87. http://www.icrc.org/ihl.nsf/INTRO/470 (Accessed December 5, 2013).

(Protocol II)Protocol Additional to the Geneva Conventions of 12 August 1949, and relating to the Protection of Victims of Non-International Armed Conflicts, June 8, 1977, International Committee of the Red Cross. Geneva, 1977, pp. 89–101. http://www.icrc.org/ihl.nsf/INTRO/475 (Accessed December 5, 2013).

Purdue, J. B. (2012) *The War of All the People: The Nexus of Latin American Radicalism and Middle Eastern Terrorism*. Washington. DC: Potomac Books.

Pye, L. W. (1981) *Guerrilla Communism in Malaya: Its Social and Political Meaning*. Westport. CT: Greenwood.

Rabinovich, R. (2013) "China to Strengthen Shadow Banking Rules." *Financial Times*. February 26. http://www.ft.com/cms/s/0/223777b6-7fec-11e2-adbd-00144feabdc0.html#axzz2PxKjSr1y.

Rajagopal, B. (2004) *International Law from Below: Development, Social Movements and Third World Resistance*. Cambridge. MA: MIT Press.

Ramage, B. S., Sheil, D., Salim, H. M. W., Fletcher, C., Mustafa, N.-Z. A., Luruthusamay, J. C., Harrison, R. D., Butod, E., Dzulkiply, A. D., Kassim, A. R., and Potts, M. D. (2013) "Pseudoreplication in Tropical Forests and the Resulting Effects on Biodiversity Conservation." *Conservation Biology*. 27(2): pp. 364–372.

Ramseur, J. L. and Hagerty, C. L. (2013) *Deepwater Horizon Oil Spill: Recent Activities and Ongoing Developments*. Congressional research Service, CRS 42942.

Rankin, A. (n/d) "Recent Trends in Organized Crime in Japan: Yakuza vs. Police and Foreign Crime Gangs - The State, The Police and The Yakuza: Control or Symbiosis?" *Japan Focus*. http://www.japanfocus.org/-Andrew-Rankin/3692# (Accessed December 1, 2013).

Rao, S. and Presenti, C. (2012) "Understanding Human Trafficking Origin: A Cross-Country Empirical Analysis." *Feminist Economics*. 18: 2, pp. 231–263.

Rasanayagam, A. (2005) *Afghanistan: A Modern History*. London: I. B. Taurus.

Rashid, T. (2006) *Contested Representation: Punjabi Women in Feminist Debate in Pakistan*. Karachi. Pakistan: Oxford University Press.

Rawls, J. (1971) *A Theory of Justice*. Cambridge. MA: Harvard University Press.

Rawnsley, A. (2013) "The G8 Could Act Radically To Stop Tax Avoidance. Don't Bet On It." *Observer*. June 13. http://www.guardian.co.uk/commentisfree/2013/jun/16/cameron-tax-avoidance-g8-summit (Accessed June 30, 2013).

Ray, G. (2007) "Revolution in the Post-Fordist Revolution: Notes on the Internet as a Weapon of the Multitude." *Third Text*. 21(1): pp. 1–8.

Reagan, R. (1983) "Remarks at a White House Ceremony Inaugurating the National Endowment for Democracy," December 16. http://www.ned.org/ronald-reagan/remarks-at-a-white-house-ceremony-inaugurating-the-national-endowment-for-democracy (Accessed June 14, 2013).

Regan, A. J. (2010) *Light Intervention: Lessons from Bougainville*. (Washington. DC: United States Institute for Peace Press.

Reich, P. C., Weinstein, S., Wild, C., and Cabanlong, A. S. (2012) "Anonymity, Actual Incidents, Cyber Attacks and Digital Immobilizations." In Reich, P. C. and Gelbstein, E. (2012), *Law, Policy and Technology: Cyberterrorism, Information Warfare and Internet Immobilization*. Hershey. PA: IGI Global, pp. 170–199.

Reid, M. (2007) *Forgotten Continent: The Battle for Latin America's Soul*. New Haven. CT: Yale University Press.

Reiter, D. and Stam, A. C. (2002) Democracies at War. New Jersey. NJ: Princeton University Press.

Renard, R. D. (1996) *The Burmese Connection: Illegal Drugs and the Making of the Golden Triangle*. Boulder: Lynne Rienner.

Reno, W. (1999) *Warlord Politics and African States*. Boulder. CO: Lynne Rienner.

Reporters Without Borders (2013a) *The Enemies of the Internet, 2013 Report*. http://surveillance.rsf.org/en/china/ (Accessed June 30, 2013).

Reporters Without Borders (2013b) "Call for International Support for Release of 35 Bloggers Jailed in Vietnam," July 24. http://en.rsf.org/vietnam-call-for-international-support-for-24-07-2013, 44968.html (Accessed November 18, 2013).

Rice, C. (2008) Keynote address, Annual Meeting of the World Economic Forum, Davos, Switzerland, January 23. www.state.gov/secretary/rm/2008/01/99624.htm (Accessed January 31, 2008).

Richards, N. M. and King, J. H. (2013) "Three Paradoxes of Big Data." *Stanford Law Review Online*. 66(3): pp. 41–46. http://www.stanfordlawreview.org/online/privacy-and-big-data/three-paradoxes-big-data (Accessed December 7, 2013).

Richardson, M. (2005) "Australia-Southeast Asia Relations and the East Asia Summit." *Australian Journal of International Affairs*. 59(3): pp. 351–369.

Richter, J. (2001) *Holding Corporations Accountable: Corporate Conduct, International Codes and Citizen Action*. London: Zed Books.

Rid, T. (2013) *Cyber War Will Not Take Place*. New York. NY: Oxford University Press.

Rid, T. (2012) "Cyber War Will Not Take Place." *Journal of Strategic Studies*. 35(1): pp. 5–32.

Riddell, R. (2007) *Does Foreign Aid Really Work?* Oxford: Oxford University Press.

Rieff, D. (2003) *A Bed for the Night: Humanitarianism in Crisis*. New York. NY: Simon and Schuster.

Rieff, D., Packer, D., Steel, R., and Kagan, R. (2008) "An Exchange: Neocon Nation?" *World Affairs Journal*. Spring. http://www.worldaffairsjournal.org/article/exchange-neocon-nation (Accessed June 20, 2012).

Rifkin, J. (1998) *Bio-tech Century: How Genetic Commerce will Change the World*. London: Phoenix.

Rigzone (2013) "Musings: PwC Says Shale Oil 'The Next Energy Revolution' – Really?" Rigzone.com. February 22. http://www.rigzone.com/news/oil_gas/a/124567/Musings_PwC_Says_Shale_Oil_The_Next_Energy_Revolution_ReallyEconomists (Accessed March 24, 2013).

Rihani, S. (2002) *Complex Systems Theory and Development Practice: Understanding Non-Linear Realities*. London: Zed Books.

Rio Tinto (2003) *Human Rights Guidance*. Rio Tinto plc and Rio Tinto Limited. http://www.cccindia.co/corecentre/Database/Docs/DocFiles/corpPub_HumanRights.pdf (Accessed April 5, 2014).

Rio Tinto v. Sarei, No. 11-649, Supreme Court of the United States (February 2012). http://www.supremecourt.gov/Search.aspx?FileName=/docketfiles/11-649.htm (Accessed January 3, 2014)

Rivera-Santos, M. and Rufin, C. (2010) "Odd Couples: Understanding the Governance of Firm-NGO Alliances. *Journal of Business Ethics*. 94(1): 55–70.

Robb, J. (2009) "Risk and Resilience in a Globalized Age: Containing Chaos." *World Politics Review*. August 17. http://www.worldpoliticsreview.com/articles/4203/risk-and-resilience-in-a-globalized-age-containing-chaos (Accessed December 6, 2013).

Robb, J. (2008) "Nation-states, Market-states and Virtual-states." In Bunker R. J. (ed.) *Criminal-States and Criminal-Soldiers*. Abingdon. UK: Routledge, pp. 29–33.

Robertson, R. (1992) *Globalization, Social Theory and Global Culture*. Thousand Oaks: SAGE.

Rodden, J. (2008) "Heuristics, Hypocrisy, and History Without Lessons: Nuremberg, War Crimes and 'Shock and Awe.'" *Journal of Human Rights*. 7: 1, pp. 34–43.

Rogers, M. and Ruppersberger, D. (2012) *Investigative report on the U.S. National Security Issues Posed by Chinese Telecommunications Companies Huawei and ZTE. Permanent Select Committee on Intelligence*. U.S. House Of Representatives, 112th Congress. October 8, pp. 7–8. http://intelligence.house.gov/sites/intelligence.house.gov/files/Huawei-ZTE%20Investigative%20Report%20%28FINAL%29.pdf (Accessed March 23, 2013).

Rogers, S. and Chalabi, M. (2013) "Afghan Civilian Casualties." *Guardian*. April 12. http://www.theguardian.com/news/datablog/2010/aug/10/afghanistan-civilian-casualties-statistics#data (Accessed November 27, 2013).

Romanelli, S. (2013) "New York's Undocumented Workers Join Forces Against Mistreatment." *Guardian*, July 23. http://www.theguardian.com/global-development/2013/jul/23/new-york-undocumented-workers-mistreatment (Accessed January 12, 2014).

Rome Statute of the International Court (2002) The Hague: ICC Public Information and Documentation Service.

Romero, J.A. et al. v. Drummond Company. US Court of Appeals, 11th Circuit. 07-14090. December, 2008. http://law.justia.com/cases/federal/appellate-courts/ca11/07-14090/200714090-2011-02-28.html (Accessed January 2, 2010).

Roosevelt, F. D. (1945) "State of the Union Address," January 6, online by Peters, G. and Woolley, J. T., The American Presidency Project. http://www.presidency.uc (Accessed October 29, 2013).

Rose-Ackerman, S. (1999) *Corruption and Government: Causes, Consequences and Reform*. Cambridge: Cambridge University Press.

Rosecrance, R. (1999) *The Rise of the Virtual State: Wealth and Power in the Coming Century*. New York. NY: Basic Books.

Rosenberg, T. (1991) *Children of Cain: Violence and the Violent in Latin America*. New York: Penguin Books.

Rostow, W. W. (1971) *Stages of Economic Growth: A Non-Communist Manifesto* (2nd edition). London: Cambridge University Press.

Roth, K. (2004) "Drawing the Line: War Rules and Law Enforcement Rules in the Fight against Terrorism." In Human Rights Watch (ed.) *World Report 2004: Human Rights and Armed Conflict*. New York: Human Rights Watch, pp. 177–193. http://www.hrw.org/legacy/wr2k4/9.htm (Accessed July 3, 2008).

Rothwell, D. R. (2010) "Australia v. Japan: JARPAII Whaling Case before the International Court of Justice." *The Hague Justice Portal*. July 2. http://www.haguejusticeportal.net/index.php?id=11840 (Accessed October 11, 2013).

Roxburgh, C., Lund, S., and Piotrowski, J. (2011) *Mapping Global Capital Markets, 2011*. McKinsey Global Institute. http://www.mckinsey.com/Insights/MGI/Research/Financial_Markets/Mapping_global_capital_markets_2011 (Accessed February 18, 2012).

RT USA, November 23, 2012. http://rt.com/usa/anonymous-stratfor-hammond-judge-440/ (Accessed October 14, 2013).

Rubinsztein-Dunlop, S. (2012) "Pistol Import Ring Exposes Customs Service," *ABC Online*. March 15. http://www.abc.net.au/news/2012-03-14/pistol-import-ring-exposes-customs-service/3889450/?site=newcastle (Accessed March 15, 2012).

Rummel, R. J. (2008) *Death by Government* (2nd edition). New Brunswick. NY: Transaction.

Rushkoff, D. (2011) "Occupy Wall Street Beta Tests and New Way of Living." *CNN*, October 25. http://edition.cnn.com/2011/10/25/ opinion/rushkoff-occupy-prototype/index.html (Accessed September 27, 2013).

Saab, B. Y. and Taylor, A. W. (2009) "Criminality and Armed Groups: A Comparative Study of FARC and Paramilitary Groups in Colombia." *Studies in Conflict and Terrorism*. 32(6): pp. 455–475.

Sadoun, B. (2007) *Political Space for Non-Governmental Organizations in the United Nations World Summit Processes*. Civil Society and Social Movements Programme Paper No. 29, United Nations Research Institute for Social Development.

Safford, F. and Palacios, M. (2002) *Colombia: Fragmented Land, Divided Society*. Oxford: Oxford University Press.

Samatar, A. I. (2011) "The Production of Somali Conflict and the Role of Internal and External Actors." In Bereketab, R. (ed.) *The Horn of Africa: Intra-State and Inter-State Conflicts and Security*. London: Pluto, pp. 3119–3528.

Sandholtz, W. (2009) "Explaining International Norm Change." In Sandholtz, W. and Kendal, S. (ed.) *International Norms and Cycles of Change*. Oxford: Oxford University Press.

Sanger, D. E. (2012) "Obama Order Sped up Wave of Cyber Attacks Against Iran." *New York Times*. June 1. http://www.nytimes.com/2012/06/01/world/middleeast/obama-ordered-wave-of-cyberattacks-against-iran.html.

Sarei v. Rio Tinto, PLC, 722 F. 3d 1109 - Court of Appeals (9th Circuit 2013). http://scholar.google.com.au/scholar_case?case=8730189957161081235&q=Rio+Tinto+v.+Sarei,+2013&hl=en&as_sdt=2006&as_vis=1 (Accessed November 12, 2013).

Sarei v. Rio Tinto, PLC, 671 F.3d 736 Court of Appeals (9th Circuit, 2011). http://scholar.google.com.au/scholar_case?case=3657655203535349515&q=Sarei+v.+Rio+Tinto+PLC&hl=en&as_sdt=2,5&as_vis=1 (Accessed June 30, 2013).

Savage, C. and Risen, J. (2010) "Federal Judge Finds N.S.A. Wiretaps Were Illegal." *New York Times*. March 31. http://www.nytimes.com/2010/04/01/us/01nsa.html?_r=0 (Accessed October 2, 2013).

Savage, K., Delesgues, L., Martin, E., and Ulfat, G. P. (2007) *Corruption Perceptions and Risks in Humanitarian Action: An Afghanistan Case Study*. London: Overseas Development Institute.

Schloenhardt, A. (2008) *The Illegal Trade in Timber and Timber Products in the Asia Pacific*. Research and Public Policy Series No. 89, Canberra: Australian Institute of Criminology.

Schmidt, E. and Cohen, J. (2013) *The New Digital Age: Reshaping the Future of People, Nations and Business*. London: John Murray.

Schneider, F., Buehn, A., and Montenegro, C. E. (2010) *Shadow Economies All Over The World: New Estimates for 162 Countries from 1999–2007*. World Bank Policy Research Working Paper 5356, July. http://econ.worldbank.org/external/default/main?pagePK=64165259&theSitePK=478060&piPK=64165421&menuPK=64166093&entityID=000158349_20101014160704 (Accessed March 19, 2012).

Schumpeter, J. (2012) *Capitalism, Socialism and Democracy*. eBook: Start Publishing.

Seccombe, M. (2013) "Abbott: Open for Business and Multinational Lawsuits." *Global Mail*. September 20. http://www.theglobalmail.org/feature/abbott-open-for-business-and-multinational-lawsuits/700/ (Accessed September 26, 2013).

Sen, A. (1999) *Development as Freedom*. Oxford: Oxford University Press.

Sewell, W. H. (2012) "What's Wrong with Economic History?" *History and Theory*. 51(October), pp. 466–476.

Shan Herald News Agency (2006) *Hand in Glove: The Burma Army and the Drug Trade in Shan State*. http://www.burmalibrary.org/docs07/HandinGlove.pdf (Accessed September 16, 2009).

Shearf, D. (2013) "With Burma in Mind, China Quietly Supports the Wa Rebels." *Voice of America*. January 25. http://www.voanews.com/content/chinese-support-for-wa-rebels-designed-to-counter-burma/1590718.html (Accessed November 9, 2013).

Shell, "Ken Saro-Wiwa." http://www.shell.com.ng/environment-society/ogoni/ken-saro-wiwa.html (Accessed June 12, 2013).

Sherlock, R. (2013) "How the Free Syrian Army Became a Largely Criminal Enterprise." *Business Insider Australia*. December 1. http://www.businessinsider.com.au/how-the-free-syrian-army-became-a-largely-criminal-enterprise-2013-11 (Accessed December 17, 2013).

Sherman Anti Trust Act 1890, U.S. Code Title 15, Chapter 1.

Shetty, S. (2014) "Changing Times," Amnesty International Website. http://amnesty.org/en/who-we-are/about-amnesty-international/changing-times (Accessed January 16, 2014).

Shiller, R. (2000) *Irrational Exuberance*. Melbourne: Scribe.

Shulsky, A. N. and Schmidt, G. J. (2002) *Silent Warfare: Understanding the World of Intelligence* (3rd edition). Dulles. VA: Potomac Books.

Silver, N. (2012) *The Signal and the Noise: The Art and Science of Prediction*. London: Allen Lane.

Simpson, G. (2007) *Law, War & Crime: War Crimes Trials and the Reinvention of International Law*. Cambridge: Polity.

Simpson, I. and Roshan, M. (2013) "U.S. soldier Manning gets 35 years for passing documents to WikiLeaks." *Reuters*. August 21. http://www.reuters.com/

article/2013/08/21/us-usa-wikileaks-manning-idUSBRE97J0JI20130821 (Accessed November 4, 2013).

Simpson, L. L. (1996) "Botulinum Toxin: A Deadly Poison Sheds Its Negative Image." *Annals of Internal Medicine*. 125(7): pp. 616–618.

Singh, C. (2013) "Al Shabab Fights the Pirates," *New York Times*, October 22. http://www.nytimes.com/2013/10/23/opinion/international/al-shabab-fights-the-pirates.html?_r=0 (Accessed January 7, 2014).

(SIPRI) Stockholm International Peace Research Institute (2013a) *SIPRI Yearbook 2013*. http://www.sipri.org/yearbook/2013/05 (Accessed December 15, 2013).

(SIPRI) Stockholm International Peace Research Institute (2013b) "Trends in International Arms Transfers, 2012." *SIPRI Fact Sheet*, March. http://www.sipri.org/research/armaments/transfers/measuring/recent-trends-in-arms-transfers (Accessed December 2, 2013).

Siracusa, J. M. (2008) *Nuclear Weapons: A Very Short Introduction*. Oxford: Oxford University Press.

Skidmore, T. E. and Smith, P. H. (2005) *Modern Latin America* (6th edition). Oxford: Oxford University Press.

Skinner, Q. (1979) *The Foundations of Modern Political Thought, Volume 1: The Renaissance*. Cambridge: Cambridge University Press.

Sklair, L. (2002) *Globalization, Capitalism and Its Alternatives*. Oxford: Oxford University Press.

Sklair, L. (2001) *Transnational Capitalist Class*. Malden. MA: Wiley-Blackwell.

Sledge, M. (2013) "Bradley Manning Uncovered U.S. Torture, Abuse, Soldiers Laughing As They Killed Innocent Civilians." *Huffington Post*. August 21. http://www.huffingtonpost.com/2013/08/21/bradley-manning-leaks_n_3788126.html (Accessed January 12, 2014).

Slim, H. (2009) "NGOs in Gaza: Humanitarianism v. Politics." *Open Democracy*. January 30. http://www.opendemocracy.net/article/ngos-in-gaza-between-humanitarianism-and-politics (Accessed October 4, 2011).

Slovik, P. (2012) "Systemically Important Banks and Capital Regulation Challenges." *OECD Economics Department Working Papers*. No. 916, OECD Publishing. doi: 10.1787/5kg0ps8cq8q6-en.

Smallberg, M. (2013) *Dangerous Liaisons: Revolving Door at SEC Creates Risk of Regulatory Capture*. Washington. DC: Project on Government Oversight. February. http://www.pogo.org/our-work/reports/sec-revolving-door.html (Accessed June 6, 2013).

(SMH) Sydney *Morning Herald* (December 25, 2013) http://www.smh.com.au/world/russia-begins-closing-cases-against-greenpeace-arctic-30-activists-20131225-hv6tz.html (Accessed January 20, 2014).

(SMH) Sydney *Morning Herald* (December 22, 2013) http://www.smh.com.au/world/charges-laid-over-bangladesh-factory-fire-20131222-hv6nv.html (Accessed January 25, 2014).

(SMH) Sydney *Morning Herald* (October 3, 2013) http://www.smh.com.au/technology/technology-news/silk-road-mastermind-ross-william-ulbrichttripped-upby-careless-online-mistake-20131003-2utky.html (Accessed October 20, 2013).

Smith, A. (1790) *An Inquiry into the Nature and Causes of the Wealth of Nations*. Public Domain eBook.

Smith, A. (1759) *The Theory of the Moral Sentiments*. University of Oxford eBook.

Smith, M. (1993) *Burma: Insurgency and the Politics of Ethnicity* (2nd edition). London: Zed Books.

Smith, R. H. (2005) *OSS: The Secret History of America's First Central Intelligence Agency* (2nd edition). Guilford. CT: Lyons Press.

Soldatov, A. and Borogan, I. (2010) *The New Nobility: The Restoration of Russia's Security State and the Enduring Legacy of the KGB*. New York. NY: Public Affairs.

Sorensen, K. (2008) *State Failure on the High Seas – Reviewing Somali Piracy*. FOI Somalia Papers: Report 3, Stockholm: Swedish Defence Research Agency.

Sørensen, E. and Torfing, J. (2008) "Theoretical Approaches to Governance Network Dynamics." In Sorensen, E. and Torfing, J. (ed.) *Theories of Democratic Network Governance*. London: Macmillan, pp. 25–42.

SpeechNow.org Et Al., vs. Federal Electoral Commission, United States Court of Appeals, District of Columbia, No. 08-5223, March 26, 2010. http://www.fec.gov/law/litigation/speechnow.shtml (Accessed March 18, 2012).

Spencer, R. (2011) "France Supplying Arms to Libyan Rebels." *Telegraph*. June 29. http://www.telegraph.co.uk/news/worldnews/africaandindianocean/libya/8606541/Francesupplying-weapons-to-Libyan-rebels.html (Accessed February 10, 2012).

Spiers, E. M. (2010) *A History of Chemical and Biological Weapons*. London: Reaktion.

Spiller, R. J. (1988) "S.L.A. Marshall and the Ratio of Fire." *The RUSI Journal*. 133(4): pp. 63–71.

Stacher, J. (2012) *Adaptable Autocrats: Regime Power in Egypt and Syria*. Stanford. CA: Stanford University Press.

Standing, G. (2011) *The Precariat: The New Dangerous Class*. London: Bloomsbury.

Standing Committee of Foreign Affairs, Defence and Trade (2008) *Australia's Involvement in Peacekeeping Operations*. Canberra: Commonwealth of Australia.

Stavenhagen, R. (2005) "Report of the Special Rapporteur on the Situation of Human Rights and Fundamental Freedoms of Indigenous People," UN General Assembly, A/60/358, September 16, 2005. daccessdds.un.org/doc/UNDOC/GEN/N05/513/14/PDF/N0551314.pdf? (Accessed April 28, 2008).

Steger, M. B. (2009) *The Rise of the Global Imaginary: Political Ideologies from the French Revolution to the Global War on Terror*. Oxford: Oxford University Press.

Steger, M. B. (2000). *Gandhi's Dilemma: Nonviolent Principles or Nationalist Power?* New York: St. Martin's.

Steger, M. B., Goodman, J., and Wilson, E. K. (2013) Justice Globalism: Ideology, Crises, Policy. London: SAGE.

Stern, J. (2003) *Terror in the Name of God: Why Religious Militants Kill*. New York: Ecco.

Stern, J. G. (2008) "Humanitarian Organizations: Accountable – Why, to Whom, for What, and How?" In Barnett, M. and Weiss, T. G. (ed.) *Humanitarianism in Question: Politics, Power, Ethics*. Ithaca. NY: Cornell University Press.

Stevenson, J. (2010) "Jihad and Piracy in Somalia." *Survival*. 52(1): pp. 27–38.

Stiglitz, J. (2010) *Freefall: Free Markets and the Sinking of the Global Economy*. London: Allen Lane.

Stiglitz, J. (2002) *Globalization and its Discontents*. New York. NY: W.W. Norton.

Stockton, N. (2005) "Preventing Corruption in Humanitarian Relief Operations." Issue Paper (Workshop C). *ADB/OECD Anti-Corruption Initiative for Asia and the Pacific*. 5th Regional Anti-Corruption Conference, September 28–30, Beijing. www.oecd.org/dataoecd/63/49/35592702.pdf (Accessed January 24, 2012).

Strange, S. (2004) *States and Markets* (2nd edition). London: Continuum (1st edition 1988).

Studwell, J. (2007) *Asian Godfathers: Money and Power in Hong Kong and Southeast Asia*. New York. NY: Atlantic Monthly Press.

Sullivan, K. (2013) "Two Years After Libya's Revolution, Government Struggles to Control Hundreds of Armed Militias." *Washington Post*. September 6. http://articles.washingtonpost.com/2013-09-06/world/41833837_1_armed-militias-libya-s-revolution (Accessed November 29, 2013).

Sunstein, C. R. (2002) *Risk and Reason: Safety, Law, and the Environment*. Cambridge: Cambridge University Press.

Suter, K. (2006) "West Papua: Indonesia's 26th Province or Australia's New Neighbor?" In Rumley, D., Forbes, V. L., and Griffin, G. (ed.) *Australia's Arc of Instability: The Political and Cultural Dynamics of Regional Security*. Springer, pp. 111–127.

Swainson, L. and McGregor, A. (2008) "Compensating for Development: Orang Asli Experiences of Malaysia's Sungei Selagnor Dam." *Asia Pacific Viewpoint*. 49(2): pp. 155–167.

Swanger, J. (2007) "Feminist Community Building in Ciudad Juárez: A Local Cultural Alternative to the Structural Violence of Globalization." *Latin American Perspectives*. 34(2): pp. 108–123.

(SWIFT) Society for Worldwide Interbank Financial Telecommunications (2012) "SWIFT Instructed To Disconnect Sanctioned Iranian Banks Following EU Council Decision," March 15. http://www.swift.com/news/press_releases/SWIFT_disconnect_Iranian_banks (Accessed November 10, 2013).

Symantec (2013) *Internet Security Threat Report, 2013*. Vol. 18. http://www.symantec.com/security_response/publications/threatreport.jsp (Accessed September 26, 2013).

Tadros, M. (2010) *Faith-Based Organizations and Service Delivery: Some Gender Conundrums*. Gender and Development Paper 11, United Nations Research Institute for Social Development. http://www.unrisd.org/80256B3C005BCCF9/search/592137C50475F6A8C12577BD004FB5A0?OpenDocument (Accessed November 6, 2013).

Taillard, M. (2012) *Economics and Modern Warfare: The Invisible Fist of the Market*. New York. NY: Palgrave Macmillan.

Taleb, N. S. (2012) *Antifragile: How to Live in a World We Don't Understand*. London: Allen Lane.

Tanaka, Y. (1996) *Hidden Horrors: Japanese War Crimes in World War II*. Boulder. CO: Westview.

Tax Justice Network (2011) *The Cost of Tax Abuse*. http://www.tackletaxhavens.com/Cost_of_Tax_Abuse_TJN_Research_23rd (Accessed March 12, 2012).

Taylor, B. (2009) "Chapter Three: Sanctioning Iran." *The Adelphi Papers*. 49(411): pp. 59–100.

Taylor, C. (2007) *Modern Social Imaginaries*. Durham. NC: Duke University Press.

Taylor, M. and Elbushra, M. E. (2006) "Research Note: Hassan al-Turabi, Osama bin Laden, and Al Qaeda in Sudan." *Terrorism and Political Violence*. 18(3): pp. 449–464.

Terry, F. (2011) "Myanmar: 'Golfing with the Generals.'" In Magone, C., Neuman, M., and Weissman, T. (ed.) *Humanitarian Negotiations Revealed: The MSF Experience*. New York. NY: Columbia University Press, pp. 109–128.

Terry, F. (2002) *Condemned to Repeat: The Paradox of Humanitarian Action*. Ithaca. NY: Cornell University Press.

Thomas, D. and Loader, B. D. (2000) "Introduction-Cybercrime: Law Enforcement, Security and Surveillance in the Information Age." In Tomas, D. and Loader, B. D. (ed.) *Cybercrime: Law Enforcement, Security and Surveillance in the Information Age*. Abingdon: Routledge, pp. 21–43.

Thomas, G. (2009a) *Gideon's Spies: The Secret History of the Mossad*. New York. NY: Thomas Dunne.

Thomas, G. (2009b) *Secret Wars: One Hundred Years of British Intelligence Inside MI5 and MI6*. New York. NY: Thomas Dunne.

Thompson, C. (2007) "The Scramble for Africa's Oil." *New Statesman*. June 14. www.newstatesman.com (Accessed December 5, 2007).

Tibi, B. (2007) "The Totalitarianism of Jihadist Islamism and Its Challenge to Europe and to Islam." *Totalitarian Movements and Political Religions*. 8, pp. 35–54.

Timberg, C. and Nakashima, E. (2013) "Agreements with Private Companies Protect U.S. Access to Cables' Data for Surveillance." *Washington Post*. July 7 (iPad edition).

Tolson, M. (2013) "Mekong Dam Threatens to Drain Lifeblood of the Region." *Nation*. November 30. http://www.nationmultimedia.com/opinion/Mekong-dam-threatens-to-drain-lifeblood-of-region-30220899.html (Accessed December 1, 2013).

Tolvanen, A. (2003) *The Legacy of Greenstone Resources in Nicaragua*. Canada: MiningWatch. http://www.miningwatch.ca/updir/Nicaragua_studies.pdf (Accessed June 30, 2008).

Trocki, K. (1999) *Opium, Empire and the Global Political Economy: A History of the Asian Opium Trade, 1750–1950*. London: Routledge.

Tubiana, J. (2013) "Sudan and South Sudan Inch Toward War," International Crisis Group, *Foreign Affairs*. October 8. http://www.crisisgroup.org/en/regions/africa/horn-of-africa/south-sudan/op-eds/tubiana-horn-of-africa-sudan-and-south-sudan-inch-toward-war.aspx (Accessed October 29, 2013).

Tudor, A. and Lucchetti, A. (2010) "Bank Tie-up Spans Oceans and Cultures." *Wall Street Journal*. Asia ed. May 7. http://online.wsj.com/article/SB100014240527487036863045752281300664542 38.html (Accessed October 29, 2012).

Twiss, S. B. (1998) "A Constructive Framework for Discussing Confucianism and Human Rights." In De Barry, W. and Weiming, T. (ed.) *Confucianism and Human Rights*. New York. NY: Columbia University Press, pp. 27–53.

Twitter (2014a) "Justin Bieber." https://twitter.com/justinbieber (Accessed January 30, 2014).

Twitter (2014b) "Occupy Wall Street." https://twitter.com/OccupyWallSt (Accessed January 30, 2014).

Tyrrell, I. R. (1991) *Woman's World/Woman's Empire: The Woman's Christian Temperance Union in International Perspective, 1880–1930*. Chapel Hill. NC: University of North Carolina Press.

(UCDP) Uppsala Conflict Data Program (n/d) http://www.pcr.uu.se/research/UCDP/ (Accessed April 26, 2013).

Uhlmann, D. M. (2009) "Environmental Crime Comes of Age: The Evolution of Criminal Enforcement in the Environmental Regulatory Scheme." *Utah Law Review*. 4, pp. 1223–1252.

(UKISC) United Kingdom Intelligence and Security Committee (2013) *Foreign Involvement in the Critical National Infrastructure: The Implications for National*

Security. UK Government, June 2013. https://www.gov.uk/government/uploads/system/uploads/attachment_data/file/205680/ISC-Report-Foreign-Investment-in-the-Critical-National-Infrastructure.pdf (Accessed June 30, 2013).

(UK JCHR) Joint Committee on Human Rights (2010) *Any of Our Business? Human Rights and the UK Private Sector: Government Response to the Committee's First Report of Session 2009-10*. HL Paper 66/HC 401, UK Parliament. http://www.publications.parliament.uk/pa/jt200910/jtselect/jtrights/66/66.pdf (Accessed July 5, 2012).

(UN) United Nations (2007) "Declaration on the Rights of Indigenous Peoples," 61/295, October 2, 2007. daccessdds.un.org/doc/UNDOC/GEN/N06/512/07/PDF/N0651207.pdf?OpenElement (Accessed February 24, 2008).

(UN DESA) United Nations Department of Economic and Social Affairs (2010) *The World's Women, 2010, Trends and Statistics*. New York. NY: United Nations.

(UN ECOSOC) United Nations Economic and Social Committee Department of Economic and Social Affairs, NGO Branch (2014) "At Your Service." http://csonet.org/ (Accessed January 12, 2014).

(UN ECOSOC) United Nations Economic and Social Committee (2013) "List of Nongovernment Organizations in Consultative Status with the Economic and Social Council as of September 1, 2013," October 4, E/2013/INF/6. http://csonet.org/content/documents/e2013inf6.pdf (Accessed January 14, 2014).

(UN ECOSOC) Economic and Social Committee (1996) *Resolution 1996/31. Consultative Relationship between the United Nations and Non-governmental Organizations*. 49th Plenary. http://www.un.org/documents/ecosoc/res/1996/eres1996-31.htm (Accessed October 4, 2008).

UN Trafficking in Persons Protocol (2000) *Protocol to Prevent, Suppress and Punish Trafficking in Persons, Especially Women and Children*, supplementing the United Nations Convention against Transnational Organized Crime, United Nations Treaty Series A-39574 entered into force December 25, 2003.

(UNCHS) United Nations Commission on Human Security (2003) *Human Security Now*. New York. NY: United Nations.

(UNCLOS) *United Nations Convention on the Law of the Sea* (1982) United Nations Treaty Series I-31363, entered into force November 16, 1994. http://www.un.org/depts/los/convention_agreements/texts/unclos/UNCLOS-TOC.htm (Accessed June 5, 2006).

(UNCTAD) United Nations Conference on Trade and Development (2012a) *World Investment Report, 2012: Towards a New Generation of Investment Policies*. Geneva: United Nations.

(UNCTAD) United Nations Conference on Trade and Development (2012b) "South-South Integration is Key to rebalancing the Global Economy." *UNCTAD Policy Briefs*. 22, February. http://unctad.org/en/docs/presspb20114_en.pdf (Accessed July 9, 2013).

(UNCTAD) United Nations Conference on Trade and Development (2011) *World Investment Report, 2011: Non-Equity Modes of International Production and Development*. Geneva: United Nations.

(UNCTAD) United Nations Conference on Trade and Development (2010) *World Investment Report, 2010: Investing in a Low Carbon Economy*. New York. NY: United Nations.

(UNCTAD) United Nations Conference on Trade and Development (2007) *World Investment Report, 2007: Transnational Corporations, Extractive Industries and Development*. New York. NY: United Nations.

(UNDP) United Nations Development Programme (1995) *Human Development Report, 1995*. New York. NY: Oxford University Press.

(UNDP) United Nations Development Programme (1994) *Human Development Report, 1994*. New York: Oxford University Press.

(UNEP) United Nations Environment Programme (2011) *Environmental Assessment of Ogniland*. Nairobi: UNEP. http://postconflict.unep.ch/publications/OEA/UNEP_OEA.pdf (Accessed January 7, 2014).

(UNEP) United Nations Environment Programme (2007) *Sudan: Post-Conflict Environmental Assessment (Synthesis Report)*. www.humanitarianreform.org/humanitarianreform/Portals/1/cluster%20approach%20page/clusters%20pages/Environment/UNEP_Sudan_synthesis_E.pdf (Accessed March 24, 2008).

(UNFPA) United Nations Population Fund (2006) *State of the World Population 2006, A Passage to Hope: Women and International Migration*. www.unfpa.org/swp/2006/english (Accessed September 12, 2007).

(UNGA) United Nations General Assembly (2005) *2005 World Summit Outcome*. Sixtieth Session, A/60/L.1. http://www.un.org/depts/dhl/resguide/r60_en.shtml (Accessed October 7, 2009).

(UNHCR) United Nations High Commissioner for Refugees (2013) "UNHCR Country Operations Profile - Colombia." http//:www.unhcr.org/pages/49e492ad6.html (Accessed November 25, 2013).

(UNHCR) United Nations High Commissioner for Refugees (2012) *The State of the World's Refugees: In Search of Solidarity*. Geneva: Office of the UN High Commissioner for Refugees. http://www.unhcr.org/pages/49c3646c4b8.html (Accessed April 19, 2013).

(UNHCR) United Nations High Commissioner for Refugees (2006a) *State of the World's Refugees: Human Displacement in the New Millennium*. Oxford: Oxford University Press.

(UNHCR) United Nations High Commissioner for Refugees (2006b) *2005 Global Refugee Trends*. Geneva: UNHCR. http://www.unhcr.org.au/pdfs/2005GlobalRefugeetrends.pdf (Accessed May 14, 2007).

United Nations Declaration on the Rights of Indigenous Peoples (2007) United National General Assembly A/Res/61/295. http://www.un.org/esa/socdev/unpfii/documents/DRIPS_en.pdf (Accessed July 9, 2009).

United Nations Global Compact (2013) *Global Corporate Sustainability Report, 2013*. New York. NY: United Nations. http://www.unglobalcompact.org/docs/about_the_gc/Global_Corporate_Sustainability_Report2013.pdf (Accessed January 5, 2014).

United Nations Mission to Investigate Allegations of the Use of Chemical Weapons in the Syrian Arab Republic (2013) *Report on the Alleged Use of Chemical Weapons in the Ghouta Area of Damascus on 21 August 2013*. A/67/997-S/2013/553 (September 13). http://unterm.un.org/DGAACS/unterm.nsf/8fa942046ff7601c85256983007ca4d8/e7e520a4b276eb5385257b4f006e48be?OpenDocument (Accessed October 7, 2013).

United Nations News Centre (2013) "Syria: UN Human Rights Chief Urges Probe into Alleged Execution of Government Soldiers." http://www.un.org/apps/news/story.asp?NewsID=45552#.Uq9qX2QW2G4 (Accessed October 7, 2013).

United States of America v. Chiquita Brands, U.S. District Court for the District of Colombia, March 14, 2007. http://www.corporatecrimereporter.com/documents/SentencingmemoFINAL.pdf (Accessed June 7, 2010).

United States of America v. HSBC and HBUS, Case 1:12, cr763, 1–3, December 11, 2012. http://www.gibsondunn.com/publications/Documents/HSBC_DPA.pdf (Accessed December 4, 2013).

(UNMOVIC) United Nations Monitoring, Inspection and Verification Commission (2007a) "Building a UN Verification Regime." In *Compendium of Iraq's Proscribed Weapons Programmes in the Chemical and Biological Missile Areas*, June. http://www.unmovic.org (Accessed March 24, 2009).

(UNMOVIC) United Nations Monitoring, Inspection and Verification Commission (2007b) "The Biological Weapons Programme." In *Compendium of Iraq's Proscribed Weapons Programmes in the Chemical and Biological Missile Areas*. http://www.unmovic.org (Accessed March 24, 2009).

(UNODC) United National Office on Drugs and Crime (2013a) *World Drug Report, 2013*. Vienna: United Nations.

(UNODC) United Nations Office on Drugs and Crime (2013b) *Patterns and Trends of Amphetamine-Type Stimulants and Other Drugs: Challenges for Asia and the Pacific. Global SMART Programme*. http://www.unodc.org/documents/southeastasiaandpacific/Publications/2013/ats-2013/2013_Regional_ATS_Report_web.pdf (Accessed November 11, 2013).

(UNODC) United National Office on Drugs and Crime (2011) *World Drug Report, 2011*. Vienna: United Nations.

(UNODC) United Nations Office on Drugs and Crime (2010) *The Globalization of Crime: A Transnational Organized Crime Threat Assessment*. Vienna: United Nations.

(UNODC) United Nations Office on Drugs and Crime (2007) *World Drug Report 2007*. Vienna: United Nations.

(UNODC) United Nations Office on Drugs and Crime (2005) *Transnational Organized Crime in the West African Region*. New York: United Nations. http://www.unodc.org/pdf/transnational_crime_west-africa-05.pdf (Accessed July 26, 2008).

(UNODC) United Nations Office on Drugs and Crime (2004) *United Nations Convention Against Transnational Organized Crime and the Protocols Thereto*. New York. NY: UNODC. http://www.unodc.org/unodc/en/treaties/CTOC/ (Accessed July 4, 2009).

(UNSC) United Nations Security Council (2013a) *Report of the Secretary-General on the Situation with Respect to Piracy and Armed Robbery at Sea off the Coast of Somalia*. S/2013/623, October 21. http://www.securitycouncilreport.org/atf/cf/%7B65BFCF9B-6D27-4E9C-8CD3-CF6E4FF96FF9%7D/s_2013_623.pdf (Accessed December 4, 2013).

(UNSC) United Nations Security Council (2013b) Security Council Resolutions. http://www.un.org/en/sc/documents/resolutions/2013.shtml (Accessed January 9, 2014).

(UNSC) United Nations Security Council (2013c) *Small Arms: September 2013 Monthly Forecast*. http://www.securitycouncilreport.org/monthly-forecast/2013-09/small_arms.php (Accessed December 4, 2013).

(UNSC) United Nations Security Council (2011a) Resolution 1973 (2011), S/RES1973 (2011), March 17. http://www.nato.int/nato_static/assets/pdf/pdf_2011_03/20110927_110311-UNSCR-1973.pdf (Accessed November 2, 2012).

(UNSC) United Nations Security Council (2011b) *Small Arms: Report of the Secretary General*. S/2011/255. http://www.securitycouncilreport.org/atf/cf/%7B65BFC

F9B-6D27-4E9C-8CD3-CF6E4FF96FF9%7D/Arms%20S%202011%20255.pdf (Accessed October 2, 2012).

Urry, J. (2003) *Global Complexity*. Cambridge: Blackwell.

(US AID) US Agency for International Development (2013) *U.S. Overseas Loans and Grants (Greenbook)*. https://explore.data.gov/Foreign-Commerce-and-Aid/U-S-Overseas-Loans-and-Grants-Greenbook-/5gah-bvex (Accessed December 7, 2013).

US Congress (2001) "Joint Declaration." 107th Congress, Public Law 1070140, 115, Stat. 224. http://www.gpo.gov/fdsys/pkg/PLAW-107publ40/pdf/PLAW-107publ40.pdf (Accessed June 29, 2013).

US Congress. House of Representatives (2011) *Communist Chinese Cyber-Attacks, Cyber-Espionage and Theft of American Technology*. 112th Congress, 1st Session, April 15, https://www.fas.org/irp/congress/2011_hr/china-cyber.pdf (Accessed July 12, 2013).

US Congress. House of Representatives (2009) *International Efforts to Combat Maritime Piracy*.111th Congress, 1st Session, April 30, 2009. http://www.foreignaffairs.house.gov (Accessed April 28, 2010).

US Congress. House of Representatives (2007a) *Protection Money: U.S. Companies, Their Employees, and Violence in Colombia*. 110th Congress, 1st Session, June 28. http://democrats.edworkforce.house.gov/hearing/protection-and-money-us-companies-their-employees-and-violence-colombia (Accessed June 30, 2010).

US Congress. House of Representatives (2007b) *Blackwater USA: Hearing before the Committee on Oversight and Government Reform*. 110th Congress, 1st Session, October 2. https://house.resource.org/110/org.c-span.201290-1.1.pdf (Accessed July 5, 2010).

US Congress. House of Representatives (2007c) *Private Military Contractors in Iraq: An Examination of Blackwater's Actions in Fallujah*. September. http://oversight-archive.waxman.house.gov/documents/20070927104643.pdf (Accessed July 7, 2010).

US Congress. House of Representatives (2001) "Uniting and Strengthening America by Providing Appropriate Tools Required to Intercept and Obstruct Terrorism (USA Patriot Act) Act of 2001." 107th Congress, 1st Session, January. http://www.gpo.gov/fdsys/pkg/BILLS-107hr3162enr/pdf/BILLS-107hr3162enr.pdf (Accessed January 14, 2014).

US Congress. Senate (2012) *U.S. Vulnerability to Money Laundering, Drugs and Terrorist Financing: HSBC Case History*. July 17. http://www.hsgac.senate.gov/subcommittees/investigations (Accessed August 31, 2012).

US Congress. Senate (1987) *Report of the Congressional Committees Investigating the Iran-Contra Affair, with Supplemental Minority, and Additional Views*. 100th Congress, 1st Session, November 17. https://ia700301.us.archive.org/19/items/reportofcongress87unit/reportofcongress87unit.pdf (Accessed November 1, 2013).

(USTR) Office of the United States Trade Representative (n/d) "Trade and Sustainable Management of Natural Resources," http://www.ustr.gov/tradetopics/environment/trade-and-sustainable-management-natural-resources (Accessed May 26, 2013).

Vatikiotis, M. (2004) "Indonesian Food Giant Undergoes a Transformation." *New York Times*, November 26. http://www.nytimes.com/2004/11/26/business/worldbusiness/26noodle.html?_r=0 (Accessed December 4, 2013).

Varese, F. (2011) *Mafias on the Move: How Organized Crime Conquers New Territories*. Princeton. NJ: Princeton University Press.

Velasco, J. L. (2005) *Insurgency, Authoritarianism, and Drug Trafficking in Mexico's "Democratization."* New York. NY: Routledge.

Verizon (2013) *Data Breach Investigations Report, 2013*. http://www.verizonenterprise.com/resources/reports/rp_data-breach-investigations-report-2013_en_xg.pdf (Accessed September 26, 2013).

Villareal, R. (2013) "Medellin: How Colombia's Second City Overcame its Drug Cartel Past." *International Business Times*. March 5. http://www.ibtimes.com/medellin-how-colombias-second-city-overcame-its-drug-cartel-past-1111226 (Accessed October 21, 2013).

Vitali, S., Glattfelder. J., and Battiston, S. (2011) "The Network of Global Corporate Control." *PLoS ONE*. 6(1): pp. 1–6.

Volcker, P. (2005) *Manipulation of the Oil-for-Food Programme by the Iraqi Regime*. Independent Inquiry into the United Nations Oil-for-Food Programme, October 27. http://www.iic.offp.org (Accessed July 12, 2010) Voon, T. and Mitchell, A. (2013) "Australia's Plain Tobacco Packaging Law at the WTO." *The Conversation*. May 15. http://theconversation.com/australias-plain-tobacco-packaging-law-at-the-wto-14043 (Accessed October 10, 2013).

Voon, T. and Mitchell, A. (2013) "Australia's Plain Tobacco Packaging Law at the WTO." *The Conversation*. May 15. http://theconversation.com/australias-plain-tobacco-packaging-law-at-the-wto-14043 (Accessed October 10, 2013).

Wainwright, E. (2003) "Responding to State Failure 'the Case of Australia and the Solomon Islands.'" *Australian Journal of International Affairs*. 57(3): pp. 485–498.

Waites, D. (2011) "Thailand's Red Shirts: Astroturf or Real Grass?" *Asian Correspondent*. April 12. http://asiancorrespondent.com/52275/thailands-red-shirts-astroturf-or-real-grass/ (Accessed February 7, 2014).

Waldo, M. A. (2009) "Two Piracies in Somalia: Why the World Ignores the Other." *Wardheer News*. January 8. http://www/wardheernews.com (Accessed April 29, 2010).

Walk Free Foundation (2013) *The Global Slavery Index, 2013*. http://www.globalslaveryindex.org/report/?download (Accessed October 16, 2013).

Wallerstein, I. (2011) *The Modern World System III, The Second Era of Great Expansion of the Capitalist World Economy, 1730s-1840s*. Berkeley. CA: University of California Press.

Wallerstein, I. (2004) *World System Analysis: An Introduction*. Durham. NC: Duke University Press.

Waltz, K. (1979) *Theory of International Politics*. Boston: McGraw-Hill.

Wang, X. F. and Chen, G. (2003) "Complex Networks: Small-World, Scale-Free and Beyond." *IEEE Circuits and Systems Magazine*. 3(1): pp. 6–20.

(WCED) World Commission on Environment and Development and Brundtland, G. H. (1987) *Report of the World Commission on Environment and Development: Our Common Future*. United Nations. http://conspect.nl/pdf/Our_Common_Future-Brundtland_Report_1987.pdf (Accessed June 12, 2013).

(WDC) Whale and Dolphin Conservation (2013) "Whaling in Norway." http://us.whales.org/issues/whaling-in-norway (Accessed October 17, 2013).

Weber, M. (2008) "Politics as a Vocation." In Dreijmalis, J., Wells, J., and Gordon, C. (ed.) *Max Weber's Complete Writings on Academic and Political Vocations*. New York. NY: Algora Publishing.

Weisbrot, M. (2011) "Haiti and the International Aid Scam." *Guardian*. April 23. http://www.theguardian.com/commentisfree/cifamerica/2011/apr/22/haiti-aid (Accessed September 2, 2013).

Weiss, T. G. (2000) "Governance, Good Governance and Global Governance: Conceptual and Actual Challenges." *Third World Quarterly*. 21(5): 795–814.

Wendt, A. (1999) *Social Theory of International Politics*. Cambridge: Cambridge University Press.

White, R. (2008) *Crimes Against Nature: Environmental Criminology and Ecological Justice*. Cullompton. UK: Willan Publishing.

Whitman, J. (2005) *The Limits of Global Governance*. London: Routledge.

Whiton, C. (2013) *Smart Power: Between Diplomacy and War*. Dulles. VA: Potomac.

(WHO) World Health Organization (2011) *WHO Report on the Global Tobacco Epidemic: Warning About the Dangers of Tobacco*. Geneva: World Health Organization.

Wiley, J. (2008) *The Banana: Empires, Trade Wars and Globalization*. Lincoln. NB: University of Nebraska Press.

Wilks, S. (2013) *The Political Power of the Business Corporation*. Cheltenham: Edward Elgar.

Wille, C. (2006) "How Many Weapons Are There in Cambodia?" *Small Arms Survey Working Paper*. Geneva: Small Arms Survey. http://www.smallarmssurvey.org (Accessed January 2, 2010).

Williams, E. et al. (2008) *Human Performance*. McLean. VA: The Mitre Corporation.

Williams, P. D. and Bellamy, A. J. (2005) "The Responsibility to Protect and the Crisis in Darfur." *Security Dialogue*. 36, pp. 27–47.

Williamson, J. (2012) "The Dollar and US Power." Paper presented to the conference Currencies of Power and the Power of Currencies: The Geopolitics of Currencies, Reserves and the Global Financial System, International Institute for Strategic Studies Seminar, September 30–October 2, 2012, 3rd Session. http://www.iiss.org/programmes/geo-economics-and-strategy/events/seminars/papers/john-williamson/ (Accessed January 6, 2013).

Willsher, K. and Melkle, J. (2013) "Arctic 30: Five Britons Arrive Back in UK from Russia." *Guardian*. December 28. http://www.theguardian.com/environment/2013/dec/27/arctic-30-five-britons-home-russia-greenpeace (Accessed January 1, 2014).

Wilson, W. (1919) "President Woodrow Wilson's Fourteen Points." January 8, *The Avalon Project: Documents in Law, History and Diplomacy*. Yale Law School. http://avalon.law.yale.edu/20th_century/wilson14.asp (Accessed October 30, 2013).

Wines, M. (2011) "Sudanese Leader is Welcomed in Visit to China." *New York Times*. June 29. http://www.nytimes.com/2011/06/30/world/asia/30china.html (Accessed November 8, 2013).

Witcher, T. (2011) "Libya Arms Threaten to Infiltrate Africa Conflicts." *Defense News*. October 21. http://www.defensenews.com/article/20111021/DEFSECT02/110210305/Libya-Arms-Threaten-Infiltrate-Africa-Conflicts (Accessed February 10, 2012).

Wiwa v. Anderson, U.S. 01 Civ. 1909, 2003. Second Amended Complaint. http://www.shellnews.net/ShellAfrica/12Sept2003.pdf (Accessed April 24, 2014).

Wiwa v. Shell, U.S. 96 Civ. 8386, 2009. http://wiwavshell.org/documents/Wiwa_v_Shell_agreements_and_orders.pdf (Accessed July 4, 2010).

World Bank (2013a) *Worldwide Governance Indicators*. http://info.worldbank.org/governance/wgi/index.aspx#home (Accessed January 9, 2014).

World Bank (2013b) *Pirate Trails: Tracking the Illicit Financial Flows from Pirate Activities off the Horn of Africa*. Washington. DC: World Bank. doi:10.1596/978-0-8213-9963-7.

World Bank (2006) *Global Development Finance: The Development Potential of Surging Capital Flows*. Washington. DC: World Bank.

World Values Survey (n/d) http://www.worldvaluessurvey.org/ (Accessed April 21, 2013).

Wuerth, I. (2013) "The Supreme Court and the Alien Tort Statute: Kiobel v. Royal Dutch Petroleum Co." *American Journal of International Law*. 107, Vanderbilt Public Law Research Paper 13–26, pp. 1–27. http://papers.ssrn.com/sol3/papers.cfm?abstract_id=2264323 (Accessed May 29, 2013).

(WV AP) World Vision Asia Pacific (2007) *World Vision's Indonesia Tsunami Response-Final Report: December 2004-December 2007*. http://reliefweb.int/sites/reliefweb.int/files/resources/52F981A33706CFF3492573A70007797D-Full_Report.pdf (Accessed January 4, 2014).

(WVA) World Vision Australia (2014) Website, FAQs. http://www.worldvision.com.au/AboutUs/Careers/CareerFAQs.aspx#836b52fe-d18b-4f8a-972c-8bb37cabc879 (Accessed January 20, 2014).

(WVI) World Vision International (2014) *World Vision International and Consolidated Affiliates, Consolidated Financial Statements, September 2013 and 2102*. Independent Auditor's Report (KPMG) file:///Users/e12723/Downloads/World%20Vision%20International%20Issued%20FS%202013.pdf (Accessed March 4, 2014).

(WVInc) World Vision Inc. (2014) Our Impact. http://www.worldvision.org/our-impact/our-faith-in-action (Accessed January 20, 2014).

Wyld, R. (2013) "Why Foreign Bribery is Important to Australian Corporations, Directors and Executives." Foreign Bribery. Johnson Winter & Slattery Lawyers, March. http://www.jws.com.au/__files/f/5456/Foreign%20Bribery%20Update%20March%202013.pdf (Accessed February 2, 2014).

Wyler, L. S. (2013) *International Drug Control Policy: Background and U.S. Responses*. Congressional Research Report, RL34543. http://www.fas.org/sgp/crs/row/RL34543.pdf (Accessed October 10, 2013).

Young, N. M. (2011) "Paying Off Khan Was 'Least Worst Option' According to Amnesty's IEC Chair." *Civil Society*, March 1. http://www.civilsociety.co.uk/governance/news/content/8481/paying_off_khan_was_least-worst_option_according_to_amnestys_iec_chair (Accessed January 3, 2014).

Young-Bruehl, E. (2006) *Why Arendt Matters*. New Haven. CT: Yale University Press.

Younglai, R. and Rampton, R. (2012) "US Pushes EU, SWIFT to Eject Iranian Banks." *Reuters*. February 15. http://www.reuters.com/article/2012/02/16/us-iran-usa-swift-idUSTRE81F00I20120216 (Accessed December 12, 2013).

Yousef, D. M. and Gismatullin, E. (2013) "Kenya Attack Stirs Complacency Fear Over Somali Pirates." *Bloomberg News*. Sep 27. http://www.bloomberg.com/news/2013-09-25/kenya-attack-stirs-complacency-fear-over-somali-pirates.html (Accessed January 12, 2014).

Zakaria, F. (1994) "Culture Is Destiny: A Conversation with Lee Kuan Yew." *Foreign Affairs*. March/April 1994, pp. 109–126. www.fareedzakaria.com/articles/other/culture.html (Accessed May 10, 2008).

Zanotti, J. (2013) *U.S. Aid to the Palestinains*. CRS, RS22967, September 30. http://www.fas.org/sgp/crs/mideast/RS22967.pdf (Accessed November 5, 2013).

Zhang, Qi and Tong, Hao (2009) "'Bribery is widespread' in Rio Case." *China Daily*. http://www.chinadaily.com.cn/china/2009-07/15/content_8428702.htm (Accessed November 4, 2011).

Index

Page numbers in **bold** refer to figures, page numbers in *italic* refer to tables.

Printed and bound by CPI Group (UK) Ltd, Croydon, CR0 4YY